Cycling and the British

Cycling and the British

A Modern History

NEIL CARTER

BLOOMSBURY ACADEMIC
LONDON • NEW YORK • OXFORD • NEW DELHI • SYDNEY

BLOOMSBURY ACADEMIC
Bloomsbury Publishing Plc
50 Bedford Square, London, WC1B 3DP, UK
1385 Broadway, New York, NY 10018, USA

BLOOMSBURY, BLOOMSBURY ACADEMIC and the Diana logo are trademarks of
Bloomsbury Publishing Plc

First published in Great Britain 2021

Copyright © Neil Carter, 2021

Neil Carter has asserted his right under the Copyright, Designs and
Patents Act, 1988, to be identified as Author of this work.

For legal purposes the acknowledgments on p. vi constitute an extension
of this copyright page.

Cover design: Terry Woodley
Cover image © Mary Evans Picture Library

All rights reserved. No part of this publication may be reproduced or transmitted
in any form or by any means, electronic or mechanical, including photocopying,
recording, or any information storage or retrieval system, without prior
permission in writing from the publishers.

Bloomsbury Publishing Plc does not have any control over, or responsibility for, any
third-party websites referred to or in this book. All internet addresses given in this
book were correct at the time of going to press. The author and publisher regret
any inconvenience caused if addresses have changed or sites have ceased to
exist, but can accept no responsibility for any such changes.

A catalogue record for this book is available from the British Library.

Library of Congress Cataloging-in-Publication Data
Names: Carter, Neil, 1967-author.
Title: Cycling and the British: a modern history / Neil Carter.
Description: London; New York: Bloomsbury Academic, 2020. |
Includes bibliographical references and index.
Identifiers: LCCN 2020033576 (print) | LCCN 2020033577 (ebook) | ISBN 9781472572097
(hardback) | ISBN 9781472572080 (paperback) | ISBN 9781472572103 (ebook) |
ISBN 9781472572110 (epub) Subjects: LCSH: Cycling–Great Britain–History. |
Cycling–Social aspects–Great Britain. | Great Britain–Social life and customs.
Classification: LCC GV1046.G7 C37 2020 (print) | LCC GV1046.G7 (ebook) |
DDC 796.60941–dc23
LC record available at https://lccn.loc.gov/2020033576
LC ebook record available at https://lccn.loc.gov/2020033577

ISBN: HB: 978-1-4725-7209-7
PB: 978-1-4725-7208-0
ePDF: 978-1-4725-7210-3
eBook: 978-1-4725-7211-0

Typeset by Deanta Global Publishing Services, Chennai, India

To find out more about our authors and books visit www.bloomsbury.com and
sign up for our newsletters.

CONTENTS

Acknowledgements vi
Abbreviations vii

Introduction 1
1   Cycling and the rise of respectable recreation 13
2   Cycling as Victorian spectacle 41
3   Cycling, Englishness and the politics of the road 69
4   Cycling and the people 89
5   The birth of British massed-start racing 115
6   Women, modernity and cycling 143
7   Cycling in the age of motoring 165
8   Cycling, politics and environmentalism 185
9   Cycling in post-industrial Britain 209
10 Elite cycling and British society 233
Conclusion 255

Notes 259
Bibliography 324
Index 343

ACKNOWLEDGEMENTS

Many people have helped in the writing and research of this book. I am grateful to all those at Bloomsbury Academic for their patience and understanding, especially Emily Drewe, Joseph Gautham, Abigail Lane and Dan Hutchins.

I am particularly grateful to Richard Holt who read numerous drafts and provided reassuring support at important times during the whole process. For other drafts, Dil Porter made typically sensible and astute suggestions.

My colleagues in the International Centre for Sports History and Culture – Martin Polley, Matt Taylor, Heather Dichter, James Panter and Rob Colls – were generous with their time and advice, while I am also grateful for the support I received from colleagues in the History Department at DMU.

Many, many thanks also to the staff at the Modern Records Centre at the University of Warwick who not only provided expert advice on its cycling archive but were also good humoured and friendly while putting up with my numerous requests and questions.

Finally, I am grateful to everyone who has been keen to share with me their stories on and insights into cycling – a number of which have been included in the book. This as much as anything has highlighted how universal cycling has been throughout the period studied.

ABBREVIATIONS

AAA	Amateur Athletic Association
AAC	Amateur Athletic Club
BAR	Best All-Rounder
BBC	British Broadcasting Corporation
BC	bicycle club
BCF	British Cycling Federation
BLRC	British League of Racing Cyclists
BMA	British Medical Association
BMX	Bicycle Motocross
BU	Bicycle Union
CC	cycling club
CM	Critical Mass
CTC	Cyclists' Touring Club
FIFA	Fédération Internationale de Football Association
HPV	human powered vehicle
ICA	International Cycling Association
IMG	International Management Group
MoT	Ministry of Transport
MSR	massed-start racing
MTB	mountain bike
NCPS	National Cycling Proficiency Scheme
NCU	National Cyclists' Union
NFC	National Fitness Council
NGO	non-governmental organisation
PED	performance enhancing drugs
RoSPA	Royal Society for the Prevention of Accidents
RRA	Road Records Association
RRC	Road Racing Council
RTTC	Road Time Trials Association
TfL	Transport for London
TT	time-trial
UCI	Union Cycliste Internationale
WRRA	Women's Road Records Association

Introduction

Since the late nineteenth century, cycling's presence in British society has been remarkably persistent. It has been a presence though that has flickered, sometimes brightly, sometimes dimly. In recent years, interest in cycling has grown exponentially, although the extent of its popularity and its impact has been contested. Its level of public awareness arguably reached a peak on 22 July 2012 when the final stage of the Tour de France took place on the Champs-Élysées in Paris. In a scene that the writer William Fotheringham called a 'surreal sight', the wearer of the yellow jersey, Bradley Wiggins, soon to be the first British winner of the race, led out Mark Cavendish, wearing the rainbow jersey as the world champion, for the final sprint, which he won. These landmark successes were quickly followed with a glut of cycling gold medals at the London Olympics. At the same time, cycling's place on the political agenda had never been higher due to a combination of a growing awareness of environmental issues and increasing concerns over well-being.

These twenty-first-century images offered a contrast with past ones of the bicycle and its place in popular culture. In December 1963, for example, *Coronation Street*, still Britain's longest-running television show, was first aired on ITV. One of the opening scenes is set at the Barlows' dinner table where the younger son, David, arrives home late from work because his bicycle had had a puncture. Later, his father is seen helping him to fix it in the backroom. While broadcast at the onset of the age of the motor car, *Coronation Street* owed more to the 1930s than to the 1960s, and as such there was more than a whiff of nostalgia about the scene, as with the programme in general. The 1930s had been a time when the bicycle was an elemental part of working-class culture. Not only was it a form of transport, but it was also used for leisure and pleasure as people, with a group of friends, with partners or just riding for their own enjoyment, could escape into the countryside on their bicycles and tandems to imbibe its fresh air and scenery.

Fast-forward over 30 years and in the video for Pulp's 1995 Britpop anthem 'Common People' there are brief shots of a Raleigh Chopper being ridden in a street. Again, with its association with the 1970s, the Chopper represents a nostalgic nod to the band's frontman Jarvis Cocker's childhood. The early 1970s, however, had represented a shift in the status of the bicycle. The dominance of the motor car in terms of its economic and cultural appeal forced major changes on the cycling industry, changing the very idea of the bicycle itself. Whereas once it was regarded as a vehicle that adults rode, and this had been reflected in its design, now bicycles had an urban edge and increasingly appealed to children. The Chopper's unique design was driven by changing consumerist tastes. It was conceived to be edgy and niche, reflecting other aspects of popular culture, in this case the motorbikes from the 1969 film *Easy Rider*. Not only does the appearance of a bicycle in these settings reveal its versatility, diversity and ubiquity since the nineteenth century, but these brief, almost subliminal appearances also highlight how it has been on the margins of British society rather than at its centre.

Cycling since the late nineteenth century has meant different things to different people at different times. This book aims to not only capture these changing meanings but also understand why people rode bicycles – and also why they did not – as well as which people rode them, in addition to analysing how different forms of cycling, whether as sport, as leisure or as a form of transport, developed. Politics and pleasure, therefore, form the centre of this book.

Cycling and the British examines individual forms of cycling – sport, leisure and transport – but it does not do so in isolation. Instead, there has been a considerable overlap between them at various times, which has shaped the development of each particular form. Like sport, cycling is one word, but many things. This book charts the shifting place of cycling in British society since 1870, when it was taken up by increasing numbers of people. It weaves together the separate and often disparate histories of cycling into a coherent whole. In order to examine its continuities and discontinuities, *Cycling and the British* traverses several historical sub-disciplines. In addition to histories of sport, leisure and technology, it also utilizes political culture, material culture and the history of transport, with a particular focus on the motor car to show how a culture of motoring shaped – and continues to shape – cycling in Britain.

The book's overall approach draws on Harry Oosterhuis's historiographical essay on the history of cycling in Western nations.[1] Oosterhuis has argued that there has been a dominant historical narrative that highlights an initial omnipresence of the bicycle, up to the 1950s, only for it to be superseded by motoring; then from the 1970s cycling's environmental qualities were increasingly promoted, which resulted in the bicycle's increasing political importance. This history, especially from when cycling became a mass activity, has been underpinned by a number of common themes: first, the impact of motoring; second, the traffic policies implemented by the state; third, the extent to which cycling and motoring have reflected changing social relations; fourth, the role of bicycle organizations, both politically and culturally; and finally, the influence of elite sport in shaping cycling cultures more generally.[2] However, there were also differences in terms of cycling levels, patterns of use and cycling cultures between nations, and this book identifies these differences within the context of the British experience.

Cycling and the British loosely adopts the above themes and framework to capture the development of a national culture of cycling in Britain since the nineteenth century. Despite general commonalities, there were significant differences in the British experience compared to its European neighbours. In the Netherlands and Denmark, for example, cycling, as a form of transport embedded in the nation's infrastructure, has characterized their cycling culture since the early twentieth century. By contrast, Britain was one of the first countries, along with America and Germany, to marginalize cycling by prioritizing motoring – a process that owed much to reasons of social status associated with each form of transport. Sport has been another of the centralizing agencies that have shaped a national cycling culture. In his history of French cycling, Hugh Dauncey has highlighted the central importance of the Tour de France to French national culture more generally.[3] Similarly, sport has been at the centre of the cycling cultures in Belgium, Italy and, to a lesser extent, Spain.[4] Stijn Knuts has argued that races like the Tour de Flanders have been crucial to the formation of regional and national identities in Belgium.[5]

Because Britain was part of that Anglo-Saxon world where cycling had been marginalized by motoring, cycling in Britain has become associated more with recreational and sporting purposes from the second half of the twentieth century. Despite occasional international successes, the power of sport to act as a national unifying agency has been largely absent in British cycling. Instead, football and cricket have been Britain's national sports, while cycling has been at the margins. Moreover, its early history goes against the grain of modern sport. Whereas Britain played the pivotal role in the early development of modern sports, in cycling it was the French who soon took over the sport's running on the international stage. With the later establishment of the Tour de France, France's ascendancy was reinforced. By contrast, the sport of cycling in Britain reflected the amateur-voluntary ethos of sport more generally, and while a de facto Tour of Britain was established in 1945 it lacked the prestige – and geography – of the Tour and the Giro d'Italia.

More recently, cycling in Britain has been characterized as a marginal, largely male activity and has carried negative overtones due to its image among the general public as an eccentric and unsafe activity. It has also been associated with either the low-social-status demographic or the well-educated and the lycra-clad middle classes. As a consequence, daily (or utilitarian) bicycle use has become a lifestyle choice, and a politicized cycling activism and subculture has developed in opposition to the dominant car culture. By contrast, in the Netherlands and Denmark because the cycling experience is so deeply embedded in their infrastructure, political activism has not been as great, because it has not been seen as necessary.[6]

Of course, the trajectory of British cycling has developed in its own contexts and has been shaped by human agency as well as by its being part of broader national narratives. *Cycling and the British* is underpinned by four overlapping core ideas, which run throughout the entire period under consideration. The first is based on the notion that riding a bicycle has been a political act in its broadest sense. The vast majority of people who rode a bicycle did not do so consciously for political reasons – although a minority did. Instead, this book is more concerned with prosaic – yet still political – questions such as why do cyclists ride on some roads and why are there cycle paths? The act of riding and where it has taken place has been a product of shifting legal and political debates around cycling, which at various times have either bolstered or diminished its cultural status. As a consequence, the book explores British political culture and the extent of the state's role in shaping cycling's history.

Political culture in Britain throughout the twentieth century largely revolved around class conflict. Not only were the economy and industrial relations characterized by tensions between workers and management, but they were underpinned by a largely undemocratic and tribal two-party political system based on conceptions of class that were perpetuated by a mainly right-wing media. Up until the 1980s, Britain had the most balanced mixed economy in the free world, with a pioneering welfare state and a concentrated business sector underpinned by an uneasy post-war political consensus. However, from the 1980s, British politics embraced a neoliberal ethos with an emphasis on 'rolling back the state', something that the Labour government between 1997 and 2010 had only partial success in stemming.[7] With an emphasis on unregulated free-market economics and a low taxation system, social and economic inequalities began to grow back to Victorian levels. By the late twentieth century, due to changes in the economic structure, political culture increasingly revolved around values as ideas of class gradually eroded without ever disappearing.[8] In particular, the issue of the environment moved up the political agenda. Thus, cycling became a site for ideas of individualism and collectivism with regard to transport politics. While the bicycle was initially seen as symbol of freedom, by the late twentieth century the car had replaced it in this regard. However, the bicycle was increasingly seen as an antidote to the environmental damage caused by motoring by a bourgeoning and university-educated middle class, while motorists and the motoring lobby saw it as a threat.

The second idea is that the history of cycling has been bound up with the changing values of the middle classes – political, social, cultural and economic. Not only did the middle classes create the modern world, but they did so in their own image.[9] For much of its history, cycling has been a mass activity, but it has been the middle classes who have largely shaped its direction and political discourse, which has stretched from the age of amateurism in the Victorian period to growing concerns over the environment by the late twentieth century. With reference to leisure, Jeff Hill has argued that it 'became implicated in the process of class consciousness at the point when middle-class people began to seek control of formerly public spaces in order to "privatise" them for approved activity'.[10] Later, through the growth of car ownership the middle classes have also shaped the nature of cycling in a negative sense. As a consequence, cycling has been little different to other areas of British society over this period. This is not to argue that the working classes, as the largest group of cyclists, have been unable to make their own cycling histories. Instead, the argument here is that these histories have been shaped within a historical context, which has been framed by middle-class values, attitudes and actions.

Third, a history of cycling is also a history of the modern world, and the bicycle was an important agent in shaping this world. The notions of modernity and the modern world are problematic for historians, given their teleological implications. Cycling, however, emerged in a period that was organized differently compared to what came before and what came after. Between 1870 and 1900, there was a greater sense of living in a peculiarly 'modern age' as urbanization and modern communication technologies, such as the railways, newspapers and the telegraph, were creating a more intimate world. Some viewed this modernity as a process of liberation, but for others there was a persistent grief at the memory of a world that had been lost. Moreover, as Eric Zuelow argues, '[m]odernity is a "condition", not a value', and one that was European in origin. It was during this period that

> [s]cience and rational thought, while certainly important at other times, hold sway to an extent never known before. Consequently, ideas about health and wellness diverge significantly from what was true previously. Aesthetic sensibilities are unique. Consumption and consumerism play a far greater role in society. The individual matters more than in the past and, partly as a consequence, governments ... are arranged much differently that they were in pre-modern times.[11]

With reference to modernity's contradictions, Jose Harris has argued these 'ambiguities are a valuable reminder that "modernity" was essentially a mental construct' rather than an objective one.[12]

Cycling itself contributed to Western modernity. Similar to later mobilities, such as motoring, aviation and skiing, cycling cultivated a modern relationship with space and the landscape through active movement.[13] Not only did travel on the bicycle collapse time and space, but cycling journeys opened up new ways of thinking about the world. For the cycling tourist, for example, a 'gaze' was constructed subject to broader social and cultural forces. In particular, one of cycling's main attractions was to escape to the countryside and for a brief time to flee from the negative aspects of urbanization and industrialization. Cycling, though, could not be perpetually modern and it became a victim of modernizing impulses through the growth of motoring, highlighting how ideas of modernity have been shaped by broader historical forces.

Finally, *Cycling and the British* examines the changing social make-up of cycling, and how it shaped social identities. It is evident, almost a cliché, that the bicycle has been an agent for social change. In particular, it has been the sheer visibility and act of riding a bicycle that has demonstrated its potential to disrupt social relations to both those riding and those watching. In particular, for women the bicycle has been an emancipatory machine.[14] Because the bicycle has essentially been democratic and relatively cheap, for the Victorian and Edwardian working classes, cycling opened up new ways of communication and thinking about the world and, importantly, their place in it. At the same time during this period, it challenged middle-class sensibilities around social hierarchies. In addition, the book explores how cycling contributed towards ideas of national identity, both through its literature and through the actual movement of people on bicycles. British society was characterized by a strong voluntary and associational culture, where cycling clubs, for example, formed their own subcultures. Other cycling subcultures not only developed along the lines of class and gender but were determined through age. Cycle speedway was an example of a DIY sport, set up from the grassroots by teenagers, while BMX was a commercialized sport that was aimed at children. Other cycling activities such as mountain biking and their links to the counterculture reflected changing political and cultural values.

This book will fill a gap in the historiography of British cycling since the nineteenth century. In comparison to other histories, it aims to bring together many of cycling's constituent parts into one account. An early history of the sport, entitled *Cycling*, was written in 1889 by George Lacy Hillier and Lord Albemarle, two key figures, especially Hillier, in its early development.[15] Hillier was a former champion cyclist as well as a militant amateur. By the 1970s histories of cycling began to emerge, some written by amateur historians such as Derek Roberts, while Andrew Ritchie has been one of the leading historians to have written on the sport of cycling in the Victorian period.[16] The first academic publication on cycling was David much-quoted article on the boom in the 1890s.[17] Further histories of cycling in Britain have also focussed on the Victorian period, partly due to the availability of sources and also because this was a period of technical innovation and rapid change.[18] There has been little work on other periods, including, surprisingly the middle years of the twentieth century when cycling was at its most popular.[19] Nevertheless, this bourgeoning literature has been buttressed by the emergence of an international cycling history community which has periodically organized conferences and published proceedings.[20]

The recent rise of the bicycle up the political agenda has been both reflected and reinforced by a growing literature on cycling. One key text, *Cycling and Society*, an edited volume of essays, analyses cycling's role in society from a variety of perspectives, including transport, geography and gender.[21] In addition, cycling's growing activism has spawned an impressive literature on the subject, especially from Rachel Aldred and Peter Cox.[22] (Cox's *Cycling: A Sociology of Vélomobility* was published just after this book was completed.[23]) His work has been part of a broader project on mobility and mobilities, which has its origins in the work of John Urry, which has mainly centred around the impact of the motor car. Reflecting its growing importance, there is now a vast academic literature on cycling in transport, health and economics journals.

One of the main strands of writings on cycling's history, which separates it from other sports, has been the focus on technology. Tracing the origins of the bicycle has attracted much attention from historians, keen to identify a key technological breakthrough.[24] This book does not attempt to follow this path, but it does recognize the importance of technology in cycling's history. The technological evolution of the bicycle was not an inevitable process, argue Bijker and Rosen. Instead, they have attributed its development to socio-technological change with consumers pressurizing manufacturers to innovate and adapt new designs that were suited to their needs.[25] Other histories of cycling have been written from different angles, including business.[26] This book draws on this literature in analysing and contextualizing the ebbs and flows in cycling's history.

The early history of the bicycle

While this book does not claim to be a history of technology, it is undeniable that technological developments have been crucial to cycling's history. As such an understanding of its beginnings would be beneficial. Early attempts to build a 'mechanical horse' actually go back to 1696. However, many accounts – albeit disputed – credit the 'draisine', aka the hobby or dandy horse, as the forerunner to the modern bicycle. Built in the early nineteenth century, a rider would sit astride this two-wheeled machine, propelling themselves with their legs using a walking-and-running motion via their feet touching the ground. It was briefly popular before its obvious limitations, in particular in going uphill, were exposed.

It is generally agreed that the first 'proper' bicycle – the velocipede – had its origins in the 1860s. The essential difference between this two-wheeler machine and the 'draisine' was that it was propelled by pedals and cranks attached to the front hub, and was a veritable machine. In 1867 the velocipede first appeared on the streets of Paris. It had been built by Pierre Michaux, a local blacksmith, though the business was underwritten by three brothers, Marius, Aime and Rene Oliver, and cost 250 francs. However, it was subsequently discovered that the sole patent pertaining to a basic bicycle had been filed in the United States in 1856 by Pierre Lallement, a citizen of Nancy. He had built and ridden a velocipede in 1863 before leaving for America two years later. David Herlihy has speculated that Lallement had struck a business relationship with the Oliver brothers before their arrangement with Michaux.[27] Whatever the story behind its origins, the velocipede began to make its mark on French society.

By 1869, cycling was also making its mark in Britain, although some saw it as a passing trend. The *Spectator* for one was not optimistic of the bicycle's future. Acknowledging that it was 'for the moment a rage', the journal doubted 'very greatly if it is more ... or [will] become a permanent addition to our means of locomotion'. In particular, there were concerns over its mechanical reliability and difficulty which could result in serious accidents, as pointed out in the *Lancet*. Moreover, because of this threat, it was not considered 'a vehicle for women'.[28]

The bicycle's early technical and manufacturing development owed much to sport. As Andrew Ritchie has pointed out, the sport of cycling was crucial in the mechanical evolution of the bicycle and subsequently as a mass product. The first cycle manufacturers were often craftsmen and professional cyclists who worked in small workshops, while early sporting competitions became testing grounds for improvements in technology, which later led to more reliable machines and greater comfort for recreational cyclists.[29] Technical developments during this early period were rapid. At first, machines were heavy with cast-iron frames and wood-spoked wheels which were rimmed with a metal band, and they were more the product of a blacksmith's workshop than an advanced manufacturing process. By 1873, however, the velocipede was transformed due to a lighter, tubular frame and wire-suspension wheels with solid rubber tyres.[30]

The perpetual quest for greater speed among professional cyclists led to further technical innovations. By 1875 the most visible innovation was the invention of the high-wheeler or 'ordinary' bicycle.[31] (For discussion of tricycles and sociables, see Chapter 1.) At this time, the size of the pedalled front wheel acted as a bicycle's gear. For these machines to increase speed and the distance covered with each pedal rotation, it was easier to increase the size of the front wheel. The ordinary was the pre-eminent bicycle design over the next 10 years; its supremacy ended with the introduction of the rear wheel chain-driven 'safety' bicycle in 1884–5 – the Starley Rover, manufactured in Coventry by John Kemp Starley, the nephew of James Starley, another early cycling inventor.[32] The safety remains the most important and influential design in the history of cycling. The safety element was in the design of two equal and much-smaller-sized wheels, which opened up cycling up to the masses, and especially women. Three years later the invention of Dunlop's pneumatic tyre would further increase the appeal of the safety. The men who rode the ordinary had been scornful of the safety's ease compared to the courage and skill required to ride a high-wheeler. However, the ordinary's brief reign had ended and cycling's age of mass participation had begun. The diamond design of the safety has remained remarkably robust and still forms the main design for most bicycles today. During the interwar period the invention of lightweight bicycles further popularized cycling among women. It was the later emergence of the mountain bike that ushered in perhaps the most innovative designs since the safety.

The emotions of cycling

What about the actual emotions of riding, its appeal and owning a bicycle? What meanings and experiences has it stimulated? Owning a bicycle can stir emotions similar to owning other inanimate objects and possessions, such as motor cars. A bicycle can become something to be treasured, to be looked after, cultivating a certain attachment towards it. To what extent a bicycle becomes an extension of someone's personality is difficult to assess, but perhaps it can be said that familiarity through riding a particular bicycle regularly can breed affection rather than contempt. Moreover, riding a bicycle has created a wide range of motivations and sensations. It may have been for sporting competitions, for utilitarian purposes or pure pleasure, or for a combination of these emotions. For some it offered the thrill of speed, for others the independence and freedom of personal mobility. Moreover, that cycling has health benefits has been a claim as old as cycling itself. From the late nineteenth century, the comparison of the human body to a thermodynamic engine was made, and it was soon realized that the bicycle converted physical energy into movement more efficiently than other forms of human locomotion. Yet meanings of cycling have changed in light of broader social and cultural contexts. Rachel Aldred has stated, 'Cycling is never "just cycling"; it is always constructed in context and the meanings of cycling – and cyclists – are often hotly contested by activists and others.'[33] This argument was true for the nineteenth century as it is for the twenty-first. In attempting to understand this history it is difficult not to agree with Richard Holt, who has stated, 'Sport is cultural as well as physical and what we do with our bodies is very much a product of what we think we ought to do with them.' While prevailing social and economic conditions can determine the extent of and changes in leisure practices, what people 'chose to do within such limits may be strongly influenced by traditions, shifting patterns of behaviour and taste that cannot be easily explained by material factors alone'.[34]

The story of Tommy Turnbull does capture some of the emotion attached to cycling, including owning a bicycle as well as providing an insight into how meanings of cycling have changed over time. Turnbull was a 29-year-old miner from South Shields during the mid-1920s. One day he set out to buy a bicycle. It was a deeply personal matter, and he was very deliberate in his selection of what would be his first bicycle. For over 3 hours he visited numerous bicycle shops in Newcastle, each on more than one occasion, much to the frustration of his friends who wanted him to make his mind up quickly. With his savings of £8, he was determined he 'wouldn't be rushed'. He had 'waited years and years for this and I wasn't going to buy anything until I was certain in my own mind that it was exactly what I wanted. It was only going to happen the once.'[35]

After buying his first bicycle, Turnbull joined a cycling club, Tyne Dock Belle Vue CC. For him club runs opened up a whole new way of thinking about life and people as well as getting out into the country and into the fresh air: 'For those like me who sometimes worked a sixteen-hours stretch in a dark and bad atmosphere and then went home to the smells of bone-yards, piggeries, factory smoke and the stink of the Tyne, a place like Corbridge or Barnard Castle was like heaven on earth.' In the countryside

> the air would be cool and fresh and the smells of flowers, blossom and meadow grass, would be all around you. ... On a bike you felt as though you were part of the countryside. ... Every week as soon as I saw the first green field I'd be breathing in and out as deeply as I could. I'd be striving to get rid of all the dust and muck from every part of my insides and trying to fill myself with sufficient sweet air to last me until the next time.[36]

Thus, while cycling held explicitly conscious political meanings for activists and aficionados, its meanings for non-activists too were not neutral, as they had been shaped by broader political and cultural forces.

Cycling's history has been an under-researched subject, something that is surprising given the wealth of primary sources held in the National Cycle Archive (MSS.328) at the University of Warwick's Modern Records Centre. The archive holds cycling newspapers, personal collections, cycling club archives as well as those of governing bodies such as the Cyclists' Touring Club (CTC) and the National Cyclists' Union (NCU). Importantly, it also holds almost complete runs of journals like *Cycling* and the *Cyclist's Touring Club Gazette*, which have been used extensively. It is arguably the most voluminous archive related to any sport, but because of the unique qualities of cycling as a leisure activity and especially a form of transport, it also holds material related to the politics of transport, such as files on Friends of the Earth. While the research for this book has leaned heavily on this vast archive, most of it has been left untouched. Another not insubstantial cycling archive consulted has been the papers of massed-start racing pioneer Percy Stallard at Wolverhampton's record office, although again much more has been left unseen. The National Archives held records relating to the relationship between cycling and the politics of transport.[37] To give further colour to the research some anecdotal material has been included. Most of this has been from friends and family. While this hardly amounts to a systematic oral history, what it does highlight is how universal riding a bike was and still is.

The book is broadly rather than strictly chronological in structure. Each chapter has its own distinct theme and as a result, there is overlap between chapters. While this is a history of British cycling, its coverage is admittedly uneven, as it is difficult to cover all parts of the UK equally. Instead, the focus is mainly on England and, at times, London. However, when looked at also in other terms, for example, class and gender, developments here have had nationwide implications regarding cycling trends and policies.

Chapter 1 begins with the emergence of cycling as a growing and then popular activity during the Victorian period. In particular, the chapter examines how cycling became a middle-class recreation and, as a consequence, how it reflected and reinforced middle-class values, especially amateurism. The Victorian period and Edwardian eras are also the setting for Chapter 2. This chapter looks at how the bicycle became part of contemporary popular culture. The main emphasis is on how the sport of cycling developed. The 1890s had precipitated a boom in cycling more generally, but it was quickly followed by a crash.

The next four chapters cover the middle years of the twentieth century. This period has been largely neglected by historians of cycling, yet it witnessed not only the highpoint of cycling's popularity but also its shifting political and cultural status. Chapter 3 examines the changing relationship between cycling and Englishness during the interwar period through the prism of transport politics. Cycling's cultural status had been firmly fixed to a rural ideology, but motoring's growing integration into the fabric of British life challenged this ideal and thus cycling's association with it. The interwar years more generally had witnessed cycling's second boom. Chapter 4 charts the birth of this popularity up until the mid-1950s and its consequence for cycling's role in British society. Cycling became a vital part of the outdoor movement as millions of people would ride their bicycle into the countryside for pleasure. Clubs also flourished, although even this essentially democratic activity was marked by demarcations of class. Chapter 5 is devoted to sport and in particular road racing. The main point here is that developments were inextricably linked with cycling's political and cultural status. Essentially, the chapter charts the development of the time trial from the late nineteenth century to the establishment of massed-start racing by the 1950s, which can be set in a narrative of tradition versus modernity. Chapter 6 is a standalone chapter on women and cycling. It mainly covers the first half of the twentieth century and highlights how cycling continued to be a symbol of female emancipation just through the sheer numbers of women who were now riding bicycles for both sporting and leisure purposes.

Boom is usually followed by bust, and Chapter 7 looks at the period between around 1955 and 1975. With the onset of the age of motoring, cycling declined as a mass activity and especially as a form of transport, a victim of post-war modernity and planning. As a consequence, cycling was forced to adapt to changing consumer tastes and look to niche markets. Chapter 8 charts the relationship between the bicycle, politics and environmentalism. The bicycle has come to represent both an anti-modernist critique and a symbol of the bourgeoning environmental movement since the early 1970s.

Chapter 9 examines the resurgence of cycling in post-industrial Britain, covering the 1970s through to the early twenty-first century. Partly as a result of changing attitudes to the environment and a growth in the health and fitness industry, cycling underwent a consumer boom in the late twentieth century. The final chapter is devoted to elite sport. It charts the rise of British cycling from the 1960s when it was still a largely amateur sport to its international dominance on the road and track in the early twenty-first century. Underpinning this transformation were a greater state investment in sport generally and the media's growing influence. With success though came doubt as British cycling was unable to escape cycling's reputation for doping. Thus, cycling has been a ubiquitous activity with many functions and meanings; this book attempts to understand the ebbs and flows of its relationship with British society.

CHAPTER 1

Cycling and the rise of respectable recreation

In February 1869 the first London to Brighton bicycle journey took place. It was also the first long-distance bicycle road ride in Great Britain. Three pioneering velocipedes riders, Charles Spencer, J. Mayall and Rowley B. Turner, took the best part of a day to cover the 50 or so miles on machines weighing between 70 and 80 pounds. They set off in the morning, stopped off in Crawley for lunch before reaching Brighton in darkness. Spencer and Mayall were gymnasts from the German Gym Club in King's Cross, and Spencer would later earn a living writing about cycling and as a bicycle instructor, teaching people how to ride these new modern machines. Spencer himself had been taught by Turner. It was Turner, then a student in Paris, who had been the first person to bring a Michaux velocipede – an iron-tired wooden boneshaker – to Britain in 1868. He then persuaded his uncle, Josiah Turner, the managing director of the European Sewing Machine Company (later Coventry Machinists Co. Ltd.), to accept an order to build 400 machines for the French market. However, with the outbreak of the Franco-Prussian War the machines were later put on the British market. The three riders were followed for part of their journey by a journalist from *The Times* in a horse-drawn carriage as the ride was, in essence, a commercial venture and an exercise in marketing, as it acted as a public demonstration of the machine's capabilities and a test of its robustness. The completion of their ride proved that the new machine was practical and road worthy. The publicity it brought to cycling and its trade ushered in a craze for this new activity, and it became a marker of modernity among the middle classes in Britain, as at the time it was only they who could afford the price of £10 to £12 for each machine.[1]

The birth and then the startling growth in popularity of cycling both reflected and reinforced many of the characteristics of the Victorian age.

Economic prosperity, entrepreneurship, national self-confidence and growing social divisions can all be found in the emergence of cycling as a mass activity. Cycling enjoyed an elevated place in social circles, which was both a cause and a product of a boom in sales of bicycles during the 1890s especially, and before the mass production of motor vehicles, cyclists enjoyed the relative freedom of the roads. The bicycle also offered a form of liberation and emancipation for women while organizations such as the Cyclists' Touring Club (CTC) and the National Cyclists' Union (NCU) established cycling as a sport and leisure activity on a national scale. While cycling eventually traversed both class and gender lines, it was initially a male, middle-class activity for participation and pleasure seeking. More generally, '[s]port became embroiled in the sophistication of a class society anxious to define its own position in a world of very raw newness'.[2] In particular, the ideology of amateurism was present within cycling as it was in many other areas of middle-class society.

While cycling offered the Victorians a modern form of pleasure and thrill seeking, its appeal was also a response to a range of contemporary anxieties. One of these was health. Holt has argued that '[m]aterial and cultural forces came together in the second half of the nineteenth century to create a new culture of the body, ingeniously fusing together the values of a striving enterprising liberal elite with the refined and restrained world of upper-class good manners and style'.[3] Summed up by the phrase *mens sana in corpore sano*, Bruce Haley has claimed that '[n]o topic more occupied the Victorian mind than Health – not religion, or politics, or Improvement, or Darwinism'. The dominant idea, reflecting new attitudes towards mental well-being, was 'total health or wholeness'. New attitudes to bodily discipline found receptive audiences in all areas of Victorian society and its institutions.[4] The birth of cycling coincided with the sports boom of the late nineteenth century. A cult of athleticism had been stimulated in the elite public schools, leading to a growth in the popularity of sports such as football and cricket, while for the middle classes in particular lawn tennis and golf took root in the bourgeoning suburbs. An increasing number of publications were devoted to physical culture and the importance of exercise in attaining a healthy mind in a healthy body.[5]

The cycling industry and the sport's enthusiasts and promoters had been keen to point out the health benefits of cycling through its link to the 'great outdoors'. The Victorian era had witnessed an exponential growth in office work, leading to the 'great indoors'. Working conditions were unhealthy due to rising levels of pollution in cities, poor ventilation and a lack of lighting. As a result, it bred a need to escape into the country. One notable medical cycling enthusiast, Dr Richardson, declared,

> I really know of nothing that has been so good for health. They [men and women] have learned how to ventilate their own bodies, how to imbibe an air free of injurious vapours and particles; while they have developed

a freedom and a strength of limb, a mental pleasure and escape from care, which have been useful alike to mind and body. In addition, they have been gainers of many good and serviceable mental qualities.[6]

Arthur Balfour, the future prime minister, later noted that in light of rapid urbanization and the diminishing boundary between the rural and the urban, especially in London, previous generations had had fewer opportunities to get out of the capital 'to enjoy by means of the cycle a breath of country air, a view of country scenery, a knowledge of the splendours of the magnificence, which English scenery presents to us'.[7]

On the flip side of its pleasures, riding a bicycle brought with it danger and the threat of injury. In 1876 one cyclist in Scotland had suffered a broken arm and other injuries after a boy threw his cap into the front wheel of his ordinary. It was noted that there had been many other serious accidents in Edinburgh due to this type of behaviour.[8] Later, there were medical warnings over the dangers of cycling. These included damage to the spine due to a crouched riding style, 'bicycle face' caused by an aching neck as well a risk of a general decline in fertility. In 1896 a series of contradictory articles in the *British Medical Journal* on the relationship between health and cycling reflected this state of affairs.[9] Much of the advice dispensed regarding exercise and its benefits for health was predicated on the notion of moderation. It was thought that excessive physical activity would lead to ill health and this also applied to cycling. Moreover, the promotion of moderation was also a reaction to the growing popularity of professional and commercial sport which contradicted the virtues of sport as seen through the eyes (and words) of an amateur elite.

Cycling, allied to its health benefits, also had a moral worth, it was argued. In 1884 E. R. Shipton, the editor of the Cycling Tourists' Club's *CTC Gazette*, proclaimed,

> Cycling is daily becoming a strong moral force, not alone in that it has enlisted the sympathies of those who seek healthful recreation at a modicum of cost but because it has appealed successfully to those in high places, and because its utilitarian nature is daily bringing it into request in a hundred different ways, all of which must gain for it a position, in the estimation of an essentially practical people, which it would otherwise for many a day have been denied.[10]

In March 1899, Balfour, in a speech addressing the National Cyclists' Union, in his capacity as its president, declared that 'there has been no more civilising invention in the memory of the present generation than the invention of the cycle. (Cheers). Open to all classes, enjoyed by both sexes and by all ages, the cycle gives us health, it gives us variety.'[11] Moreover, riding a bicycle was not only a healthy and pleasurable experience; it was a marker of Victorian middle-class status. Despite Balfour's claim, at a time of rapid social change, cycling carried meanings of respectability and aspiration, which often made it a site of both social inclusion and exclusion. For Richardson, for example, cycling produced character-building qualities, such as perseverance and courage, which were important characteristics of the middle-class gentleman.[12] It was in this social and cultural context that cycling emerged as a pastime.

Victorian cyclists and cycling organizations

In terms of the extent of cycling's popularity, the period from 1870 to 1900 can be divided into two phases: before and after the craze of the 1890s. At its height from 1895 to 1897, it was estimated that there were 1.5 million cyclists in Britain.[13] According to Rubenstein, 'There is no doubt that almost everyone who could afford a bicycle and who was not physically incapacitated rode avidly during the "boom" of 1895-97.'[14] Women in particular were to the fore during the boom. In 1890 a Ladies' Cycling Club was briefly formed, before the years 1895 to 1898 witnessed the establishment of numerous female cycling clubs across the country with a national body, the Lady Cyclists' Association, formed in 1895. Yet few of these clubs survived the boom and many disbanded, reflecting general trends within cycling.[15]

While much of the history of cycling has been written from the perspective of the 1890s, the 'anti-diluvium period' remains important as the pre-1890s established some of the social and cultural trends that shaped cycling deep in to the twentieth century. How many people actually rode bicycles and tricycles during this early period? In 1877 one estimate put the figure at 40,000. By 1888 it had grown to an estimate of 300,000 to 400,000 cyclists.[16] As way of comparison, in 1884 there were only around 4,000 bicycles in France, but by 1893 this figure had increased to 132,276, rising in 1898 to 376,117.[17] Early meets and parades had helped to popularize cycling, drawing large crowds and interest from the press. One of the first had been the Hampton Court meeting. It was first staged in 1874 with 40 cyclists; two years later there were over 400, most belonging to a club. In 1876 they rode two-by-two from Hampton to Teddington, then on to Bushey Park before returning to Hampton. Another indication of cycling's bourgeoning popularity was the emergence of instructors. An early pioneer was the aforementioned Charles Spencer. Spencer was a journalist and president of the Middlesex Bicycle Club and his gymnasium was the first school for teaching bicycling. In 1870 he published a guide for beginners, *The Bicycle: Its Use and Action*.[18] By the late 1880s there were cycling schools in most urban areas.[19] In another social context, the early bicycle also drew comparisons with the horse as a 'steed of steel' or 'iron steed', for example. It reflected how now owning bicycle carried similar social and economic connotations to owning a horse, as the rider could look down on those, literally and metaphorically, who could not own one.[20]

Britain was still a localized and rural country during the nineteenth century.[21] Yet like the railways, the bicycle was opening up the nation. The bicycle allowed a rider to discover new roads as well as new villages and towns. In June 1873 Spencer and three other members of his club rode for the first time from London to John O'Groats, a journey of about 800 miles, which took two weeks. In July 1880 Henry Blackwell and C. A. Harman, both of Canonbury CC, completed the first 'End-to-End' on bicycles, taking 13 days to ride 889 miles from Land's End to John O'Groats.[22] In 1878 two national cycling organizations had been formed: the Bicycle Union, later renamed the National Cyclists' Union in 1883, and the Bicycle Touring Club, later renamed the Cyclists' Touring Club also in 1883.[23] By 1899 the membership of the CTC was over 60,000 and that of the NCU, based on its individual members and affiliated clubs, had exceeded 70,000.[24] However, the vast majority of cyclists were unattached, because unlike members of team and many individual sports, they did not need to belong to a club; they instead could make their own fun due to the freedom cycling offered. Moreover, it was not compulsory for clubs to join these bodies.

Underpinning the early development of cycling was the growth of an increasingly affluent suburban middle class, comprised mainly of young men, who were eager to embrace modern technology. The late nineteenth century had witnessed a growth in the middle classes more generally. In 1880 it was estimated that the non-manual class accounted for 16.7 per cent of the working population, a figure that had increased to 26.6 per cent by 1913. While there was a modest increase in some professions such as the clergy and the law, there were exponential rises elsewhere. For example, the number of civil servants grew by nearly 170 per cent.[25] Between 1881 and 1911, the number of commercial clerks in England and Wales – male and female – rose from 181,457 to 477,535.[26] Male clerks and other members of the lower middle classes were at the forefront of the 1890s sporting mania. Places of work were used for organizing sporting activities, while clerks also had the requisite skills in running clubs.[27]

The middle-class cycling fraternity was not homogenous. In H. G. Wells' comic novel *The Wheels of Chance: A Bicycling Idyll*, published at the height of the boom in 1896, the hero Hoopdriver, was a draper's assistant. He represented a classic member of the socially aspiring lower middle classes. While he planned to spend his holidays on a cycling tour in the south of England, he was unable to afford a modern diamond-frame bicycle, and kept falling off his older model, which resulted in badly bruised legs. Despite the democratic nature of cycling, the novel highlights the stark class divisions between its main characters. While Hoopdriver aspires to respectability, he is looked down upon by the acquaintances of the novel's upper-middle-class heroine. Wells was one of a number of literary figures who made cycling the subject of one of their novels. Another was J. K. Jerome and his story of *Three Men on a Bummel*. Although a similarly comic story, it concerned the adventures of three middle-class gentlemen on a cycling tour in Europe. The playwright George Bernard Shaw was also a regular cyclist who was accompanied on his rides by his Fabian friends, Sidney and Beatrice Webb.[28] Another substantial literary figure who cycled was Henry James. James began riding in Torquay in 1895 on 'a battered Humber', and cycling even provided the inspiration for some of his work.[29]

In the early days of cycling, it had been only some members of the middle classes who could afford to buy brand new machines, as a velocipede, an ordinary and especially a sociable or tricycle were initially far out of the price range of working people. In 1869 the first advertisement for a velocipede appeared in the *English Mechanic*. The cost of a No. 1 with a 32-inch front wheel was £10, with a No. 4 (48-inch front wheel) at £14.[30] By 1883 a Humber No. 3 Racer Bicycle – an ordinary – was advertised at £18 while two years later £32 was the price for a new Humber No. 5, Ordinary Tandem.[31] Doctors had been one of the first groups of people to use a bicycle for work purposes. Previously many rural doctors had used a horse, but from the 1870s, the expense of keeping one had increased considerably and only elite members of the profession could afford a horse.[32] The bicycle would be only an intermediate stage in doctors' transition from horses to mechanical transport, as they later took to the motor car with great speed. The bicycle's cultural status was further highlighted by the adverse reaction it generated, which included numerous reports of working-class boys throwing stones at the riders.

During the boom summers of 1895 and 1896, cycling gained popularity among the upper echelons of British society.[33] Battersea Park and Rotten Row in Hyde Park became fashionable locations for London society, and particularly striking were the hundreds of young women who had taken up this new activity. In addition, politicians and leading entertainers were willingly photographed on a bike. In 1895, as a mark of cycling's social respectability, Arthur Balfour became president of the NCU.[34] Balfour at the time was the leader of the House of Commons and the First Lord of the Treasury, before becoming Tory prime minister in 1902. In 1899 it was claimed that over 100 MPs were members of the CTC and that all six vice-chancellors of Cambridge university were cyclists.[35] In that year, new candidates for membership of the CTC included the Duchess of Connaught and her daughters, Ladies Torrens, Bentinck, Meredyth, Vincent and Blaine plus Baroness Von Lepel.[36] In 1899, it was noted that the Bishop of Stepney cycled early in the morning when there was little traffic.[37]

Another indicator of the growth in cycling's popularity was an increase in bicycle theft. In 1904, for example, it was reported that Edward Levene had been sentenced for receiving over 200 stolen bicycles. He kept what was apparently a respectable bicycle business in Tottenham Court Road, the speciality of which was second-hand machines. Cycle thieves evidently knew it and brought stolen cycles there knowing there was a ready market.

Levene at once altered the machines – changing handlebars, saddles and easily transferable parts, even re-enamelling, so that identification was almost impossible.[38]

Early cycling clubs were very keen to project and protect the virtues of the gentleman–amateur and at the same time maintain a social exclusivity. The creed of amateurism ran strongly through virtually all early cycling clubs, especially when it came to the issue of professionals. It was during this period that amateurism, as an ideology, shaped social and cultural attitudes not just in sport where it has been most commonly associated, but also within society more generally. As Holt has argued, 'Amateurism was an important and distinctive element in the ideology of the British elite.'[39] This gentleman-amateur creed was composed of unwritten codes of behaviour and conventions. It was lubricated by an arcane language honed in all-male elite public schools, and was in evidence throughout the British establishment. Indeed, the British 'constitution' – Britain does not have a written constitution – has been a mixture of laws, customs and rituals, which have evolved over the centuries. With reference to the Victorian middle classes, amateurism provided legitimacy for 'marking social difference, confirming class boundaries, controlling property, organisations and membership and asserting power'.[40] As a more class-based society began to develop from the mid-Victorian period, amateurism was accompanied by snobbishness, hypocrisy and double standards that were emblematic of class.[41]

Many early cycling clubs were also part of 'a male-dominated associational world'.[42] Voluntary associational life more generally was an important feature of civil society in urban Victorian Britain.[43] For the urban middle classes, clubs were part of a wide-ranging network of voluntary societies. Not only did networks provide an opportunity to reaffirm middle-class identity, but especially through voluntary and philanthropic work they were also used for professional and social advancement.[44] Clubs formed the backbone of Britain's early cycling culture. In 1873 there were seven bicycle clubs in London with 22 in the provinces. By 1877 these figures had increased to 23 and 100, respectively, and it was estimated that there were 230 clubs nationwide in 1879.[45] The journalist Henry Sturmey calculated that this equated to between 8,000 and 9,000 club members. In 1898, following the mid-nineties boom, Sturmey estimated that there were 1,816 clubs in Britain, with 256 in London and, based on an average membership of 71 members, there was a total membership of 128,936.[46] Yet it is worth noting that this still only amounted to around 10 per cent of the estimated number of people who then rode a bicycle.

The origins and motivations for forming individual clubs were varied. The earliest cycling club may have been the Liverpool Velocipede Club formed in 1868, while the London-based Pickwick Club was formed in 1870. Named after Dickens' novel *The Pickwick Papers*, its membership was restricted because all members were named after characters in the book. Peterborough CC, the oldest active club, was formed in 1874, the same year as the first club in Yorkshire, Bradford Bicycle Club, was formed.[47] In 1876 clubs were formed in Chichester, Hastings and St. Leonards, Darlington and Leek. Clubs sprung up all over the British Isles. Ireland's first club, the Amateur Velocipede Club, was founded in Dublin in 1869, but was short-lived and folded in 1873. The 1870s witnessed the formation of clubs across Ireland, including in 1874, the Ariel Bicycle Club, the first in Ulster. In that same year the first club in Limerick was formed.[48] Most clubs were geographical in origin, but some clubs had other motivations. The Vegetarian Cycling Club was formed in 1887, for example, to promote the healthy virtues of a meat-free diet. After a year it had over 100 members.[49] In 1895 the Temperance Society in Leicester added a cycling club to its portfolio of activities.[50]

As a feature of civil society more generally, some clubs had greater social pretensions than others. One such elite institution was the Amateur Athletic Club (AAC). Formed in December 1865 as a private club, its select membership was open only to army and naval officers, members of the civil service, the universities, the Bar and the principal 'London Clubs'. Anyone else had to go through a ballot, and thus could be 'black-balled' if their social make-up did not satisfy the membership.[51] The social make-up and rules of early cycling clubs reflected these social aspirations. The loftily named Amateur Bicycle Club was formed in 1871 and prospective members had to meet two basic qualifications: that 'he be a Gentleman-Amateur' and that he own a bicycle. Not only was the prohibitive cost of a bicycle a form of exclusion, but the deliberately vague notion and aspiration of a gentleman–amateur further provided upper-middle-class networks with their own kind of cultural legitimation.[52] The Edinburgh Bicycle Club, formed in 1874, soon changed its name to incorporate 'Amateur' in the title. Ironically, the Amateur Bicycle Club did the opposite, changing its to 'London'. Clubs made up their own rules and the Edinburgh club initially disallowed its members from joining other local clubs.[53] The first club formed in industrial Middlesbrough was the Middlesbrough Bicycle Club in 1877. Unsurprisingly, the club's initial membership of 20 was socially exclusive. The first president was one of the town's 'ironmasters', John Gjers, while another two ironmasters were club officials. Four lived in the suburban and affluent area of Southfields Villas. Middle-class professionals also sat on the committee. By 1881 membership had increased to 80 and the club had its own premises, which included a billiard table, reinforcing both the idea of the club and the sense of exclusivity.[54]

Some early cycling clubs put in place a de facto 'black-balling' system. At the Temple Bicycle Club's 1877 annual general meeting, for example, there was concern over how 'to remove any possible doubts as to the Temple Bicycle Club having any members on its books not qualified by the rules of the club to be members, or its having discreditable members'. New and stringent rules were introduced pertaining to the election of new members, which were intended to 'establish the Temple Bicycle Club on such a solid basis as to justly entitle it to a position among the first amateur bicycle clubs of the day'.[55] In 1882 the North London Tricycle Club was formed 'for ladies and gentlemen tricyclists' and it was stated that 'undesirable persons will be kept out by the observance of the "personal acquaintance" qualification'.[56] As cycling's popularity expanded, the motivations of new clubs reflected a more socially aspirant society as well as the values of social exclusion. In her study of the Catford Cycling Club, Geraldine Biddle-Perry has linked its formation in 1886 with the emergence of recreational cycling 'as a conduit of social aspiration for an expanding suburban clerical class in Britain'.[57] As a consequence, it is unsurprising that the ideology of amateurism took root in suburban cycling clubs.

In addition to aspirations of social mobility, for some groups cycling was overtly political and acted as an expression of class politics. Of course, for the vast majority of cyclists riding a bike was an unconscious political act; however, some cyclists literally used their bicycles to spread political messages. The most famous of these groups was the socialist Clarion cycling clubs. The 1880s had been a period of social and political unrest, which had led to the creation of a new wave of trade unions for unskilled workers and the formation of socialist organizations. The first Clarion club was formed in 1894 in Birmingham, through the efforts of Tom Groom, and all clubs later came under the umbrella of the National Clarion Cycling Club (formed in 1895). By the end of the year four other Clarion clubs or sections had been formed in Stoke-on-Trent, Liverpool, Bradford and Barnsley. In 1914, Clarion sections numbered over 200 with a total membership of over 6,000.[58] One famous member was Colin Veitch. He was a socialist who played professional football for Newcastle United and was a member of both the city's Clarion choir and the cycling club.[59] At first the intentions of Clarion cyclists were highly political. As 'the travelling prophets of a new era', according to Robert Blatchford, the founder of the *Clarion* newspaper, they delivered copies of his *Merrie England* as well as the *Clarion* and leaflets for socialist candidates during elections. However, these cyclists were in a minority and the clubs soon complemented politics with a mixture of leisurely rides, touring and sport.[60]

On sheer numbers alone the Clarion clubs, it could be argued, failed in their mission to spread the socialist message, especially when compared with the recreational clubs of the Social Democratic Party (SPD) in Germany. By 1914 over 600,000 Germans belonged to workers' leisure and cultural organizations, including 150,000 to its cycling section, the *Arbeitererradfahrerbund Solidarität*.[61] Yet the contrast here owed as much to political culture as a devotion to the socialist cause, and highlighted the importance of voluntarism within British civil society. McKibbin, in arguing why there was no Marxism in Britain before 1914, has shown how a rich and diverse associational culture was a contributory factor to its non-appearance. In addition, the commercialization of leisure gave British workers a greater choice of leisure interests than their European counterparts.[62] For many socialists, leisure was a 'problem'. Chris Waters has argued that socialists promoted a message of rational recreation when it came to leisure activities.[63] Anxieties over the use of leisure by the masses in this period had not been confined to socialists. Social elites, such as Matthew Arnold, for example, similarly believed that the growth of mass entertainments posed a danger to the moral and physical health of the nation and that instead leisure should be worthy.

Similar to amateurism, socialists disliked intensely the commercialization of leisure, but in their case, it was how it took the British worker away from the main task of making a socialist society. Robert Blatchford himself in his tract *Merrie England* was wary of how the workers' extra leisure time should be spent. By contrast, middle-class values that were attached to leisure and popular culture were anathema to many of the working classes who had already developed their own rich associational culture.[64] However, the Clarion clubs' relative lack of popularity and political impact also discounts the idea that working-class members of British cycling clubs forsook politics, which was clearly not the case. Indeed, one of the founders of the Labour Party, Will Thorne (MP for South-West Ham), had been a cyclist as well as a boxer and athlete.[65] The voluntary nature of cycling, therefore, shaped its future governance.

The right-wing equivalent to the National Clarion Cycling Club was the Primrose League Cycling Corps, formed in 1894, which mainly organized runs and concerts rather than competitive athletics.[66] Established in 1883, the Primrose League was a social club, built on the pillars of the Empire and the Church.[67] By 1900, it had over 1.5 million members with the rank and file drawn predominantly from members of the lower middle and middle classes; the leadership was drawn from local notables, and in 1899 Arthur Balfour was elected its president.[68] However, there were working-class members who reflected that strain of popular conservatism and pleasure seeking, which could be found in all parts of the working classes. During the 1890s the Conservative Party was 'militantly populist, taking the side of popular culture against middle-class busy bodies who wanted to reform it', and as a result, the values of conservatism complemented late-Victorian mass culture, including the cycling boom.[69]

The Cyclists' Touring Club: A national middle-class identity

In 1878 the CTC was formed, combining at a stroke two modern middle-class fashions: cycling and tourism. Very quickly the club established itself as an agency for the formation of a national middle-class identity and a haven for those across the broad spectrum of the middle classes who wanted to reinforce their middle-class credentials. More pertinently, the formation of the club contributed to the birth of modern tourism. Similar to cycling, tourism was a product of modernity, and shared analogous patterns of consumption, ideas about health and notions of aesthetics. In particular, the bicycle 'opened up the notion that leisure travel to almost anyplace could be available to virtually anybody'.[70] Underpinning this growth was the assumption of tourism's health-giving properties, *mens sana in corpore sano*. Middle-class tourism was also perceived as a form of rational recreation, which complemented ideas of self-improvement as it was supposed to make people more educated, cultured and healthy.[71]

The CTC facilitated this growing middle-class tourist market. It appointed both chief consuls and consuls for its 'divisions' in both the British Isles and overseas, and they provided information to its members about roads, hotels and places of interest. The first club handbook was published in 1879. It listed the hotels and cycle repair shops where members could receive a discount, and by 1897 the CTC had agreements with 4,500 hotels and hostels across the UK. Guides and maps were later produced, plus road maps, while the *CTC Gazette* was a fount of knowledge. It contained accounts of tours, advice on touring, cycling fashions and a flourishing letters' page, which frequently published robust debates on contemporary issues related to both cycling and society.[72]

The CTC quickly gained in popularity. At the end of its first year it had 144 members. By 1883 this number had risen to 10,627 and grew to 22,316 in 1886. Interestingly, the numbers then tailed off, falling to 16,343 in 1895, before more than tripling to reach 60,449 in 1899, although it would dip sharply again, to 15,474 by 1913.[73] What about the CTC's socio-occupational make-up? In 1884 its membership revealed a mix of generally middle-class and lower-middle-class occupations.[74] It included 10 members of the nobility with the professions accounting for 1,037 and more strikingly, men from the trades – commerce and manufacturers, as well as artisans – making up the bulk of the membership, 7,357. Professionals included doctors (224 members) and lawyers (228). However, the largest group of workers were socially aspiring clerks and managers (1,994).

The make-up of the CTC reflected not only a diversification within the middle classes but also a hierarchy and stratification. Officials from upper-middle-class backgrounds were proportionately greater in number than those from the lower end when compared to the membership more generally. In 1884, the CTC was divided into 35 divisions, which included 8 outside Britain. Each was represented by one or a number of councillors. In 1884 there were 63 councillors to be elected, with 72 men nominated. In terms of their occupational breakdown, there were 14 from the professions plus nine titled nominees including five who considered themselves a 'gentleman'. There was also a sprinkling of students, engineers and clerks, as well as two artisans – a joiner and a miller. However, those from trade and commerce accounted for the greatest number of nominees with 29.[75] Between 1878 and 1899, 648 people had served on the CTC council, including 58 lawyers; 38 clergymen; 32 professors and teachers; 30 doctors and surgeons; and 26 army officers.[76]

Senior CTC officials were from similarly elitist backgrounds. In 1897, for example, the club's chairman, Kendall Burnett (born, 1854), was a Scot, reflecting its national reach. A member of the gentry, his father was the largest landowner in Aberdeenshire. A high-achieving student, who had been educated at the universities of Oxford and Edinburgh, Burnett later qualified as a solicitor and practised in Aberdeen. He took his first cycling lesson at the age of 13, and joined the CTC in 1879 from when he worked his way up the club's hierarchy. In 1882 he became a chief consul in Scotland before getting elected as the chairman of the council in 1889. He was described as belonging to 'the strong, silent class of men who have made Britain what she is today – the men who live by deeds, and not by words'. He was also an important figure within the county's middle-class networks as president of the Aberdeenshire Chess Association and who had previously been the captain of its county cricket club.[77] In the same year, the CTC's vice chairman was William Cosens (born, 1846). He had also been a keen cyclist from the early days. He first began riding in 1869 and was an original member of the CTC. Educated at private schools, he later became the manager of the London and County bank in Hertford. His father was a landowner and farmer. From the outset, he worked his way up the CTC ranks through serving on various committees and in a number of roles, before his election as vice chairman in 1895. These roles included a chief consul, a member of the Finance Committee and the Map and Road Book Committee. He held many other public positions, including as treasurer of the Board of Hertfordshire Technical Instruction Association, treasurer of the Hertfordshire Arts Society and treasurer of the Rural District Council.[78] In 1897 the club treasurer was William Gurney, then its second longest-serving official. He had joined the CTC at its origin in 1878 and was elected treasurer in 1882. Born in Bradford he attended Doncaster Grammar School, before moving back to Bradford to work in its textile industry. An early enthusiast for cycling and touring, he had been a founder of Bradford BC and the inaugural North of England meet at Harrogate in 1877, which subsequently led to the formation of the CTC a year later. He also played a formative role at the NCU in West Yorkshire. In 1885 he helped establish the West Riding Centre and was elected its chairman in 1889.[79]

Amateurism ran deep within the CTC. Peter Borsay has argued that the membership and leadership of middle-class clubs and societies acted as a source of recruitment for a pluralistic governing elite, who shared a common set of values, including gentlemanly amateurism.[80] From the outset, the CTC's rules unashamedly stated: 'Any AMATEUR Bicyclist or Tricyclist – lady or gentleman – is eligible for election to the Bicycle Touring Club.'[81] As a consequence, there was a strict screening process for prospective new members with membership lists published each month in the *CTC Gazette*. The exclusion of professionals was the main objective, although this definition was wide ranging. It was directed not only at professional cyclists but also at those with links to the cycling trade, including instructors, which it was feared would give the CTC a whiff of commercialism. On occasions, established members wrote in to question the amateur credentials of new ones.[82] In 1889, for example, it was claimed by Mr C. W. Nairn that Mr Plaum should be debarred because he had worked as an agent for Humber, the cycling manufacturer.[83] Scrutiny was not restricted to professional cyclists, but also included sport more generally. In 1882 it was declared that if a bicyclist or tricyclist had run in foot races for money then they are 'no longer an amateur rider. A professional in one branch of sport is a professional in all.'[84] In 1889 it was reported that a professional cricketer had wished to join a local cycling club, and in turn had applied to join the CTC. The *CTC Gazette* argued that if the amateur regulation was not enforced then 'it will of course be apparent if the conditions of things were otherwise, the athletic world would soon resolve itself into chaos'. If the professional cricketer joined, it was claimed that this was acceptable but if he competed against other club members for a prize they would risk losing their amateur status.[85] (There was the potential delicious irony that Arthur Balfour would have been unable to join the CTC as he had once played golf against a professional.[86]) The CTC's exclusion of professional cyclists lasted until 1930, reflecting not only the residual appeal of the gentleman–amateur, but also middle-class anxieties over their status and lingering suspicions over professional athletes.[87]

The appeal of cycling's male, middle-class sociability was not confined to Britain. The sharing of middle-class values was a reflection of the wider growth of the professional classes, which transcended national boundaries. In the late nineteenth century, Anglophilia was common throughout the globe and many of the middle classes in different countries were influenced by British culture and ideology. Other countries were keen to adopt not only British sports but also the codes of behaviour associated with a gentleman–amateur. During the early 1880s there were reciprocal relations between British and American cyclists, especially those who rode under the flag of the League of American Wheelmen (LAW). The LAW had been founded in 1880, while an American division of the CTC was also established. In that year the members of the LAW toured Britain and it was concluded with a presentation and dinner in their honour by the CTC.[88]

Middle-class values at a transnational level were further reinforced through touring. In July 1897 an International Touring Congress was held in Amsterdam and Belgium with the objective of forming an International Union of Touring Clubs. Attended by a CTC delegate, in his opening address the president of the Netherlands Cyclists' Union, Edo Bergsma, who was also the burgomaster of Enschedé, 'expressed the hope that their deliberations would tend not only to the development of international cycle touring, but to the encouragement of a feeling on international friendship and esteem'.[89] An international league was formed a year later and its inaugural congress took place in 1899 in London. The Congress also revealed typical British sensibilities about its perceived place in world affairs. The CTC, similar to British football associations' attitudes to the formation of FIFA in 1904, had been cooler in its enthusiasm. It reflected wider British feelings of not only superiority in the Victorian period but also anxieties over a perceived threat to its position. The British representative was quick to remind the other delegates that the CTC was the '*doyen*' of touring clubs. Without a hint of irony or modesty, 'he could without egotism say that the Clubs of the various delegates present were but offshoots of the parent body'. He also pointed out that nearly all international cyclists who toured, 'no matter to what nationality they belonged, joined the CTC'. Moreover, when other touring clubs were formed, the CTC – generously – did not raise any objections, responding that imitation was the greatest form of flattery. Instead, the CTC was there to observe and would not pledge itself to abide by the decisions of the Congress.[90]

In a wider sense, the Congress highlighted both a growing demand for the freedom of movement of people across Europe and the increasing importance and organization of the tourism industry. As David Edgerton notes, in 1900 the UK was relatively cosmopolitan and liberal, and conducted free trade with Europe and the rest of the world.[91] One of the motivations behind the Congress had been to smooth the travel of cycling tourists through the removal of all custom barriers to international touring. In 1891 the CTC had reached its own agreement with the French government for its members; if members produced their membership card at customs, a certificate of re-exportation was not required for their bicycle. After its introduction over 50,000 CTC members had made use of it by 1897. In addition, the Congress wanted to standardize and simplify touring in different countries. This would entail offering the same benefits to all members at hotels and hostelries across Europe, plus uniformity over danger signs, handbooks and maps.[92]

Cycling club culture

What did club cyclists do during this early period? What activities did they undertake and what culture/s did they generate? Club life was organized around an annual calendar of club runs, racing and social occasions. Initially, clubs offered opportunities for male sociability, in particular the weekly run. The first run of the Edinburgh Amateur Bicycle Club (EABC) took place in April 1874 and comprised six members. It was later agreed to meet at Haymarket at 3.30 pm every Saturday. On one early run four members plus two 'strangers' rode across the Sean Bridge and then rode on to Camond Bridge 'where they refreshed themselves' before carrying on to Queensferry. Following a short stay, again no doubt for refreshment, they left and arrived home at 7.00 pm. Early reports of these rides were notable for their remarks on (unsurprisingly) the weather and also the condition of the roads, which were sometimes described as soft, heavy or splendid.[93]

Club life was not just riding and racing, it was also for talking, arguing, reminiscing, eating, drinking, writing articles for magazines, organizing dances, putting on plays and musical evenings, as well as probably high jinks, and possibly some 'sinful pleasures'.[94] The EABC also held social occasions. In January 1884, at the Imperial Hotel, a smoking concert took place with 60 'gentlemen' where '[a] most enjoyable evening was passed and a first rate time was had with songs, pianoforte, solos and duets, ... and recitations'.[95] On winter evenings, for many clubs, the club room, which was often in a pub, was a place where members could meet friends. These types of fraternal experiences demonstrated the complex interrelationships of male middle-class society, creating 'layered identities' in sport, as in other aspects of cultural life.[96] For many cyclists, the season began with the Easter club tour. For some clubs this was a long-held tradition by the twentieth century. In 1900 the Stanley Club held its 22nd Easter tour with club rides to Warwick via Wendover, Aylesbury and Banbury. Two days later the party cycled to Oxford before getting the train back to London.[97]

All clubs had a captain and at first their role was a prestigious one. Some clubs initially selected the captain and other officials via the annual club championship. In 1874 the EABC stipulated that 'on the last Saturday of May every year there shall be a race of not less than 40 miles for the Captaincy, Sub-captaincy and 1st and 2nd Committee men, and the gentlemen who win shall, along with the secretary, also acting as treasurer, constitute the committee of management'.[98] On Saturday, 29 May 1875, a handicap race was run on a road between Bathgate and Edinburgh. The eventual winner was Mr Nicol who had started a minute before the runner-up, Mr Reid, a starter from scratch; they assumed the positions of captain and sub-captain, respectively. It was noted that two other riders who started on scratch had accidents within minutes.[99]

Early club rules had distinctly militaristic overtones, especially in regard to the club runs. In 1877 the EABC's military connections extended to its president, one Captain Colquhoun; by 1884 he was a colonel.[100] An EABC club run in the 1870s and 1880s shared similar characteristics with hunting. The members rode out with the 'senior officer' while another officer was appointed as the 'whipper-in' – a hunting term for handling a pack of hounds. A series of whistle signals were used to 'control the pack'. One whistle from the leader and riders had to mount and ride in single file. Once mounted, two whistles signalled that everyone had to change to double file; three and they had to dismount. The whipper-in controlled the run's pace; one whistle meant slow down, two to speed up. No other member could use their whistles unless in an emergency. On club runs the captain's command was final. No rider could pass him, or the 'officer in command', without his permission. Any member infringing this rule would be fined and a second offence could result in expulsion from the club.[101]

By the early twentieth century the novelty and the strict controls of the club run had begun to wear off. This trend no doubt reflected cycling's growing popularity among the masses, and a lack of deference to invented middle-class conventions. In addition, cycling's inherent independent nature encouraged freedom and inhibited conformity. One cycling journalist claimed that '[i]t is not pleasant to ride in drives, to halt and eat where ordered, frequently to spend the greater part of a fine evening in a stuffy, smoky room, bored by amateurish efforts to entertain, in company with perhaps many who are not altogether congenial'. Some clubs looked at other ways to keep members interested. The Sharrow Club in Sheffield organized a monthly visit to a place of historical interest with one member acting as a guide.[102]

Cycling and the Victorian female body

One of the key arguments made about cycling's growing popularity was that it acted as a form of emancipation for the late-nineteenth-century woman. As Ina Zweiniger-Bargielowska has pointed out, 'The emergence of a strong, fit modern women challenged established ideas of feminine weakness and the rise of female sport and physical culture contributed towards the liberating of the female body.'[103] Cycling brought women not only the freedom of physical movement but also the freedom of social intercourse as it allowed the opportunity to meet members of the opposite sex outside the surveillance of the family. Of course, this was not the complete picture. Cycling – as with physical culture more generally – was a minor activity for women, mainly restricted to the middle classes. For the majority of women, who came from working-class backgrounds, life was one of remitting toil and hard work.[104] Any leisure was 'interwoven with their day-to-day routines and social and familial responsibilities'.[105] They were therefore excluded – more so than men – from this new craze and leisure practices in general on grounds of time and money. Technology, combined with the dictates of female fashion, were major factors in the early development of women's cycling. The invention and subsequent popularity of the ordinary made cycling for any middle-class woman impractical when the dictates of prevailing fashion and expected female behaviour were taken into account. One unsuccessful experiment, dating from 1869, was a tandem adapted with a rear seat side saddle, in theory, allowing middle-class women to both retain their dignity and also replicate the female style for riding a horse.[106]

It is difficult to know how many women took up cycling during this period. As with their male counterparts, it is likely most female cyclists did not join a club. However, some figures from the CTC can give a sense of cycling's growing popularity among women at the time. In October 1880 out of 3,500 CTC members only two were females.[107] The first had been the wife of the CTC secretary, J. A. Cotterell. Interestingly, there was no debate over her membership as the constitution had not stipulated that the CTC was a male-only club. It may also have been the case that many men were in favour of their wives, daughters and sisters joining the CTC. Davidoff and Hall have noted how middle-class Victorian fathers formed intense relationships with their children, which included going for walks with them and teaching them skills.[108] By 1884 women still made up only 2.7 per cent (342) of the club's 12,514 members.[109] Five years later, membership stood at 20,098 with 231 female cyclists (4.36 per cent) joining out of a total of 5,291 new members. By 1904, with membership at 38,487, there had been an exponential increase in female members and in that year, women made up 29 per cent (1,846) of the club's new additions (6,353).[110]

The sheer visibility of female cyclists was a contributory factor in shaping ideas of the late-nineteenth-century 'New Woman' and as a consequence helped to 'destabilise and reshape gender relations'. Debates over women's bodies revolved around the themes of beauty, health and fitness. The promotion of a fit, healthy female body not only challenged medical theories, but also overlapped with middle-class notions of femininity. In reality, dominant medical discourses regarding women and physical exercise were constantly in flux and as much related to class as gender.[111] Initially, debate among doctors had revolved around both contemporary medical theories, especially eugenics, and attitudes towards the role of (middle-class) women in Victorian society. It was contended that the human body had only a limited, non-renewable amount of energy (the 'vitalistic theory') and that women had to conserve theirs for their essential purpose in life – to bear children. Moreover, a patriarchal prudery meant that doctors – virtually all male at this time – had a cultural preference for refined women who were expected to conform to 'ladylike' forms of behaviour and certainly not overstrain themselves through physical exercise. However, due to the wider acceptance of new medical ideas the human body was increasingly being compared to a machine, which required maintenance and doctors began to realize that exercise for women was beneficial to their health and ability to reproduce. Female cyclists, and also writers, therefore, challenged the discourse of the 'eternally wounded women'.[112] As part of the growing fashion for physical culture, cycling promoted femininity among British women. How vigorous though and what form of exercise and physical culture should be promoted continued to be part of the debate, and would in particular shape the development of sport in women's cycling.[113]

One brief and largely overlooked episode in the history of female cycling – and cycling more generally – was the emergence of the tricycle and the sociable.[114] The tricycle stimulated a growth in the number of female cyclists. As a consequence, 'the tricycle provided the beachhead for women cyclists' in establishing and legitimizing their presence in public spaces, such as parks and streets, as cyclists. For female cyclists, therefore, this period was a harbinger of the 'safety' bicycle boom in the 1890s.[115] The tricycle was also an important moment in the technological innovation of cycling, and as Glen Norcliffe has argued 'the tricycle is a vehicle of considerable historical significance in its own right'.[116] During the 1880s there was a surge in demand for tricycles and sociables. They filled a historical gap in the market between the dominance of the male-only ordinary and the safety bicycle revolution. It was claimed that '[n]o man is more popular in his set than he who owns a sociable tricycle. Its possession seems to confer upon a badge of respectability equivalent to that proverbially attributed to the man who "keeps a gig".'[117]

Even before the invention of the ordinary, a number of 3- and 4-wheel machines had been built. One of their attractions was that they provided greater stability than two wheelers. In the 1870s, James Starley was the first inventor to successfully put a tricycle into production.[118] It was an attempt to promote a safer form of cycling, which was then largely restricted to fit young men. In 1877, through further experimentation, Starley invented both the first sociable, the Lever Tricycle, and then more successfully and importantly the Salvoquadricycle. It was driven by a chain – later used for the safety – and made cycling a more comfortable and faster experience. The 'Salvo' was the main reason for the tricycle's popularity and another design converted it into a two-seater machine.[119] In 1882 *The Tricyclist*, edited by G. Lacy Hillier, began publication to tap into its bourgeoning popularity. In its very first editorial Hillier pronounced, 'Great as are the capabilities of the bicycle for economic and rapid transit, it is certain that ... the tricycle will in the future find favour with a very much larger section of the public.'[120]

Tricycle and sociable machines allowed women to participate in cycling in a particular context. First, unsurprisingly, given their price (as discussed earlier), riding these machines was limited to only a small section of the middle classes, and was seen as a more practical and respectable activity for a woman than riding a bicycle. To a certain extent, riding a tricycle or sociable in the 1880s was an extension of married life. A companionate marriage was about intimacy and leisure as husband and wife were expected to spend a great deal of time in each other's company, and sharing a sociable fulfilled this expectation.[121] However, it was anticipated that the husband would perform most of the physical effort, mirroring how 'Victorian middle-class culture was constructed around a heavily polarized understanding of gender'.[122] In the 1882 summer edition of *Girl's Own Paper*, an image of a young woman riding a tricycle with her brother indicated how it was deemed necessary for females to be accompanied by a male member of her family.[123] Any espousal of tricycling's health benefits for women was usually sprinkled with 'patriarchal prudery'. *The Tricyclist's* first editorial, in its appeal for new recruits, declared, 'The fair sex, for once, can participate in the sport. Of purely athletic and health-giving pursuits over sisters have but little choice.' Tricycling, it was argued, was a more robust activity but one in which female members of polite society could participate and with greater benefits for health than

> [t]he mild inanities of croquet and the enjoyable game of tennis, which require two players at least, seem, with the exception of an occasional pull on the river by those fortunate enough to be able to indulge in it, to be the only open air pursuits likely to aid a healthy development. But tricycling (already finding favour with the fair sex) offers an extensive field of health-giving enjoyment. Picnic and sketching parties composed of a few fair tricyclists and a suitable escort are by no means unheard of. Paterfamilias jogs down the road on a sociable, with a daughter by his side; pairs of sisters glide along in search of health and exercise; and the British public are rapidly becoming accustomed to the fair 'Velocipediste' or 'Tricyclenne'. When once the 'conspicuousness' has worn off, many more ladies will take to the sport.[124]

Yet tricycles also offered some women individual opportunities for independence. One early female tricyclist was Elizabeth Garrett-Anderson, the first woman to qualify as a physician and surgeon. Her enthusiasm for cycling was perhaps unsurprising as she was 'strongly in favour of athletic and gymnastic exercises for ladies' and a notable critic of the vitalistic medical theory.[125] A member of the South London Tricycle Club, she was made a vice-president of the club, which later appointed a four-woman 'ladies' committee. The club also had two other women on its main committee of four. Hillier commented, 'This is highly necessary in tricycle clubs, so as to enable ladies to have some say in the management without which they can hardly be expected to take a strong interest in the club.'[126] One particularly energetic female tricyclist was Miss Jessie Choice who also wrote a column in the *Tricyclist* under the nom-de-plume 'Dottings by Dot'. Another member of the South London TC, in 1882 it was enthusiastically reported that, she rode a front-wheel steering single tricycle up Central Hill in Sydenham.[127] In the same year she recounted her journey to Brighton from South London.[128] The following year she was one of three female tricyclists who rode over 100 miles in 24 hours with one Mrs Allen of Birmingham setting a new record of 153 miles.[129]

The growth in female cycling had attracted the attention of male cyclists, albeit this particular gaze was also couched in contemporary attitudes towards women. In 1884, in his speech at the Stanley Show's second annual supper, the president of the NCU, Viscount Bury, was particularly glad 'to notice ladies present and to know that they were taking to tricycling with so much energy'. He was also 'astonished when he thought that some of them had ridden over 100 miles in the day, and considered it an astounding proof of the energy and determination which was stored within those *apparently* frail and tender forms'. He was unable though to pass comment without making reference to the connection between healthy exercise and beauty with a reference to the women in ancient Greece who took part in athletic exercises, which led to the 'classical beauty of form' and that 'the use of the tricycle by ladies would tend to the development of similar physical conditions.'[130]

Whereas bicycle clubs were male-only because the machines were only suitable for men to ride, tricycle clubs at first enthusiastically recruited female members. However, as female numbers increased so did tensions between the sexes. To a certain extent, these tensions reflected a clash between contemporary male perceptions of a woman's role and physical capabilities as well as women's growing social status. In 1869, single women ratepayers had received the right to vote in the Municipal Franchise Act while charity work was increasingly a space where women, such as Josephine Butler, were able to exert political influence. In 1883 Choice complained that the committee of the North London Tricycle Club had stated that in its opinion 'it is undesirable for lady-members to attend the winter club-runs, unless on sociable tricycles'.[131] She declared, 'I take up arms against this resolution … because it seems to me that we ladies have just at present need to stand up for our rights.' She added,

> Please do not exclaim my cynical masculine reader, 'Oh, you go in for woman's rights!' and think that by ridicule you can answer or silence us. Lately I have been sorry to notice an expression among clubmen unfavourable to lady-members.

Among 'clubmen' there had been a sense that the 'novelty' of female members had worn off, and that they now went too slow on club runs, so they were left behind (a claim that would be repeated throughout the twentieth century). She later appealed for others to join her on a women's-only run on single tricycles.

Another source of tension was smoking. Women from the upper-middle classes did not do it and did not like being in the same room when men were smoking. However, it was a regular ritual of cycling club dinners and socials as well as something men did after taking tea on a club run. Choice believed that women were in general too polite to ask men to stop smoking and would suffer in silence, although at one dinner, 'a prominent tricyclist and his wife left immediately [after] men began smoking'.[132] Hillier, as an arch proponent of amateurism in all its social exclusiveness, seized on the issue of smoking to promote – and remind his readers – that tricycle clubs were elitist bodies. The rise in membership of clubs had meant a decline in social exclusivity. Men could mix in any company but for women it was different because

> they suffer considerably if suddenly mixed up with others of the same sex but of lower social status, and we can hardly expect lady riders to go in

much for the sociability of club life whilst the fad for numerical strength alone is carried to the extent it is just at this time by some TCs.[133]

For Hillier, tricycle clubs were different and this 'straining for numbers' had an adverse impact on monitoring the social exclusivity of clubs. He argued,

> It is impossible in such gigantic bodies to check the candidates for election as fully as they should be checked. Personal acquaintance is not insisted on and the rapid downward gradations soon make the lengthy list of members look very mixed when carefully examined. A properly exclusive club cannot be a large one to commence with but it possesses within itself all the necessary qualities for a steady and healthy development.[134]

He questioned whether these members lower down the social scale were acquainted with the etiquette of smoking in the company of the 'softer sex'. He called on tricycle clubs to ensure their success 'that a certain amount of exclusiveness should regulate its qualification for membership and maintain as much as possible an equal social status amongst the members'. Similar to the regulations of the Amateur Athletic Club, he argued that for the success of a tricycle club there should be a mandatory clause on its proposal form that required information on the candidates' occupation or business, and 'by its means to keep the club as much as possible confined to the same strata of society'.[135] How this issue impinged on the number of females taking up cycling is unclear. However, it highlighted how the popularity of cycling could also threaten the elitist sensibilities of some of its influential figures; something that would accelerate during the 1890s.

Cycling styles and fashions

Victorian body cultures were not confined to health. Importantly for the amateur cyclist, style was just as important as cycling's health benefits for both men and women. Amateurism was also an aesthetic as 'the amateur sportsman came to stand for the ideal type of new English gentleman'.[136] Much emphasis was placed on a cyclist's riding style on leisure rides. Debates over style intensified in the 1890s due to increase in the number of working-class cyclists. Reflecting social tensions more widely, riding in a certain way offered an opportunity for the middle-class amateur to distinguish themselves from these 'furious' riders who were usually from the working classes. There were numerous images in *Cycling* of working-class cyclists hunched over the bicycle in contrast to middle-class men and women riding with an upright posture. This ideal manifested itself not only in the desire for the well-proportioned athletic body but also in forms of attire. Sartorial elegance – or at least this objective – continued to be an important aspect of cycling culture as it traversed the social spectrum.[137]

Initially, uniforms with a military bearing were important to middle-class cycling clubs as they fostered 'a sense of distinction through an elite form of togetherness'.[138] At the early Hampton parades most cyclists wore a military-style uniform. Debates over the choice of uniform and badge were common among members of many clubs. In 1874, for example, the EABC chose a Maltese Cross as its badge and dark purple as the colour of its uniform.[139] On its inception in 1883, the uniform or 'club costume' of the North Ormesby and Middlesbrough CC similarly reflected military tastes. It 'consisted of a dark green velvet jacket and knickers to match, with black stockings and hunting cap'. Club captains dressed according to their position, and in the case of the North Ormesby and Middlesbrough CC his cap was decorated with a gold cord, while other club officers wore silver cords.[140]

Much ink was spilt in the columns of the *CTC Gazette* over that club's uniform. Almost from its formation the CTC had insisted that members should wear one. In 1880 regulations were issued to members that it was compulsory to wear either the uniform or a badge. The uniform itself consisted of the following: 'Dark Green Devonshire Serge Jacket, Norfolk shape, Knickerbockers and Stanley Helmet of the same, Green Stockings and White Gloves. The club badge shall be fixed to the cap'. Moreover, reflecting ideas of hierarchy borrowed from the military, there were various small gradations within the uniform to distinguish members and club officials. Thus, each club consul had to wear 'a small piece of scarlet velvet under the badge, to project visibly out to a small degree on each side, so that the said consuls may be more easily recognised'. Not only this, but the consul could only buy the scarlet velvet from the CTC secretary. Meanwhile the club's president, vice-president and treasurer were to wear purple, while the chief consuls and secretary wore blue velvet. The badge – it would be changed in 1886 to its present design – was a small silver shield with the club's name. Even here there were gradations. Consuls were to have a small letter 'C' on their badges, while club officers wore gilt badges.[141]

The importance of the uniform to the CTC was further underlined when it appointed a uniform committee in 1882 due to ongoing complaints about its impracticality. The realities of enforcing uniform regulations as well as the impracticality of wearing one for cycling highlighted how the bicycle's ubiquity was a source of its ambiguity and the different meanings that cycling held. Whereas some regarded the uniform as a status symbol, for others cycling was a practical form of transport. In 1885 one member, a 'professional man', found the uniform 'useless' for practical purposes for someone like himself who rode his bicycle daily.[142] Moreover, as uniforms were purchased through the club, it made the CTC a trading concern, which in turn made many members uncomfortable due to this association with commercialism. The uniform was formally abandoned in 1907, although CTC members had begun to discard it by 1892.[143] An examination of photographs of groups of cyclists over the 1870–1900 period illustrates how the uniform was phased out, which highlighted how cycling's popularity had led to a liberalization of dress conventions.

Nevertheless, there continued to be an informal cycling dress code, which was part of cycling's commercialization. Stores such as Selfridges and Harrod's began to sell bicycles along with the specialist sporting goods retailer Gamage's.[144] Gamage's sold bicycles along with a range of fashionable cycling clothing with the intention of targeting young suburban club cyclists from the middle and lower middle classes. For his holidays, H. G. Wells's Hoopdriver bought himself a new brown cycling suit, which consisted of 'a handsome Norfolk jacket thing for 30s' and a pair of thick chequered stockings.[145] As Biddle-Perry has argued, 'Sport was a key factor in repositioning male consumers as subjects whose sexual and class identities could be expressed through appropriate forms of fashionable consumption.'[146]

To a large extent, debates over British women's attire for cycling from the nineteenth century, and up until the interwar period, were guided by the unwritten principle that '[a] lady should inwardly dress like a gentleman but outwardly look like a lady'.[147] While fashion and appearance were important, there was just as greater emphasis on the practicality of riding a bicycle or tricycle, but in the context of what was presumed a middle-class woman – who was not supposed to perspire or show any sign of bare legs – should wear in the late nineteenth century. Debates over the attire of female cyclists began to gather pace from the 1880s. In 1881 the Society for Rational Dress was formed. It was a response to new medical theories about lighter dress, the changing social and economic position of middle-class women and opposition to voluminous skirts, tight corsets and high heels. More women were also working, which necessitated leaving the home, while there was a growing awareness of the benefits of health and exercise, for which cycling was in the vanguard. However, French female cyclists had actually predated the rush to rationals. As early as 1869 some had eschewed long skirts due to their unsuitability for riding a velocipede, going on to wear tights and knickerbockers. Yet all this did was to confirm to the English the alleged immorality of French women and so it did not catch on.[148]

In 1882 Jessica Choice believed that women needed to present 'an elegant appearance when riding' and that '[m]any ladies are induced to ride from seeing a graceful lady-rider, or are deterred from doing so by an ungraceful one'. She behoved 'all those, therefore, who have the success of our sport at heart, to study appearance as much as possible; to be careful to adopt the most suitable and becoming dress'.[149] Men were also keen to participate in these debates. One early male self-appointed expert on women's dress had advised his wife on her style of dress when riding a tricycle and added that '[l]ady tricyclists should look as nearly as possible as though no alteration had been made in their ordinary dress; but for health and comfort sake the stereotyped underclothing must be radically altered'. One female tricyclist also stressed that dress should be practical. She had first worn a long

Newmarket coat, but found it too long and uncomfortable. Now she wore a wide skirt made from plain dark wool with little or no trimming. It was made extra long, but not long enough to catch on the treadles. She also wore a plain felt hat as well as boots, which she preferred to shoes as they soon got dirty. For her undergarment, she wore a merino wool rather than itchy flannel. Another female tricyclist preached simplicity. Fewer garments would mean 'the greater will be comfort, her freedom, and her happiness on the wheel; and the more eagerly will she set out upon each fresh excursion'.[150]

In 1883 around 50 female CTC members (plus a few male officials) held a meeting at the Masonic Hall in London to discuss a uniform for women. The chair of the meeting was Viscountess Harberton who was also president of the Rational Dress Society and later a supporter of women's suffrage.[151] Any proposed uniform had to strike a balance. It had to be practical and suited to 'the taking of healthy athletic exercise, with its concomitant need of freedom of movement' and keeping warm. At the meeting, a number of options for the uniform were discussed: a divided skirt; a long plain overskirt with an opening of five buttons; and loose trousers to match the colour of the dress chosen. An overskirt of walking length was recommended while Norfolk jackets, straw hats and black woollen stockings made up the remainder of the uniform. There was criticism of the choice of trousers over knickerbockers, but it suggested that even in the 1880s cutting edge fashion was far ahead of public ideas of what constituted proper female dress for cycling.[152]

It was the invention of the safety bicycle and the subsequent boom in female cyclists in the 1890s which gave dress reform greater public attention. It was during this decade that the idea of the New Woman emerged. Women's physical empowerment redefined femininity as the modern women embraced physical liberation as well as demands for greater access to education, wider employment opportunities and full rights as a citizen.[153] Moreover, riding a bicycle changed the social dynamics for women as it now meant riding astride and riding without a chaperone. The craze for women's cycling in this decade reflected this aggressive femininity and highlighted debates over rational dress. In Wells's *The Wheels of Chance*, Hoopdriver had been impressed with the heroine wearing 'rationals'. Yet it also reflected cycling's class divide. In September 1893 Tessie Reynolds wore rational dress, that is, knickerbockers, and rode from Brighton to London and back. It caused a sensation in the press, but for most it was a step too far in terms of a new fashion. While sport more generally provided a forum for female dress reform, most women cared little about it. As a consequence, long skirts, numerous petticoats, high heels and tight-laced corsets 'remained the sporting costume of Victorian women'. Moreover, most British women were not particularly emancipated in the ideas of dress reform or sympathetic to feminism. In general, 'while women engaged in games partly in order to enjoy a certain bodily freedom, they had no intention of sacrificing beauty for comfort', as sport for women was an opportunity to meet a future partner.154 Virtually all cycling and women's magazines continued to advise readers to stick to skirts. In 1909 it was declared by one journal that the fashion for rational dress was at an end.155 It would be the First World War that would revive it.156

Touring, landscape and Englishness

For many middle-class cyclists, in addition to its health-giving qualities, the essence of touring by bicycle was that it was distinctive and had a sense of romance and adventure compared to other travellers. In 1897 it was claimed that

> [f]or it is very true that that extremely modern person, the cyclist of to-day, stands almost alone among modern travellers in that he can, if he have [sic] the mind for it, still extract some romance from the manner of his journey. The railway passenger is, so to speak, packed like a parcel at one end and delivered at the other: wind and weather matter nothing to him, he encounters no adventures, and learns absolutely nothing of the places through which he passes.157

It was no coincidence that James T. Lightwood's 1928 history of the CTC was subtitled *Being the Romance of Fifty Years' Cycling*. Touring offered an opportunity to discover the nation. But what kind of nation did cyclists find? More pertinently what did they seek to find and in what context was the 'gaze' of the touring cyclist formed? To what extent were these based around contemporary notions of Britain and its constituent parts? Tourism is as much about preconditioned ideas as specific places and spaces; here modernity mixed with a sense of nostalgia, and touring by bicycle reinforced as much as reshaped ideas of what it meant to be British.158

The process of what constituted important British landmarks was in itself a social and cultural construction. By the nineteenth century there were sustained efforts by the state to identify the places and peoples of Britain, which had implications for how the English especially perceived their country, its landscape, its history and its heritage. The Local Government Act of 1888, for example, buttressed the ancient idea of the county, while, through architects, English history became identified with a certain look of the land. These sensibilities were underpinned by the fact that Britain was an island nation, with a sense it needed to be defended.159 Above all Ordnance Survey maps were important in framing a sense of identity. The mapping survey of Britain was completed in 1911 while there were sewerage and telegraphic networks that assisted in a process of standardization. By 1919 all British roads had been coded.160 As Colls observes, 'Once in the people's hands,

OS maps conferred a kind of geographical citizenship, a flattened-out, decentred, whole-people, Whole Island of Great Britain view of themselves and others.'[161] Moreover, '[a]ll people enjoyed the right to read these maps and use these roads. ... [Cycling] the country, and looking upon it, and learning about, and naming it, became mass pleasures.'[162]

In 1903, highlighting the importance of maps for touring cyclists, the CTC collaborated with Bartholomew's in producing a new map especially for cyclists. It was intended that this issue would indicate the topography from a cyclist's perspective including every road in Britain, the whereabouts of dangerous hills and descents and the inclusion of places of interest worth visiting.[163] Ideas of Britain and antiquarian perceptions of its history were found in the literature of cycling touring. During the boom, the *Daily Mail* published regular tourist columns, but it was in the pages of the *CTC Gazette* where the link between tourism, cycling and ideas of national identity was fortified.

Touring more generally was a constituent element of self-improvement for the Victorian middle classes. Reflecting notions of 'Smilesian' 'self-help', touring would broaden the mind it was believed, and guidebooks were designed to achieve this worthy and respectable middle-class objective. Nevertheless, guidebooks were designed to mediate to tourists the meanings of particular views, locations, landscapes, buildings, relics, ruins and other notable sites. In particular, cycling tourist literature made a major contribution to the idealization of the 'view'. This idealization had its roots in the late eighteenth century, when the growth in mountaineering ushered in the idea of the picturesque tour. The emergence of mountaineering as a leisure practice, especially in the Lake District, and its links with the literature of the romantic poets had played a crucial role in legitimizing the cultural importance of 'the view'. Mountaineers were able to 'see' in new ways, which increased a romantic sensibility, such as Dorothy Wordsworth's ascent of Scafell Pike.[164] Of course, as one writer in the *CTC Gazette* pointed out, the passion for mountain scenery was a modern development because for someone who worked on the land, views of hills and lakes were 'bound up in his mind with the idea of painful physical effort'.[165]

For many cyclists, touring represented what Alun Howkins has argued was 'the ideology of England', and because of rapid urbanization 'Englishness is to a remarkable degree rural. Most importantly a large part of the English ideal is rural.'[166] In France there was a similar transformation in the countryside, alongside criticism of the degenerative effects of urbanization. A love of the countryside was built into the school curriculum and an image was constructed that rural France was becoming more civilized.[167] Cycling illuminated increasingly complex relationships between the urban and the rural as well as the contradictory values of modernity more generally. Cycling during the fin de siècle was part of 'a wider anti-urbanism' that was evident across Western Europe.[168]

The CTC through its raison d'être and journal bolstered these ideas. Not only did the journal offer practical advice on touring, such as clothes to be worn on tour, but its pages were also filled with accounts of tours taken in both Britain and Europe. These accounts also acted as a history of the British Isles that reinforced this rural idyll. The first account of a tour in the *CTC Gazette*, 'Across Dartmoor to the Land's End', appeared in 1881 in a soon-to-be-regular column, 'Wheel Wanderings'. After the two cyclists crossed the Tamar into Cornwall it was noted that the county began

> with a very long and stony hill which ends on Hingston Down, so called from some battle in which the Saxton chieftain, Hengist, is said to have figured. From this point a fine view may be obtained over the two counties; the rocky 'tors' of Dartmoor forming a magnificent background to the east.[169]

Thus, in a couple of sentences, it captured a sense of ancient history in combination with an idealized view of the landscape. These guidebooks were written in an era of nationalism and their accounts of historic sites gave a distinctive sense of the past. Histories were important in framing and shaping national identities. Guidebook histories, therefore, were not neutral, and instead were an early form of projecting a sense of heritage.

Ideas of Englishness were also formed through the new fashion for photography, and many accounts of tours in the *CTC Gazette* were accompanied with photographs. During the 1880s the bicycle and the camera were exemplars of modernity. There was a fusion between both inventions, as the term 'cyclo-photographers' entered the lexicon. Unsurprisingly, both cameras and bicycles were also expensive, and it was only the middle and upper classes that could afford them. Initially the gear was expensive, bulky and heavy, weighing up to 50 lbs and was best suited for carrying by tricycles and sociables. By the mid-1890s, cheaper, smaller and lighter cameras that held film rolls had been developed, complementing the invention of the safety bicycle. Moreover, the bicycle was a key agent of the photographic survey movement, which recorded English heritage between 1885 and 1918. The mobile independence of cyclists allowed them to take photographs – up to a point – whenever and wherever they liked, what Sara Dominici has termed the 'moving gaze'.[170] It was these images, along with touring accounts, that later became a staple diet for cycling publications, further buttressing the link between cycling, Englishness and a rural ideology.

Before the boom period of the 1890s, cycling was a not insignificant element of middle-class life and culture in Victorian Britain. Indeed, through amateurism, it was an important agency in reinforcing middle-class identity at a time of growing social tensions. Of course, it was also a source of pleasure, but one which disrupted gender relations, especially regarding middle-class women. By the 1890s cycling had been transformed from its emergence as a minor leisure pursuit in the 1870s to a mass activity. It cut across classes and moved away from its middle-class origins to become a mass-participation recreation. By the 1890s, the democratic nature of cycling meant that it appealed to people across the social spectrum who had different motivations, whether racers (or scorchers), tourists, recreationalist cyclists or utilitarian cyclists. Instead, cycling's meanings were complex and contradictory with its recreational function just one aspect. The following chapter analyses cycling as a form of spectacle, especially sport and its place in Victorian and Edwardian popular culture.

CHAPTER 2

Cycling as Victorian spectacle

On 18 May 1889 William Hume, captain of the Belfast Cruisers Cycling Club, easily won four races at the Queen's College sport meeting held at the North of Ireland Cricket Club in Belfast. It was a landmark event in the history of cycling in terms of both technology and sports. Not only was Hume riding a safety bicycle, but it was fitted with pneumatic tyres. Within a few years, the previously dominant ordinary would become redundant and the newly enhanced safety would be the choice not only of racing cyclists but also, more importantly for the industry, of the general public. The pneumatic tyre had been invented in 1887. Its inventor, the non-cycling Scottish-born Belfast veterinarian, John Boyd Dunlop, had fitted them to his son's tricycle, before patenting his invention the following year. Although the Rover Safety bicycle first appeared on the market in 1885, it had been disadvantaged because of the increased vibration from the smaller, same-sized wheels, and the 'High-Wheeler' had continued to be the principal design for racing. This situation quickly changed after Hume's success with 'sausage tyres', and would have far-reaching consequences for cycling.[1]

Later in July 1889, at the Liverpool Police athletic meeting, Hume would become the first rider to race on pneumatics in England where he won two races. In the immediate aftermath of Hume's successes, other Irish riders – the 'Irish Brigade' – briefly dominated British cycling. The previously dominant Du Cros family of racers switched immediately from the ordinary to the safety, now equipped with pneumatics, after they had been defeated by Hume in Belfast. At the 1890 NCU national championships, held at Paddington in London, Robert Mercredy won all four titles. In 1889, highlighting the close link between the sport of cycling, the cycling industry and technological innovation, Harvey Du Cros became the chairman of the first Dunlop company, The Pneumatic Tyre and Booth's Cycle Agency, Ltd, and in 1891 he set up a branch of Dunlop's in Chicago. Not only was this a highly symbolic episode, but it also marked the end of the era of 'early cycling' and ushered in an era of mass cycling in which sport would be a key component.[2] Andrew Ritchie, with much justification, has claimed that because of the increased comfort they afforded, '[t]he pneumatic tire became the key factor in the bicycle racing and recreational cycling boom of the 1890s vehicles'.[3] There was subsequently a rapid growth in the bicycle industry.[4] It was claimed that in 1896 the 1.5 million cyclists in Britain were supporting a cycling industry worth £75 million and employing 50,000 men. The Dunlop Tyre Company was sold for £3 million while over 30 bicycle companies were capitalized for a total of £10 million. Importantly, the weight of a bicycle was dramatically reduced, making cycling a more appealing pastime for women.[5] Nevertheless, the rise in cycling's popularity, as a sport, a recreational activity and as a form of transport, would also make it a site for social conflict. The sporting arena would see professional-amateur tensions, while the growing number of cyclists on the roads created both practical and social anxieties. These tensions would continue to echo through the twentieth century and in the case of the rights of cyclists to ride on the road to the present day.

The bicycle and Victorian society

Late Victorian Britain had been marked by both rapid urbanization and industrialization. The landscape literally changed from a rural to an urban society as the population of Britain more than doubled from 14 million in 1837 to 29 million by 1901. There was also a corresponding increase in urban density. In 1851, for the first time, a majority of Britons lived in urban areas; by 1901 this figure had risen to around 80 per cent.[6] These transformative processes had a marked influence on how people worked and how Britons spent their leisure time, which provided concentrated markets for leisure entrepreneurs to exploit. Importantly, despite great poverty and social inequalities, many workers had more money and time to spend on leisure activities with per capita wages about 50 per cent higher in 1901 than in 1851. In 1886 it was estimated that the weekly wages of carpenters were about 30 shillings per week (approx. £75 per annum); of labourers, about 20 shillings (approx. £50 per annum); and of coal hewers, about 30 shillings (approx. £75 per annum). In 1906 foremen, in a variety of industries, earned between £86 and £134 per year.[7] A series of Factory Acts had, albeit unevenly and slowly, seen a reduction in hours for workers in some occupations, which provided more opportunities for sport and leisure. Moreover, Victorian Britain was a young society. In 1851 half of the population was under 20 with only a quarter over 45, which added to the potential for spending money and time on sport and leisure activities.[8] The bicycle therefore became an appropriate modern machine for a bourgeoning young population.

Even before the boom of the 1890s, working-class cyclists had been more abundant in numbers, riding earlier than has previously been thought. In 1885 one 'professional man' living in a country town observed that everybody rides 'from bricklayers to baronets'.[9] In his study of cycling in the north-east between 1869 and 1914, Robert Goodall, while he found regional differences between colliery villages in the South Durham coalfield and North Yorkshire market towns, has claimed that 'in essence, lord or labourer could be found awheel anywhere in the land, although not riding together'.[10] Working-class cyclists took advantage of a thriving second-hand market in bicycles as the back pages of cycling journals listed dozens of machines up for sale. Out of the price range for many when brand new, bicycles became more affordable second-hand. Advertisements from 1883 and 1884 in Middlesbrough's *North-Eastern Daily Gazette* for second-hand bicycles displayed a range in prices from £2 15s to £13 for a bicycle which had been 'scarcely ridden'. Young's Bicycle Repository was advertising boys' machines for £2 15s and adult ones from between £3 10s to £11 10s.[11] By the 1880s bicycles and tricycles in Middlesbrough were sold via agents. The mass production of bicycles later allowed prices to fall further. In addition, the emergence of working-class credit and hire-purchase schemes were used extensively by both cycle dealers and mail order companies. By 1899, one major firm was selling bicycles at £8 15s, then within the price range of many working-class people.[12]

The commercialization of cycling was reflected in the growth of working-class clubs. In his study of Northumberland mining communities, Alan Metcalfe has calculated that between 1891 and 1914 approximately 49 clubs were formed with many organized and run by miners. In 1890 the Astley Club of Seaton Delaval, for example, was founded through the efforts of two miners, aged 20 and 23. Of its 15 members, 12 were miners and the others were a railway signalman, a butcher's apprentice and a blacksmith. Different clubs though had different motivations, which appealed to other groups within Northumberland. Sport was closely tied to traditional practices, such as competition and betting, while the development of touring clubs appealed to groups that espoused the values of rational recreation. Some developed in association with the temperance movement, Mechanics' Institutes, churches and youth groups,[13] while by 1898 the Primrose League Cycling Corps was attached to the North Shields Habitation.[14]

Cycling machines also became associated with workers. Postmen were one group of workers who have been associated in the popular imagination with the bicycle. As early as 1880 the Post Office had purchased a few velocipedes as an experiment, while some tricycles were used in Coventry. In 1882 the 'Centre Cycle' appeared in Horsham and was used by local postal service workers. Designed by a local architect, it was nicknamed the 'hen and chickens'. The machine was a kind of ordinary with a large wheel in the centre and two small wheels at each end, allowing it to support a large basket. The centre cycle did not catch on nationally. It was not until

1895 with the establishment of 67 nationwide cycling posts that the bicycle became a significant part of the postal service.[15] In 1899 the Post Office announced plans for the formation of a cycling corps, offering a financial concession to those workers that used the bike for work.[16] In the same year, a special police cycling corps was formed in Hertfordshire. Composed of younger policemen, cycling allowed them to patrol the roads and country lanes more easily, but there was unease among cyclists in general about their purpose.[17]

With the surge in its popularity combined with its ubiquity, the bicycle embedded itself in Victorian popular culture more generally. One writer referred to the boom as a 'Cycling Epidemic' another as 'Cyclomania'.[18] For another – probably tongue-in-cheek – society had become 'cyclised', being subject to a process of 'cyclisation' which went hand in hand with civilization.[19] The bicycle was adapted to suit activities beyond sport and recreational cycling. In 1884, for example, a Lincolnshire couple rode to the church on a tandem tricycle for their wedding. Once married, they 'mounted their steed and set off home'.[20] In 1898 a group of cyclists had attempted to cross the Channel to Boulogne on a water cycle, but were prevented from doing so by heavy winds.[21] Meanwhile, the Stanley Show became not just an important event for the industry but also a major social occasion. In particular the Stanley Club dinner was the great social function of the cycling year. In 1897 the banquet – the 23rd – was held at the Hotel Metropole.[22]

Initially the spectacle of meets and parades, like the Hampton Court meeting, had helped to popularize cycling, drawing large crowds and interest from the press. Meets were also held in county Durham where they increased cycling's appeal and stature.[23] Between 1877 and 1903 until its demise, the most prestigious meeting in this period was the Harrogate camp, which took place over the August Bank Holiday. It catered for middle-class sociability as well as fun and games and was later run by the CTC.[24] Fancy dress was one activity in addition to races, while each tent had its own theme.[25] In 1884 the meeting consisted of various activities. On Saturday there was some racing, while on Sunday morning some cyclists rode to neighbouring towns. In the afternoon there was a church service on site accompanied by a choir of cyclists. On Monday morning there was a procession of machines, which included women and numbered over 1,000 participants. The afternoon witnessed more racing. The following day there was a tennis tournament, before people departed.[26] During the 1890s the florally decorated bicycle was a common sight at cycling carnivals and club parades.[27] In 1899 Chester held a masquerade cycle parade, which was over a mile in length.[28] Parades were not to everyone's taste though, and in 1899 there was opposition to cyclists' church parades from a Newcastle Presbyterian committee.[29]

Publications on cycling added to its cultural legitimacy as a sport, a recreational activity and importantly, a form of transport. Not only did the spectacle of cycle racing attract the attention of the press who provided vivid accounts of this new fad and its heroes' exploits, but newspapers and periodicals were boosted by advertising income from manufacturers. Indeed, some cycling events were invented purely to advertise the machines used. The first periodical solely devoted to cycling was *The Bicyclist*, a monthly, first published in 1875. Others soon followed, including weeklies such as *Bicycling News* (1876), the *Bicycle Journal* (1876), the *Cyclist* (1879) and the *Tricyclist* (1882). Between 1875 and 1914 there had been 29 failed cycling newspapers published in London alone, highlighting both cycling's boom and its later decline.[30] Other sporting papers, such as *Athletic News*, the *Field*, *Sportsman*, *Sporting Life* and *Scottish Umpire*, also devoted considerable coverage to the sport.[31] The weekly journal *Cycling* was founded in 1891 and has proved to be cycling's most enduring publication. Its first editor, until 1892, was Charles Sisley. Unsurprisingly, he was a cycling enthusiast and had been an energetic race organizer and secretary of the Catford Cycling Club.[32] In 1896, at the height of the sport's popularity, *Cycling* sold over 41,000 copies. Cycling activities were regularly reported in daily and weekly newspapers. Society and women's journals devoted regular columns to cycling while there were two popular national cycle exhibitions, the National plus the Stanley.[33] For a number of years the *Daily Mail*, which was founded in 1896, ran a cycling column on touring and racing news, written by Sisley. Its founder, Viscount Rothermere, later Lord Northcliffe, had himself began his career as a journalist on *Bicycling News*.

As an icon of popular culture, the bicycle was not confined to the road or race tracks. In the London music halls, artists and artistes were keen to associate themselves with the bicycle.[34] In 1892 cycling was given its own song, 'Daisy Bell', the lyrics of which were sung by adults – and twisted by schoolboys for decades after. Trick cycling developed as a music-hall act. An early exponent was 'Albin'. His real name was Dumphrey and he started cycling on a boneshaker. His act involved riding a giant ordinary, which was about eight feet in height. He pedalled the cranks through stilts fixed to the forks. Albin toured Europe and he appeared at the Crystal Palace on numerous occasions. In 1879 he provided some in-house entertainment during a six-day race at the Agricultural Hall.[35] In 1882 he went on a 12-month tour with the Barnum and Bailey circus in the United States. Two years later he appeared at the Westminster Aquarium with a partner, riding a tandem bicycle, similar to a Rucker tandem, which had the front wheels of two ordinary bicycles. The rear rider then unclipped the back wheel and rode it as a unicycle.[36] The performances of trick riders continued to attract the crowds. At the Aquarium, a popular cycling venue, one such rider, 'Minting', rode up a spiral incline from the floor to the roof, then across a narrow plank to the other side of the building and down again to the floor.[37] Cycling entertainment was also extended to comedy acts, such as the three Powers Brothers from America who in 1899 toured Britain and that year performed in front of the Prince of Wales at the Alhambra.[38]

In addition to his novel, *The Wheels of Chance*, H. G. Wells was actually a member of the CTC. 'There is no place more delightful as a holiday resort than the environs of a well-made roadster bicycle,'[39] he once claimed. He wrote for the *CTC Gazette* and even the machine in his 1895 novel *The Time Machine* bore some resemblance to a bicycle as it had a saddle and handlebars. In 1888 Wells had written a short story based on a time machine, 'The Chronic Argonauts', but the machine later 'evolved into a kind of bicycle', which reflected 'the extraordinary public impact of the "freedom machine"' and its place, as a symbol of modernity or in this case the future, in the popular consciousness of Victorian society.[40]

The Boer War had coincided with the popularity of cycling. Unsurprisingly given the wave of patriotism and jingoism that accompanied the conflict the bicycle's military potential was promoted. By 1899 it was claimed that there were nearly 2,000 cycling sections attached to local volunteer regiments and the following year the army had its own purpose-built bicycle.[41] That year a Major Liles offered to raise a corps of cyclists who would serve as marksmen in South Africa, but he was turned down by the War Office.[42] During the First World War the NCU secretary was of the belief that cyclists had special qualities for warfare, such as scouting and as despatch riders. He claimed that they were not recruiting in vast numbers because they were hoping the War Office would form cyclist battalions.[43] But as the war developed the bicycle was almost useless in that type of warfare.

The origins of the sport of cycling

Cycling was at the forefront of the Victorian sporting revolution. Sport in turn was crucial to the early development of cycling, especially in driving forward technological innovation. Central to improvements in the manufacture of the bicycle was sporting competition. It was those riders who became reliant on cycling for a living who were at the forefront of this process, not only as professional athletes but also as manufacturers in their own right. One professional cyclist who built bicycles was John Keen. At his workshop he was continually tinkering with his machine in the quest for greater efficiency and speed.[44] Because of the bicycle's novelty, cycling was as much spectacle as it was sport at first. Part of the attraction was for the public to witness the speed as well as the thrills and spills of this modern invention. Competition though quickly added to cycling's appeal.[45]

Sport more generally was part of the rapid expansion in late nineteenth-century leisure industries, alongside the music hall, seaside resorts and the bourgeoning newspaper industry. There was an explosion in the numbers watching and playing sports as well the codification of older sports such as football (association and rugby) and boxing, as well as the invention of new sports, like cycling. What Tony Collins has described as a 'sporting industrial revolution' took place in which the sports industry consisted of millions of consumers in the form of spectators and readers of newspapers, thousands of workers in the form of professional athletes, armies of journalists to promote it, plus sports entrepreneurs, sporting goods manufacturers and retailers. This rapid commercialization of sport had been predicated on three key elements: a unified national culture, a mass popular press and importantly an industrial working class.[46]

As a sporting form, cycling has been versatile and adaptable, offering a wide variety of events and competitions, both on the track and on the road. However, this variety and ubiquity has been both a strength and a weakness. Cycling promoters have had to continually invent different events, such as six-day races, to maintain its appeal. On the road, not only were races held over different distances, but there were also challenges against the clock, which ranged from the One Hour Record to the 'End to End' – Land's End to John O'Groats. There were also separate races and records for those who rode tricycles and later tandems, plus those for pacing and later non-pacing (as discussed further).

The early history of track cycling as a professional sport can be divided into two periods. First, from the mid-1870s to the late 1880s professional bicycle racing attracted large numbers of spectators, especially from the working classes and was arguably the most popular sport in the country. However, by the late 1880s the sport had declined due to the growing appeal of football, rugby and cricket. Second, during the 1890s, professional track racing enjoyed a revival, especially in London, on the back of the boom. However, this was short-lived and by 1900 it attained the status of a minority sport. While track racing continued, it also became a relatively minor form of the sport of cycling – only revived in Britain in the twenty-first century due to Olympic success.

In its first phase of popularity, professional cycling shared many of the characteristics of premodern sports, like cricket, pugilism and pedestrianism. Initially, it had been promoters and the professionals themselves who organized bicycle races and meetings. Similar to pugilism and pedestrianism, riders issued challenges to rivals through newspapers. In 1878, for example, in a letter published in the *Sporting Life* Sam Rowson challenged David Stanton, then known as 'the long-distance champion', to a match over six days at the Agricultural Hall in London for £10 and his title.[47] In these years the two main early centres of cycling were Wolverhampton and Leicester. The Molineux Grounds, at the time a Victorian pleasure garden (now the home of Wolverhampton Wanderers FC), hosted numerous races. Publicans were early examples of sporting entrepreneurs and these races were under the management of local publican, O. E. McGregor.[43] Large crowds were attracted to Molineux to watch early stars such as Keen, James Moore and Stanton. On Boxing Day 1875, for example, it was estimated that there were 18,000 spectators to watch championship races between the early professionals.[49] Another early track was at Crystal Palace in Sydenham. It had a long association with cycling, stretching back to 1869 when the first cycle show in Britain was held. In 1880 the first Crystal Palace track was opened. A 'cinder-path', it was built round a shallow ornamental lake and on occasions riders fell in. It later fell into dis-use and like other cycling tracks became a football ground – the one where the FA Cup final was played between 1895 and 1914.[50]

Cycling attracted the largest sporting crowds in Leicester during the 1880s. Racing took place at two tracks: one in Belgrave, the other at a multi-sports complex in Aylestone owned by Leicestershire County Cricket Club, which included a cycling track and cricket ground. The sport's popularity was partly generated by – and then dependent on – the rivalry between Fred Wood from Leicester and Richard Howell from Wolverhampton between 1883 and 1886. Identification with local riders was cultivated by the local press. In 1884 there was a crowd of 12,000 at Aylestone to watch their 25-mile 'bicycle championship of the world'. So-called world championships during this era were merely inventions of promoters to increase public interest and draw the crowds, rather than verifiable races. Ultimately, this form of the sport was not sustainable as a commercial entity. First, there were only about 20 regular professionals during the 1880s who competed for insufficient prize money. Attempts to form a professional cyclists' association in 1883 and 1887 came to nothing and this lack of a national sporting bureaucracy meant that the professional side of the sport was unable to organize and standardize national competitions, which had been a factor behind the popularity of football. In addition, a national governing body could act to curb professional sport's self-destructive qualities, especially the spectre of gambling and race fixing.[51] At times, it was also not the most spectator friendly of sport due to the length of some of the races and the tactics sometimes employed by riders. Moreover, by the 1890s local identity found a more deep-rooted expression in support of a team sport than for local riders.[52]

During the 1870s there was also an increasing amateur presence in the sport, ushering in a period of professional–amateur tensions mirroring those in other sports. In 1871 the first amateur cycling championships had been held at Lillie Bridge under the aegis of the AAC. The club's first objective had been to own a ground free from professionals with its annual championships open to all 'gentleman-amateurs'.[53] The AAC had strict rules on professionalism. On its formation in 1866 it inserted a clause in its constitution forbidding mechanics, artisans and labourers from joining the club. As consequence, the AAC, later emulated by the Amateur Rowing Association, specifically barred these workers on the basis that their occupations provided them with a physical advantage over the supposedly more delicate gentleman amateurs.

In 1873 both the Dark Blue Bicycle Club (Oxford University) and Cambridge University BC were formed with the first inter-varsity match taking place that same year. One outstanding amateur cyclist was Ion

Keith-Falconer. Keith-Falconer, the brother of the Earl of Kintore, was born into the Scottish aristocracy and embodied the ideal of muscular Christianity. In 1874 he went to Cambridge where he read theology and was a founder member of its bicycle club. He later became a professor of Arabic at Cambridge before undertaking missionary work in the Middle East. As a cyclist he won the 2-mile national championship in 1878 and the 50-mile championship in 1882. Moreover, in that year he rode from Land's End to John O'Groats in 13 days.[54] Despite his immaculate amateur credentials – he was also a member of the London Amateur Bicycle Club – Keith-Falconer had not been immune from commercialism. In 1874 he wrote a report for the *Field* about his ride from Bournemouth to Hitchin in which he advertised both the machine and the hat he wore to prevent sunstroke. He died in 1887 after catching a fever in Aden where he was buried.[55]

The formation of the Bicycle Union (BU) in 1878 came out of a dissatisfaction among members of the amateur bicycling fraternity with the AAC's control of its national championships.[56] It was the first of many splits within the world of British cycling. It also points to fractures within the middle classes more generally as member of this group lower down the social scale were becoming increasingly assertive about their place in society. At the BU's initial meeting at the Guildhall Tavern, 30 clubs were represented who comprised cycling's social elite.[57] G. F. Cobb, from the Cambridge University club, was its first chairman. In its constitution the BU sought to accommodate professional cyclists through a licencing system. At the same time, it set down clear rules on what constituted professionalism. In this case, it did not exclude mechanics and artisans. The *Athletic News* commented somewhat sarcastically, 'It appears therefore that the Bicycle Union has taken the somewhat liberal view not to exclude artisans, mechanics, etc. from competing as amateurs.'[58] The BU's rules though were still typical of how sporting bodies defined the boundaries between professionalism and amateurism. While there were strict conditions applied to the definition of professionalism, amateurism was only defined against these conditions, in a negative sense; there was no 'positive' definition of what constituted an amateur.

The personal relations between professional and amateur cyclists were more complex. According to Huggins, the motivations of middle-class sportsmen and their attitudes to the working classes and sport varied depending on their particular context.[59] During the 1870s there were some occasions when amateurs and professionals raced each other. In May 1879, for example, in a 2-mile race staged at Cambridge University between two amateurs and two professionals, Ion Keith-Falconer defeated the professional champion John Keen, which also involved Herbert Cortis and another professional, Fred Cooper.[60] Typically though this was another example of amateur hypocrisy. Any amateur racing against a professional was usually no longer considered an amateur. However, in this case the BU made an exception.[61]

The most prominent cycling figure of the period up to 1900 was George Lacy Hillier (1856–1941). A devout amateur, he nonetheless was able to make a healthy living from cycling through his journalism and, as a result of stock market speculation, on various bicycle companies. Ritchie notes that despite this overwhelming hypocrisy, he 'remained resolutely committed to British-style amateurism as a moral crusade'.[62] Unsurprisingly, he was at the centre of professional–amateur tensions throughout the period. Hillier, born in Chichester in 1856, began riding in 1874 and joined the Stanley Club in 1878. He later played a role in the foundation and the running of both the Bicycle Union and the Bicycle Touring Club. In 1881 he won all the amateur BU championships riding an ordinary. He later became a journalist. In 1882 *The Tricyclist* was launched with him as its editor. In 1885 it was amalgamated with *Bicycling News* and *Wheel Life* where he remained editor until 1891.[63] Hillier later promoted cycling meetings through the London County Cycling and Athletic Club Ltd., and was a director of the Herne Hill track. Another famous sporting administrator of the time, Pa Jackson, had set up the Corinthians Football Club in 1882. While it professed to uphold the ideals of amateurism, Jackson similarly profited from the matches he organized.[64] Of his journalism it was said, '[I]t has to be admitted that Hillier was a man of strong prejudice, and he rather allowed them to dominate his opinions.'[65] His articles

> waged continual war against innovations which afterwards became universally popular and created revolutions in the cycling world. He inveighed against the safety bicycle, advocated the 'separation of the classes' in racing ... in 1888, Hillier ranged his forces against the pneumatic tyre, wrote scathingly about it and ... had no belief in its future. Later, he heaped ridicule on the motorcar.[66]

Ultimately perhaps he may have been nostalgic for the time when amateurs like himself dominated the cycling landscape and when working-class professionals knew their place. It was a common feeling among other amateur administrators in sports such as football and rugby union and the middle classes more generally, which reflected their growing anxieties over the rising assertiveness of the working classes. Moreover, given the hypocrisy of his financial interests in cycling, it also reflected how the ideology of amateurism was a veneer for these broader social tensions.

'To root out the evil of professionalism', the NCU put in place arrangements with the Amateur Athletic Association plus other amateur bodies such as the Swimming Association of GB. The relationship with the AAA was mainly for practical reasons as many cycling competitions were staged alongside athletics events. The relationship also reflected how the ideology of amateurism was enshrined in both bodies' constitutions. In 1884, for example, they drew up a 'Black List' of irregular cycling meetings not held under NCU and AAA rules. Riders who competed at them were liable to be suspended by both organizations.⁶⁷ Because the NCU also catered for professional cyclists, relations were sensitive and in 1885 a dispute with the AAA briefly flared up. Later, a similar dispute over professional cyclists competing at the same meeting as amateur runners led to a more serious fracture in the relationship. As a result, a competing body was formed, the National Athletic Union in 1910. Two years later though the rift was healed.⁶⁸ Nevertheless, what these disputes demonstrated was how amateurism continued to act as the defining ideology for British sport more generally during this period, and its influence would continue deep into the twentieth century.

While the NCU was an overwhelmingly amateur-dominated organization, that it also catered for professionals was not unusual in the Victorian sporting world. However, not all professional cyclists joined it, preferring instead to organize their own meetings. Cricket had both professional and amateur players, although the game was run by the MCC, a socially elite organization. In 1885 the Football Association legalized professionalism, despite a governing body dominated by the amateur ethos. Rugby union followed a different path. It was more militant in enforcing amateur regulations and in 1895 the Northern Union broke away. To a certain extent, the uneasy relationship between amateurs and professionals in cycling reflected that while some sports had a cross-class appeal, they like other areas of popular culture such as the music hall, were still divided along class lines. There was also a growing marginalization of professional cyclists. During the 1890s, amateur opposition towards professionals, particularly in the form of the NCU, stiffened. This opposition would stretch to road racing (as discussed further). As Tony Collins has argued, for certain sections of the middle classes the amateur ethos, and its emphasis on an obedience of authority and authority's ability to regulate who could and could not play, were positive and attractive features.⁶⁹

The 1890s boom not only briefly reinvigorated professional track racing but also modernized cycling as a sport. Andrew Ritchie argues, 'The bicycle racing that emerged in the 1890s – new, exciting and fashionably technological – had many of the characteristics of modern sport.'⁷⁰ It acquired a workforce in the form of professional riders, some in teams, who were paid by trade manufacturers and who publicized their products in the growing cycling press. Another aspect of cycling's modernity was its ability to fulfil the public's obsession with speed. *Cycling*, for example, regularly published an updated list of records – world, British amateur and British professional – for track and road as well as for tricycles and later tandems.⁷¹ Sprint racing continued to form the backbone of amateur and professional track cycling, but the sheer number and bewildering range of records served the interests of the cycling industry as record attempts generated publicity for bicycle and tyre companies. In particular, the pacing of riders in record attempts became a popular feature of track racing. In the Cuca Cocoa 24-hour race – significant in itself as a commercially sponsored event – for example, riders were paced by teams of tandems, triplets and quadruplets. In its 1894 edition, Frank Shortland set a world record of 460 miles at the Herne Hill track. In terms of road racing, however, the British sport of cycling would take a different direction compared to its European counterparts.

During the 1890s, there was a surge in the building of cycling tracks. These self-enclosed arenas allowed promoters to charge spectators an entrance fee. Between 1886 and 1900 around 40 purpose-built cycling tracks were laid in Britain, with eight in London (plus the White City in 1908).[72] In London, bicycle racing had initially taken place at existing athletics venues such as Lillie Bridge, Stamford Bridge and Balham before the first purpose track was built at the Paddington Recreation Ground in 1888.[73] Others followed at the National Athletic Ground, Kensal Rise (1890), Herne Hill (1891), Putney (1891), Catford Cycle and Athletic Ground (1895), Wood Green (1895), Crystal Palace (1896) and the Memorial Ground, Canning Town (1897). This spurt of track building briefly elevated London to the hotbed of world track cycling. Most of these tracks or velodromes – Putney was the first to use the title in 1895 – were multipurpose and also used for athletics and football. As commercial ventures, each track advertised itself as the fastest through record-breaking achievements, leading to improvements in track engineering with the development of banking and the use of concrete rather than cinders as the surface.[74] The tracks attracted crowds on occasions of up to 18,000 to witness record-breaking attempts and world-class racers such as the black American Major Taylor.

The new Crystal Palace track (or path) was opened in 1896. To accommodate record-breaking attempts, it was cement surfaced and measured three laps to the mile. The track became a magnet for record breaking and hence it provided commercial opportunities for manufacturers to advertise their machines. Between 1896 and 1898, it housed the trade's biggest and most expensive team of pacemakers, who were sponsored by Dunlop. This group, which numbered up to 50 riders, trained twice a day, and was supported by a staff of trainers and mechanics.[75] It was the promoters and trade teams who managed the professional riders. Pacers were in demand. Poole and Co.'s Ibex Quad was advertised as '[t]he instrument that has been pacing most of the record breakers this season'.[76]

The Wood Green track was another purely business venture. It was built and owned by the North London Track Co., which launched a share issue, and '[t]his Company has a splendid opportunity of earning good dividends and there is every prospect of investments therein proving sound and remunerative', claimed a journalist in *Cycling* keen to promote investment.[77] The proprietary company was the department store Gamage's, and Gamage himself was its chairman.[78] The first cycling meeting took place on Whitsuntide Monday in 1895. Other meetings were run under the banner of particular clubs or at holiday times. In May 1896 the North London CC held an open mixed meeting, combining amateurs and professionals. The programme was typical, consisting of a 25-mile club handicap, a 5-mile handicap for professionals, a mile and a half-mile amateur handicaps. There were also various record attempts, including a successful one at the 10-mile amateur tandem, which at various times was paced by the Poole Quad and the Chase tandem. The crowd though was a disappointing 2,000 to 3,000.[79] In addition to the racing, the track staged a variety of novelties, such as trick riding in between races. Another promotional gimmick was the Fowler Sextuplet. It was built by an American company and appeared at Wood Green in 1896 as part of its tour of Britain. Its team of six riders had earlier defeated an express train over half a mile.[80] In 1897 Samuel Franklin Cody held one of his Wild West shows at Wood Green. It not only comprised shooting, driving and various performances with horses, but also a race between a horse and a bicycle.[81] At the Catford track a year later the show had attracted 7,000 people.[82] The need to bring in other entertainments was common among many sports, but in cycling there was a growing sense that the sport could not pay for itself.

In reality, professional cyclists in the north and elsewhere were not overly concerned about gaining a licence with the amateur-based NCU. A demand for the sport could be found in all cities and towns, and also many villages. Northumberland's mining village publicans, for example, built several enclosed tracks during the early 1880s and charged an entrance fee. The sport's popularity in the county reached a peak between 1888 and 1900 and then disappeared just as quickly. During these years cycling in Northumberland had been based around a core of 17 clubs who owned and ran seven tracks, five within a 2-mile radius of Seaton Delaval. The New Delaval Black Diamond Amateur Bicycle Club, formed in 1886, took its name from a local pub, the Black Diamond. A year later it acquired a field for an enclosed track from the local coal company. It hosted many club events. Between April and September there were weekly races for club members and also four to five annual meets, which attracted racers from all over the north-east. Yet very quickly, as Metcalfe argues, 'the bottom had fallen out of racing'. Few races took place in 1894 and little income was generated. The next year the cycling club disbanded and a football club, Newsham Villa Football Club, moved in.[83]

At an even smaller level was the ironstone mining village of Lingdale in the north-east. Lingdale had sprung up during the 1870s due to the discovery of ironstone in east Cleveland, and in 1876 a school was opened. The mine was owned by the Quaker Joseph Pease who also sponsored community events. The nearby mining village of Brotton had hosted an annual Flower Show, which had included sports, since the 1870s.[84] As Gregson and Huggins have argued these events were more reflective of a northern tradition of professional sport rather than any subversion of amateurism. These events could take gate money and they often mixed open and 'amateur' races – even the local horticultural events had similar categories – with cash offered to the professionals while the amateurs could compete for potentially valuable cups and medals and sell them on later for profit. The inclusion of handicap races deliberately encouraged gambling.[85] For amateurs, gambling was seen as an adjunct to professionalism. In 1897, on one occasion, the police had attempted to stop betting at a club meeting, but the bookmakers immediately formed a circle around the police and began to sing hymns; the police decided to take no action.[86] A breach of the rules was taken seriously by the NCU. In 1914 John James Smith of Houghton-le-Spring was sentenced to one month in prison after being found guilty of fraud by obtaining two prizes at a Southport sports meeting after entering himself under a false name.[87]

By 1881 Lingdale was hosting similar annual community events at its Recreation Grounds.[88] In 1886 the breathlessly named Lingdale and Stanghow Horticultural and Industrial and Athletic Society held its annual meeting with a number of foot races run for money. The 140-yard handicap, for example, attracted 40 men who competed for a first prize of £5. Other events included a mile handicap plus horse leaping and pony leaping.[89] The following year the event was tellingly renamed the Lingdale and Stanghow Horticultural and Industrial and Bicycle Society. Foot races still took place, but the main feature was now the 5-mile bicycle race (off scratch) for the championship of Cleveland in addition to the horticultural prizes. The disappointing crowd of 500, due to the wet weather, also witnessed 1-mile and 2-mile handicap bicycle races. The winner of the 5-mile championship race in a nine-man field was G. Carter of North Ormesby CC. His time was 17 minutes, 34 seconds and he was presented with the Lingdale Silver Cup, worth £10 10s. The cup had to be won three years in seven years to be the outright property of the holder, a feat Carter completed in 1892.[90] The Lingdale event became established throughout the region with clubs organizing club runs to watch their members compete in the races.

In 1897 a new track at Lingdale was opened by Alfred Pease MP; the previous one had been designated as the site for the mine's shale (slag) heap. The new cinder track measured four laps to a mile with 130-yard straights and the ends were banked six feet high.[91] In 1898, such was the reputation of the track that it was chosen as the venue for the NCU's North Yorkshire and South Durham centre 25-mile championship.[92] In opening the new track, Pease, who was himself a member of the CTC, espoused the values of rational recreation and amateurism. While he was aware of the criticisms of 'foot-racing' and 'cycle-racing' due to their links with gambling (and by extension, professionalism), he argued that 'it was the duty of those who believed that healthy sports and exercises were good for the physical wellbeing of the people to see that the people had the opportunities of indulging in those physical exercises and that the competitions were carried out under fair auspices'. He added, 'Where there were able committees controlling operations of a club they ought to secure fair play and prevent any degradation of those great national sports.'[93]

After 1903 though it seems that the annual cycling event had come to an end as there are no further references. Why was this? The mining industry was hit by intermittent slumps, which created high unemployment in mono-industry villages. It was also possible that a run of bad weather dampened enthusiasm and the number of cyclists who had been attracted to the event to support fellow club members. There was a Lingdale and Stanghow cycling club, but it is unknown if it ever used the track for sport. It may have been that the club favoured touring and/or club runs. It was also possible that the growing grip of amateurism was having an impact on professionalism, although nearby Liverton Mines had begun its own annual horticulture and sports events soon after. In addition, the popularity of football in that part of the world had increasingly taken a grip, which put cycling in the shade. Football was played on the site of the cycling track and even today it is still known as 'The Track', despite no one in living memory ever having witnessed any cycling on it.[94]

The 1890s cycling boom also witnessed and created a demand for women's professional racing. It was a brief craze, but at the time some riders earned more than male racers. There were about 80 professional female cyclists – track and road, and trick cyclists – who came from mainly Britain, France and America with audiences attracted by both the sight of scantily dressed women and their cycling skills.[95] Simpson argues that as much as a novelty their value can be seen in the commercial context of cycle racing during the boom where there were 'mutually beneficial relationships between audiences, racers, and investors' who included entrepreneurs, retailers and manufacturers. In other words, women racers were exploited as a commercial opportunity for the cycling industry as bicycles for women was seen as a potential area for growth in the market during the 1890s. The images of women racers were used to advertise bicycles as well as costumes. They also became associated with the socially progressive 'New Woman' of the period, reflecting a 'gendered expression of modernity'. While few people seemed to have taken women's racing seriously, the riders themselves did, as many trained hard for competition.[96] The idea of the New Woman did not find favour with everyone. In 1897 a proposal to grant full degrees to women at Cambridge University was met with outrage by some male students. In protest they hoisted an effigy of a female cyclist, dressed in rational costume, a symbol of the New Woman. The resolution was defeated.[97]

As we have seen in Chapter 1, the invention of the safety bicycle was a seminal technological breakthrough in the relationship between women and cycling. The ordinary, due largely to its dimensions and the dictates of female fashion, inhibited women from riding bicycles, and instead, many were confined to riding a tricycle or sociable with a male partner. While riding a safety was a form of liberalization and the sight of women riding a bicycle became commonplace, racing was a different matter. Athletic competition had been deemed socially and medically unacceptable for women, while there was also a fear of accidents. However, the relationship between femininity and athleticism was in constant flux, and professional female athletes were not uncommon. Female natationists, who performed 'ornamental and scientific swimming' feats, were key to the commercial success of the Beckwith troupe, for example. In 1880 Agnes Beckwith completed a 100-hours swim in six days, while she also competed in races against other female swimmers.[98] Moreover, in America Louise Armaindo was a successful female high-wheeler racer. A circus performer and pedestrienne, she and a few other women began to race in the 1870s and 1880s.[99]

As early as 1868, there had been women races in Paris, although this was as much to do with male voyeurism as organized sport.[100] Nevertheless, there were some women who had sporting inclinations. In 1887, for example, Mrs Welch, a member of Thornaby CC on Teesside, began racing. She specialized in long-distance events and was still competing in 1895.[101] There were also some early commercial enterprises. In 1889 the Seaton Delaval track in Northumberland had hosted five American female cyclists who competed against local champions. Miss Lottie Stanley, an 18-year-old professional from Pittsburgh, gave the local male champion G. H. Symington, a miner, a 28-yard start and beat him by a foot.[102]

In the 1890s London was the main focus of women's racing. In May 1896 Olympia staged both men's and women's international racing. England's Zelle Pattison won the five-laps handicap with compatriot Jessie Gambley coming second and two French women third and fourth.[103] The main venue that staged regular women's races was the Royal Aquarium.[104] In 1897 a six-day race was held for both men and women. Riding for three and a half hours per day 'large crowds' witnessed a close – possibly stage-managed – finish between Mss. Anderson, Pattison and Blackburn. Each rode 380 miles and six laps (the men's winner rode 391 miles), with Anderson winning by half a wheel.[105] The reactions to women competing were mixed. In 1895 the local NCU centre threatened to withdraw Hartlepools Social CC's permit for its sports day if it allowed the running of a 'ladies' race'. On the other hand, in 1897 the Norton Bicycle Gymkhana permitted female competitors.[106] Not all women were in favour women racing. One critic was Elizabeth Robins Pennell. In 1894, she noted that a team of American female professionals who travelled to Britain 'met with the failure they deserved'.[107]

Cycling and the state

The growing popularity of cycling in the nineteenth century had necessitated a closer relationship with the state. The state, either informally or through direct intervention, has been a prime agent in framing cycling's history and, partly because of its relationship with the state, has shaped cycling's ongoing meanings and discourses. The legal status of cycling as a mode of transport itself on the Queen's highways and byways was established in 1888 through the Local Government Act. The conferring of legality followed a 20-year period, coinciding with a period of increasing road traffic and rapid urbanization, in which cycling's popularity grew, but its existence became increasingly contested. Moreover, these tensions also shaped the history of the sport of road racing.

First, while a pastoral and rural image of the nineteenth-century cyclist having the road to him or herself has persisted, cyclists were actually competing for room in an expanding transport network – a reason for the perpetuation of this image of cycling. The nineteenth century may have been the age of the train, but it did not mean there was a reduction of traffic on the road. On the contrary, as Barker and Gerhold point out, the railways helped to generate more short-distance road traffic despite capturing more of the freight and passenger market. It was this gap in the market for short-distance journeys that the cycling industry aimed to fill. Road transport grew exponentially and in particular there was a concentration of activity around London. It has been estimated, for example, that the number of commercial vehicles on Britain's roads in 1851 was 161,000. This figure grew to 388,000 in 1881 and 702,000 in 1901.[108]

Road traffic consisted of various forms of transport, both old, such as horse-powered vehicles, and more modern mechanized forms. Barker and Gerhold have stated that the Victorian age was as much a horse-drawn society as it was the age of the railways. In 1888 there were 11,500 cabs and public carriages in London while in total there were over 400,000 horse-drawn vehicles. It was estimated that in 1901 there were still 1.8 million working horses on the roads. Mechanized road vehicles, using steam to power them, had first made their appearance on British roads in the 1850s. However, because of the noise, which frightened horses and other road users, and the pollution they emitted, the speed of traction engines was regulated by an act of Parliament in 1865 – 4 mph in the countryside and 2 mph in urban areas. In 1878 the English Highways and Locomotives Amendment Act – the Red Flag Act – stipulated that a man had to walk ahead with a red flag to warn pedestrians and other road users alike. The roads were further congested with the expansion of the electricity network in the 1890s where there was a rapid expansion in electric tramways in Britain's towns and cities, especially London.

The rapid growth in the transport network was also a prime agency in accelerating urbanization. Thus, diminishing space was a constant issue for cyclists in urban Britain, especially when compared to other countries. In 1896 it was noted that cycling in Chicago was much more popular than in Britain, partly due to a 13-mile stretch of asphalt road on which nothing but light carriages and bicycles were allowed. 'Alvena', the female cycling columnist, wondered 'Would that we could do likewise!' in exasperation at the lack of similar facilities in Britain.[109] By contrast, with the exception of Paris, France was still a mainly rural country where the roads were largely empty. This emptiness would be a factor in the later success of the Tour de

France, which aimed to bring the country together and forge a national identity in a way that was unlikely in Britain, due to it greater urban and population density.

Debates over the legality and status of cycling can be dated from its inception. Initially, concerns and tensions were raised over the bicycle's impact on other forms of transport, especially horses. In 1878 a coachman on the 'St. Albans' tried to lasso cyclists, such was his frustration at the manner of their riding, while the term 'furious riding' had been recorded in Hansard as early as 1870.[110] In the year of their formations both the NCU and the CTC were faced with a potential crisis in the form of the Highways and Locomotives Act (1878), which contained an amendment that aimed to ban cycling on the public highway. The debate in Parliament in many ways set the future confrontational tone of the discourse over cycling on public roads. It was proposed that bicycles should be regulated on the highways unless fitted with a bell and whistle for riders to forewarn other road users, especially horse-driven vehicles. Riders, it was also suggested, should use lights. Wilbraham Egerton MP wanted to go further and prohibit 'riding furiously, or racing, against time or otherwise' of bicycles (and other vehicles) due to the possibility of endangering 'the lives and limbs of passengers riding on the highway'. In response to these proposals, London cyclists had objected, reflecting both the influence that elite London clubs held and the political lobbying process, led by the NCU.[111] The NCU had appointed a solicitor and lobbied the government with the aid of two civil servants plus the MP for Coventry, which was then the industry's main hub.[112]

In addition, cycling was perhaps fortunate that Viscount Bury (1832–94, also known as William Coutts Keppel, and later the Earl of Albemarle) was a keen cyclist. President of the NCU between 1883 and 1885, he was an undersecretary for war under Disraeli and again under Lord Salisbury, between 1885 and 1886. He was also an acquaintance of G. Lacy Hillier with whom he co-authored *Cycling*, an early history of the sport in 1887.[113] Bury's political connections would come in handy when cycling was finally declared legal under the 1888 Local Government Act. Previous provisions were repealed, and bicycles and tricycles were declared carriages 'within the meaning of the Highways Act' but with the proviso that they had to carry a (front) lamp and forewarn other road users when they were overtaking them.[114]

Set against this political background, the two main cycling bodies – the NCU and the CTC – developed into effective lobbyists, which had important consequences for recreational and utilitarian cyclists alike.[115] Peter Cox has referred to the CTC before the interwar period as 'a polite, middle-class club' but this tends to underestimate the vigorous efforts from their foundation of the CTC as well as the NCU in campaigning for the rights of the cyclist.[116] For cycling to gain respectability, in the eyes of the law, cycling organizations were aware of the need to assuage tensions on the road. Concerns over the status and legality of cycling had been prominent features of the NCU's original objects in 1878, which aimed to secure justice for cyclists and safeguard their rights on the road.[117] As early as 1880 the CTC set out 10 rules in their members' own highway code. Not only did the rules of the road have to be 'most strictly followed out' but in response to regular complaints extra care had to be taken when cyclists met horses. Regulation nine, for example, stipulated:

> In meeting or passing restive horses a dismount should only be made if requested, as sudden dismounts often have the worst effect. A slow pace and a few words form the best course. The rider should always keep as far away from the horse as possible.[118]

The NCU and the CTC also both monitored any legislative moves in Parliament and at local government level that affected cycling, and its solicitors were instructed to make representations when necessary. In addition, their official organs and supporters in the press responded, often vehemently, to criticism of cycling and were quick to defend what they saw as their rights. The *CTC Gazette* carried a regular column of court cases involving cyclists while in 1910 the NCU drew up a 'Dogs' Black List' and in three years it had recorded hundreds of incidents where cyclists had been attacked by dogs and caused an accident. The worst culprit was the Irish terrier.[119] By 1900 the NCU had fought 891 legal cases, winning 505 and losing 99.[120] In 1899 the NCU challenged Thames Conservancy on the prohibition of cyclists from riding on towpaths.[121] The following year its challenge to the legality of the watering of tramway lines because of the accidents it caused to cyclists was the subject of a *Daily Mail* editorial.[122] Yet some matters were also quite prosaic. Railway companies, for example, were continually lobbied for better rates for the conveyance of bicycles on trains[123] while arguments over the use of cyclists' lights/lamps would run deep into the twentieth century. In general, adopting a liberal position, cyclists were against any form of compulsion. One argument being that pedestrians should also carry tail lights.[124]

Any justification of the cyclist's cause was usually couched in the language of cycling's utility, whether in terms of its physical and mental health benefits, locomotion advantages or claims that it was an important aspect of the British character. In 1899, to highlight the cultural and economic importance of cycling at the time, a conference took place between the NCU, UK cycle manufacturers and the Railway Clearing House authorities. It was claimed at the time to be 'the most important fixture of the kind that has ever been held in connection with cycling interests in this country'. Nearly 100 Parliamentarians had written in support of cycling's deputation, which included MPs such as Herbert Gladstone plus industry representatives and officials from the NCU.[125] A Cyclists' Parliamentary and Municipal

Association had been formed in 1897[126] while in 1901 the NCU London centre claimed that out of 1,362 borough councillors within its locale, 204 supported the NCU.[127]

Another recurring issue included resistance to a tax on bicycles, which was also a reflection of political culture. State intervention in France had seen taxes on bikes, but in Britain this was anathema given its liberal tradition and free trade outlook. Nevertheless, with a commensurate rise in its popularity and criticism, cycling came under increasing public scrutiny. There were various motivations behind calls for taxing the bicycle. One correspondent, echoing future debates over motoring, claimed that cyclists should be registered because it was a dangerous activity and had become a public nuisance with reference to the death of a young girl from riding a tricycle.[128] There were further intermittent calls to tax the bicycle, none of which succeeded. Resistance was fierce from the cycling authorities – and probably also from the manufacturers.[129] A *CTC Gazette* editorial responded in typical style:

> To insist upon the purchase of a licence would be to seriously hamper the growth of a pastime which has done more than any introduction of the present century to maintain the healthful and manly attributes which have secured for England the proud position she occupies among the nations.[130]

Respectability was important for cycling organizations. It reflected not only prevailing middle-class sensibilities among these organizations but also a fear of state sanctions. The conduct of cyclists, therefore, was closely monitored both externally by the police and also by cyclists themselves. In an attempt to assuage any dangers for cyclists on the road, but also to placate the authorities both the NCU and the CTC voluntarily erected danger boards on roads to warn cyclists of steep descents and sharp corners.[131] A defence of the rights of cyclists was tempered with regular complaints over the behaviour of some fellow 'wheelmen' due to the prospect of the damage to cycling's reputation. In 1884, for example, one letter to the editor of the *CTC Gazette* identified two classes of cyclists who caused the most accidents. First, there was the 'tyro' who, it was claimed, cycled down hills without caution and ended up falling off head-first – 'a header'. Second, there was – echoing cycling's similarities with horse riding – 'the galloping snob' or more appropriately 'the cad on castors'. It was claimed, with exaggeration,

> There is no difficulty in recognising one of them. He generally rides at a furious rate, utterly regardless of the safety or comfort of other travellers whether driving, cycling or on foot. He takes a delight in startling pedestrians or nervous drivers by rushing them at full speed without previously notifying his presence, or else, perhaps, he makes a fiendish

noise with a bugle, a weapon generally carried by these gentlemen, almost in the ear of the unlucky traveller. On reaching a hill, although he has no knowledge of the gradient, up goes his legs over the handles, and away he goes – a yell or shriek of the bugle greets anyone who imagines he has a prescriptive right to any portion of the road. But horror! The hill is getting steeper! He cannot put his legs down without releasing the brake.[132]

The subject of 'furious riding' became an ongoing issue. A *Punch* cartoon was a reference to a notorious incident in July 1897 when Arthur Evans was 'hooked off' his bike by a plain-clothes policeman. Evans, the police claimed, had been travelling at around 30 mph down Prescot Brow, a notorious steep gradient near Liverpool, which had become a speeding trap.[133] Despite claims from his solicitor that Evans could have been killed he was fined for 'furiously riding a bicycle'.[134]

In 1896 the Red Flag restrictions were removed on motorized transport, ushering in a new era of both modern motoring and transport politics.[135] By 1904 there were 8,465 cars in use, rising to 53,196 in 1910 and in 1914 to 132,015, which was then part of a total of 388,860 motor vehicles on the road.[136] This visibly changed not only cultural perceptions of cycling but also the practicalities of riding a bicycle on the road. Cyclists were very sensitive about their rights and fiercely defended them, especially in light of future transport developments. There was also a sense of loss, summed up by James Blair, the chairman of the NCU's London centre, when he argued that 'the coming of the motor-car has stripped the highway of much of its charm for many formerly ardent cyclists'.[137] It was not long before the cycling bodies were voicing concerns, such as at the Royal Commission on Motor-Cars in 1905, over the impact of the motor car, in terms of their dangers to cyclists and also how cars with metal-studded tyres were damaging the roads.[138] As a sign of the divisions to come, a letter to the *Daily News* promoted the idea of a Pedestrian and Cyclist's Protection Society.[139]

By the early twentieth century, the police were beginning to clamp down on speeding, both by bicycles and by cars. In 1901, the NCU urged touring cyclists to boycott Reigate in Surrey in response to what they felt was an overzealous clampdown on speeding cyclists and motorists. During one week in October 47 cyclists and 13 motorists were 'roped in' by the police and fined.[140] The response of the NCU though further underlined its concern that cycling should been seen as respectable as it argued 'that the enemy of the pastime of cycling is the "scorcher", and we are more anxious to put down the evil than the Reigate Bench'.[141] In one sense it highlighted cycling's popularity and how it had become integrated into political discourse and part of everyday life. In 1901, for example, the NCU and the CTC vigorously opposed a clause by the Blackpool Corporation seeking powers to prevent cyclists under the age of 16 from cycling in certain streets.[142]

Debates over the maintenance of the roads were a reflection of cycling's changing place in British political culture. In 1886 the CTC and the NCU had formed the Roads Improvement Association (RIA), following complaints about the dust produced by cyclists. Later, the CTC was represented by William Rees Jeffreys who became the RIA's most influential figure and the leading authority on road building in the first half of the twentieth century. Between 1902 and 1907 he had been responsible for the tar trials, which led to the replacement of the dusty macadam roads with the dustless 'blacktops'. By 1914 the RIA had been taken over by the motor industry as the number of motor cars on the roads increased exponentially. It was an early indication of how the bicycle would be increasingly metaphorically and literally squeezed from UK roads as the RIA morphed into the road lobby, which for much of the twentieth century was the most politically powerful in Britain.[143]

As the animosities between motor-car drivers and cyclists grew, tensions were increasingly riven with notions of class. Only the wealthy could afford cars, including members of the judiciary, and in 1906 the death of a cyclist who had been knocked down by one Lieutenant Paton at Windlesham, was summarized in a dismissive tone by the magistrate, 'No matter how fast the car was going the driver was not responsible for the cyclist's death.'[144] It was a tone that would raise the hackles of cyclists and cycling bodies for decades to come. In 1911 Royal Automobile Club proposed that cyclists should be compelled to carry number plates – an idea vigorously rejected by cycling organizations on the grounds that it would lead to registration and taxation.[145]

Road racing and the birth of the time trial

By the 1890s cycling and politics became interlinked with a debate over the legality of road racing on Britain's increasingly crowded highways. Criticism of the sport had arisen not only from people and bodies outside of cycling, such as the police, but also from many within the cycling world itself. Ultimately, this dispute led to the invention of the time trial in 1895 and set the culture of British cycling deep into the twentieth century. Thus, the time trial was an invented tradition and its origins owed much not only to prevailing political debates over cycling as a legal form of transport but also to the underlying professional–amateur tensions within the cycling world.

Tensions had been building throughout the 1880s. In 1888, the same year that cycling was declared a legal carriage of the road, the NCU voted to no longer recognize road records; it was soon replaced by the Road Records' Association (RRA). However, the RRA became responsible for individual records rather than any form of mass-start races. It is reasonable to conclude that the NCU's decision was linked to its long-running campaign to defend the rights of cyclists and that the growing controversy over road racing was potentially detrimental to its legal status. Yet opposition to road racing was also linked to an inherent amateur ideal, which resulted in a distaste for cycling's growing commercial practices and its links with the trade. Road racing over long distances had provided great opportunities for manufacturers, both to test and to improve on the technology of their bicycles, and to promote them due to record-breaking feats. Moreover, the cyclists, who usually came from the working classes, were able to capitalize on their successes.[145]

As early as 1883 the NCU had publicly stated its opposition to road racing as it was 'inimical to the true interests of the sport'.[147] Unsurprisingly, Hillier, as one of the most vocal defenders of the amateur ideal, was one of road racing's earliest and fiercest critics.[148] Another, Elizabeth Pennell, writing in the *New Review* in 1891, described road racing as 'the worst evil which has sprung up in connection with cycle racing'. As much as any danger, what underpinned this view was her distaste for the commercial aspect of this new sport and 'its cheap sort of notoriety and advertisement for absolutely thoughtless manufacturers'. Moreover, there was also the spectre of one cyclist 'hounded on by a lot of pacemakers clearing the road for him'. She believed, highlighting the class divisions within cycling, that '[t]he vast mass of cyclists would be grateful if the authorities would step in and suppress the whole business'.[149]

The middle-class members of the CTC had been another source of this increasing opposition to racing on the roads. A series of editorials in the *CTC Gazette* in 1889 reflected genuine concerns over any potential efforts to overturn cycling's hard-won legal status, gained the previous year. However, they also highlighted the different meanings cycling held for those who owned and rode a bicycle. The subsequent criticisms of its editor, E. R. Shipton, unsurprisingly reflected the interests of a body that was mainly interested in cycling as a leisurely activity and, thus, in middle-class respectability. Under the title of 'The Road Racing Scandal', he angrily pronounced that

> the selfish and short-sighted policy of the road-racing fraternity has developed into what threatens to be a serious attempt on the part of the police to hamper the legitimate use of the roads by the more sober-minded section of wheelmen.[150]

He also proclaimed, 'The respectable section of cycling journalism, like the outside press, is naturally dead against the illegal but growing practice of racing upon the highway', while also referring to how, for 'the rational road user' – the 'more respectable element of wheeldom' – 'how sickening all this must be' so soon after the cycling had been legalized that 'a set of thoughtless monomaniacs' put it under threat.[151] Widespread criticism of road racing in the cycling press was a major contributory factor in its decline. In Northumberland, for example, racing on the county's highways was banned by the county council in 1891. In 1890 over 50 per cent of challenge matches had been held on the county roads; by 1891 racing had disappeared from the roads and had moved on to enclosed tracks.[152] Even the *Athletic News*, normally supportive of professional sport, was cautious about racing on the roads. In 1888, it had prophetically suggested that it would be shrewder for club races to take place 'on the quiet' (which is later what happened), rather than advertise them in the press.[153]

The NCU's ban on road racing was finally confirmed in 1897 when it finally banned any of its licenced riders to participate in any races or paced record attempts on the road. Road racing continued, however, just not under the aegis of the NCU. In protest, the North Road Club, the sport's most prestigious club, seceded from the NCU and with other elite clubs went its own way.[154] In terms of the internal politics of cycling it was a decision that the NCU never really recovered from due to its loss of authority. Its abdication from road racing left a vacuum in how the sport in Britain was run. Road racing was now in the hands of a small band of clubs. With the continuation of road racing, albeit at a very low level in the 1890s, it would allow for other parties to challenge its status.

Britain and international cycling

While the first cycling road race took place in 1869 and was won by James Moore, a Parisian-based Briton, it was in the 1890s that the sport became international. The now-acknowledged first major road-race classic was the 1891 Bordeaux to Paris over 590 kilometres. British riders, experienced from riding 12-hour and 24-hour time trials on British roads, filled the first four places. The winner was G. P. Mills in 26 hours 35 minutes; second, Montague Holbein, 27 hours 50 minutes; third, S. F. Edge, 30 hours 13 minutes; and fourth, J. E. L. Bates, 30 hours 13 minutes. However, these British de facto professionals – Mills rode for the Humber company – were only competing against French amateurs. In order to attract the best international field, and to comply with the British definition of amateurism, the race organizers allowed only French amateurs. If the British riders had ridden against professionals their amateur status would have been revoked.

Many of British cycling's leading figures were fully aware of international developments, especially in France, and in 1892 an international governing body was formed. The International Cycling Association (ICA) was founded by a prominent journalist, Henry Sturmey. The ICA was formed 2 years before the International Olympic Committee and 12 years before FIFA, highlighting how cycling itself was in the vanguard of the development of modern international sport and that Britain was the leading cycling nation as well as the world's dominant political and military power.

The ICA was underpinned by the NCU's strict definition of amateurism. Unsurprisingly, Hillier had helped to draft the governing rules. The definition was followed not only by the NCU but also by the League of American Wheelmen. In 1893 the inaugural world championships were held in Chicago. At first, they were amateur-only, but in 1895 professionals were included. France would also join the ICA, but it was only represented by its amateur governing body, the Union des Sociétés Françaises de Sports Athlétiques. France's cycling governing body, the Union Velocipedique de France, did not abide by the British and American amateur definition. The de facto exclusion of the French was also an NCU reaction to the growing commercialism associated with road racing. In addition to Bordeaux-Paris, other massed-start races emerged including Liège–Bastogne–Liège in 1892 and in 1896 Paris-Roubaix. In 1900, led by the French, the Union Cycliste Internationale (UCI) usurped the ICA as international cycling's governing body. It was a symbolic moment. It reflected the growing strength of cycling as an international, professional and commercial sport in Europe, whereas the ICA had wanted to shape cycling, like other sports, very much in the mould of British amateurism. The staging of the first Tour de France in 1903 reinforced France's position as the pre-eminent cycling nation, while Britain became increasingly marginalized.[155]

The end of the boom

British cycling's golden era was over by the early twentieth century. The sport faded in light of the growing dominance and popularity of football, while the rise of the motor car transformed perceptions of cycling's cultural status. To cater for the growth of motoring, in 1899 *Cycling* changed its name to *Cycling and Moting*, accompanied now with images of record-breaking attempts by motor cars. In 1899 it published a photograph of a group of motorists among the stones at Stonehenge at Easter.[156] It was symbolic of a shift in the nature of modernity, with the middle classes confidently laying claim to this ancient monument through modern means.

Underpinning these developments was how cycling's rapid commercialization became a victim of laissez-faire Victorian speculation. During the mid-1890s, at the height of the cycle mania, a flotation bubble was created by cycle company promoters such as E. T. Hooley. In the peak year of 1896 the value of new share issues in the cycle and related industries accounted for 13.4 per cent of the total value of all new share issues; it dropped to 4 per cent in 1897. Public shares were issued in invariably unsuitable small cycling firms at a rapid rate. In Birmingham alone in 1896 and 1897, at the peak of the boom, there was a conversion rate to joint-stock status of about four cycle firms a week.[157] In total there were over 300 flotation issues by cycle, motor vehicle and related industries between 1882 and 1914.[158] After 1897, however, supply exceeded demand, a situation exacerbated by American manufacturers flooding the market with cheaper standardized bicycles. Thus, the boom turned into depression, leaving many firms who had overstretched themselves going bust as their values crashed. Those firms which had floated at the top of the boom had based their capitalization on the high profits earned during the cycle mania, but too many had acquired very high and unrealistic terms for their businesses. By 1897 the newly floated companies that emerged were burdened with a capital base that required high profits to satisfy the expectations of shareholders in terms of high dividends.[159]

With the downturn in the bicycle industry in 1897, many of its major manufacturers, such as Humber (1898), Rover (1904) and Singer (1905), diversified into motor-vehicle production.[160] Because motor cycles shared a lineage with the bicycle, a Cycle and Motor Cycle Manufacturers and Traders' Union Ltd. was formed in 1900. The bicycle design also stabilized and became standardized around the black roadster with little differentiation among models. As a consequence, from 1904 the National Cycle Show was discontinued.[161] By contrast, the design of motor vehicles was at the same stage the cycling industry had reached in the 1880s and 1890s when there was lots of creativity and a sense of something new. The most important and successful figure in the history of British motoring, William Morris, later Lord Nuffield, had begun his career making bicycles in a shed in his parent's back garden in 1893. Another car magnate, Herbert Austin, had established the Longbridge plant, based on Henry Ford's mass-production techniques in 1905. A painting by Robert Johnson shows Austin leaning on his bicycle after discovering the empty factory site, which would become his Longbridge plant. Similar to J. W. M. Turner's 1838 painting *The Fighting Temeraire*, it indicated a changing of the guard and a shift from the old to the modern.

In the sporting world, the emergence and then subsequent disappearance of cycling tracks had reflected the industry's speculation bubble. In London, both Catford and Wood Green tracks closed in 1900 and after 1914 only Paddington and Herne Hill survived. After one final year of cycling, Wood Green was eventually sold to property developers after failing to find a professional football club to play at the grounds during the winter.[162] One of the new cycling tracks – the Memorial Ground – had been responsible for the origins of one football club, Thames Ironworks, which was formed in 1895. In 1900, it morphed into West Ham United. After a few seasons playing at the capacious Memorial Grounds, which it was claimed could hold 120,000 spectators, West Ham later moved to the Boleyn Ground in 1904.[163]

The 'talk of decadence in path racing' was nationwide, the *Athletic News* noted in 1913. The cycling tracks at Celtic Park and Villa Park were closed in that year, in the case of Villa Park in order to redevelop the stadium for football only.[164] It was an indication that there was a lack of demand for cycling among the working classes, and that football was now, and would remain, the national sport. In 1901 the attendance for the FA Cup final was over 100,000 for the first time as the Edwardian period witnessed a boom in the sport.

Cycling had also lost its lustre as its claims to modernity were usurped by a growing motorization. In 1900 the Wood Green track had actually staged motor cycle races.[165] The shift in modern tastes was reflected in cycling events themselves. Out went the pacing quad teams which were replaced with motor cycles. While the speed of cyclists increased there was no longer the sense that the bicycle was the fastest form of locomotion.[166] Moreover, the spectacle of racing was increasingly criticized by fans and critics alike, especially the tactic of 'crawling' and 'loafing' employed by the riders who wanted to exploit the advantage of drafting rivals.

The sport of cycling did not disappear. Indeed, in 1911 it was claimed, albeit unlikely, that there were between 70,000 and 80,000 cyclists affiliated to the NCU.[167] While road racing became an almost subterranean sport, track racing continued. In 1904, Crystal Palace staged the world championships. Furthermore, Bill Bailey won the world amateur sprint amateur championship on four occasions, between 1909 and 1911 and in 1913.[168] There were other moments when it seemed cycling was undergoing a revival. In 1909, for example, a new 24-hour race was staged at the Olympic stadium for *The Weekly Dispatch* Cup, organized by the NCU and sponsored by the newspaper, which attracted a crowd of 15,000. As it was staged under lights, it was promoted as the biggest and most spectacular cycle race ever staged in Britain, with the best long-distance amateur riders from England and France, and the first race of its type for 15 years.[169] The race was an impressive exercise in organization. Each rider was allowed up to 30 pacemakers, making a total of 360, while 500 officials were involved.[170] However, the event was not renewed after 1910. A key factor in the difference in the status of cycling in Britain and that in France was, inevitably, amateurism. Whereas in France it was practically 'non-existent', in Britain it continued to act as a middle-class control on cycling's commercialization and expansion.

Despite this cultural shift, Nicholas Oddy has persuasively argued that rather than the period between 1900 and 1920 being seen as a 'dark age', the early-twentieth-century cyclist pushed 'personal mechanized transport into a new phase of modernity'.[171] A subtle but important change subsequently took place regarding the image of the bicycle. The car, associated with the upper and middle classes, had replaced the bicycle as the most visible vehicle on the road in the minds of both the public and the authorities; however, the bicycle was no longer seen as the threat it was once perceived in the nineteenth century. Even in 1913, when Britain was the most affluent car market in Europe, the number of registered cars was 175,300. By contrast, the number of bicycles could be measured in the millions.[172] Instead, cycling was increasingly considered the most democratic form of transport and 'unremarkable', giving cyclists the cloak of anonymity.[173]

CHAPTER 3

Cycling, Englishness and the politics of the road

In 1940 the old Etonian George Orwell started to solve the riddle of Englishness according to Rob Colls.[1] The following year, in his patriotic essay 'England Your England', Orwell identified 'old maids cycling to Holy Communion through the mists of the autumn morning' as not just a fragment but a characteristic fragment of 'the English scene'.[2] In 1993 John Major revived this image of old maids on bicycles as he (unsuccessfully) attempted to ease Tory fears over Britain's ever closer relationship with Europe. Thus, cycling was linked with invincible green suburbs and long shadows on county grounds in Major's wistful vision of Britain.[3] Yet despite its place in these defences of England and Britain, cycling was seen as a peripheral and peculiar, even an eccentric, activity. More pertinently to the status of cycling in 1940, one fragment of the English scene that Major did not re-invoke from Orwell's essay was 'the to-and-fro of the lorries on the Great North Road'. Why might this have been important? Previously at the centre of cycling's early identity and history, the Great North Road had now been appropriated by motor traffic. A clue to this symbolism and cycling's transformation and subsequent marginalization can be found at Poplars Corner.

Poplars Corner is situated on the northbound A1 in Bedfordshire, just off the A603 and just before Girtford Bridge near Sandy. After the first right turn, at the fork of the road stands a small memorial garden now largely obscured due to the tall poplar trees and an overgrowth of vegetation. Here is situated the Bidlake Memorial Garden. In September 1933 *Cycling* had announced that 'Our beloved "Biddy" is dead'.[4] 'Biddy' – Frederick Thomas (FT) Bidlake – was widely acknowledged as the greatest cyclist of his generation.[5] This moniker reflected the different perceptions of cycling at this time. While in the twenty-first century it would almost certainly be attributed to an elite athlete, Bidlake was recognized for his all-round role in shaping the place and perception of cycling in British life. He was a leading cycling journalist, timekeeper, administrator and advocate, but his most lasting legacy was that he was chiefly responsible for inventing the time trial. The time trial would capture much of the essence of British cycling for decades. Even after the emergence of mass-start racing (see Chapter 5), the time trial remained a peculiarly British tradition and contrasted with the sporting culture of other European cycling nations. Rather than sport, this chapter is concerned with Bidlake and others' championing of cycling as a middle-class discovery of the countryside and how this sensibility clashed with and persisted in opposition to the onward march of modernity, namely in the form of the motor car.

Bidlake's Garden of Remembrance was opened in 1934 with his memorial stone unveiled at the same time.[6] The event was highly emblematic in how it represented cycling's past and present. Bidlake's death came at a time when there were growing concerns over cycling's place in national life among its leading figures. In particular, an increase in motor traffic had led to an exponential rise in the deaths of cyclists. Moreover, these developments were a reflection of wider cultural change, which revolved around notions of Englishness. Bidlake's memorial captured a sense of loss or perhaps more accurately a world that was rapidly disappearing.

Cycling had been an active agency in the construction of Englishness in the Victorian period but during the interwar years, ideas of Englishness mutated. In the nineteenth century, a rural mythology had been reinforced through the thousands of cyclists who either toured or pottered around the English countryside away from polluted urban areas, breathing in fresh air on open roads, which were traffic free. These notions were further reinforced by the members of cycling's hierarchy, whose values and cycling's place in society were formed in the late nineteenth century. Through the interwar years, they would continue to promote and project a particular vision of cycling that would have implications for not only their sport but also the politics of the road. A sense of loss for this rural idyll was perhaps greater in Britain considering it was still the most industrialized and urbanized country in Western Europe, if not the world. By 1935 only 7 per cent of England's and Wales' occupied population worked in agriculture, compared to around 20 per cent in the Netherlands, 30 per cent in Germany and 38 per cent in France.[7]

This particular backward-looking sensibility was not representative of cycling or cyclists as a whole as it was largely middle class in its source and projection. However, it provided a cultural legitimacy for the cycling authorities to position themselves in opposition to emerging post-war ideas about the relationship between Englishness and landscape as well as the perceived and real growing menace of the motor car. Cycling became part of a wider struggle for the preservation of the countryside, or at least a certain perception of it. In 1926 Patrick Abercrombie formed the Council for the Preservation of Rural England. A progressive town planner, he was keen to protect 'the national scenery' at the same time. He argued that '[t]he greatest historical monument that we possess, the most essential thing which *is* England, is the Countryside, the Market Towns, the Village, the Hedgerow Trees, the Lanes, the Copses, the Streams and the Farmstead.'[8]

An interwar movement emerged based around the planning and preservation of the English landscape, which combined nostalgia with progress. The relationship between Englishness and landscape shifted from those of freedom and independence in the nineteenth century – ideally suited to the qualities of the bicycle – to one framed around an idea of progressive planning and good citizenship. As a consequence, rural leisure was now to be defined as orderly and modern. At the centre of this shift towards the management of the countryside was motoring. Reflecting its growing cultural and economic importance, the car now had 'moved into the symbolically safe hands of the middle classes',[9] which contrasted with the 'reckless modernity' represented by Mr Toad in Kenneth Grahame's *The Wind in the Willows*. A 'motoring pastoral' ideal emerged in which preservationists now 'projected their own sense of modern Englishness and modern citizenship'.[10]

In a number of ways, this management of preservation reflected the changing values of the middle classes more widely during the mid-twentieth century. McKibbin has shown how there was not only an increase in size, but also a substantial change in the composition of the middle classes, and by 1931 they made up around 22 per cent of the occupied population, about 9 to 10 million people. There had been a growth in salaried professions and especially clerical workers who formed the bulk of this increase. More pertinently, the culture of the middle classes changed with the emergence of a predominantly technical–scientific–commercial–managerial middle class, which thought itself as self-consciously modern. As a result, a confident individualist democracy developed based on expertise and public engagement.[11] Many people from this group also aspired to own a car.

Bidlake was one of the early middle-class cycling administrators who represented a different set of values. This was unsurprising, given that they were part of the pioneering generation who wanted to hold on to those principles at its origins. It was *their* sport after all, they had invented it, and in many ways they captured the spirit of those times. Born into a middle-class family in 1867, like his father, Bidlake was awarded a degree from London University. He was initially a private tutor before turning to journalism and joined *Cycling* on its foundation in 1891. Journalists were important figures in a number of sports. J. J. Bentley, for example, a leading football administrator and later president of the Football League, was an editor of the *Athletic News*. Bidlake combined his journalism with cycling. From 1887, when he joined, he was a leading member of the elite North Road Club, which up to the 1920s was the sport's leading club. Bidlake also raced. He was a champion tricyclist who set records for 50 miles, 100 miles, 12 hours and 24 hours on both the track and the road, culminating in riding 410 miles in 24 hours at Herne Hill velodrome in 1893. He would later become known as the father of the time trial (see Chapter 5).[12]

Other pioneers were part of cycling's unitary civic culture. Many of them were officials in cycling bodies and members of their various committees. Through regular meetings this identity was reinforced. Life as a cycling official was also something different to their everyday lives. It was more exciting and came with the opportunity to travel and meet new people and especially to ingratiate themselves with people from a higher social background. As with football administrators by the interwar years, for many committeemen cycling 'had ceased to be merely a hobby or an interest long ago: it had become a way of life; almost a surrogate profession in itself'.[13] Another early stalwart was W. P. (William Pagan) 'Billy' Cook (1870–1936) who was described in grand terms as 'a cyclist, first, last, and always'.[14] Cook was also a journalist, who for a time (1890–9) worked in America. He had earlier joined the Anfield Bicycle Club – 'the greatest of the northern clubs' – and at the time of his death had been its president since 1921 after serving as secretary and on the club committee. It was claimed that he rode at least 10,000 miles every year.[15] On a national level he had been elected a vice-president of the CTC in 1924, while in 1934 he was elected as cycling's representative on the Transport Advisory Committee. His other cycling duties and roles had included past-president of the Fellowship of Old-Time Cyclists, president of the Road Records Association, as well as one of its official timekeepers. Cook also acted as a conservator of both the Cyclists' War Memorial (discussed further) and the Bidlake Memorial Prize.[16]

Following the death of Bidlake George Herbert Stancer (1878–1962) took on his mantle as the Grand Old Man of cycling and the chief defender of its traditional rights and values. Like Bidlake, he was also a member of the North Road CC, rode on the road and the track, and was a keen tricyclist who later became president of the Tricycle Association. Between 1910 and 1919 he was the editor of *Cycling*, but he quit this position to become the secretary of the CTC in 1920, a post he held until 1945. From 1934 he resumed his weekly column, 'Out and About' – first published in 1907 – in *Cycling* while also writing under the nom de plume of 'Robin Hood' in the *CTC Gazette*. He not only held a powerful position through his journalism and the CTC but was also an important figure in the administration of the sport. In 1936, for example, he was elected president of the Road Records Association. In 1912 he founded and became the inaugural president of the Century Road Club, a position he held to his death in 1962. In 1911 *Cycling* had organized a 'Century' competition for 'hard-riding' tourist cyclists who rode the greatest number of one-day centuries during the year. The interest it generated had led to the club's formation.[17] In 1953 he was awarded the gold medal of the Alliance Internationale de Tourisme for the cause of international cycle touring. For his services to cycling, he was awarded an OBE in 1954.[18]

Cook and Stancer were present at the unveiling ceremony for the Bidlake Memorial Garden, which took place on 23 September 1934. Around 4,000 people were in attendance to witness the Garden of Remembrance being declared officially opened and his memorial tablet unveiled. It was akin to a state event for cycling with many important figures closely associated with the sport, as well as trade interests, present. The proceedings were conducted by the vicar of Sandy, the Reverend T. H. Strong, who gave his blessing to the memorial, while there were also speeches from Stancer and Cook, who performed the unveiling.[19] The Bidlake Memorial Prize, inaugurated in 1934, was bestowed with great prestige and acknowledged as the 'highest recognition of merit in the cycling world'.

Cycling, the rural idyll and cultural legitimacy

Cycling endured rather than embraced the brave new world of motoring. The pages of its periodicals provided much of the cultural legitimacy for cycling's response and political stance as well as capturing its mood among many of its community. *Cycling* itself preached the values of conservatism and consensus. The drawings of Frank Patterson, in particular, presented an ever-present rural idyll, which cemented a distinct relationship between cycling and the British (mainly English) countryside in the popular consciousness for over 50 years. Patterson's illustrations appeared in *Cycling* from 1893 up to and including the year of his death in 1952; from 1925 he also drew for the *CTC Gazette*. His sketches represented an extreme ruralism: such were their uncompromising eulogizing of a mythical and fading English rural landscape. *Cycling* aptly if unconsciously described how he 'imprisons the open air atmosphere' in its pages.[20] Yet while he attempted to capture and keep alive this particular notion of Englishness, shaped in a pre-industrial age, it was at odds with a landscape increasingly subject to an industrial economy.

Tim Hilton, a dedicated cyclist for over 40 years and art critic for the *Guardian* and *Independent*, has argued that Patterson 'had an enormous but imprecise effect on the nature of English cycling'. This was surprising given that Patterson was a recluse. He gave up cycling in 1906 and his drawings were mainly based on postcards sent to him by members of the public who asked him to sketch their favourite locations. Instead 'the purpose of his art was to embalm the England he had known as a boy', although it was an England that only existed in his imagination. His style, based on very thin, elongated pen lines, 'described rural scenes, landscapes and quaint country buildings'. The scenes were immemorial. His illustrations seemed to 'record the spirit of some past time, not an actual moment'. The drawings always included a cyclist or a bicycle (leaning against a tree or fence) and depicted images and scenery that appealed to old-time cyclists. They included the Welsh hills, the Lake and Peak districts and the Great North Road as well as market towns with coaching inns, castles, thatched country pubs, remote parish churches and cycling the final miles home by moonlight. Tellingly, roads were traffic free while cyclists were usually alone and male. The only sport represented was the time trial. Patterson also evoked the period after the First World War. As Hilton points out, the 'emptiness of his drawings, which make much use of white space, reflected a real emptiness in rural England. Fathers and sons from so many villages had left for foreign fields, never to return', which gave his drawings a phantasmagorical quality.[21]

The trauma of the First World War did not elicit a uniform response. While for some it created a sense of the need to rebuild and plan for a better society, for many others there was just a desire to return to the state of affairs before August 1914. These two competing tensions would be central to ideas of Englishness during the interwar years. One example of the war's ever presence in the pages of *Cycling* appeared in 1934. It was an illustration, for once based on Patterson's own experience it was claimed, which illustrated a cyclist observing the 11 November two-minute silence. Dressed in the traditional cycling uniform of a jacket and plus fours, he had been fixing a puncture and interrupted this job to pay his respects. It was set deep in the countryside, where in the same picture a shepherd and his dog, attending their flock, can also been seen observing the silence.[22] His work in maintaining these particular ideas of England were also deemed important during the Second World War and in 1944 he was awarded the Bidlake Memorial Prize.

Writers on cycling further reinforced Patterson's sense of pastoral sentimentality. Unconsciously, they reflected wider cultural discourses and ideological tensions during the interwar period, which revolved around opposition to modernity. According to Anthony Bateman, common among critics, in particular the F. R. Leavis-led Scrutiny group, was a 'tendency to both celebrate and bemoan the loss of the rural "organic" community'. In this sense, writers and lecturers on cycling shared similarities with cricket writers, especially Neville Cardus, who began writing for the *Manchester Guardian* in 1921. Cardus's work, Bateman has argued, provided cultural gatekeepers with 'images of how they believed England and Englishness should be reproduced'.[23]

Other members of cycling's literati fulfilled a similar function by proselytizing cycling's physical and psychic benefits. Cycling lectures had been inaugurated in 1897 in Liverpool when the secretary of its District Association (DA), T. Lee Lloyd, gave a lantern lecture. Other DAs soon followed, and lectures became an integral part of cycling clubs' winter social programmes.[24] This particular 'canon' appropriated and reinforced middle-class values of cycling 'as a socially healthy leisure pursuit'. At the same time the canon excluded 'bad cycling', namely, a working-class cycling culture, and projected an image of what Tom Bray has called 'good' cycling based around issues of health and the environment.[25] One such member of this canon was William Fitzwater Wray, better known by his pen name, 'Kuklos'. Kuklos wrote regular weekend columns in the *Daily News* and *Daily Herald* and also during the interwar years wrote *The Kuklos Annual and Handbook for Cyclists and Other Roadfarers*.

The doyen of the group was Walter MacGregor Robinson (1877–1956), aka 'Wayfarer'. Another long-time member of the elite Anfield Bicycle Club, Robinson became an apostle for cycling as a pastime and fired the imagination of many readers in the interwar period. Wayfarer, it was stated, was 'a great cyclist within the broader meaning of the term because, like most of us, he evinced a spiritual outlook synonymously called sportsmanship which is the hall-mark of the better citizen'.[26] Accounts of his tours throughout Britain reinforced a pastoral image and were part of what Alison Light has argued was the literature of convalescence in the early post-war years.[27] Robinson had joined *Cycling* in 1912 but he established his reputation with an article in *Cycling* titled, 'Over the Top: Crossing the Berwyn Mountains in March', published on 8 May 1919. It charted his 'heroic adventure' with W. P. Cook in wintry conditions cycling over Nant Rhyd Wilym, a challenging pass in the mid-Wales Berwyn Mountains. His vivid account of the journey, it was claimed, inspired many other cyclists to explore the great outdoors and go off the beaten track. In honour of Wayfarer's touring exploits a memorial was erected on the pass by the Rough Stuff Fellowship (a body devoted to off-road cycling).[28] Moreover, Robinson's experiences as a solider during the First World War encapsulated and added to a general sense of longing for the British countryside. He recalled how as a soldier in the trenches he found his 'thoughts constantly straying homewards' where he 'visualised bits of England and Wales with which I was familiar and revisited them in spirit'. Staring out into the bleak No Man's Land he said, 'It was not difficult to fit a piece of the South Down, or of the New Forest, or of Warwickshire into the landscape spread out in front of me.'[29]

Wayfarer's nationwide lantern lectures on his cycling tours were an early post-war sensation. By 1924 he was broadcasting his lectures on the wireless in the Birmingham area.[30] These lectures were variously titled 'The Open Road' and 'The Lure of the Road'. In March 1922 1,100 people attended a lecture in London, held at the Memorial Hall in Farringdon Street. Robinson initially spoke for an hour on the joys of the 'Open Road' before showing the audience a series of lantern slides. They included images of Cheshire, Shropshire, Fenland, Ireland and the 'grandest bits' of North and mid-Wales.[31] He was not alone and other lecturers, such as A. W. Rumney, further reinforced cycling pastoral image in the popular imagination.[32] While Wayfarer in 1924 began a new series, 'The English Wonderland', Kuklos was giving a lantern lecture on 'Old English Inns' for the CTC's Birmingham and Midland DA in association with the Walsall Photographic Society.[33]

Importantly, these ideals were transferred through their authority within the cycling world. In addition to this 'abiding delight in the "eternal hills" and a lively consciousness of the First Cause', Wayfarer was a ferocious defender of the cyclist's rights on the public highway through his column in *Cycling*, 'Roadside Reflections'.[34] Robinson was also a member of the CTC Council from 1924 to 1946 and was elected vice-president in 1945.

In addition to this sense of loss promoted through the pages of *Cycling* and also the *CTC Gazette*, the establishment of the Old Time Fellowship in 1916 further reinforced a longing for the past. Lucy Newlyn has argued nostalgia is both a form of mental therapy and a sickness of the mind, and these qualities were evident in the Fellowship.[35] Its annual summer meet usually consisted of a ride out to Ripley in Surrey, while its annual dinner was augmented with a speech by an old-timer. In 1920 the speech was given by Dr E. B. Turner, who had not only been a record-breaking cyclist, but also played football for England and had been president of the Amateur Athletic Association.[36] This annual gathering was as an exercise in sociability for its members, many of whom had ridden in the 1870s. *Cycling*'s readers were reminded, with reference to Ripley, that the old-timers were 'wheeling on ground which was hallowed in the memory of every old-timer, for had not the Surrey village been called, way back in the seventies, "the Mecca of all cyclists"!' Its eldest member was 88 and included the arch defender of amateurism, G. Lacy Hillier.[37] However, it represented not only a passing of generations but also a yearning for a time when cycling enjoyed a more elevated place in British society. It was this sensibility that continued to shape attitudes among those who ran the sport and its governing bodies during the interwar period. Most of members of the Fellowship had been linked to the world of the ordinary and, with reference to the emergence of motoring, cycling's legality as a carriage of the road under the 1888 Local Government Act was continually invoked in political debates. The Fellowship embodied a sense of loss through an image of Britain (especially England and Southern England even more so) in which cycling's place was relatively unchallenged. Ironically, once a symbol of nineteenth-century modernity, cycling, at least in the minds of its elite, was increasingly represented as an antidote to creeping mechanization. While it did not represent the fracture that had taken place in football, for example, with the formation of the Amateur Football Association in 1907,[38] the Fellowship harked back to the 'Golden Age' of the ordinary. Before most other sports, cycling had an awareness of its own heritage. The racing of ordinaries became a feature of cycling meets in the early twentieth century, for example, while in the 1930s the journalist H. W. J Bartleet donated his collection of old cycling machines to the city of Coventry. Bartleet had little connection with the city but his motivation stemmed from its previous status as the centre of the cycling industry.[39]

In addition to official cycling organs, ideas of ruralism were also conveyed through the diaries of individual cyclists. The journals of David Hamilton, a school teacher, not only included accounts of his tours over his long life but were also dotted with pictures, images and illustrations of rural England, including canals, rivers, woodland scenes, plus panoramic views. A member of the CTC and also a communist, his entry for 12 August 1923 read:

> After breakfast and a wash etc. I left about 7.45am carrying on across the plain passed Stonehenge in the bright rays of the morning sun. I had a puncture soon after on a loose hill. Leaving the broad undulating plains of Wiltshire, I cut across a few miles of Dorset into Somerset, famed for its beautiful churches. Its villages are no less attractive, lying in hollows through which the road sharply winds.

The entry provides a suggestion of what John Urry has called the 'Tourist's Gaze', where views have been socially and culturally constructed; how Hamilton's accounts had been shaped by preconceived ideas of what constituted an idyllic scene.[40]

The establishment of the Bidlake Memorial Garden had also reflected a culture of memorialization in interwar Britain. In 1921 cycling erected its own war memorial in Meriden. Two years earlier an appeal for £1000 had been launched. It was driven by many leading cycling figures who felt 'that something must be done on a national scale to commemorate the supreme sacrifice that so many cyclists have made' and a national memorial was a 'ways and means of perpetuating the memory of fallen wheelmen'.[41] There had been local memorials. In 1920 a stained-glass window and a tablet were unveiled at St. Barnabas Church, in Jesmond, Newcastle, which was dedicated to the 170 officers and men of the Northern Cyclist Battalion who died in the war.[42] The erection of memorials for sportsmen who lost their lives during the conflict was not unique to cycling and each held different meanings for each sport. Tony Collins has argued that rugby union's war memorials and commemoration were 'the means by which [it] paid homage to itself as the embodiment of middle-class tradition and stability in a post-war world in which these certainties were being challenged'.[43] Cycling lacked rugby union's militaristic and imperial sentiments and despite cycling units having a role early in the war, it did not glorify its links with the military. Moreover, cycling had a greater working-class demographic than rugby union. Nevertheless, cycling's commemoration, like rugby union, was both couched in the language of sacrifice and rooted in a past, which would reflect its own post-war anxieties. It was a past strongly based on a rural vision, and at the same time underpinned underlying class tensions as the middle classes attempted to reassert their values in the post-war period.

While rugby union conveyed an imperial message, cycling instead invoked ideas of fraternity and its links with rural England, sentiments strongly supported in the letters' pages of *Cycling*. One *Cycling* editorial, in defence of the memorial, stated:

It was sentiment which called our fellow wheelmen from the serenity of England's leafy lanes; it was sentiment that sent them to endure the cold, the heat, the hunger, the filth and the weariness of war; and it was sentiment that led to the last sacrifice.[44]

Similarly, H. Collings Young, the fund's honorary secretary, claimed,

> We cyclists, perhaps more than the devotees of any other sport or pastime, have a strong feeling of sympathy and comradeship, one with the other, and it is up to us, in spite of the many calls upon our purses at the present time to contribute our offering, be it however small, that the result may be in every way a worthy tribute to our Glorious Dead.[45]

After the First World War there was a widespread belief that the countryside 'was the ultimate repository of the national character'.[46] Memorials and other imagery acted as representations for a pre-1914 English rural idyll that had been lost as well as a form of guilt for those that survived the war, and who were now having fun on their bikes, their comrades, like ghosts, riding beside them.

The Cyclists' War Memorial itself was a relatively plain obelisk, but this also reflected middle-class notions of what constituted cycling. Instead of a (working-class) racing cyclist, the memorial was designed to appeal to all cyclists, especially the touring cyclist. Of particular significance was the memorial's site, the Warwickshire village of Meriden, located between Birmingham and Coventry because, as *Cycling* noted, Meriden was 'commonly accepted as the "centre of England"'.[47] The memorial held in May, rather than November, became a popular annual event with some cyclists riding through the night to attend.[48] After noting how the Catford CC's memorial run to the Cenotaph had made 'a strong appeal to the imagination', Wayfarer encouraged all cyclists to do the same for the Cyclists' War Memorial.[49] Despite the practical benefits of this site, which allowed cyclists from all parts of the country to visit the memorial, it was this veneration for the centre of England and the meanings that accompanied it that reinforced cycling's pastoral image. Thus, the memorial illuminated how the cycling hierarchy perceived cycling's place in a particular English, rural idyll – a vision that excluded working-class cyclists. Instead, the site – metaphorically in middle England – was designed to appeal to a genteel, middle-class image of cycling.[50] Meriden's place in cycling's mythology was further buttressed with the construction of memorial on the same village green to Wayfarer, who died in 1956. In commemoration of his service to cycling, the CTC erected a stone-backed bench at the opposite end of the green at Meriden, appropriately perhaps facing the Cyclists' War Memorial with the inscription: 'His devotion to the pastime of cycling inspired many to enjoy the countryside and the open road.'

The connection between cycling and pastoralism was maintained during the Second World War. The idea of cycling, its utility as a form of transport and its social and health benefits were kept firmly in the public consciousness through a series of programmes on BBC radio. The broadcasting of sport during the Second World War brought 'a comfortable familiarity' to listeners for the overall purpose of maintaining civilian morale, and these programmes on cycling reflected this broader objective.[51] The person behind these broadcasts was Alex Josey, the assistant editor of *Cycling* and later the founder of the Pedal Club, who was known under the pseudonym KMD.[52] The broadcasts perpetuated the 'Wayfarer' idealization of cycling from the interwar years as cycling was presented in educational, moderate and consensual terms with some broadcasts providing advice on how to ride and look after bicycles.

His broadcasts had actually begun in 1938 and continued until 1942. They were usually in the form of 15-minute talks with some slotted in between *Children's Hour* and the 6.00 pm news on the Home Service, with others on the Forces Programme. Sport was just one facet of cycling that was broadcast. There was also a propaganda element to some programmes such as 'How the Cyclist Is Helping', which was broadcast on 29 August 1940.[53] It promoted the worth of the bicycle to the war effort, especially as a messenger for the National Defence Services, as well as highlighting the voluntary cycling corps. In response to the formation of bicycle detachments for the Home Guard, Josey provided a history of the bicycle during wartime.[54] There was also a general programme on the history of cycling as well as one devoted to sport in 1941. It was broadcast on the Forces Programme, which indicated that this station may have been a more receptive audience for sport. Some of his programmes need to be seen in the context of the decline in use of the car and acted as a message to persuade people to take up cycling for the war effort. In addition, the value of cycling was broadcast on a number of programmes on the *Health Magazine*, which was produced for the Home Service by Janet Quigley. Later a producer for *Woman's Hour* and *Today*, Quigley had socialist sympathies and was keen to use 'indirect propaganda' through featuring references to certain subjects. She was especially keen on the role of the housewife and motherhood, but also recognized the worth of cycling.[55]

Cycle paths and the transformation of Englishness

In 1940 George Orwell had unconsciously noted the role of the Great North Road – now a major trunk road – in the transformation of Englishness. During the interwar years, the cycle path equally acted as a site for this shift over ideas of English identity. At one end of the spectrum, cycle paths reflected a modern and managed Englishness, as Matless has outlined; at the other, for the cycling authorities they represented a restriction on and a violation of a cyclist's freedom and independence, and the subsequent association with cycling uninhibited in the countryside, a right hard won in the nineteenth century. As much as this marginalization of the bicycle, cycle paths confirmed the cultural supremacy of the motor car, which in turn would have long-term – mainly post-1945 – ramifications for perceptions and the activity of cycling. The conflict over cycle paths, therefore, marked an important physical and cultural moment in the history of cycling's place in British society.

Debates over road safety and the role of the motoring lobby can be explained in terms of class and power as both O'Connell and Cox have argued.[56] Yet this episode over cycle paths can also reveal the changing role and status of cycling more generally in Britain, which was increasingly presented as a proletarian activity. The debate was slightly complicated as the basis for the objections of the cycling authorities to cycle paths was the long-held belief of equal rights for cyclists to the road, partly based around a particular notion of Englishness, which was borne out of the nineteenth-century middle classes. Thus, the growing cultural (and political) power of motoring was as much as a reflection of changing social structures that had been shaped by modernity and consumption.

In 1934 the first cycle path in Britain was laid along Western Avenue in London. It was a 2.5-mile stretch between Hangar Lane and Greenford Road. By 1938 41 miles of cycle tracks had been laid across the country with a further 54 miles under construction.[57] The Ministry of Transport aimed to build 50 miles of cycle paths every year for the next five years.[58] Other cycle tracks included a 12-mile stretch along the A64 York to Malton road with a further 12.5-mile path under construction between York and Tadcaster along the same road.[59] The pattern of cycle paths was patchy, however, especially when it was compared to the total of 170,000 miles of public roads in Britain at that time.

The idea of cycle paths had partly been a response by the government to the growing levels of motor traffic. Car and motor-vehicle (including motor cycles) ownership levels grew steadily from low levels in the early twentieth century. In particular, car ownership grew rapidly in the 1930s. In 1920 there were a total of 650,000 motor vehicles in the UK, which included 187,000 cars. By 1930 these figures had increased to 2.3 million and 1.1 million, respectively; in 1935 they were 2.6 million and 1.5 million; and 3.1 million and 2 million by 1939.[60] Plowden has proclaimed, 'The 1930s were perhaps the classic period of motoring as a middle-class occupation.'[61] A post-war Automobile Association survey suggested that at least half of car owners were members of the AB social group in 1939. Although owning a car outright was still out of the reach of the vast majority of the working classes,[62] during the thirties the costs of motoring decreased substantially, making car ownership more affordable to more members of the middle classes.[63] Growing car ownership reinforced what Trainor has identified as the emergence of a national middle-class culture. The traditional division between 'Town' and 'Country' gradually faded and in its place there was an 'increasingly geographically unified middle class in which London institutions and fashions set the pace, but to which the provinces made a major contribution'.[64] One such institution that was part of the glue that created this new national middle-class identity, and which added to the idea of a motoring pastoral, was the Automobile Association. Its membership grew exponentially from 36,000 in 1918 to 680,000 by 1939.[65]

However, the most striking feature of motoring during the 1930s was the rise in road casualties. Throughout the 1930s fatalities from road accidents hovered around the 6,000 to 7,000 mark, while there was a sharp peak in casualties, rising from 178,000 in 1930 to 232,000 by 1934.[66] In 1933, 1,324 cyclists had been killed with over 80 per cent of the fatalities due to collisions with motor vehicles.[67] Between 1928 and 1933, regarding the rise in road accidents generally, cyclists accounted for 54 per cent of the increase in injuries and 62 per cent of the increase in fatalities. By 1935, one in four of those injured and nearly one in five of those killed on the roads was a pedal cyclist; and of the increase in road accidents, between 1928 and 1933, 54 per cent of the injuries and 62 per cent of the deaths were cyclists.[68] Road safety became a political issue and the problem centred around the private motor car. 'Middle-Class Killers' was the apt title of a chapter in William Plowden's book *The Motor Car and Politics*, highlighting both the political and the social dimensions to the issue.

The idea of and debates over cycling paths can be dated back to the turn of the twentieth century. In 1908, highlighting a growing acknowledgement of the issue, engineers called for the separation of automobile and bicycle lanes at the First International Road Congress in Paris.[69] Even at an early stage discourse over cycle paths pointed to the nub of future debates and tensions, which revolved around the rights of cyclists. In 1901 Bristol's city council was 'seriously proposing to make cycle tracks along the edges of the streets', emulating other places, which had already laid cycle paths. In that same year, it was reported that a cycle path of 2 miles with a width of 10 feet and composed of sand and cinders had recently been built in Sydney. Its cost of £100 had been met by public subscription In Washington DC another publicly subscribed cycle path 5 to 6 miles in length was built at a cost of £600. Another cycle path near Minneapolis, which ran out of the city for 10 miles, was also built from public subscription. In addition, it was reported that 'there is a splendid cycle path in the Golden Gate Park' in San Francisco funded entirely by the government.[70] Interestingly, it was noted that cycle paths in Belgium were a product of 'horribly bad roads'. By contrast, due partly to the work of the Roads Improvement Association, roads in England were generally in comparatively better condition – an irony in itself as this organization had been established by cyclists, but was later taken over by supporters of motoring. It not only negated the necessity of cycle paths in England, but further reinforced among cyclists their right to ride on the road. Nevertheless, as early as 1901, it was prophesized that

> [i]n England we have no cycle tracks of this kind but it seems probable that in the near future we shall have to take the question into consideration. With the increase in vehicular traffic it becomes evident that city cycling in the future will only be indulged in at tremendous risk to life and limb.[71]

On each occasion cycle paths were proposed as a solution, it was vigorously opposed by cycling grandees. It was not as if important cycling figures were anti-car as a number had connections with motoring stretching back to its early days. Bidlake had been a motoring journalist for the *Athletic News* and in 1900 he had taken part in the 1,000 miles motor trial of that year for which Stancer was one of the local organizers. John Urry and H. W. Bartleet were also drivers, as was the editor of *Cycling*, Harry England.[72] Instead, the political debate was shaped by class tensions in two areas. First, there was the conflict between middle-class motorists and working-class cyclists. Second, there was an intra-class conflict within the middle classes, which highlighted a shift in middle-class values, represented by cycling and motoring advocates. Cycle paths was just one restrictive measure that cyclists contested during this period. In addition to motorists, there was also criticism of coroners. It was felt that because many of them, as members of the middle class, owned cars they were biased towards motorists at hearings on traffic accidents.[73]

The issue of cycle tracks/paths was again raised in cycling circles after the First World War. In 1920 it was mooted that the Ministry of Transport had considered building 'specially-prepared tracks for cyclists' to run alongside a new road around Croydon.[74] 'Robin Hood', aka G. H. Stancer, was unsurprisingly wary of this potential development on two accounts. First, he feared that cyclists themselves would have to pay for cycle paths through taxation, and second, there was a fear that it was a scheme 'to get rid of us altogether'. He reiterated how '[t]he road is our rightful heritage, and we shall not be squeezed off it without a struggle – least of all at our own expense!'[75] Wayfarer also set the tone for the forthcoming debate. Responding to the prospect of cycle tracks, he launched a similarly passionate defence, invoking a cyclist's 'inalienable right' to ride on the highway. While 'special cycling tracks' in cities were another story, like those he had experienced in Copenhagen, he claimed – prophetically – that

> the real cycling is done in the country and not in towns and cities, and if it is ever seriously proposed to construct these tracks along the open road, cyclists will sit up and take notice.[76]

Instead, he called on the minister of transport to '[r]egulate your traffic so that it keeps on the right side of the roads with due consideration for the owners and other users thereof'.

In 1922 the Roads Improvement Association made a tentative enquiry about whether the CTC would be in favour of cycle paths, but it was met with a brusque response. Instead, and highlighting how proprietorial the cycling authorities were over the roads, an editorial recommended that motor vehicles have their own exclusive roads built for them.[77] Cycle paths were not a matter of urgency in government circles. In 1927, one member of the public, Mr Wright Miller, wrote to the Ministry of Transport outlining his plans for cycle paths; he would continue to be a regular letter writer to the ministry throughout the interwar years. He was actually a member of the CTC and admitted he was in a small minority of cyclists who favoured cycle paths, albeit so long as they were built to the appropriate quality. The minister rejected his proposal.[78]

As late as January 1933 the minister of transport (then John Pybus) was rebuffing any suggestions regarding the construction of cycle paths.[79] By November of that year, however, attitudes were hardening towards cyclists as they came under increasing scrutiny. In particular, it was claimed that the total number of fatal accidents in which cyclists were a contributory factor was high, and in practically all of them they were the victim.[80] The new minister of transport, Oliver Stanley, when questioned over allowing cyclists to use footpaths, doubted its advisability, but then declared, 'I am prepared to consider any proposal submitted to me by the appropriate highway authority for the provision of separate tracks for pedal cyclists.'[81] A narrative was emerging within government and Whitehall circles that rather than road casualties being the fault of motorists, cyclists needed saving from themselves.

Leslie Hore-Belisha, minister of transport between 1934 and 1937, was the person associated with the introduction of cycle paths. He had a flair for publicity and was the first minister to grapple with the problems of the motor car. He introduced pelican crossings and the 'Belisha beacons' while also bringing in the driving test and revising the highway code.[82] Importantly, he brought the control of major trunk roads under central government. In 1935 a five-year road building plan was announced, at a cost of £100 million, while the 1936 Trunk Roads Act effectively nationalized 4,500 miles of roads.[83] Belisha was not sympathetic to cyclists, at one point referring to them as 'hysterical prima donnas'.[84] He would become a focus of cyclists' ire. In December 1934 Hore-Belisha opened the Western Avenue cycle path. His speech reflected – at least in the eyes of cycling figures – a rhetoric of an acceptance of dangerous motorists and that instead of legislating against them, it emphasized how cyclists were being excluded from using the roads for their own good. He proclaimed that 'cyclists may use these paths with safety and motorists will know that the cyclists will not be on the road'. Hore-Belisha added, 'This is an honest attempt to try and save these people's [cyclists'] lives. It is no use saying that the motorist should not go so fast when the cyclist is dead!'[85] One Conservative MP, Marcus Samuel, reinforcing this rhetoric, also argued,

I do think that cyclists, for their own sakes, should be pleased to have some special rights to some part of the road where if anything happens to them through other people's neglect, there should be no doubt whatever as to who is to blame.[86]

Part of the context behind these debates was the state of the British economy. In his 1935 memorandum on relieving unemployment, former prime minister David Lloyd George argued that '[f]ar-reaching reforms of our road conditions are needed with an urgency that cannot be overstated' to stimulate the economy. For Lloyd George, of the 'greatest urgency', in light of the growing accident rate concerning cyclists, was 'the provision of special tracks for cyclists'. Similar to Hore-Belisha, he added that 'pedal cyclists … are to-day regarded as constituting the major part of the problem of road accidents', thus further reinforcing the idea that cyclists were the problem, not motor vehicles.[87]

Ranged against cycling was an increasingly influential and powerful motoring lobby.[88] Initially, the motor car had received a bad press. Criticism was framed in terms of class, particularly those drivers who were deemed as irresponsible members of the nouveau riche and derided as road hogs, a la Toad of Toad Hall. During the 1920s car ownership continued to be dominated by a significant minority of the population, but as car ownership began to spread down the social classes, criticism from motoring journals was increasingly muted. Moreover, the motor industry's importance to the national interest and economic value increased. In 1935 Lloyd George stated that motor vehicles 'have long become an indispensable factor in our national economy'.[89] In 1939 1.4 million jobs were directly or indirectly linked to the industry, while the car industry brought significant inward investment, such as the Ford factory at Dagenham that opened in 1931. By the late 1930s it was also increasingly evident that the motor industry would play an important military role in any future war.[90]

Central to debates over road accidents was the speed limit. As early as 1903 the motoring lobby had persuaded the state to raise the speed limit from 12 mph to 20 mph.[91] In 1930 the Road Traffic Act abolished the 20-mph limit, only for a 30-mph limit to be introduced following the Road Traffic Act of 1934 despite an exponential rise in road fatalities. The 1934 Road Traffic Act was the last piece of traffic legislation with regard to private motoring during the interwar years. After this there was increasing emphasis placed on propaganda and the education of all road users, culminating in an 'ideology of road safety'.[92] From 1926 the Ministry of Transport had published weekly updates of traffic accidents and fatalities.[93] Whether by accident or design, these figures further highlighted the dangers of the road and made the subject a regular feature of public discourse. The statistics not only ushered in a sense of panic and created a climate of 'something must be done' but also forced the relevant parties to respond via public relations.

In the field of public relations, motoring organizations were more resourceful than their cycling counterparts and had more members than the latter; motoring also had powerful lobbyists among the press, especially the *Daily Mail*. In his motoring column the record-breaking motorist Malcolm Campbell, for example, insisted that cyclists must use the tracks for the sake of safety.[94] By the late 1930s the motoring lobby had successfully implanted the idea that it was 'individual drivers who were the fundamental cause of increasing danger on the roads, not the mode of individual transport being used'[95] – the emphasis on the action of individuals being a classic public relations tactic to divert attention away from institutional difficulties. As a consequence, there was increased emphasis on the safety of pedestrians and cyclists, which obscured, if not eliminated, the inherent danger of motor vehicles. Similar to how Matless described the construction of a modern Englishness through a greater emphasis on planning and order, a rhetoric of road safety emerged that revolved around a need for planning and education. At the centre of this process was the National Safety First Association, which was funded by motoring organizations. Thus, road safety campaigns were not politically neutral, but instead ideologically designed to neuter criticism of the car.[96] It was this rhetoric of safety that has dominated debate around cycling both as a sport and as a leisure activity ever since.

The cycling community – in its organized form – was not prepared to accept these developments. The CTC had declined an invitation to the opening of the Western Avenue cycle path while the NCU had accepted their invite, but had also made clear its opposition to the paths.[97] In particular, cycling opinion makers feared that the use of these paths would become compulsory for cyclists. There had also been suggestions in Parliament that pedestrian footpaths be given over to cyclists. In a typically robust defence of cyclists' rights, Stancer warned that cycle paths were ultimately designed to exclude them from any public roads that were lined with cycle paths. He argued that this now happened in France, while also claiming that cycle paths there and in Belgium were of a lower standard than in Holland, which was commonly used as the exemplar in this area.[98] In his capacity as secretary of the CTC, Stancer invoked the notion of cyclists as British citizens as well as ratepayers to reiterate his opposition: 'Cyclists do not consider that such paths are either necessary or desirable and are apprehensive that this is merely the first step towards depriving them of their common right as British citizens to the use of the public highway.'[99]

A national campaign against cycle paths was organized. To a certain extent, it reflected new forms of citizenship, which had been a product of the expansion in the franchise since 1918. Membership of both the NCU and the CTC increased considerably during the thirties (see Chapter 4) and created a more engaged and active community. In 1935 there were a number of large meetings around the country protesting against cycle paths while at the same time criticizing speeding motorists as the cause of the rise in accidents.[100] In March 3,000 people attended a joint meeting at Picton Hall and St. George's

Hall in Liverpool, where senior figures such as Wayfarer led the debate.[101] Following a personal message in *Cycling*, in which Hore-Belisha outlined the government's commitment to the safety of the cyclist, Kuklos responded by arguing that Hore-Belisha's plans for cycle paths had been a sop to the motoring lobby who were to face a speed limit. Kuklos demanded no let-up in the protests of cyclists. In combative terms, he declared,

> We must attack all the time, and not be content with rearguard actions. If and when a cycle path appears, constructed by an occasional, short-sighted and mis-guided local authority, it should be systematically picketed at weekends by responsible cyclists, armed with leaflet for the thoughtless and irresponsible 'pushbikist', to point out how he is selling his birthright for a mess of asphalt. Let militant committees be formed everywhere, from CTC, NCU, Clarion and the local clubs.[102]

This collective action created the momentum for the formation of the Fellowship of the Wheel the following year. It was a movement set up by the CTC, NCU and the Clarion club, but it was also open to unattached cyclists, to protect the rights of the cyclist on the highway.[103] By July it had over 50,000 members.[104] Yet cycling bodies were hardly firebrands. Later, the CTC distributed 5 million leaflets to cyclists explaining to them the requirements of the law, relative to the Highway Code, and that cyclists should use courtesy towards other road users.[105] The desire for respectability was still important both in the perception of cycling as a law-abiding activity and in how they conducted business.

It was not all conflict. In 1937 the CTC and the NCU formed a joint committee with the motoring organization, The Order of the Road, to discuss improving the etiquette of all road users and to promote 'a spirit of co-operation'.[106] At a luncheon held at London's Savoy Hotel representatives of each organization gave a speech. For the CTC, Stancer suggested that the time had come for the building of motor-vehicle-only roads, that is, motorways, arguing that the road system could not cope with the growth in traffic. In this sense, it marked an acceptance of the car's cultural supremacy and a need for practical solutions. Moreover, it further reflected how a modernity that revolved around planning was in the ascendancy.[107]

Post-war European developments concerning cycle paths provided a contrast with those in Britain. In 1934 it was reported that there was to be a major building programme of cycle paths in Germany under the control of the Reichsgemeinschaft fur Radfahrwegebaus E.V, the Association of the Reich for the Construction of Cycle Paths.[108] However, it was in the Netherlands where cycle paths were integrated most successfully into the transport infrastructure. Cycling occupied a central role in Dutch society and culture in a way that it never did or has in Britain. In 1921, in a special supplement, *The Times* was effusive in its praise for Dutch attitudes and policies towards cycling. Both in urban areas and the countryside the bicycle was the main form of transport. Because of this, and because cycling was also the most popular form of touring, the country's cyclists were supported by an extensive network of cycle paths. Running parallel with practically every main road were special cycle paths, which totalled over 1,500 miles. More paths were laid out across fields and woodland areas, covering a distance of over 1,000 miles.[109] Dutch cycle paths were regarded as the best in Europe in terms of their width and the smoothness of their surface.[110] Moreover, they catered for a large cycling population. In 1935 it was estimated that there were 3.3 million bicycles in Holland out of a population of 8.4 million, equating to 4 in 10 people owning one. By contrast, there were 90,000 cars (0.01 per cent owned a car) from a total of 183,000 motor vehicles.[111] In comparison the approximate figures for the UK were – a still not unimpressive – 20 to 25 per cent regarding bicycle ownership and 4 per cent for car ownership.

It would be easy to attribute the Netherlands' cycling network to its largely flat topography. Its success though was due to political factors as well as the Netherlands' neutrality in the First World War. In particular, as Anne-Katrin Ebert has outlined, the Dutch touring association, the Nederlandsche Algemeene Wielrijders Bond (ANWB) – in complete contrast to the CTC in Britain – was the prime lobbyist for the construction of cycling lanes.[112] Importantly, unlike in Britain, the ANWB comprised both cyclists and motorists. Moreover, the ANWB, which was dominated by the Dutch upper middle classes, offered a different vision of the benefits of cycling compared to the CTC. Whereas the CTC was built on nineteenth-century liberal values of individualism and self-improvement, the ANWB promoted the Dutch liberal values of self-control, balance and composure. As a consequence, as Ebert argues, '[b]icycle path construction was neither an environmental nor a social project, but was brought about by the efforts of a social elite that used bicycle tourism to strengthen national identity and increase social restraint'.[113] The Dutch reaction to the objections of the British cycling authorities to cycle paths was one of incredulity. In 1935, an article in the ANWB's journal *De Kampion*, stated, 'With all stubbornness they object to this new measure and the arguments, which they put up are in our eyes nearly ridiculous.'[114]

Yet unlike in the Netherlands, the debate over cycle paths in Britain was driven by economic interests and cultural perceptions over who had a right to use the roads. The publication of the Alness committee report, *Prevention of Road Accidents*, in 1939 confirmed the greater emphasis placed on motoring, or in the eyes of cyclists a bias and a prejudice against them. The Alness committee had been composed of a group of Lords and its chair had asked every witness about cycling. By this time, the CTC through Stancer had almost accepted the inevitable, but did insist on cycle paths of good quality. Yet the report's recommendations on cycling were underpinned with an emphasis on getting cyclists off the roads for their own safety. Motorists by contrast, according to Carlton Reid, were favourably treated. The intervention of war saw the mothballing of plans for an extensive network of cycle paths.[115]

Cycling's political and cultural marginalization mirrored changing ideas of Englishness during the thirties. Despite its growth as the most popular form of transport by 1939, cycling was increasingly shunted literally and metaphorically away from the centre of the road to its edges. In his classic 1934 *English Journey*, J. B. Priestley identified three 'Englands'. The first was what he termed 'byways England', slow, rural and benign; the second harsh, ugly and industrial; while the third, modern, was more reflective of a developing consumer, car-owning, suburban dwelling society. Cycling's cultural gatekeepers had been natural defenders of 'byways England' which struggled to reconcile a planned modernity at odds with the England of their youth, and which would continue to challenge ideas of ruralism associated with cycling. It was this contrast that would continue to shape the place of cycling in British society, as well as the tone of the debate over its status, not just for the rest of the 1900s but also into the twenty-first century.

CHAPTER 4

Cycling and the people

David Kynaston has observed that the first 10 years or so after the Second World War were a 'truly golden age' for cycling.[1] In many ways, this golden age had started during the interwar years. While the late Victorian period was characterized by roads free of cars, pioneering technical innovations and high society's fleeting association with the bicycle, it was the interwar period that ushered in mass cycling where more people rode bicycles more often than ever before or since. In his seminal work *The Uses of Literacy*, Richard Hoggart argued that cycling had a positive impact on working-class culture as through it working people 'could still react positively to both the challenge of their environments and the useful possibilities of cheap mass-production'.[2] The bicycle became increasingly ubiquitous, democratic and, importantly, a major form of transport for millions of workers, or, as they were called by the cycling cognoscenti, 'utilitarians'. The interwar years through to the mid-1950s ushered in a period of great popularity for the bicycle in various ways. Similar to rambling, its popularity was grassroots in origin and was largely a product of the outdoor movement. Touring regained its popularity, and there was a relaxation of wider social conventions, including cycling attire for both males and females. The bicycle, as a symbol of freedom, encapsulated some of the broader changes in British life more generally.

The period from around 1918 to 1950 was one of political transformation. In particular, it was during these years that the British thought of themselves as 'democratic'.[3] At a social and economic level, however, 'England was emphatically a working-class country', despite changes in the occupational structure of the working classes. A decline in those working in the primary industries was offset by a growth in the newer metal industries, in the motor industry and in building and engineering. As a result, while the working classes continued to be deeply marked by interwar unemployment, by the

1940s their prosperity and political influence – partly due to the Second World War – 'had no historic precedent'.[4] However, ever-present social tensions bookended the period as anti-working-class sensibilities among the middle classes, evident at the end of the First World War, resurfaced after 1945.[5]

During this period, the values and enduring appeal of cycling for many of its enthusiasts were remarkably consistent, and comprised companionship, hard exercise and fresh air. To a certain extent, this appeal reflected prevailing ideas of Britishness that revolved around modesty, respectability and conviviality – an image of cycling that was evident right up until the mid-1950s when in terms of status cycling declined. These qualities and cycling's appeal were portrayed in a British Transport Film in 1955, titled 'Cyclists Special'.[6] It was made in conjunction with the CTC and aimed to advertise both cycling and British Railways' London Midland Region. The short 15-minute film featured a number of CTC members from in and around the London area taking an excursion to Rugby from where various cycling parties rode to different parts of the Midlands. The film evoked a wistful image of rural England and had more than a whiff of Victorian Britain about it. The film's consensual and educational tone emphasized the virtues of companionship and sociability among the group as well as highlighting historical sites, such as Kenilworth Castle, where members took photographs. One member suffered a puncture, but as the narrator pointed out, in the spirit of cycling's fraternity, all the members of the group stopped to assist. The film also attempted to depict other so-called British characteristics. Typical of the Whiggish history so prevalent in cycling publications, when some cyclists reached the monument of the Battle of Naseby, its outcome was described as 'a typical English blooming mixture', which, in consensual terms, is then related to a cycling club. 'You know it's a funny thing but if you think about it, its clubs like these that bring out all the qualities that stamp themselves in the British character', where

> only the humming of tyres and the talk that arises between solicitor and carpenter, teacher and typesetter, electrician and radiographer; between people of all ages, ranks and station who rediscover their common humanity in finding countryside, exercise and companionship all in one.[7]

While the film promoted a rural vision of England and of a cohesive and peaceful society, it also represented a critique of modernity. (The train here, ironically, was seen as an agency in the promotion of the English countryside.) As a nod to the opposition to interwar ribbon developments, for example, it was noted that 'Rugby is not one of those towns that sprawls a rash of semi-detached villas across the land. It still keeps within its bounds; snug, packed with respect for the country out of which it has grown.' Even more telling, in the film the roads were almost devoid of any cars. Away from the main roads it was noted, Rugby was only 5 or 10 minutes from 'the quiet countryside as most cyclists go cycling to find'. For each group, it was claimed that '[t]he tree-lined lanes welcome these friendly processions that bring no exhaust fumes, no petrol fumes, no racket or blaring of horns'. There was an antediluvian quality about the film – a moment when Britain was on the cusp of change before the motor car would come to dominate the roads.

The revival of cycling

Cycling's popularity and visibility had inevitably suffered a dip due to the millions of men who were called up for duty on the Western Front. Indeed, it was women that kept cycling in the public eye during the Great War (see Chapter 6). By 1923, however, the *Manchester Guardian* had identified Easter as signalling 'the revival of bicycling'. It noted that bicycles old and new, in groups and clubs, had showed up on the roads 'in numbers that vouch for the survival of the bicycle'. Moreover, many commentators had been surprised by the increased number of cyclists touring abroad.[8] What was behind this revival? In reality, cycling numbers had been growing since demobilization, as more men again took up riding. For the interwar more generally, economic factors were important as part of a wider demand for leisure among the working classes. The purchasing power of consumers and the number of paid holidays of workers were increasing, while the working week was falling during the interwar period. Simply put, 'there was more money in working-class hands to be spent on recreation, and more time available in which to enjoy recreational activities'.[9]

In 1923 it had been estimated that there were 5 million cyclists in the country, a figure that rose to 10 to 12 million by 1939. This growth had been reflected in the manufacturing of bicycles. Despite a dip from the boom in 1896 to 1912, output almost trebled between 1924 and 1937 when 2,057,000 bicycles were built.[10] Following the boom there had been a downturn and a period of consolidation and amalgamations within the bicycling industry. During the interwar years there were nine major companies with three – Raleigh, Hercules and BSA – responsible for 55 per cent of cycle production. Hercules was then the largest company producing 600,000 cycles in 1935, nearly twice as many as Raleigh. A wider range of models were introduced to cater for the growing market, although there were still only four standard designs: the roadster; the racer; the tourist; and the semi-sports.[11] One innovation was the lightweight bicycle, which was particularly suited to female riders.[12] Manufacturers, for reasons of mass production, had initially continued to concentrate on producing standard roadsters largely for utilitarian purposes. However, there was an increasing demand to satisfy consumer tastes. As a result, new bicycles incorporated design features which intended to make riding more pleasurable in an attempt to revive cycling as a pastime. At first, there was a focus on racing, but 'lightweight' roadster machines, which incorporated new ideas and components, began to appear.[13] By 1932, lightweight bicycles had their own show, held in October at the Royal Horticultural Hall.[14]

An increase in the number of clubs and the membership of governing bodies mirrored cycling's growth. In 1934 it was estimated that there were over 100,000 cyclists who were members of various organized bodies.[15] The number of clubs affiliated to the NCU had doubled over the interwar years, from 836 in 1926 to 1,790 by 1936,[16] and its membership similarly expanded over the same period from 24,500 to 55,930.[17] From its peak in 1899 of 60,000, CTC membership had dropped to 8,546 by 1918, but numbers grew steadily thereafter. Membership reached 20,000 in 1925 and then 38,000 in 1936.[18] Cycling witnessed a further spurt in its popularity during and after the Second World War, as a result of the sharp decline in motoring levels. In 1939 there had been 3.2 million vehicles with licences (including over 400,000 bicycles and tricycles, for work purposes) with private cars accounting for 2 million. But mainly because of petrol rationing, by 1944 these totals had shrunk to 1.6 million and 0.75 million, respectively.[19] As a consequence, it forced many people to cycle to work. On Good Friday in 1940 it was reported that the roads were comparatively empty.[20] By 1948 the membership of the various cycling organizations reached record levels. The NCU had nearly 60,000 members while the CTC, with its 50 DAs had nearly as many. The Road Time Trials Council (RTTC) membership numbered nearly 30,000 with a similar number, members of the National Clarion Association.[21] In 1950 the NCU's membership peaked at over 66,000.[22]

In the wake of the damage of British cities from the Blitz, a new sport was even born, cycle speedway. A post-war teenage craze, it had a DIY culture with bikes made from spare parts and the tracks out of bomb sites. As much a breeding ground for speedway riders as for cycling, it was characterized literally by some rough and tumble. By 1949 it was estimated that there were between 30,000 and 100,000 'teenage enthusiasts' with 200 clubs in East London alone. Results were published in the tabloid newspapers and some races were televised by the BBC as the sport spread across the country. By the late 1950s the craze had faded as the bomb sites were redeveloped, the riders did their national service and speedway itself declined in popularity.[23]

For many people though cycling was not about sport or being part of an organization. Instead, because of its innate freedom, it was a spontaneous activity, which could mean just pottering about or day outings. Even cycling holidays required little planning. At the end of the war cycling was still a pervasive part of British life. In 1944 one survey had found that 26 per cent of adults owned a bicycle.[24] The presence of the bicycle was evident in many facets of everyday life. Patterns of cycling though were not uniform across the country. Cycling was more popular in the flatter regions such as East Anglia, the south-central region and the Midlands – the centre of the bicycle industry – than in the hillier environs of Scotland, Wales and the north-east of England.²⁵ Nor was it evenly distributed across the population. Interestingly, in terms of social class, it was found that those in middle income groups were more regular bike riders than those in the highest and lowest groups, while men – 42 per cent – were more likely to use or own a bicycle than women – 19 per cent.²⁶

It was the sheer banality of cycling during this period that was striking, along with how familiarity bred contempt for the bicycle. During the interwar years cycling was the most common form of 'autonomous vehicular mobility'.²⁷ Its growing proletarian image was reinforced through the sight of men and women cycling to and from work. Coventry may have been the centre of the British car industry, but according to Peter Bailey one of his abiding childhood memories was the 'dense surging columns of pedalling workers released from the factories at the end of the day'.²⁸ Pioneering design critic Reynar Banham was from a working-class background in interwar Norwich. He recalled, 'I came from a cycling community. ... I was a bob-ender in the days when a bob-ender meant a certain class of person. ... Anyone who knows Norwich knows that the cycling was king of the road there, and all other traffic had to stand aside when the cyclists got loose.'²⁹ Tony Mason recalls how his father cycled to work in Gainsborough by pedalling with one leg. Unable to bend the other leg, he had a specially made bar to rest his foot on.³⁰ In the 1940s the average journey to work – 5 miles – was now double the distance of the 1890s,³¹ yet in 1944 27 per cent of workers, who owned a bicycle, still regularly cycled to work. A higher percentage of those cycling to work was to be found in agriculture, munitions industries, construction, transport and clerical occupations.³² As a harbinger of things to come, between 1940 and 1959, the use of the bicycle for the journey to work declined slightly from 19.6 per cent to 16 per cent, while the use of a car increased from 6 per cent to 16 per cent.³³ In 1948 it was estimated that there were around 10 million people who owned a bicycle,³⁴ while in 1950 there were just over 2 million cars, confirming its image as a middle-class luxury.³⁵

In addition to work and leisure, the bicycle had other uses, including experiencing historical events. On 7 May 1945, Tom Flinn, after hearing the constant din of hooters from the docks and factory sirens in London's East End in anticipation of the announcement of VE Day, 'went for a short run round on the bike through the streets of East and West Ham and saw many jubilant crowds dancing round bonfires to the playing of pianos and much home-made music'. He also noted that '[a]ll pubs were doing good business'.³⁶ The bicycle also acted as a transformative social agent for children, in terms of status and their own experiences. For some children having their first bike became a kind of rite of passage. Tony Mason was given a new bike by his parents in 1949 as a reward for passing his 11-plus for entry into Gainsborough Grammar School. Teddy Carter, because he could not afford one, built his own fixed wheel bicycle from parts he found in a local dump. In her study of teenagers in the early 1950s, Pearl

Jephcott claims, 'A cycling craze was on at the same time of the Enquiry; and a large proportion of both boys and girls had the use of a bicycle.'[37] The bike fulfilled various roles for the teenagers, generally complementing without being the dominant part of their lives. Jephcott noted that for many of the teenagers cycling was 'a strictly local activity'. Those who pursued 'energetic cycling', that is, sport and long-distance touring, were in the minority. The bicycle was 'regarded as essential for making street encounters' and for girls a bicycle also enabled them 'to pick up boys more easily than if they were on foot'.[38] Cycling offered opportunities for teenagers to extend their horizons. One boy, Arthur, was part of a group of eight boys who all had bikes and would go off to the woods for the day on Saturdays and Sundays. Two brothers, Ted and Sammy, aged 17 and 15 respectively, 'became madly keen on week-end cycling expeditions' despite their mother's reservations. By contrast Harry (17) had 'a constant and absorbing passion' for cycle racing. His parents had been keen cyclists and gave him his first bicycle when he was 14. Within a year he was racing in time trials and winning races. On the evidence of one week in April 1950 his life revolved around cycling, whether this was racing, club runs, training or evenings at the club. As for other interests, it was said that he liked girls 'but a serious one would have diverted cash and time from the bike, so he had decided to keep heart-free'.[39]

The democratization of cycling was perhaps no better illustrated in the public domain than the sight of soldiers injured during the First World War riding bicycles. The war had increased both the visibility and the awareness of disability in Britain on an unprecedented scale. Of those who survived the war and returned home, over 41,000 men had limbs amputated during the war; 69 per cent lost one leg, 28 per cent lost one arm and nearly 3 per cent had lost both legs or both arms. Another 272,000 suffered injuries in the arms or legs while 60,500 were wounded in the head or eyes and 89,000 men sustained other serious damage to their bodies.[40] However, by 1930 the well of sympathy for soldiers with mutilated bodies was running dry due to the increasing competition for limited economic sources with disabled civilians.[41]

In early 1918 the CTC had launched an appeal to its members to send any spare bicycles to Preparatory and Fitting Hospitals for 'disabled sailors and soldiers'.[42] After the First World War a number of articles appeared in the trade press concerned with the provision of special cycles and motor cycles for the disabled and some manufacturers produced models catering for this demand.[43] Some men were keen to cycle again and wrote to the cycling press asking for advice about specialist machines.[44] In 1920 a disabled cyclists' rally took place in Regent's Park, London. The event was sponsored by *The Motor Cycle and Cycle Trader*, and the 90 machines on display acted as an advertisement for this growing market. All were hand-propelled tricycles – rather than bicycles – with some designs having a motor fixed.[45] This was not a completely new idea as in the nineteenth century machines had been constructed for 'cripples' to be powered by the use of the arms and hands only.[46] Some injured soldiers who had cycled before the war adapted their machines themselves. One former serviceman, who had lost a leg and who was also a cycling engineer, inserted a footrest from the bottom bracket. Between June and October in 1920 he claimed to have ridden over 1,000 miles.[47]

Perhaps the most visible example of the relationship between cycling and disability was through the exploits of Walter Greaves. In 1936 Greaves rode a world record 45,383 miles in a calendar year, despite having the use of only one arm.[48] Born in 1907, instead of the Great War, his left arm had been amputated just above the elbow following a road accident when he was 14. Greaves was a talented cyclist and like many similar record attempts at the time, it was an exercise in advertising. During the year Greaves rode a specially adapted – it had half a handlebar – 'Three Spires' bicycle for Coventry Bicycles Ltd. At a stroke, he became a professional cyclist, but his motivations were obvious, as at the time he was an unemployed motor mechanic.[49] Greaves was also noted for being a committed vegetarian and a member of the Vegetarian Cycling and Athletic Club. One of his aims had been to show the benefits of his daily diet, which consisted of 'a pound and a half of wholemeal bread with butter, 2lbs of apples, 1.5lbs of tomatoes, 7–8 pints of milk, up to 10 pints of water, orange juice and the occasional ginger beer'.[50]

On 6 January he received a civic send-off in Bradford at the start of his journey and throughout the year, as part of the advertising campaign, he visited various locations around the country where at times he was met by crowds and local cyclists and feted by local dignitaries. As part of the ride, and for extra publicity, he attempted other records and established routes such as Land's End to John O'Groats. On completing six months in the saddle, he was received in Doncaster by Alderman Charles Theobald and escorted by members of 10 cycling clubs.[51] For setting a new English record in October he was given a civic reception in Lincoln. He was welcomed by the town's mayor, Councillor J. J. Leamy, and one Mrs English placed a garland of chrysanthemums round his neck and Mr F. Elvidge welcomed him on behalf of Lincoln cyclists. Greaves, typical of civic protocol, responded with a few words thanking Lincolnshire cyclists for turning out in such numbers.[52] His record ride finished in his home town of Bradford on 31 December. Initially, he had set off that day from York with several hundred cyclists plus the lord mayor in attendance. He arrived in Bradford's Town Hall square shortly before midnight where he was greeted by around 5,000 people. This civic event was combined with commercial interests. Greaves was presented with the 'Three Spires' trophy by the lord mayor, George Carter, while other industry interests were present. These included the presentation by the Bradford cycle trade of the Trivelox Cup and the Middlemore Cup from a comedian, Albert Modley, while in recognition of his feat he received three cheques from Coventry Bicycles.

To what extent Greaves changed perceptions of disability is difficult to assess. In virtually all newspaper reports, he was referred to as the 'one-armed cyclist' while his visit to Sunderland in July was advertised as something akin to the arrival of a circus freak show. 'Walter Greaves the one-armed cyclist … . The most amazing cyclist in the world. Please note he has one arm only.'[53] One report referred to him as the 'Bicycling Superman', another, 'Greaves – One-Armed Wonder'.[54] Greaves's feat though did capture the imagination of the public and cycling manufacturers saw the potential benefits of such a record attempt. A craze for year-long cycling records ensued. The following year there was a competition between two riders on two different hemispheres. In England, the veteran French cyclist Rene Menzies rode 61,561 miles on a Rudge-Whitworth bicycle.[55] Despite smashing Greaves's record, he was pipped by the Australian Ossie Nicholson, who completed 62,855.6 miles. In 1938, in a widely publicized attempt, Billie Dovey, also on a Rudge-Whitworth, would set a new record for women (see Chapter 6).[56]

Greaves later opened his own shop in Bradford where he made and sold bicycles. His most famous design was a racer, 'King of the Mountains'. A member of the Clarion Club, he was someone who held strong communist views, although he had a reputation for not being very communal with fellow cyclists.[57] He had joined West Bradford CC in 1932 before he started his own, Airedale Olympic in 1948. He had also continued his cycling career, although in 1937 he had been unable to attract any sponsors in a bid to regain the world record. In 1942 he was a founder member of the British League of Racing Cyclists (BLRC) and in 1945, he took part in the first Brighton-Glasgow Victory Marathon, organized by the BLRC (see Chapter 5).[58] His motivation was perhaps partly driven by the refusal of the Road Time Trials Council to reinstate his amateur status, as he had received payment for his record ride.[59] Greaves later promoted cycling in Bradford, before turning his talents to folk music, which included 'What Lloyd George Gave Me', a song about the granting of the old-age pension.

Mass cycling and social demarcations

Despite attaining the status of a mass activity, there were various social demarcations among the cycling population. Clubs and cycling bodies, for example, revealed class tensions. Voluntary association continued to play an important role in class formation. Depending on the type of voluntary association, there was 'a fashioning of an a-political consciousness that enabled some of the continuing fractions within class'.[60] Of course, this was a relatively unconscious political process for the majority of cyclists. Within the cycling community at large any fractions within class were not generally reflected in the social activities of clubs and groups as there was little difference. Instead, it suggests that cyclists wanted to enjoy them with like-minded people. A typical example of cycling activities featured at the Clarion cyclists' annual Whitsun Camp in 1937. Jointly organized by the unions of the Midlands, Wales and Southern Counties, it took place in the Cotswold at Cirencester in Gloucestershire with over 250 'Clarionettes' in attendance. There was a variety of activities that mixed sport with the recreational, and included men and women's tug of war competitions, runs and rambles, plus a time trial.[61]

In addition to the long-standing middle-class clubs who had formed in the nineteenth century, new ones emerged from working-class backgrounds, such as the workplace as well as those that had their origins in workers' politics. In the mid-1930s, for example, the 40 or so clubs that made up the North Yorkshire and South Durham centre of the NCU included Bishop Auckland Cyclists and Tourists Club; Hartlepool Co-operative CC; Darlington Workmen's Club and Institute CC; Darlington Stooperdale Employees Club; Middlesbrough Clarion CC; and Richmond CC.[62] The two clubs that had the largest affiliated membership in the whole of the NCU were Teesside-based: Stockton Wheelers and Middlesbrough Co-operative CC, both with 211 members each.[63]

While the demarcations of class in all clubs were not clear cut, the working classes had different values than middle-class bodies, which sometimes created difficulties in terms of mixing socially and an acceptance of the aims of the club.[64] The working class of course was not itself a homogenous body. Whereas the growth of organized labour increasingly politicized workers, others aspired to middle-class cultural values. While its social make-up was not entirely clear, one of the original members of the South Lancashire Road Club (formed in 1935) was a farm labourer, yet most of the original members were from Sale, a well-to-do Cheshire town, who paid a 2d weekly fee. A post-war monthly column, 'Club Personalities', in *Awheel*, the club magazine of the Solihull CC – an affluent town near Birmingham – featured those from working-class backgrounds, which included toolmakers and carpenters. One member had worked as a waiter in a Birmingham hotel, while another worked at the local grocery store and delivered goods on a box tricycle.[65]

The London-based Comet CC was formed in 1904. According to Arthur Cook, who joined in 1924, it was a working-class club, which included 'cabinetmakers, bakers, printers, shop assistants [and] a couple of railway locomotive firemen'. Most of its male-only members came from Hoxton, Islington and Walthamstow in North London and 'hardly any of them had got beyond Standard VII when leaving school'. On its formation – allegedly around a lamp post in Hoxton – the club used a pub the Downham Arms just off Southgate Road as its headquarters. Cook's first impressions were that he 'found them a very goodhearted crowd, one or two a bit rough and ready maybe but all friendly and generous minded men'.[66] Interestingly, he refers to the Comet as not being rated as a 'first-class' club, which confirms the existence of a social hierarchy among cycling clubs, not dissimilar to rugby union.

Different cycling activities – sport and touring – were also enjoyed across the social spectrum. However, while the CTC still projected a middle-class identity, its membership during the interwar years 'had become much more proletarian'.[67] Despite the best efforts of publications like *Cycling* and the *CTC Gazette* to promote cycling as a homogenous fraternity, some class tensions rose to the surface. Social tensions generally had been growing since the end of the First World War. Employer opposition to the demands of an increasingly powerful and assertive trade unions movement had created industrial unrest, which culminated in the General Strike in May 1926. Strains were evident within and between cycling bodies (for sport, see Chapter 5). Many of the CTC and NCU administrators still promoted Victorian ideas of rational recreation and deference, so it was unsurprising that there were clashes with the growing numbers of politically aware cyclists from the working classes. In 1918, for example, there had been inside criticism of the 'practical monopoly by the professional and leisured classes of representation upon [the CTC] council'. A resolution put forward at a council meeting made an appeal to make it more democratic and hence more attractive to the working classes, who, it reminded council members, 'constitute an overwhelming majority of the cyclists of this country'.[68] The resolution was not adopted but was later carried at the AGM by a 20–19 vote. The motion had been opposed by R. D. Maddox who argued – in contradictory terms – that the CTC was

> a national club and one for all sorts and conditions of men and women, and he objected to any form of class legislation such as was indicated by the resolution. Their club appealed to all and any such attempt to limit it to any one class was to be deprecated very strongly.[69]

For some left-wing cyclists the CTC was seen as part of the establishment. A Clarion splinter group – from the Midlands – which briefly but confusingly produced a monthly paper titled *The Clarion Cyclist*, attacked the CTC for claiming that it was non-political when instead 'it glorifies capitalism and religion by electing kings and landowners as its patrons and presidents'.[70] In terms of the CTC's patrons and presidents this was not incorrect. While the CTC membership was increasingly working class in make-up, it was still founded on Victorian ideas of middle-class respectability. In 1930 a brief spat broke out between the editor of the *CTC Gazette* and cycling grandee G. H. Stancer and the cycling council of the British Workers' Sport Federation (BWSF).[71] It was reported that on their Sunday runs BWSF cyclists were heard shouting 'mass slogans':

> One, two, three, four
> Who are we for?

We are for the workers' sport
Down with the bosses' sport
Workers' sport!'

It reflected the BWSF's increasingly communist outlook, and drew some sarcastic criticism from Stancer, who did not like the peace and quiet of the countryside being disturbed.[72] In response, the BWSF referred to the CTC's 'middle-class officials and writers', and in provocative terms claimed: 'We shall show that we are not just an ordinary cycling club, but an organization of young and enthusiastic fighters against the snobocracy and corruption of capitalist sport.'[73] However, criticism from the fringes can usually be the loudest and there was little sign of open rebellion within the massed ranks of the CTC.

Behind the formation of the British Workers' Sports Federation in 1923 had originally been cyclists of the Clarion club, whose secretary, Tom Groom, was a committed internationalist.[74] Indeed, the emergence of the labour sport movement in interwar Britain was largely due to the Clarion Cycling Club (CCC). The National Workers' Sport Association (NWSA), for example, was formed in 1930, and by 1936 had a membership of 13,000, although 8,000 of this number was accounted for by the CCC. Interestingly, the NWSA, in contrast to the BWSF, put a greater emphasis on the sporting side of cycling rather than its recreational qualities. By the 1930s, CCC members had become just as interested in competitive cycling, as its recreational qualities. Similar to CTC members who enjoyed 'hard riding', some Clarion cyclists formed their own 'speed' sections.[75] It was a state of affairs that ironically mirrored similar tensions within each body over sport and recreational cycling. During the 1930s the Clarion Club enjoyed a revival in membership. In 1931 it had been as low as 1,915, but its rise mirrored cycling's popularity more generally. The CCC became a not insignificant part of the cycling scene during the thirties, almost part of the cycling establishment. The club, joined with other bodies to oppose cycle paths and even had its own stand at the London lightweight cycle show.[76] Moreover, the CCC protested against the lack of municipal sporting provision, including cycle tracks.[77]

Communist cycling clubs such as Red Wheelers and Spartacus CC were also formed, while in 1931, the title of Spartacus was given to the BWSF's cycling section. The popularity of cycling on the far political left not only reflected the prevailing class tensions of the period; it also highlighted ideological differences between socialists and communists who ascribed different meanings to cycling. The Communist Party of Great Britain had been formed in 1920. For many of its small number of members cycling offered an opportunity to reinforce a communist identity.[78] While cycling (and recreational activities generally) exhibited continuities with the Clarion tradition, leisure activity for communists was dialectical. They defined themselves against what they opposed, which included both 'bourgeois' leisure and leisure defined by the socialist and social-democratic tradition.[79] For socialists and social-democrats, leisure was primarily a matter for the individual, but for communists this seemed naïve. Leisure was always political for them and never free from political struggle. Instead, participation in leisure was 'always meant to further communist political aims' and also offered opportunities for recruitment. Cycling in particular lent itself to this wider communist agenda. It had practical uses in political disputes, such as spreading the word of industrial action in local coalfields. The bicycle also represented class struggle. Whereas it was seen as a proletarian machine, car ownership was for the middle classes. Bicycle rides were also ascribed with a different meaning by communists. Instead of imbibing the rural idyll, they provided opportunities to reinforce class awareness, for example, seeing the large residences of the idle rich provided a sharp contrast to city slums.[80] Typically for far left political groups, there was a schism within the ranks, when in 1936 members of the Eastern section of the Spartacus club defected en masse to the Clarion.[81] The working classes were never a homogenous body, nor were they overtly political; politics became important for the majority when it was deemed to matter. At the same time, working-class cyclists did not have to specifically belong to left-wing cycling organizations to hold left-leaning views.

Class was not the only line of demarcation. Religious cycling clubs were also formed in the early twentieth century, although similar to early football clubs, members may have joined just to ride a bike rather than to worship. Cycling crossed the religious divide. In 1900 a Protestant Reform CC had been formed[82] with Catholic St. Christopher's clubs formed in Glasgow, Leeds and Manchester during the 1930s. Other clubs had links to the Church of England. St. Michael & All Angels Cycling Club, for example, was attached to an Anglican church in Walthamstow, while St. George's Gravesend Cycle Club was affiliated to the town's church of the same name. Masonic cycling clubs were formed and there was also a Jewish presence in the British cycling scene.[83] In 1938 it was claimed that a then defunct all-Jewish club had been formed in Leeds 'years ago',[84] while in 1950 the Brent Jewish Road Club was formed in North London.[85] In 1934 the British Maccabi Association had been founded on the idea that sport could play a role in combating Jewish physical, social and spiritual decline.[86] In 1958 it formed a new cycling club, the National Maccabi Cycling Centre. Open to both sexes, it affiliated to cycling's governing bodies and was especially keen on the sporting side. The club's jersey colours were royal blue and white with the word 'Maccabi' on the back.[87] Jews were also members of non-Jewish clubs, which may have been part of the longer-term drift of younger Jews away from their community and religion.[88] In 1939 Lutz Durlacher came to England, aged 12, as a Kinder Transport refugee. His parents were murdered at Auschwitz. Durlacher became a long-standing member of the Solihull Cycling Club and competed in various events on the track and on the road and also competed at the 1957 Maccabiah Games. He worked as a waiter in a Birmingham hotel before setting up his own business as a manufacturer of racing jerseys.[89]

Cycling and associational life

What was the appeal of cycling during this period? Beyond any political motivations, for the vast majority of its enthusiasts cycling was a way of life. Importantly, through its network of clubs and various associations it provided and reinforced sociability. While the practice of cycling itself was the main attraction, a clubbable environment was, for many, another important aspect of the sport's sub-culture. Both the NCU and the CTC were really umbrella organizations as people did not join them specifically. Instead, the club or section that they joined was affiliated to the NCU or the CTC, respectively; these cyclists by default became members of the national governing bodies. It was at the grassroots, in the clubs and DA sections, where associational life in cycling flourished and the bonds of friendship and fraternity were forged. Tim Hilton claimed that he, like most cyclists of his generation, was 'brought up within local divisions of the CTC' and then joined a specialist cycling club to race.[90] Each group and club had its own dynamic, their own customs and culture which emerged out of the habits and traditions of the members. The early objectives of the Hitchin club (the Nomads) were to hold regular club runs on Sundays, plus weekend and holiday tours; to get a clubroom; and to put on a full time-trials programme.[91] It was said that the Comet CC was 'based mainly on the principle of friendship and comradeship' and its first rule was 'to promote sport and sociability'. Even in 1987 Arthur Cook would still claim that 'this spirit of good fellowship holds throughout the whole cycling world. Once a cyclist always a cyclist. ... They never forget.'[92]

One of the defining characteristics of a club's identity was its gender mix. Different clubs had different rules regarding the admittance of women. Arthur Cook felt that those clubs that admitted women were oriented more towards social activities, such as dances and concerts, than towards 'hard-riding'. The Nomads CC, for example, admitted women from its foundation in 1931.[93] The Forest CC was formed in 1900 and had initially been a mixed-sex club, but in 1912 it decided to exclude women.[94] Similarly, the formation of the Essex Roads CC in 1903 had been in part due to a rejection of female members. The club was essentially a breakaway from the then fashionable Walthamstow Town CC, which had both male and female members but did not cater for the needs of those members who were much keener on racing. As a result, an all-male amateur racing club was formed, initially made up of young men from Walthamstow.[95]

For the committed cyclist there existed a cycling calendar. It had its own, unique rhythm, which revolved around certain events, milestones and activities. The signal to mark the start of a new year was the 'opening run'. For the Comet CC, in East London, this was the first Sunday in March during the interwar years. The Comet was not the only East London club to hold an opening run on this day. Arthur Cook recalled that there would be other large groups of cyclists, all along the Epping Road.[96] These runs were usually announced in advance in the cycling press, such was their significance. In 1922 it was important enough for three clubs, the Socialist, Eclipse and Unicorn CCs, to invite both men and women on their opening runs.[97]

Throughout the year club runs continued to form the staple of club life. They would usually start at a regular point with tea taken at selected café before embarking on the journey home. In July 1924 the *CTC Gazette* listed around 600 runs by its DAs for that month alone. There was a variety, which included night rides, map-reading contests and 'surprise' runs, while some catered for different types of riders such as women and tandems. Because it was the summer the list also included mid-week evening runs. 'Runs' demanded a certain road etiquette. The Loiterer's Section of the CTC's North Metropolitan District Association, for example, attracted up to 40 cyclists for their summer runs for which the secretary warned that 'it seems only courteous that the runs should be conducted in a manner to cause the least possible interference with other road users'. The section was split into groups of 8 to 10 with a rear marshal appointed to check for stragglers. For members who found the pace too fast, it was felt that their leader would be considerate enough to slow down. The secretary was also keen that 'in order to uphold the prestige of the club, I feel sure that members will do their best to keep in formation of two-abreast and not straggle over the road unnecessarily'.[98] Even club runs could have their moments of drama. In December 1935, the members of the South Lancashire Road Club got lost on a night run to Ellesmere where it was recorded that 'we all contracted a touch of the "bonk" and so decided to bed down under a hedge' before continuing on to Ellesmere.[99] Completion of three runs was sufficient for membership to the Comet. Arthur Cook's election was confirmed with an initiation ceremony in the clubroom at which he was made to stand up and was introduced amid loud cheers followed by handshakes all round.[100]

For some cycling groups, because they were also sporting clubs, there was a balance to be struck between etiquette and excitement. The role of the captain was still important in this respect. Tim Hilton recalled how his captain was a useful time triallist who set a fast pace on club runs as well as devising difficult runs, which included some off-riding sections through local forests in the West Midlands.[101] On Comet club runs the captain also led at his own pace. There was also a fine of 6d for passing him without permission. On Arthur Cook's first club run with the Comet the captain yelled 'Pass me' at the bottom of a hill, allowing others to 'scorch' up it and down the other side. At the South Lancashire Road Club the captain decided when everyone should dismount going uphill.[102]

In addition to its regular club runs, the Comet Club's cycling programme, included the all-night ride, which took place in mid-summer. Setting off from London in the middle of the night, they would travel to the south coast, first to Worthing then on to Brighton for lunch, starting back in the late afternoon and would arrive back in London in the late evening. Another annual event became the February 100-mile 'training spin', which was mainly for the racing men. There were also fun runs, which included surprise runs, paperchases and detective contests. Many clubs embarked on tours at Easter and on bank holidays, especially Whitsuntide. In 1926 the Comet began touring in the Isle of Wight when 18 members set off. Touring by bicycle was increasingly seen as a cheaper form of holiday and grew in popularity as more workers gained paid holidays.

Of course, most touring by cyclists was undertaken by those not linked to clubs. Touring by bike gave working-class people a sense of freedom and the opportunity to discover new places on relatively cheap terms. Eric Porter, born in Walthamstow in 1914, was a keen cyclist during the late 1920s and early 1930s. Eric, who first worked as a clerk in a solicitor's office, took many cycling holidays and trips with either friends from school or the 4th Walthamstow Boy Scouts. A number of them took camping holidays to the Isle of Wight, which would entail a midnight start from the Bell Corner in Walthamstow and riding across London to catch an early-morning ferry from Portsmouth to Ryde. On another occasion, he had a cycling holiday in Scotland after travelling by ship for two days up the east coast. Eric also rode a tandem and later travelled from London to Herefordshire to visit relatives. On one occasion, when staying overnight at a pub, he met his future wife, who worked in the local village.[103]

Cycling was one part of club life. 'The Loiterers' was a section of the CTC's North Metropolitan District Association that held a wide range of social activities throughout the year. In 1938 the section attended the Alexandra Palace Gymkhana, which acted as part of the CTC's recruitment campaign, and where the Loiterers also played a game of cycling polo. In May there was a map-reading contest while for the social Sunday in August the section organized a treasure hunt. There were also well-attended lantern lectures, a general-knowledge quiz, a whist drive and a dance in the club room. Interestingly, the secretary did not think that dances appealed to the majority of (probably male) members, who instead preferred to play table tennis and darts or discuss cycling matters.[104] Each club and section were organic in their development and usually dependent on the voluntary efforts of young people. In 1927 Rochdale, the CTC's 4th Manchester DA Section was formed. One of its founders described the runs of those 'first mad months' as 'effervescent'. The section's average age was 18 and they tried many different activities. In its first year there were 'three official tours, two of them camping. There were all-night runs, an 8-hour, dinners, sports days, trips to caves, weekend runs and a gamut of activities', including 'memorable suppers and dinners' held at Mrs Beard's Dog Hill establishment. Within two years membership had risen to over 100, enabling it to form subsections, which included a Bachelors' Section, a Women's Section and a Cave and Crag Section. The section held long-distance weekends, cycling as far east as Robin Hood's Bay and Saltburn, and Haweswater in the Lakes. It also did some racing – 24- and 12-hour time trials.[105]

Tensions sometimes emerged among members over the direction of their club. By the interwar years, some CTC sections had 'Hardriders' groups who organized time trials for those members who had liking for sport. In 1928 a racing club for Yorkshire CTC members only was formed under the name of Yorkshire Century CC.[106] Some touring cyclists had not been in favour of this drift. In 1925 'Ikonklast', writing in *Cycling*, felt that racing spoilt club life as it should be 'for the propagation and enjoyment of cycling, not a gang of roughnecks, who talk, think and do nothing but racing'.[107] He complained,

> Nearly all clubs now cater exclusively for the racing man (and woman), or else are pestered by a militant racing minority to sacrifice their social programmes in favour of an ever-increasing round of races and hill-climbs. Racing spoils club life, and ... spoils cycling.

He added that '[t]he whole face of cycling is being blighted by a small horde of howling speed fiends' who 'only live for publicity'.[108] His piece stirred considerable comment on both sides of the argument. An editorial, in typically paternalistic tones, warned riders from both camps about any 'indecorous behaviour', and to consider the public by keeping the noise down when out cycling.[109] On the face of it these differences of opinion may have reflected class divisions, but not necessarily as middle-class cyclists participated in sporting competition, while the working classes also enjoyed the recreational side. The South Lancashire Road Club was more inclined to racing and on his time with the club, J. E. Ford recalled,

> Curiously also, looking back, was the complete disinterest in places of historic or scenery interest. The club swept along the sea fronts, but never paid any attention to beaches or swimming. The lakes [district] were merely interludes at the foot of important climbs to which full attention was given. Thus, we continued our narrow existence.[110]

Club identity was also shaped through the regular production of a magazine or newsletter, which reported on its activities and reinforced a club's mythology, while a clubroom – usually a room in a pub – and a club weekend retreat provided opportunities for sociability. The Comet CC held its weekly meetings on Wednesday evenings in the Downham Arms, just off Southgate Road in North London. Later, in 1938 the club established its own country hut at Stansted, Essex, which acted as a base for both racing and touring into North Essex and Hertfordshire. In her study of female climbing, Carol Osborne identified how a distinctive 'hut life' emerged 'where women could live out their identities as climbers without inhibition or censure', away from male expectations.[111] The club rooms and weekend retreats offered similar opportunities for cyclists, mainly male but also female. At the Comet clubroom, social evenings would include renditions of music-hall songs, such as Marie Lloyd's 'My Old Man', with a regular turn from the landlady, Mrs Clement, who had 'tread the boards'.[112] Some of cycling's most popular tunes included 'Widdicombe Fair', 'Bobby Shaftoe' and 'Clementine', the lyrics for which could be adapted for club purposes.[113] Because female members were not allowed by some clubs, like the Comet, it provided opportunities for male sociability – and high-jinx.[114] Arthur Cook recounted the tale of a dead rat being slipped into the saddle bag of a fellow member one Sunday evening.[115] Cook claimed in defence of the all-male Comet, 'Although well able to speak the local lingo and to record the latest bawdy joke or limerick, I never, never, never heard any one of them use what my church-going parents would call a "wicked word" in a lady's presence.'[116] 'The Loiterers also used a pub for regular meetings. Members were expected to observe certain standards of behaviour as respectability remained an important objective for clubs. In 1938 the secretary, in the section's journal, advised

> members not to make too much noise at the clubroom. Underneath is the Billiard Room and Saloon Bar. There is no objection to the use of the piano so long as members do not practice their scales on it and otherwise hammer the keyboard. A few members seem to think that the chairs make fine drums. I must ask them to think again.[117]

There was a long tradition of clubhouses in the Clarion Cycling Club. The first 'socialist guesthouse' had been opened in Bucklow Hill in Cheshire in 1897. Its lease was not renewed in 1902 after local people objected to the socialist values of the club and complained to the landlord. A new clubhouse was subsequently found at Handforth in Cheshire and would be the club's principal venue from 1903 until its closure in 1936. The clubhouse offered the opportunity for cyclists to escape the polluted city air. Its motto was 'Co-operation for pleasure, intellectual recreation and interchange of opinions and ideas', which meant playing some games, immersing themselves in socialist literature in the library plus evening entertainment. After the First World War, six Clarion clubhouses had been acquired by 1920. By 1939, however, due to the expense of their upkeep, only three remained, and by 1960 only the Yorkshire Clarion Clubhouse at Menston was left.[118]

While cycling was a largely apolitical activity, cycling groups could act as forums for political debate. This was unsurprising as just cycling on the roads heightened political awareness due to ever-increasing traffic accidents and congestion. In the previous chapter, it was shown how grassroots cyclists were mobilized in opposition to cycle paths. In 1945, the Loiterers' clubroom programme squeezed in formal discussions of Labour's and the Liberals' 1945 election manifestos. On 16 May there was a group discussion of Colonel Dew's policies and two weeks later, one on the Tottenham South MP, Fred Messer.[119] As with most people, the cyclists were only interested in politics when it mattered to them, and the clubroom programme over those few weeks also included the music group and dancing tuition. Of more interest were the subsequent preparations for VE Day, while in August it was stated that 'post-general election' discussions were to move temporarily away from politics to matters which concerned cycling directly, such as road safety.[120]

The cycling year was rounded off with the social season. These consisted of a mixture of dances and gatherings, which concluded with the club dinner, usually in January or February. These were a combination of decorum and informality, with men wearing suits and women in gowns. In addition, the club prizes were usually awarded by an honoured guest. In 1956, for example, C. E. Green, the president of the Tricycle Association, was to be the guest at the South Lancashire Road Club's annual dinner.[121] Numerous toasts followed to the club, its visitors, the reigning monarch and 'Uncle Tom Cobbley and all' due to a series of cross-toasting.[122] By the 1950s, important female cyclists were guests of honour, such as Lillian Dredge, the first Women RRA record breaker, who gave the toast at the 4th annual dinner of the Forty Plus Club.[123]

Cycling and the outdoor movement

The expansion of cycling was a key agency in the development of the outdoor – or 'back to the countryside' – movement. Cycling both complemented and buttressed the growth of camping and the later creation of the Youth Hostels Association (YHA) in 1930. Its founding had been underpinned by nineteenth-century ideas of rational recreation through the ethos of Quakerism, and a desire to promote a pro-rural/anti-urban English ideology. Unsurprisingly, it was an initiative enthusiastically supported by the cycling authorities.[124] The *CTC Gazette*, on commenting on the rise of youth hostels, observed, 'That there is some growing realisation of what we are losing by our flagrant commercialism is shown in the rise of numerous societies for the preservation of England.'[125]

By 1939 the YHA had a membership of 83,418 with 297 affiliated hostels.[126] At a shilling per night, the YHA attracted growing numbers of young cyclists to the countryside who could cycle from one hostel to another. Annual membership was 3s for those over 25 and 2s 6d for those under 25, with special reduced rates for 11- to 16-year olds.[127] In 1935 the YHA secretary had estimated that around 30 per cent of users were cyclists – this percentage increased during the winter months – and in many areas cyclists formed the backbone of the movement.[128] The outdoor movement itself was marked by social differences. Hoggart argued that walking was a middle-class activity while cycling was typically working class.[129] It is likely that YHA membership in general was disproportionately from the lower middle class.[130] Nevertheless, while many cycling clubs had their own huts and weekend retreats, the YHA allowed many unattached recreational cyclists to plan their own cycling tours as it provided relatively cheap accommodation to cater to the growing demand for holidays among the masses.

The benefits of the YHA for cycling were soon recognized, and it became an integral part of the cycling culture due to an 'urge towards "weekending"'. In 1935 it was noted that since 1925 for cyclists, '[c]amping and hostels have revolutionised week-ending and touring by permitting many who could never afford extended excursions'.[131] Some cycling clubs even had their own hostel sections. In 1931 Rochdale founded what may have been the first 'Youth Hostel' section in the CTC, continuing its camping runs in a new guise, while seven years later, in his end-of-year report, the secretary of the South Lancashire Road Club, stated, 'The hostel section of the club is still as active as ever.'[132] Moreover, in joining the YHA it opened up opportunities for many cyclists to tour in Europe, where there were over 3,000 hostels by 1935.[133]

Underpinning the benefits of touring through the YHA was a paternalistic tone. In 1938, for example, *Cycling* provided a map of GB hostels and a guide on what the YHA offered and its rules, and set out its own list of what a touring cyclist should carry. It was later noted that many of the European YHAs accommodated the monolingual British. While the handbooks were written in the language of that particular country, they usually had an English glossary. In addition, at many hostels there was usually someone able to translate. 'The language obstacles are all part of the adventure, and patience and good humour will overcome almost all difficulties,' it was optimistically stated.[134] Eileen Sheridan (see Chapter 6) in advocating the benefits of the YHA, stressed how 'sensible parents of young teenagers' should plan a youth hostel holiday with care. If the children were beginners 'don't let them try to overdo the mileage each day, for their holiday would be spoilt'.[135]

Another activity that enhanced the cycling experience was photography. The rise in photography's popularity had coincided with late-nineteenth-century industrialization and urbanization, which had engendered a sense of loss.[136] Thus, the pictures these amateur cycle photographers were taking – or at least they were encouraged to do so – were usually of the English countryside and sites of historical importance. Not only were they reinforcing the English 'Wayfareresque' pastoral idyll, but post-1918 photography provided an opportunity to re-capture pastoral sensibilities that might have been feared lost during the Great War. In 1920 it was claimed that '[c]ycling and photography are most certainly twin pastimes, and the full benefit to be derived from one can only be obtained by indulging in the other also'.[137] Many cyclists, usually those of a touring bent, combined riding with photography, and unlike 'hard-riding' this was a more leisurely activity. As camera prices came down and the technology improved, photography became increasingly popular during the interwar years. Moreover, photography was seen as a respectable and socially aspiring pastime – not just a middle-class one but also among the working classes. Taking photographs and later showing them off to friends and family, along with the camera that took them, was an indication of social mobility and aspiration. Owning a camera was akin to having a wireless or, in the early post-war period, a television in the house.

Cycling periodicals gave readers regular advice on how and what type of photographs to take.[138] During the thirties, some clubs held special photography runs and also held competitions. Photography was a serious business for the Loiterers, a section of the CTC's North Metropolitan DA. In July 1938 it was announced that the section was to hold a photographic run once a month to encourage the use of cameras. These runs were to be shorter than usual to enable members to have time for their photography. It was suggested that it would be best to take a 'photographic ramble', leaving the bicycles and walking across the fields taking a picnic lunch. A photographic competition was conducted with the aim of including the best in a section photo album. Photos had to be of a 'good standard', which included ones of 'members or of the interesting scenery in the districts in which we ride'. A photo of a large group of members was to be the frontispiece.[139]

The shift to shorts: Male cycling fashion

In 1930, 'Wayfarer', aka Walter MacGregor Robinson, one of cycling's eminent figures and journalists, declared that after years of resistance he had undergone a Damascene conversion. He had begun to wear shorts. He asked himself, 'What is my frank and considered opinion of the garments? Well, *they are the goods.*' So enamoured was he with these 'abbreviated clothes' that he threatened to wear them all the time, even during the off-season.[140] It was an emblematic moment in the culture of interwar cycling and to a certain extent confirmed the unshackling of some of cycling's Victorian constraints. By the end of the 1930s a strict, albeit informal, dress code for road cyclists, consisting of a jacket and plus fours (or twos or sixes), had been replaced by a more sporting and casual look. It was a shift that was highlighted in the changing images of male cyclists in advertisements. In this sense, cycling fashion was challenging prevailing notions of masculinity (for female cycling and fashion see Chapter 6).

This change and ensuing debates can be placed in the context of a wider movement for dress reform following the First World War. In general, men's dress – in contrast to that of women's – had remained very conservative with the wearing of tight collars and heavy, thick garments, regardless of season. Dress reformers, especially Arbuthnot Lane, wanted to liberate men from the constraints of tradition. Ina Zweiniger-Bargielowska has argued, 'The campaign to improve men's health, efficiency, and appearance by means of hygienic dress was part of the reconstruction of the male body in the interwar years.' 'The advocacy of a new male dress code of lighter clothing, shorts and open-neck shirts subverted hegemonic masculinity.'[141]

Of course, the dilution – for some – of this dress code had been partly a result of the growing number of men riding bicycles in their work clothes while track cyclists had been wearing shorts for decades. However, in light of what constituted 'a cyclist', this shift to shorts had not been without debate among male cyclists. (Men – naturally – also had views on women wearing shorts). In 1920 one correspondent was fulsome in his praise of wearing shorts as they were both healthy and comfortable, and urged other riders to adopt 'this sensible garment'.[142] One of the reasons for cyclists' initial reluctance was that shorts were then seen as for boys only. For many men, riding a bike was a serious adult activity that should be reflected in the attire of male cyclists. In addition, the wearing of shorts invoked ideas of effeminacy and sexual deviance.[143] Those that did wear shorts often attracted ridicule and banter from both children and fellow cyclists, by being compared to Boy Scouts, and were called names such as 'Watney's', 'Beaver' and 'Scoutmaster'.[144] Arthur Cook recalls the first time he wore a pair, 'The boys seized me and lavishly anointed my legs with plum and apple jam.'[145] As Zweiniger-Bargielowska has argued, 'Ridicule acted as a defence mechanism, which reassured conventionally dressed men of their hegemonic position.'[146]

In 1924, there was a heated debate over what constituted the 'proper' cycling dress in the letters' pages of *Cycling*, highlighting the significance of dress codes in locating masculinity. There were some complaints that the wearing of shorts lowered the tone of the pastime, while others lauded their advantages. *Cycling*, in typically paternalistic tones, continued to uphold the sanctity of the traditional uniform, while acknowledging the popularity of shorts. The craving for respectability continued to be a powerful urge among cycling authorities and a suit and/or uniform for cyclists was one way of protecting and projecting this image.[147] Arthur Cook recalled once seeing 'a group of highly respectable older cyclists' led by '"His Highness" FT Bidlake'. Bidlake 'looked like a bishop ... clad in black and rode bolt upright on a genteel-looking bike'.[148] In a September 1924 editorial, 'shortists' were reminded that cycling 'has its recognized special costume, consisting of ordinary knickers or breeches, and we have no doubt that these represent the full extent to which most cyclists are prepared to depart from the conventionality of long trousers'.[149] Some cyclists continued to dress in formal apparel even during the 1930s. Working-class Comet members, for example, wore collars and ties on club runs. Interestingly, Cook commented that the sticklers for this dress code were the skilled and manual workers, whereas those, like Cook, who were white-collar workers, wore open-necked shirts and no ties. It was later claimed that many riders wore a little black bow tie, which may have been copied from the elite clubs who rode on the north of London roads.[150] It reflected the persistence of the respectable working-class tradition of wearing your 'Sunday best' on special occasions as well as the opportunity to get out of wearing dirty work clothes.

Cycling, the state and citizenship

Cycling's enhanced place in national life can be gauged through an examination of three events. First, in 1923 there was a National Bicycle Week; second, the National Fitness Council, 1937–9; and third, the Festival of Britain in 1951. Each of these events reflected changing ideas of citizenship in which cycling became part of the dynamics of power, linking individuals to government and state. Moreover, they also highlighted the changing role of the state in twentieth-century British society. Between 1910 and 1950 there was a mixed economy of welfare, made up of both voluntary activity and the state. By its end there had been a decisive shift towards the state as the main component. However, this was not a linear process as the traditions of voluntarism remained strong and the trend towards incorporation was subject to checks and restraints as some organizations wanted to retain independence, while others took advantage of state funding.[151]

Following the First World War, there had been a desire to create a more democratic society. It resulted in leisure, along with other rights such as health and welfare, becoming increasingly associated with 'a shared active citizenship and social well-being'.[152] In the Victorian period notions of citizenship had been tied to ideas of individual self-improvement, which bypassed issues of welfare and social inequalities.[153] In this sense, leisure practices such as cycling – at least among its governing bodies – were inscribed with middle-class values based on rational recreation, which promoted health by encouraging the masses to visit the rural idyll and liberate themselves from urban squalor.[154] However, the emphasis now was increasingly on the individual to engage in public spiritedness and to carry out wider social and civic duties.[155]

National Bicycle Week was held from 27 May to 2 June in 1923. The initiative, copied from an American event a few years previously, was a joint effort between manufacturers and cycling bodies to drum up greater publicity for cycling.[156] Its aims were ambitious: it wanted to 'bring 5 million cyclists into the fold of "enthusiastic wheel-folk"'.[157] In many ways, this was an attempt to reassert the place of the bike and the values of cycling in national life after the Great War. *Cycling* claimed it as 'a serious and genuine campaign, aimed at spreading the gospel of cycling and bringing the merits of the sport and pastime before the general public'.[158]

A week of 'really intensive "'boosting"' ensued across the country as interested parties were encouraged to organize rallies, parades, races and cycling demonstrations of all kinds. On 28 May, for example, a parade and sports had been organized for boys and girls in Aberdeen, while in Cardiff, there was a parade of school children on bicycles with prizes for the best-dressed machine.[159] In addition, a film, *History of the Bicycle*, was shown throughout England. During the week, both the NCU and the CTC organized relay (or radial) rides across the country with each carrying a message from the lord mayor of London to the mayor of each town. Updates of the progress of the CTC relay were illustrated on a large map in Selfridges' shop window. In an attempt to curry favour with the establishment, the members of the CTC relay visited Buckingham Palace to pass on birthday congratulations to the King. The week culminated in a mass gathering of 5,000 cyclists at Hyde Park.[160]

The National Fitness Council was a product of the 1937 Physical Training and Recreation Act. A national fitness campaign had begun in 1935. Its aims revolved around concerns over the health and fitness of young people, especially those in the unemployment blackspots. In effect, it achieved little due to the onset of war. However, it was a radical departure for a British government. Civic culture was based on a strong voluntary principle and this intervention was at odds with previous laissez-faire notions. In particular, modern sport had been a product of the Victorian amateur-voluntary ethos. Whereas the National Bicycle Week was a voluntary event, here voluntary bodies became an extension of the state for the purpose of government policy, namely public health, reflecting a change in the nature of political culture. Moreover, in comparison to 1930s totalitarian regimes, the civil culture of games playing conveyed ideas about freedom, and the national fitness schemes can be placed in this larger context of a British citizenship. Given cycling's obvious health benefits, it was unsurprising that cycling bodies were keen to get involved. In this sense, they reflected the status of other voluntary associations, which 'became important venues for the practical and symbolic enactment of "active citizenship"', which assisted both a democratization of the political system and social relations.[161]

In a bid to the National Fitness Council (NFC) for funding, the NCU's ambitious plans were underpinned by an educational tone among the schemes proposed, such as 'Physical Fitness Proficiency Rides' and 'Lectures on Cycling'. Lectures included 'how to ride a cycle properly', learning the Highway Code and the theoretical side of physical fitness as well as educational travel talks.[162] The NFC, though, rejected this initial bid and the NCU was advised to put in a joint bid with the CTC, which it did. The proposed NCU lectures had been 'aimed at youngsters just leaving school'.[163] The emphasis on youth had been a growing concern during the interwar years. In 1939 cycling interests were represented at a youth fitness conference, where 'recommendations were made on many subjects affecting the Youth of the Country'. These included hours and conditions of work, nutrition, medical facilities and facilities for recreation.[164]

A later trimmed-down proposal to the NFC, in conjunction with the CTC focussed on the employment of a national organizer who would liaise with local centres, give talks aided by films, encourage cycling among adult institutes and also give cycling demonstrations as a means of improving physical fitness. The person selected was J. E. Holdsworth, who was already an influential NCU official. One example of his work was the Cyclists' Good Fellowship Week, in June 1939, where he organized '825 separate community runs for beginners, utility riders and embryo cyclists'. These were conducted by cycling experts who would act as leaders to go out into the country on the rides and would instruct cyclists in the rules of the road and taught how to enjoy cycling for health.[165]

Rather than health, the 1951 Festival of Britain was designed to be 'a tonic for the nation'. Richard Weight has identified three reasons for its staging. First, it aimed to assuage the effects of austerity; second, it aimed to trumpet British achievements and to show people home and abroad that Britain was still a power to reckon with after the war; and, third, the government wanted to restore its ailing popularity.[166]

As well as 'a moment of modernity', the Festival was 'a concerted effort of national imagining at a time of great change for the British nation'.[167] To a certain extent, cycling's inclusion cemented its place in British society. *Cycling* had proudly proclaimed, 'Every feature of national life can play its part in the Festival of Britain and it will already have been noted that cycling is prominent in the arrangements of special gala days throughout the country.'[168] In addition, a six-day race was staged at Wembley's Empire Pool,[169] while there was a Festival of Cycling, mainly for club cyclists, held in Birmingham and Cannock in June. This event was not dissimilar to other events held by cycling clubs throughout the spring and summer. Held at the local Dunlop Sports Ground, it was an all-weekend event supported by manufacturers, cycling bodies – the CTC, NCU and the Clarion – as well as the cycling press and Gaumont-Odeon Cinemas with a number of local politicians in attendance. The programme included 'a Grand Cycling Pageant, a cabaret of visual turns and a stupendous Firework Display', plus various competitive events. On the Sunday there was an open-air service, and a bicycle polo match was held.[170] At the Festival itself in London, five British bicycles were part of the transport display at the Transport and Communications Pavilion.[171] The Festival had also been designed to revive British tourism and to mark the occasion a scenic atlas was produced by Reginald Wellbye '[i]ntroducing Britain to our festival year visitors who may wish to seek out its beauties easily and quickly'. Typically, given how *Cycling* promoted an English rural idyll, the first area selected was the Sussex and the Home Counties.[172]

To a certain extent, the bicycle had acted as a continuum for this rural idyll since the Victorian period. However, during this period, it became emblematic of a more cohesive and democratic society. The era of mass cycling was characterized by the club run with groups of riders cycling on relatively empty country roads. The sheer numbers and visibility of cyclists could not be ignored and ensured cycling's place in national life. Cycling clubs and communities were a reflection of a healthy associational culture, itself shaped by a political culture based on a voluntary-liberal tradition. Unsurprisingly perhaps, cycling's popularity and health-giving properties were incorporated into broader welfare policies. Moreover, the bicycle had become a mass consumer product, now affordable by the majority of the population. However, this general picture was also marked by social tensions, while the meanings of cycling were in constant flux, as ideas of modernity clashed with traditional notions of what cycling meant to the British. This particular dialectic would be particularly evident in the following chapter on developments within the sport of cycling.

CHAPTER 5

The birth of British massed-start racing

In June 1942 a massed-start bicycle race took place in Britain between Llangollen and Wolverhampton. While not the first race of its type to take place on British roads, it was the most significant. The race had been organized by the Wolverhampton cyclist and bicycle trader Percy Stallard. 'Road sport' in British cycling had usually meant the unpaced time trial not massed-start racing. This race marked a shift from the deep-rooted amateur ethos of British cycling to an embrace of the modernizing impulses found in European road racing. In particular, the Tour de France began to hold an increasing fascination and appeal among British cyclists. However, rather than a quick divorce from British cycling's Victorian roots, this cultural shift proved more of a protracted and torturous separation. The official divorce settlement came in 1959 with the formation of the British Cycling Federation (BCF), but in reality it had been a complex and lengthy process.

The shift to massed-start racing was a moment of modernity for cycling in Britain. However, 'British modernity was always a balancing act between innovation and tradition', which was characterized by 'extraordinarily contradictory impulses towards the modern'.[1] Looking at the British experience of modernity after 1945, Conekin et al. have argued that it 'was never a linear history of progressive advance'. Instead, 'the most striking feature of so many modernizing projects pioneered during this period is that they were continually compromised and contested'.[2] Some members of the British cycling fraternity were beginning to modernize self-consciously through its embrace of massed-start racing by moving away from its time-trial roots, but this process of modernization was contested – fiercely, in terms of the conflict within the sport over massed-start racing. Moreover, as the conflict had its roots during the Victorian era, it highlighted how British cycling culture revolved around the ideas of amateurism and voluntarism, as well as an idealized and pastoral vision of England.

The time trial and the British tradition of road racing

First, how did the time trial come to embody British cycling? The time trial conflated the rural imagery of cycling, as seen in the illustrations of Frank Patterson, with values that reflected the British amateur ethos. All road racing in Britain was amateur, due to a lack of public demand and the tight control cycling bodies held over the sport more generally. Moreover, because it was unpaced, it was a purely individual sport where cyclists had to race without any assistance and provided a contrast with professional road racing on the continent where the team ethos and especially the use of tactics were frowned upon. Instead, British time trials were considered 'real contests of speed and stamina from which tactics are noticeably absent' and in which 'each competitor rides his own race'.[3]

Nevertheless, the time trial was an invented tradition – a historical accident. The first time trial was run in 1895 and it was commonly acknowledged to have been thought up by F. T. Bidlake. As outlined in Chapter 2, it was essentially a pragmatic and practical solution borne out of difficult circumstances for cycling at the time. The meanings later attached to the sport were conveyed by those members of the cycling establishment who sought to justify its existence in the face of opposition, initially from the law and later from massed-start racing. Before the time trial's invention, road racing had begun to grow in popularity from the late 1880s with the invention of the safety and the pneumatic tyre. However, due to police pressure over the running of races on increasingly congested roads, it led the NCU to withdraw its governance of road racing and road records in 1888. Road racing was never legally banned by the authorities, but cycling authorities were pressurized into curtailing racing on the roads. Over the next nine years the NCU, supported by the likes of G. Lacy Hillier, continually opposed road racing before, in 1897, it suspended any NCU-licensed riders who took part in a road race or a paced record attempt. Underpinning this call for the suspension of road racing was the amateur ethos of the NCU which led to a fear of road racing becoming commercialized like track racing had during the boom of the 1890s.[4] Control over road racing passed to a small body of clubs, including the North Road Club, which had resigned from the NCU to pursue road racing.[5] In 1894, following an incident during a race on the North Road involving Bidlake and those pacing him with an oncoming horse and carriage, the North Road Club itself abandoned racing and admitted the dangerous nature of their racing.[6] It was this incident that led to Bidlake coming up with the idea of an unpaced time trial, designed to prevent the bunching of cyclists on the roads.

Time trialling became a subterranean-like activity. Its aim was for the cyclists to be as inconspicuous as possible to the general public so as to keep cycling on the right side of the law. Time trials took place early on Sunday mornings in country lanes with no advance publicity. Instead, each event had a code that identified the time, location and course, which was surreptitiously passed on to competitors.[7] In this sense they were not dissimilar to the organization of prize fights in the early 1800s and late-twentieth-century raves. To maintain the pretence, cyclists had to wear a costume to cover the whole body. It comprised an alpaca jacket plus tights to give the impression that they were not racing, but instead out for a run in the countryside. Debates over what time triallists should wear continued deep into the interwar years. At the Road Racing Council's 1935 AGM, a motion to permit the wearing of shorts in time trials was heavily defeated.[8] In 1936 there had been complaints about some of the elite time triallists riding with their jacket sleeves turned up to the elbows. One correspondent, G. W. Lee, insisted sternly, 'Everyone – even the "cracks" – should abide by this rule.'[9] Nevertheless, given the later preference for cyclists to wear shorts in the 1930s, there was an increasing sense that this uniform was outdated – a vestige of the Victorian era – as by then most cyclists were wearing shorts. As Frank Southall wryly commented in 1938,

> This inconspicuous business has always amused me because a man in black tights and alpaca can be picked out easily on the road, while if the competitors were allowed to use light touring shorts and ankle socks, they would not look a lot different from thousands of other cyclists who ride down the road at the weekends.[10]

It was only during the war that the rules were relaxed. The wearing of socks was permitted in 1942 while the wearing of ankle socks was approved for the following year. The RTTC noted – without irony – that '[t]hese modifications do not appear to have resulted in any harmful effects'.[11]

Despite the NCU's late-nineteenth-century abdication from running road racing, time trialling soon prospered, albeit among a small number of clubs. These included the North Road, Bath Road, Yorkshire, Midlands and Anfield clubs.[12] Moreover, the NCU also ceded control over the administration of long-distance road records. In 1888 the Road Records Association was formed, which was dominated by members of the same clubs. These clubs organized their own events, which were open to other riders, and came to be seen as the 'classic' races of the British road-racing season.[13] Before 1914 riders from the elite clubs generally dominated these races. Moreover, these clubs were supported in the main cycling periodicals, as a number of their journalists were members of these clubs, including Bidlake and Stancer.

The time trial was an important reason behind the rejuvenation of cycling in interwar Britain. It was embraced by the growing number of working-class cyclists – many of whom were veterans of the First World War – and in addition to the club run, time trials became an integral feature of club life. It also reflected a working-class preference for sport over the leisure aspect of cycling. The extent of the increase in time trials is difficult to measure – mainly because of the secrecy that surrounded the sport. However, by 1921 it was noted that road racing's chief problem would be its 'extraordinary popularity', which would lead to 'the embarrassment of promoters and followers of a sport that thrives upon the unostentatious manner in which it is conducted'.[14] The increase in the number of 'open' time trials staged and the large fields – over 100 – competing were increasingly viewed dimly by the leading clubs. This popularity had undermined their 'unwritten rules of road racing', namely its inconspicuous nature, and raised concerns over perceived threats to cycling's legal status and its reputation as a safe activity. In May 1920, following 'the great success' of the North London CC open '50' and the anticipation of future large entries for forthcoming road events, *Cycling* had invoked a note of caution. An editorial criticized an advertisement in a national newspaper publicizing the event and reminded readers that road racing was organized by the clubs for the clubs. As a result, it was 'not wise to admit the outside public into the charmed circle *before* the event. It is sufficient to astonish them *afterwards* with a tale of the deeds that were performed'. It further advised the promoters of these events to ensure that the start and finishes were in secluded byroads, not the main highway.[15] Bidlake himself further underlined this caution following a warning issued by the Metropolitan Police concerning cyclists riding in groups abreast.[16] For the sport of cycling to remain legitimate, he stated that 'it is also absolutely necessary to avoid publicity'.[17] Yet this desire was also linked to the time trial's wider meanings:

> The game is one for the personal enjoyment of the participants and not a spectacular entertainment for sight-seers. Road racing wants no gathering of the public and events of which the dates are fixed and the starting and finishing points become known suffer if crowds collect, as it happened that a mere lane is left between spectators for a finish or a crowd at the start may incommode other traffic, and create the 'nuisance or obstruction' which the police warn us to avoid if we wish to escape interference.[18]

The peculiarities of the British time trial were no better epitomized than at the 1922 world championships, which took place on Merseyside. It was the first time they had been held in Britain since Crystal Palace in 1904, and they would be the last until 1970 when Leicester hosted the event. This gap in itself would be a pointer to the development of elite cycling in Britain and its divergence compared to the continent. In addition to the track events held at New Brighton, a road race, organized by the Anfield BC, was to be held in the form of an unpaced time trial for amateur riders. Beforehand, the British-style conditions imposed on the race caused much bemusement and concern at the UCI 'when the delegates were informed that the event must be held quietly and without publicity, and that full road costumes must be worn'.[19] The NCU delegate Percy Low reassured the UCI Congress that 'everything possible would be done to help the visiting competitors to follow the English conditions, and the promotion of the race will proceed on the lines already arranged'.[20] In its preview of the championships, *Cycling*'s editorial reiterated the establishment view regarding the road race:

> For the success of the event it is essential that the course, and particularly the finish, should be kept free from congestion, and with that object we have consistently declined to answer any inquiries as to the locale or date of the road championship.[21]

The world championships road race – held on the roads of Shropshire – brought a British 1-2-3.[22] 'Disappointment' was expressed at the foreign competition while at the same time there was an acknowledgement that having to race in English-style 'complete costume' in the English weather was a disadvantage for foreign riders.[23]

In response to the growing post-war popularity of time trialling the Road Racing Council (RRC) was formed in 1922. S. H. Moxham, then president of the North Road Club, noted that 'the increase in the number of open events had given rise to a feeling amongst the more prominent Clubs that some measure of co-operation was desirable'. However, the RRC was essentially a self-appointed body, which comprised members of those elite clubs that had founded the sport and who were determined to maintain control over time trials in the face of its popularity among the working classes. At the inaugural meeting there were representatives from the Anfield BC, in the form of W. P. Cook, while Bidlake was the representative of the North Road CC.[24] Membership of the RRC was open to any club that organized an 'open' time-trial event. Unsurprisingly, given that it acted as a cheerleader for the sport's establishment, *Cycling* 'heartily' welcomed the new governing body, later claiming it was 'one of the most important events in the modern history of road sport'.[25] Prospective members were also expected to meet certain conditions, which included the prescribing of suitable costume; the avoidance of undue publicity; and the adoption of a non-advertising regulation.[26] The RRC, made up of middle-class cycling figures, was not universally liked. It was paternalistic in both its make-up and in the tone and manner of its administration of road racing, and the reaction of other clubs to it reflected the broader social tensions of early post-First World War British society. Arthur Cook recalled how officials at his club, the predominantly working-class Comet CC, were unhappy 'at the way this group of "big-heads" from a very small number of clubs had assumed authority'. He continued:

There was tension due to the superior complex which seemed to be adopted by the largely white-collar members of the Road Racing Council towards the Comet's mainly working-class chaps. I know that one or two of our officials deeply resented this feeling at the time.[27]

In particular Comet CC officials disliked the limit on entries to 100 – a figure designed to act as a brake on the sport's popularity.

To a certain extent, the RRC highlighted the changing nature of amateurism. The amateur ethos was never monolithic. Rather than having a strict definition, it was always defined against something and thus was constantly in flux, adapting itself to the changing values of the middle classes. Initially, in the nineteenth century amateurism acted as a form of social exclusion before it became defined against professionalism and commercialism in sport. The RRC, in trying to maintain control over cycling, established a set of values that other, mainly working-class cyclists, had to abide by. In response to criticism of the RRC and the growing popularity of time trialling, the Road Time Trials Council was eventually formed in 1938. Arthur Cook welcomed its creation. He described the RTTC as 'formed on a truly democratic basis'.[28] The RTTC was open to all clubs and was run through the election of district councils. By the end of 1938 1,064 clubs had affiliated and approximating 10,000 cyclists took part in time trials, which now took place on Saturdays as well as Sundays due to the demand.[29]

However, despite this change in governance, the values of the RTTC remained strongly paternalistic and wedded to an amateur ethos in how it viewed road racing and cycling more generally.[30] Commenting on the 1947 season, the RTTC noted, 'Once again the enormous interest and enthusiasm shown testifies to the magnetic attraction of the time-trial sport in its clean, quiet and unobtrusive character as laid down by the clubs through the council.'[31] The RTTC continued to see itself as a trustee of the traditions of the British time trial. In 1948 it declared, 'The British TT sport run in an atmosphere of pure comradeship and clean physical endeavour and with an absence of profit motive is the envy of the sporting world.' In order to preserve the sport's welfare and future, it encouraged clubs to maintain its traditional features. The RTTC urged promoters to fix start times soon after day break, particularly as it has gained 'favour with the authorities, namely, the use of the roads at an hour when the least interference with public amenities is affected'. Early-morning starts, though, could be a possible of source of unnecessary noise and it was urged that riders and helpers 'restrain their voices in built-up areas or when passing houses'. Moreover, cyclists had to always observe the law of the roads, including new developments such as traffic lights and one-way roads.[32] In 1949, in order to uphold this reputation, an 'outbreak of press publicity' was criticized as it had given prior information about the times and locations of time trials. This advertising had attracted 'needlessly large crowds' and risked interference from the authorities. The offending journalists were criticized for their 'cynical disregard ... for the welfare of the sport'.³³ Despite a relaxation in its traditional dress code, in 1950, the RTTC still insisted, 'Competitors must be completely clothed from neck to just above the knees in a costume [all in black] that includes a separate jacket or jersey with at least quarter sleeves.'³⁴

Its resolve in upholding amateurism was equally strongly. Following the end of the war on the Western Front an 80-mile TT called the Nations Road Race was to be run in France in celebration in September 1945. However, as it was a race between amateurs and professionals the RTTC (along with the NCU) ruled that 'amateurs not be allowed to ride against professionals in the same race'.³⁵ In 1947 a Paris-to-London race was run at Whitsun. The RTTC, however, complained about the spectre of commercialism hanging over it. Not only was the French portion of the race sponsored by a bicycle component-manufacturing company, but the company name was used for publicizing the event. Further contrary to the RTTC's and NCU's amateur regulations, all riders – English and French – were advertised in French journals as having used this company's components.³⁶ The RTTC's attitude towards amateurism was even more militant than the NCU's. In 1945 the NCU had allowed amateurs 'to accept cycle accessories as prizes' in its events, but the RTTC's definition on amateurism remained unchanged. It noted in censorious terms, 'It was not the first time that the NCU/RTTC rule on this matter had differed.'³⁷ In 1948 the RTTC criticized the 'system of money payments' in massed-start racing (as discussed further). In particular, it wanted to draw the attention of young riders to the ruling that the 'acceptance of such payments would endanger their chances of possible reinstatement to the amateur ranks of any recognized cycling body'.³⁸ Any riders who had accepted money or sponsorship from the trade were banned from competing as amateurs in RTTC events as 'with the thousands of members of our affiliated clubs who follow the sport as a pure hobby in a spirit of honest amateurism'.³⁹

Further proof of time trialling's popularity in Britain had been the establishment of the Best All-Rounder trophy in 1930, which was sponsored by *Cycling*.⁴⁰ An indication of a creeping modernity within cycling, it was an award that catered to the demand for competition among the growing body of working-class cyclists. The idea had actually been put forward by a famous 'old-timer', Leon Meredith. The BAR (Best All-Rounder) was decided by the fastest average time over various distances. In the end, three distances were used: 50 miles, 100 miles and 12 hours.⁴¹ Races took place over different courses over the season.⁴² The RRC had declined to run the competition and *Cycling* was more than happy to stand in. The BAR marked a further change in cycling's power relations. Previously prestigious races, such as the Bath Road CC 100 and the North Road CC 24 hours, declined in status as other races became just as important in the context of the BAR competition.⁴³

The greater preponderance of working-class cyclists was reflected by BAR winners. Two small surveys of the 12 leading male cyclists in both 1932 and 1935 (three riders appeared in both) revealed that nearly all were from working-class to lower-middle-class backgrounds. Their occupations included police constable; radio engineer; plasterer; bicycle maker; coach trimmer; clerk; butcher; mechanic; joiner; cinema operator; traveller; commission agent; tarmacadam worker; and fruit grower. Interestingly, it was noted that all were virtually non-smokers and total abstainers, who had regular massages. Few were fully committed to club life, such as touring and the club run, indicating how competitive cyclists were devoting more of their time to racing.[44] Winner of the best all-around team in 1936 and 1937 was Monckton CC from the coal mining village of Royston in South Yorkshire. Out of the three, there were two miners and the manager of a bicycle shop. The youngest at 21 was Harry 'Shake' Earnshaw. He was a miner who started work at 4.30 am; he occasionally smoked and liked a glass of beer. The other miner was Alfred Martin who was aged 24. He began his training early in the year riding 25 to 30 miles once or twice a week. Once he felt he was fit enough he would stop training.[45]

In the 1932 sample the plasterer among them had been Frank Southall (1904–64) the most successful and popular British cyclist of the interwar period. Southall, from South London, was a specialist in the time trial and won the first four editions of the BAR competition from its inception in 1930. For his first BAR title, after competing in the Charlotteville '50', the University '100' and the Polytechnic '12', all of which he won, his average speed was 21.141 mph. On Southall's inaugural victory, an editorial in *Cycling* gushed,

> [N]o name appearing on our first All-Rounder trophy could be more fittingly representative of the sport of road racing, or more symbolic of the highest form of athletic prowess, than that of this great rider whose amazing deeds have made him famous throughout the world.[46]

A member of Norwood Paragons CC in South London, Southall also won silver at the 1928 Olympics road race (a time trial) and in 1932 a bronze in the team pursuit.

To celebrate the BAR, *Cycling* established an awards ceremony – the 'All-Rounder concert'.[47] It was an early example of a sporting award; football's first was the Football Writers' Association's 'Footballer of the Year' Award in 1948. The first concert took place at the Queen's Hall in 1931 with an audience of 2,000. Due to its popularity, the following year it was moved to the capacious Royal Albert Hall, which could hold 7,000. The BAR concert, similar to other sporting awards that would follow, 'became a ritual in which the [cycling] world literally and metaphorically appeared dressed in its best clothes and showed itself to the public in the kindest possible light'.[48] The BAR concert, with its mixture of formal dress and public speaking, belonged to a mode of civic culture and citizenship that had emerged in the late nineteenth century and continued through the 1960s and as such they were a reaffirmation of Britishness and British values.[49] But it was also cycling's 'big night out', which, because it was a concert, had an air of informality, not dissimilar to the annual cycling club dinner.[50]

The 1938 concert was typical.[51] In between the giving of awards the audience was entertained by contemporary variety acts, and included some audience participation. The BAR winner in 1937 had been Yorkshire's Cyril Heppleston and after he received his trophy the audience spontaneously began singing the county's unofficial anthem, 'On Ilkla Moor Baht'at'. As part of the concert's rituals, Heppleston, like other past BAR winners, signed the 'Golden Book of Cycling' on stage. The evening also held roller racing for the Mrs RE Dangerfield Cup (the wife of *Cycling's* proprietor). In a 'packed programme' there was a mixture of music and variety acts, which was designed to appeal to all tastes, organized by Harry Goodwin, the magazine's advertisement manager. The music included recitals by Edward Holmes on the venue's 175-ton organ, dance melodies from Bobby Howell and his Band and xylophone solos by Doris Cuban, while Elsa Carlisle sang a few 'old favourites'. There were acrobats and tumblers in the form of the Seven Aus Tokay troupe plus Donovan and Hayes, a juggler, Bela Kremo and comedians, Ames and Arno. The Arthur family performed some trick cycling; the Temple Belles provided some high stepping and rhythmic dancing while by contrast Dora and Chela gave an exhibition of ballroom dancing. Johnny Nit gave a tap-dancing exhibition with Pop, White and Swagger providing a burlesque dance turn. The grand finale consisted of the Dagenham Girl Pipers and their bagpipes, with Frederick Yeomans singing 'Land of Hope and Glory'. The evening finished with all the other musicians leading a rendition of 'Auld Lang Syne', with the entire audience holding hands and singing.[52]

Yet this particular cycling culture, framed around the values of amateurism and voluntarism, was coming under threat during the 1930s. In particular, the spectre of professionalism was beginning to rear its ugly head, which would reflect an increasing commercialism in sport more generally. Frank Southall won the first four BARs, the last in 1933, and his later career reflected the changing trajectory of British cycling. According to Billy Mills, 1934 marked 'the beginning of the great record-breaking war between the big cycle making companies', who employed the best riders as professionals to attack all Road Records Association (RRA) records.[53] Southall himself was the catalyst having turned professional with Hercules Cycle Company in 1933. Its owner, Edmund Crane, had been keen to promote Hercules through various racing competitions and road record attempts.[54] Southall was then at the height of his fame, the most popular cyclist in Britain and the obvious choice.[55]

During Southall's professional career he largely restricted himself to breaking record distances up to 24 hours. In the following March he set his first professional record – the RRA dealt with both professional and amateur marks – at 50 miles in 1 hour 46 minutes 31 seconds.[56] Over the course of the year Southall broke six other records: 24 hours (457 miles); Land's End-London (15 hours 8 minutes); 12 hours (253 miles); London-York (9 hours); 100 miles (3 hours 55 minutes 33 seconds); and London-Portsmouth (6 hours 49 minutes 17 seconds).[57] Highlighting his new professional status, he posed with his bicycle in a double-spread advertisement, which noted how he had 'pulverised' and 'shattered' previous records in 'astonishing' times.

However, Southall had a rival of equal stature. While Hercules had declared Southall's achievements as a great success for the company, a few weeks later the Australian Hubert Opperman – riding for BSA – announced he was coming to Britain to challenge RRA records. In 1934 he set new marks for the End-to-End and the 1,000 miles records, for which he was selected as the first winner of the Bidlake Memorial Prize.[58] In 1935 Opperman returned with two team mates who launched another record-breaking campaign on RRA marks. Opperman himself regained the 24-hour record that Southall had set and then beat the Londoner's Land's End to London time by nearly an hour, while Ernie Milliken broke Southall's London-Brighton and back record in 4 hours, 49 minutes, 2 seconds.[59] A month later Southall regained the London-Brighton and back record by 58 seconds.[60] It all added to the hyperbole around cycling, increasing its public profile. *Cycling*'s editor, Harry England, was fawning in his praise of the Australians and put their success down to 'a fighting spirit and a capacity for taking punishment'. He then confusingly implied British racing was too soft before clarifying that there was no need for cyclists to 'hurt' themselves if they trained properly.[61]

Other British riders followed Southall into the professional ranks. In 1936, for example, Sid Ferris of the Vegetarian CC, a three-times winner of North Road '24', signed a three-year professional contract with Sturmey-Archer Gears Ltd.[62] By 1937 there were six professionals in Britain: Southall, Ferris, J. W. Torry, Syd Cozens (1908–85), H. Grant and H. James, although only Southall and Ferris were road riders. While this was small-scale compared to the Europeans, others would follow, as well as a number of female riders (see Chapter 6), reflecting the 1930s cycling boom more generally. Harry Earnshaw, for example, turned professional in 1939 with the Hercules bicycle company, who employed a team of six professionals including Marguerite Wilson. Professional road racers and their trainers carefully planned their record attempts and would camp at the start for weeks if necessary, waiting for the ideal weather, mainly a tail wind. As a consequence, record times fell dramatically.[63] To a certain extent, it echoed the record-breaking attempts and preparation of cyclists in the late nineteenth century, complete with pacing teams.

Traditionally, it had been track riders who had turned professional, but even here the numbers were low. In 1923, for example, it was reported that there were only two professionals in the country, the most famous being the sprinter Bill Bailey, and they mainly raced on the continent. Syd

Cozens, twice runner-up in the world amateur championships, had been a sprinter on the track and turned professional in 1931.[64] Track racing in Britain was regaining some of the popularity it had lost after the boom of the late 1890s. In 1934, and up to 1939, for example, London staged professional six-day races, the first since 1923.[65] Inevitably, British cycling administrators were wary if not sniffy about this relative lurch towards professionalism and commercialism. Safeguards, stretching back into the 1890s, had been put in place to prevent professionalism contaminating amateur cycling in Britain. First, once a rider turned professional there was no going back to the amateur ranks. Furthermore, at the time 95 per cent of cycling meetings included running events. As running events came under the even stricter amateur rules of the AAA, and as per an agreement with the NCU, it meant no professional cyclists were allowed to compete at these events, depriving them of the oxygen of competition. Typical of middle-class paternalistic attitudes towards workers, H. N. Crowe, the secretary of the NCU, was also quick to remind budding track professionals of their 'responsibilities' to provide entertainment and not to expect to earn vast sums of money.[66] Ultimately, the biggest factor was that there wasn't a large demand for regular professional racing in 1930s Britain. The British sporting marketplace was becoming increasingly crowded. In addition to the national sports of football and cricket, new ones such as speedway were emerging, which had greater public appeal.

The rise of massed-start racing

During the 1930s massed-start racing (MSR) began to challenge the supremacy of the time trial. This contest can be seen as part of broader modernizing tendencies within cycling, which culminated in the formation of the BLRC in 1942, as well as planting the seeds for a decline in deference towards the sport's amateur administrators and culture. The BLRC's formation marked the start of a shift in the culture of road racing, away from its British amateur, time-trial-based tradition to a greater emphasis on modern, professional massed-start racing, as practised in Europe. From the late nineteenth century, European countries had staged increasingly high-profile, professional races, especially the Tour de France and the Giro d'Italia, in addition to one-day classic races such as Paris-Roubaix (the 'Hell of the North') and Liège-Bastogne-Liège. By contrast, by 1930 British road racing had its own cosy domestic sub-culture, which revolved around the time trial and was largely detached from international developments. Although British cycling did not deliberately pursue a policy of 'splendid isolation', nor did it adopt the brave new world of sporting modernity. By contrast the Tour de France fully embraced modernity while cycling in Britain – which had been a pioneer of professionalism – now remained devoted to the amateur ethos. In France it had been the media that had created the Tour through the newspaper *L'Auto* – what Hugh Dauncey has termed the 'sports-media-industrial complex'.[67] The aim of road racing in Britain was to remain as unobtrusive as possible whereas for the Tour maximum exposure was the main objective for its organizers.

How did the change in British cycling come about? To a certain extent, it can be placed in the broader context of international sport during the 1930s. During this decade there was a 'significant internationalisation' in elite, high-achievement sport. Barbara Keys has argued that 'a truly transnational culture was established, one that attained an existence independent of the countries participating in it'. As a result, elite athletes

> competed more and more in a system constrained by international norms and standards. Their fans, their training regimens, the rules that governed their sports, and the competitors against whom they measured themselves were part of an increasingly global culture.[68]

Highlighting this shift towards transnationalism, from 1930 cyclists rode for national teams in the Tour de France instead of for trade manufacturers.[69] Not only did the Tour attract cyclists from neighbouring countries such as Italy and Belgium, but in 1928 Hugh Opperman became the first Australian to ride in the race. To a certain extent, MSR represented a generational shift among younger cyclists who had been exposed to modern cycling tastes and fashions during this period, especially the Tour de France.

Ironically, it was the traditionally conservative British cycling press, which was at the forefront of unconsciously promoting European cycling culture and giving it a cultural legitimacy. Sport and the media, historically, have had a symbiotic relationship. In his work on American football, Michael Oriard has shown how the narratives of journalists have framed meanings of sport, while similarly, Christopher Thompson has argued how the image and the success of the Tour de France was based around journalistic accounts of the suffering and heroism of cyclists.[70] After the First World War, British coverage was initially provided by an exile, Vernon Blake. Blake was a sculptor by occupation who had been a member of the North Road Club and won the Anfield BC '100' in 1894.[71] In 1919 he provided a lengthy reflection on the first post-war tour.[72] Every year after, the journal carried reports and importantly images of the Tour, in terms of both the scenery and the racing, although it did not necessarily provide up-to-date coverage at first. *Cycling*'s accounts of the Tour to a certain extent were contradictory. Since the nineteenth-century British (middle-class) cyclists had had a love affair with France and the French countryside, yet for British cycling's conservative elite, European cycling as a sport represented 'the other'. An accompanying illustration of the 1919 Tour referred to how this 'typical French road-racing scene presented a very great contrast to English methods'. It was noted that 'the riders wear the scanty clothing of the race path [track] and travel in groups while an official motorcar follows in close attendance. ... French professionals are extraordinarily skilful and are able to negotiate roads that to the ordinary rider would seem impassable ... and frequently perform wonderful feats of endurance.'[73]

Paradoxically, the Tour was popular with members of the cycling establishment. Writing in the *CTC Gazette* in 1923, G. H. Stancer had declared in uncharacteristically hyperbolic terms, 'Be it known that the Tour de France is, in reality, a road race – the greatest, longest, hardest, most wonderful road race in the world.'[74] In 1925 he further commented, 'It is clear that the Tour de France grips the French nation in a way that has no counterpart over here. Our cup finals and test matches are trivial by comparison.'[75] In 1937 Jessie Springall, the honorary secretary of the Women's RRA, 'tackled the Galibier', 'a week before the Tour de France contingent was due, so were able to form an impression of the conditions prevailing there at the time of the greatest of all road races'.[76] Stancer though, along with other members of the British cycling establishment, would never countenance a massed-start race of any type on British roads. In the early 1920s this prospect was inconceivable and for him to enjoy the Tour was to do so safe in the knowledge that the British way of cycling – and with all the cultural peculiarities it entailed – was in no danger. At this stage the Tour was something exotic, an oddity and a curiosity to the British, and European riders belonged to a different world of cycling.

However, the lure of MSR in terms of its thrills and the lust for speed was not altogether unsurprising as these desires could even be found in the normally peaceful club runs. In 1924 Arthur Cook recalled how on his first club run the captain had initially led at a sedate pace but when they reached the foot of Barnet Hill he shouted out 'Pass me' with the result of the other riders 'tearing up the hill like so many demons' and continuing in a bunch at a similar pace on to their morning stop at Shenley.[77] In 1938 one *Cycling* reader complained of 'unofficial' massed road races that were 'indulged in whenever racing clubs go out'. On one Sunday evening he had witnessed over 20 riders riding into Otley at 30 mph. In the same month the South Lancashire Road Club cancelled its 100-mile reliability trial because it was stated that these types of rides had developed 'into nothing short of massed-start races on the public roads'. It was decided that 'in the best interests of the Time Trial game to abandon the project'.[78]

Moreover, the cycling press was increasingly promoting the virtues of MSR. At the inaugural Isle of Man MSR in 1936, reflecting a tabloid style of journalism, there was a graphic description that attempted to encapsulate the 'thrills and spills' of the race.

> Faster and faster, the rider gains momentum. He flattens himself to streamline his body over his machine. Down, and down, and down – thirties, forties, forty-fives ... it's a job to hold the front wheel down ... water is streaming from his eyes. Here comes the corner; he sees its

approaching madly through water-blurred eyes. What a crowd of people! Steady with the brake – he can't afford to lose time, they are too far ahead. He's round; no, he's going too fast! Nearly, nearly; steady, man … he's going too fast … he'll crash. … He's over … heavens … crash … thud …

The bicycle lays twisted in the sandbags that pad the corner. The rider is struggling to his feet … dazed and there's blood. … He grabs his bicycle, straightens the frame. Other riders are sweeping by. Quickly he mounts: the crowd cheers and he pedals madly in pursuit.[79]

Massed-start races in England had predated the 1942 race, but these were under the sanction of the NCU and therefore took place on enclosed circuits. The first one was at the Brooklands motor-racing circuit in 1933. The race had been a response to criticism from those British cyclists, notably Percy Stallard, who had ridden in road-race world championships and felt that they were at a disadvantage to their European rivals because of their lack of experience in MSR. Because Brooklands was an enclosed circuit it did not contravene the regulations of NCU races on the public highway.[80] During the 1920s amateur world championship road races held by the UCI had fluctuated between a time trial and an MSR, before the massed-start race became the preferred form. The first Brooklands race was notable for an artificially made hill, something that was criticized because it was foreign to British riders, who were used to riding at a steady pace on relatively flat roads. Later venues for MSR included Donnington Park's motor-racing circuit, Crystal Palace and the grounds of Blenheim Palace. In Ireland MSR took place at Phoenix Park. In 1936 the Isle of Man staged its first MSR, which was won by Charles Holland. The International, as it later became known, created considerable interest due to the presence of French riders giving the British an opportunity to measure themselves against continental opposition. Unlike mainland Britain, public roads could be legally closed on the Isle of Man through an act of the House of Keys. The Isle of Man TT motorbike races had been taking place since 1907 as a consequence.[81]

Despite the later claims made for Percy Stallard, the first MSR on public roads in Britain actually took place in Scotland. In July 1934 it was announced that a Scottish newspaper was to promote a massed-start race. It was claimed that '[m]assed-start races are what the public wants but only outside of Britain, principally on the Continent, have such events been run'.[82] Organized in association with the Cowal Highland Games, the Scottish race started at Duntocher, 8 miles from Glasgow, with the route running via Balloch and Arrochar to Dunoon, the finish. It was also claimed that the race had been organized with the blessing of the NCU, but this was quickly denied. Nevertheless, for a few years it was the only massed-start race that took place on British roads. The race caused a split in Scottish cycling. It was supported by the Mid-Scotland Time-Trials Association, but riders who were members of the West of Scotland TTA had been subsequently banned, because it was believed that the race would bring 'unwanted attention' on time trials.[83] By 1937 the race had been sanctioned by the Scottish Amateur Cycling Association but under certain conditions, which included a limit of 30 riders and riders having to wear tights.[84] In 1938 there was an even more ambitious proposal – a 'Tour de Scotland' – a three-day stage race that was to be called the Empire Exhibition Race. It was to be sponsored by Associated Newspapers to publicize the Empire Exhibition, which was to be held in Glasgow that year. The towns to be included on the route were Glasgow, Edinburgh, Stirling, Dundee, Aberdeen and Inverness.[85] Much to the alarm within English time-trial circles, a letter had been published in the Scottish newspaper *The Record and Mail*, from H. N. Crowe the secretary of the NCU, which seemed to endorse the race.[86] However, later that month the race was cancelled by the SACA.[87]

As a further boost to the status and cultural legitimacy of MSR in Britain, in 1937 Charles Holland and Bill Burl became the first British riders to take part in the Tour de France.[88] On top of the growing mania for record breaking during the mid-thirties, this first for British cycling highlighted the cycling boom more generally. Holland was a star of both MSR and the time trial. In 1934 he had finished fourth (later promoted to third) in the World Amateur Road Race and won the BAR in 1936.[89] In 1937, he had just turned professional and was to write his own column in *Cycling* during the Tour, which was unlikely described as 'the most remarkable story that has ever been presented in the history of cycling journalism in this country'.[90] Even before the 1937 Tour began, there was a history of the race as well as a preview of that year's edition, which was written as a guide for British readers. Holland provided accounts of his first three days on the Tour and further updates until the 14th stage when he was forced to retire. In one report, for domestic consumption, the race's founder, Henri Desgrange, was quoted as saying that Holland had 'all the characteristics of the English people – courage, tenacity, strength and a fine physique'.[91] Holland revealed that he received lots of 'fan mail' from people from France and Belgium. He was astounded at their depth of knowledge of 'the bicycle game', including among schoolgirls. One Belgian had written to say that their son had a union jack flying on their house and it would be there as long as Holland was in the Tour.[92] To cater for both the technologically inclined among the cycling fraternity and the fashion for MSR, the bicycle Holland rode in the Tour was featured in an article, 'Massed Start Bicycle Measurements'.[93]

The trend for MSR accelerated towards the end of the 1930s. In 1938 there were 35 races staged in Britain, compared to six the year before.[94] In the same year the NCU staged its first MSR national championship at Donnington. The race was run over 34 laps of the circuit (equating to 106 miles), in front of a crowd of 4,000, and was notable because the first two riders, Jack Holmes and James Fancourt, both members of the Yorkshire Road Club, attempted to dead-heat. The NCU was not having any of this and awarded the race to Holmes, who was judged to have crossed the line first.[95] Of course, MSR paled in comparison to the plethora of time trials organized around the country on a weekend, but it did highlight a growing trend towards this European form of the sport.[96]

Complementing the growth of MSR, European cycling influences were becoming more visible on British roads. In 1936 it was noted, in somewhat sniffy terms, that '[t]he Continental racing man has had a decided influence on English cycling. Deep bars, large frames, derailleur gears and goggles are all Continental features nowadays to be seen occasionally on English roads.'[97] These changing tastes were reflected in the bicycle trade. In 1938 it was noted that the French bicycle industry had sold over 4,000 machines in England whereas three years previously it could not sell 10.[98] The contrast with the image of time trialling could hardly have been more different. The time trial was associated with the solitude of the rider on quiet country lanes and the emphasis of man against the clock. In 1938 it was being reported that hundreds of British cyclists went to France to watch stages of the 'Tour' while one *Cycling* reader even advocated the entry of a British team.[99] It was perhaps then not so surprising when in his 1943 book *Cricket Country*, a paean to English pastoralism, the poet Edmund Blunden presumed of his readers that 'I daresay you have heard of this Tour [de France], which in ordinary times catches the imagination of France in a manner probably beyond that of even a Cup Final or Grand National here.'[100]

Ideas of Europe and cycling on the continent took a firmer hold in the British cycling sub-culture in post-1945 Britain, partly due to the increasing availability of French sports publications. The first British rider to win a stage at the Tour de France, Brian Robinson, said that he used to read *Miroir des Sports*, 'with all the pictures of the big professional riders. And I used to think – boy, if I could only be among this lot.'[101] Another French publication was the *Miroir-Sprint*.[102] It was the weekly sports paper of the French communist party.[103] Tim Hilton recalled how like many racing cyclists he was a connoisseur of its photographs, along with another paper, *But et club*. As a consequence, they 'became aficionados of the Tour de France through a love of magazine illustration', as well as gaining an education about cycling more generally in France.[104]

Those riders who later joined the BLRC in the early fifties had little respect for the traditional British culture of touring and youth hostelling, but instead wanted to adopt a European-style aesthetic. A 'Leaguer' could be identified, Tim Hilton claimed, by 'his position on the bike, his continental equipment, his preference for derailleur gears ... Italian road jersey and dark glasses'.[105] Less likely – or he was merely being autobiographical – Hilton claimed that a 'Leaguer' was a fan of modern jazz, frequented coffee bars and would go out with a girl from the local art school, as well as being a snappy dresser on and off the bike.

The reception of MSR among the cycling hierarchy changed when it was increasingly perceived to pose a threat to their ideas and values, and just what they thought constituted road racing on British roads. In many ways the traditionalists were correct in thinking British was best. In 1938 *Cycling* published a survey to establish the most popular aspects of cycling. Touring was top at 27 per cent, while club riding, with 24 per cent, was second. MSR was in sixth with 3.1 per cent, while time trialling was more popular, in fourth at 14 per cent.[106] However, commissioning a survey was also an indication of its growing defensiveness over the threat of MSR and an attempt to reaffirm the traditional British cycling culture. Underpinning these attitudes was an underlying amateur ethos and the strongly held belief that English riders preferred time trials. More than anything perhaps this stout defence of British time trialling reflected wider cultural anxieties within society over the impact of modernity. In 1941 J. B. Priestley, in an article promoting leisure as a worthy pursuit, offered an anti-modern critique of sports such as greyhound racing and speedway – 'dirt track performance'. To a certain extent, the defence of the time trial against the brasher, more commercial and colourful MSR was part of this debate.[107]

Unsurprisingly, international developments were met with British resistance and scepticism. On the announcement that the 1936 Olympics road race would be a massed-start race rather than a time trial, it was typically declared in *Cycling* that there should be the 'strongest possible protest' as '[t]he Olympic Games were the last stronghold of the genuine international trial of road-riding ability, free from tactics or bunching'.[108] The NCU later lobbied the UCI to replace massed-start races in favour of time trials for championship races.[109] Under the subheading 'The Time Trial Is Best', a Harry England editorial claimed that the Tour de France was a 'festival of self-punishment'. Instead, '[o]ur style of road sport happens to suit the English tradition of fair play. It gives every rider an equal chance and is devoid of the element of fluke or freak.' He also asserted that the time trial 'did not suit the Continental demand for spectacularism and that '[i]n this country we may be thankful that we are free to concentrate on strict fairness and accuracy'.[110] Antipathy to commercialism also underpinned opposition to MSR.

The journalist KMD, aka Alex Josey, was another notable critic of MSR and a stout defender of time trials. This was perhaps unsurprising as he was also the secretary of the RTTC.[111] In 1936 he noted the 'continental flavour that is creeping into the sport, into our accessories [wearing continental-style clothing], into the design of our bicycles'. What was his reaction? Was it doing the sport, that is, British road racing, any good? After a good deal of thought, he believed not. Indeed, for him the answer was simple. Those 'who are trying hard to destroy the present system of British road sport' aimed to replace it with 'gate-paying massed-start races for parties who were only in the commercial aspect of it'. Instead his mantra was 'Let's be British', based around a belief in the amateur-voluntary tradition of the time trial where nearly all officials were honorary. Other British values that were transmitted through the time trial included individualism as the time trial was 'enjoyable and clean and where a rider can be assured that if he is good enough he will always win'. By contrast, '[t]here is a lot about [MSR] that will never appeal to us Britishers, whose thoughts about sportsmanship do not always correspond with those of the foreigner'. He quoted Hugh Opperman who claimed that when he rode in the Tour de France a rider caught him by getting a tow from a car. The Tour's publicity caravan, created in 1930, was particularly distasteful. Josey admitted that continental riders were superior to their British counterparts on account of their professional, but he also predicted the demise of MSR on the continent due to impending traffic congestion and that European countries would switch to the British system.[112]

The formation of the British League of Racing Cyclists

The development of British massed-start racing can be set in a number of contexts. First, there was the ongoing debates over road safety. Cycling's great and the good were opposed to staging MSR on public roads due to the potential for bad publicity if accidents occurred involving cyclists in a massed-start road race. In this sense, the yearning for MSR, along with Stallard's actions, and later the formation of the BLRC reflected a broader pattern of political dissent in the recreational sphere, most notably the Kinder Scout trespass in 1932. Growing demand for more access to the countryside became part of a general reform movement, which culminated in the National Parks and Access to the Countryside Act of 1949.[113] Finally, a number of sports, such as cricket and rugby union, experienced some form of disruption during the Second World War as normally strict conventions were loosened at the time, although there was an expectation among administrators that they would return to the status quo after 1945.[114]

Percy Stallard (1909–2001) was steeped in cycling. He was actually born in his father's Wolverhampton bicycle shop, which he later inherited.[115] During the 1930s he had been one of the leading cyclists in Britain and an MSR pioneer who by 1938 had ridden in six massed-start races on the continent.[116] He was also known for his cantankerous reputation. In 1943, he resigned (and at the same time, was sacked) as the BLRC's national organizer only a few months after it was set up for criticizing the organization of a BLRC race in the press.[117] He rode in the first massed-start race at Brooklands motor-racing circuit in 1933 and was subsequently selected for the British team for the world amateur road-race championships, in which he finished eleventh.[118] The following year he was sixth and in 1935, twelfth. In 1934 he won the second MSR to take place at Donnington[119] and 12 months later he was selected by the NCU as one of four riders to represent England in an international MSR in France.[120] In the same year he again won the Donnington Park trial over 49 miles.[121]

Like Stallard, some of his fellow riders felt that the NCU should take MSR more seriously. They demanded greater financial assistance from cycling manufacturers to assist in setting up specific MSR training camps or even a club, a move highly unlikely given that this had the whiff of commercialism in light of the NCU's strict amateur stance. While praising the NCU for popularizing MSR in Britain (on enclosed circuits), Stallard wanted a more professional approach and for riders to be under stricter control during championships. Originally a member of Wolverhampton Wheelers, due to his interest in MSR, in 1938 Stallard formed a new club Wolverhampton Racing Club, and became its secretary.[122] With this club he developed a more aggressive form of racing tactics, which he adopted following his continental experiences.[123]

Inspired by the Llangollen to Wolverhampton race, the BLRC was formed on 15 November 1942. Its early years, indeed its entire existence, was taken up with a struggle not just over the control of cycling, but for many the soul of the sport. Riders who joined the BLRC were automatically 'proclaimed', that is, banned, by the NCU and the RTTC, and it was only in 1959 that this 'civil war' would come to an official end when the BLRC and the NCU amalgamated to form the BCF.[124] The BLRC's formation, however, was another marker in the modernization of British cycling, and acted as a site for the tensions between the forces of cycling tradition and modernity. Whereas the other governing bodies reflected the more conservative values associated with the Victorian era, the BLRC from the outset projected a more modern and democratic outlook of cycling.

There were 24 founding members of the BLRC – 22 men and 2 women – who effectively amalgamated three racing leagues: London, Midland and the North.[125] Although the cycling establishment branded the League as rebels, it was initially run by stalwarts of other cycling bodies. In addition to Stallard, there was Charles Fox, the general secretary of the Yorkshire Road Club, who was appointed the BLRC's first honorary secretary, and Syd Copley, previously the secretary of the RTTC Yorkshire's District.[126] The record-breaking cyclist, Walter Greaves, was appointed vice chairman. Fox's successor was Jimmy Kain, the president of Ealing CC. A cyclist from the 1890s, who had ridden at the Memorial Grounds track near West Ham, he also ran a cycling business in Ealing with his wife, Brenda, a keen cyclist herself.[127] He later became the general secretary of the Ligue Internationale De Cyclisime (formed in 1948). In December 1942, Kain had resigned his position as the honorary treasurer of the RTTC's London West District Council in protest against what he perceived as the 'autocratic' stance of the NCU regarding the control of road sport and the RTTC's intransigence over the issue of massed-start racing.[128] Kain would become the BLRC's public voice. In addition, the BLRC gained the support of the editors of other cycling journalists such as Billy Mills at *The Bicycle* and *The Cyclist*'s F. J. Camm. By the end of 1943, 22 clubs had affiliated to the League and it had a membership of 643 with 384 registered for racing.[129] Clubs joined from around the country. In 1944 the West Hants RC resigned from the RTTC and joined the BLRC,[130] while in that same year the editor of the *Metropolitan and Home Counties Gazette* came out in favour of the BLRC and MSR.[131] The following year a BLRC section was formed on Tyneside which 'attracted considerable support'.[132] The League itself was organized into sections: London (248 members); Midland (185); East Midlands (8); and Northern (202). The largest club was Ealing CC with 126 members while Bradford Racing CC had the most registered riders with 65.[133]

How did the BLRC modernize the sport of cycling in Britain? At its initial meeting it set out its credentials by stating that '[c]ompetitors attire for all events may consist of a sleeved vest and track shorts'.[134] In adopting this European look it immediately contrasted with the RTTC uniform. (Ironically, a month previously the RTTC had relaxed its regulations to allow 'bare knees'.[135]) From the start the BLRC had a mixed racing programme. It included time trials and cyclo-cross as well as 'classic' massed-start races. It also catered for women and junior riders. In 1943 the first BLRC MSR national championship for men was held, finishing in Harrogate and won by Ernie Clements. The first women's BLRC national title, albeit a time trial, was held in 1944,[136] although a woman's race was included in the programme of the BLRC-organized Grand Prix de la Bastille race in Battersea Park in July 1944.[137] By 1947 over 70 events had been organized, including 20 massed-start races.[138] Races included the Tour of the Peaks, which in 1943 was an 82-mile race from Buxton and back. With more than a nod to the Tour de France and its emphasis on suffering, a poster stated 'see the notorious Snake Pass and Mam Tor conquered'.[139]

By 1955 the BLRC programme had expanded considerably with over 800 events organized. There were four races that lasted three days and seven of two days duration. Fifteen events had been organized for professionals and independents with around 70 for amateurs and independents.[140] In 1954 the BLRC had organized the first Amateur Circuit of Britain, which was sponsored by the Quaker Oats Food Company.[141] By 1956 the BLRC had a total membership of 5,412 with 637 clubs affiliated to the League.[142] The most visible feature of British cycling's modernity though was the establishment – a la Tour de France – of a national stage race.[143] The first de facto Tour of Britain had been run in August 1945 as the Brighton to Glasgow Marathon, although the first official race began in 1951 when it was sponsored by the *Daily Express*.[144] Not only was it a stage race similar to the Tour de France, but it was also a commercially run event.[145]

Cycling's great split

Unsurprisingly, the BLRC and MSR were vigorously opposed by other cycling organizations and created tensions among the sport's governing bodies and clubs at the grassroots. In 1945 the NCU had even requested that the Bicycle Polo Association not accept BLRC clubs to its membership.[146] To what extent the split in cycling revealed clear class fractures is unclear. The vast majority of the cyclists were from working-class and lower-middle-class backgrounds, and while NCU and RTTC administrators came from middle-class backgrounds, so did some of the supporters of MSR. Splits in sports, such as football and rugby, have scarred the British sporting landscape.[147] Moreover, a split had taken place within cycling's middle-class ranks following the NCU's decision in 1897 to ban any riders who took part in road races. The splits in football and rugby were largely a product of middle-class anxieties over their status in the sport and society more generally. This was not the case with the split over MSR. Instead, rather than over social class, it was more of a value-driven and generational split, which revolved around the idea of what constituted cycling in Britain. Certainly, *Cycling* was anti-MSR but MSR was also supported by other cycling journalists and magazines, such as *The Bicycle*. By 1944 even *Cycling*, which had initially self-censored itself by ignoring BLRC events, had begun to report on them, much to the disappointment of the RTTC.[148]

For the RTTC, MSR represented an existential threat to cycling as they knew it and imagined it, not only as a sport, but also the entire cycling culture, which was based on an amateur ethos. In 1948, due to the rise in popularity of MSR, it warned, 'Its [MSR] existence is now a definite menace not only to TT [time-trial] sport in its present state of freedom from interference, but to all cycling club and party riding.' In particular, there was a dislike of MSR because of its 'regimentation by the police' that threatened 'the whole of club cycling'.[149] By contrast, the RTTC's attitude was that it would 'not seek, need or desire any such "assistance" because its events are normally conducted in a manner which is perfectly safe'. Instead, the RTTC was keen to emphasize its amateur-voluntary heritage, stressing that

> [t]he most important lesson of the whole episode however is the paramount necessity for English road trials to be controlled only by the clubs themselves through their council, which is a body without any commercial or financial interest in the way the sport is held and has no other object except to preserve the sport for the sake of the members. That is why the events are governed by regulations which will ensure absence from interference and so safeguard the sport's future.[150]

Cycling was unlike other sports. Football and cricket grounds required the licence of governing bodies; this controlled who could and could not play on them. In 1921, for example, the FA had banned women's football from its registered grounds. The issue over MSR was that it took place on the public highway where no governing body could claim jurisdiction. Instead it was the law that took precedence. Almost immediately following the Llangollen to Wolverhampton race, the government had expressed concerns about MSR. During the war, the Ministry for War Transport under Herbert Morrison was keen that the roads – albeit relatively empty due to petrol rationing – were as free from congestion as possible.[151] Therefore, the RTTC and NCU continued to express fears that if massed-start racing on the road was not prohibited, cycling itself – albeit highly unlikely – could be banned. State displeasure continued to be expressed over MSR, but much to the frustration of the RTTC and NCU it was not banned after the war.

In 1952 the NCU 'legalized' MSR. By this time, it had little choice as denying the growing popularity of MSR was taking on Canute-like proportions, something tacitly recognized by both the RTTC and the NCU. Their argument that MSR posed a legal threat to cycling itself was increasingly hollow, although in the case of the RTTC it was as much about the threat to an idealized form of cycling in the form of the time trial. For the NCU their decision was largely motivated by political expediency. The NCU's move followed a key meeting between an NCU delegation and officials from the Ministry of Transport (MoT) and the Home Office in January 1952. The MoT explained that it had had received many complaints from the police about MSR but only one from a member of the public, and crucially, the MoT had 'to have regard to the liberty of the subject [i.e. the BLRC] to use the roads as he chose so long as he did not inconvenience other road users by his actions'.[152] In other words, in their dealings with the BLRC, the police were merely doing their jobs and keeping the roads clear for others. Moreover, police action was largely a local matter. While BLRC races had been warned away from Surrey and some Yorkshire roads, they were welcomed in Brighton due to tourism.[153] In addition, the MoT had praised the BLRC for the 'skilful and expert fashion' in how it promoted its races and avoided incidents: 'the Tour of Britain in particular was a model in this respect'. Furthermore, the 1951 edition of the race had received national press and radio coverage, and 'so far as NCU opinion was concerned this seemed to be the last straw'.[154] Moreover, as the international representative of British cycling the NCU's position had been weakened due to the successful promotion of this event. Why did the NCU ban MSR on open roads, yet the authorities permitted the Tour of Britain, it was asked at the UCI. As for its members, it became increasingly difficult for the NCU to convince them that MSR was going to be banned when they witnessed MSR taking place due to police and local authority cooperation. The drift in favour of MSR was also reflected in voting on the issue at NCU general council meetings. In 1947 4 voted for MSR and 37 against. By 1951 it had been 30 to 39.[155]

Ironically, when the Ministry officials were asked about their attitude if the NCU decided to promote MSR, the MoT said it would deplore it, while suggesting that as the police regarded MSR as a nuisance more might ban it as they did in Surrey.[156] The NCU's decision to legalize would be followed by a period of in-fighting between it and the BLRC for control of MSR until 1959. At the same time, the legal status of MSR was increasingly subjected to the scrutiny of law in light of rising traffic levels. A number of Parliamentary papers were published that proposed the banning of MSR, but all were resisted. It was only in 1960 with the introduction of the Cycle Racing on Highways regulations that road racing – both time trialling and MSR – was, under certain conditions, given a legal stamp of approval.[157]

What was the impact of the emergence of massed-start racing at the grassroots? Among clubs, from the outset the split created tensions which continued right up until the formation of the BCF in 1959. In 1943, for example, it was claimed that over 90 per cent of clubs were against MSR, albeit in the pro-NCU *Cycling*.[158] In its 1943 handbook Barnesbury CC (Tyneside) presented both sides of the argument, which echoed those in the cycling press. Stallard both assured its readers of the safety in staging massed-start races while playing the patriotism card, as he claimed it would improve Britain's chances at international cycling championships. The other view, from the secretary of the local NCU centre, predictably revolved around the dangers of massed-start races on the public highways.[159] In 1948 the South Lancashire Road Club split over the issue when eight of its members broke away to form the South Lancashire Racing Club in order to race under BLRC rules. They included committee member J. E. Ford and the club's two international riders, Eric Mitchell and Mr A. W. Stanway.[160] In November 1948, at a special general meeting, it had been proposed that the South Lancashire Road Club would 'transfer to BLRC ruling with a view to regaining lost membership'.[161] However, as J. E. Ford recounted, 'While a majority of active members … were all for the BLRC, the crucial meeting at which the vote was taken to convert the club was affected by the sudden appearance of many dormant members who carried the day for staying in the NCU.'[162] Resignations followed, which were accepted without regret, indicating the depth of feeling. As a consequence, the Road Club continued with time trialling.[163] By 1955, however, there had been sea change with overwhelming support for the club to join the BLRC, as it would provide 'a better programme of Massed-start events for the enthusiasts of the club'.[164]

In 1947, commenting on the split, the editorial of Solihull CC's magazine was critical of both the NCU and 'the rebels', as it referred to the BLRC.[165] A year later the sale of any BLRC publications at club functions had been prohibited, although it did point to some sympathy with MSR within the club.[166] Feelings ran deep in the Solihull CC with BLRC members also banned from joining club runs.[167] Solihull CC had split following the formation of the Midlands-based Concorde Racing CC in 1948, which catered for massed-start racing.[168] One of its early recruits from Solihull was Bob Maitland. Maitland was its star rider having won a silver medal at the 1948 Olympics in the team road race (on a closed circuit) and his 'defection' gave rise to what one member referred to as an 'attitude of sectarianism against cyclists of other clubs', which meant those in the BLRC. For many it created much anguish and undermined 'cycling's fellowship'. In 1950 one Solihull member, Len Cross, who had just returned from his national service, observed that in light of the split 'the fact remains that there is in the club an unhealthy atmosphere which in some cases amounts to little less that hatred of those ex-club members'.[169] He continued,

> I came across this feeling quite early last year when – after having been out with the Concorde CC all day, I was completely shunned by the other members of the [Solihull] club for the rest of the evening. For weeks after this incident members came up to me and with a sneer said, 'Ah, I thought you were in the Concorde.' So this loathsome undercurrent ran through the club during the season and even reared its ugly head at the AGM. The whole thing culminated (as far as I was concerned) in the despicable attitude adopted on the club night prior to the Club New Year's Party when a certain member was told that Concorde people were not wanted (even if they were personal friends).

Cross further pleaded:

> Where, may I ask, is the club spirit? What is the purpose of a club? Is it to foster hatred and bear malice against other people and organisations because we the Solihull CC think, rightly or wrongly, that other people should not have done as they did. Fellow members – I was introduced to cycling and to the Solihull CC by those very members who broke away. I count them among my best friends, much of what I know today in the sphere of cycling I owe to those same people. Surely I am not expected to 'cock a snoot' and put on a 'greater than thou' attitude, if that is so then it's time I got out of the Solihull. Let us fight by all means in friendly rivalry and sportsmanship but let us always remember and respect people whose names linked with the Solihull CC made it a household word in the cycling world.

Ironically, on 29 June 1952 it was the Solihull CC, in collaboration with the NCU's Birmingham and Midland Centre, which organized the first MSR on the public highways under the aegis of the NCU.[170]

These very localized disputes were reflective of the depth of feelings that the split created at club level nationwide. Moreover, loyalty to the club can be a powerful emotion, whatever the preferences of its individual members, and it can also engender a sense of betrayal if anyone is perceived to have undermined its values. Tensions can also be the product of a shift in a perceived natural order – in this case the emergence of the BLRC and MSR – with some in favour of this change while others preferred the status quo. Even when the other bodies began to sanction BLRC events there were still tensions between the two camps. Tom Simpson, after winning the BLRC hill championship, entered the RTTC equivalent. Half a minute before he was to begin his climb the chief judge, Pat Shaw, informed him he had to fix a locking ring to his bike, Simpson shouted, 'Just because I won the BLRC hill climb you want to disqualify me.'[171] Even years after the formation of the BCF, former 'Leaguers' out on their bikes would salute each other with 'Up the League'.

The split indicated broader changes in post-war society where there was a shift away from Victorian values, represented by the NCU. Instead, MSR offered the allure of modernity, with its nod to Europe, its colour and 'ballyhoo' no less. While many Britons quietly held xenophobic views towards Europeans, in the post-war period more Britons came into contact with Europe than ever before. As a result, these experiences established the idea of Europe more deeply in the popular consciousness. Exhibitions at the 1951 Festival of Britain, for example, had helped to popularize European-style outdoor eating and drinking.[172] The war and later the British Army on the Rhine of course had forced millions of British men onto the mainland, but the relationship between Britain began to change on a number of levels. First, there was Britain's attempt at joining the Common Market, then the rejection of its application by de Gaulle in 1963, before eventually joining in 1973. Second, more British people were taking their holidays 'abroad', especially in Spain as flights became cheaper. Third, television was also bringing Europe closer to home, especially after the start of European football competitions.

To a certain extent, the changing nature of the sport of cycling was symbolized at a lavish concert at the Royal Albert Hall to mark the Diamond Jubilee of *Cycling* in January 1951.[173] While it was also an opportunity to look forward, much of the evening was backward looking, and a throwback to the halcyon days of the 1930s when the Albert Hall had been the venue ostensibly to celebrate the winner of that year's BAR. On the face of it the awards' ceremonies were a reaffirmation of Britishness and British values forged during the interwar years, but the entire style of the event represented a different kind of Britain. Harry Goodwin, the long-time promoter of the sport at the Herne Hill track, was the MC for a mixed programme of cycling-related events and variety acts, which reflected both contemporary popular tastes. The variety acts, interspersed throughout the evening, included acrobats, singers and tumblers such as the Great Alexander Troupe; Tumbling Whirlwind of the Seven Volants; the Jackson Girls; Topper Martin, a juggler; and a roller-skating act, the Orlandos. Bringing a sense of nostalgia were the trick cyclists, Annell and Brask, who in Victorian costume rode a unicycle and an ordinary on to the stage. The show also included some typically British communal singing of the cyclists' anthem, 'Daisy Bell', before the evening ended with a rendition of Auld Lang Syne. To add further to the entertainment two cycling rollers contests were held. Typically, in light of the continuing social divisions in and the organization of sport more generally, there was one for amateurs and one for professionals. Roller contests had begun in the interwars and had been popularized on the initiative of *Cycling*. Eddie Lane was the winner of the amateur contest, a 1-mile invitation scratch roller race, which had four heats and then a final. The Race of the Champions, for the professionals, was won by Reg Harris, who defeated France's Maurice Verdeun and Sid Patterson of Australia. Prizes were presented to 12 riders and gave an insight into the sport at that time. Trophies were still mainly awarded for unpaced time trials – 100 miles, 12 hours and 24 hours – while the BAR for the second successive year was Ken Joy. A women's BAR had been established in 1948 and like Joy, Eileen Sheridan was rewarded for her second successive title. *Cycling* had its own award for cyclist of the year – the *Flying Cyclist Trophy*, which went to Reg Harris, world sprint champion. More significant to British cycling's post-war story was an award to Gordon Thomas as the 'most meritorious massed-start rider'.

This reference to massed-start racing was further reinforced with the evening's highlight, the appearance of its special guest, Fausto Coppi. Known as *Il Campionissimo* in his native Italy, Coppi was then the most famous cyclist in the world. He had already won the Tour de France in 1949 and the Giro d'Italia on three occasions in addition to numerous one-day classic races, including Milan-San Remo three times. He was famed for his style on the bicycle, but it was how he won many races in spectacular and dramatic fashion, usually due to his long-range attacks, that forged the Coppi legend.[174] Coppi's appearance was awkward, mainly because he spoke little English and Goodwin's grasp of Italian was limited. Nevertheless, the audience knew who he was and he received a 'tremendous' welcome when he was introduced to them. When asked about how a young British cyclist might become a champion, he replied, 'Ride a bicycle; ride a bicycle; ride a bicycle.' He then gave a riding exhibition on a set of revolving rollers painted in the Italian colours of red, green and white, allowing the audience to view in full 'the Coppi style'. Coppi had not been the first 'foreigner' to appear at one of these occasions. In the past Kramer of America, Denmark's Ellegard and Belgium's world champion sprinter Jef Scherens had been invited guests. Nevertheless, as an indication of shifting cycling tastes, Coppi's appearance was a different matter when taking into account his status and that his realm was massed-start racing, which up to the 1930s represented the antithesis for British cycling's hierarchy. Even Harry England, *Cycling*'s traditionally conservative editor, was fawning in his praise of Coppi. He commented that his roller exhibition was 'the same action of the complete bike rider' that he had admired when he had been watching the road classics where I have been privileged to watch him racing.'[175]

In 1955 the first British team rode in the Tour de France and four years later Brian Robinson became the first British cyclist to win a stage in the race. It was further evidence of a growing shift in British cycling towards a more modern and European style of racing. This shift had also reflected a classic struggle between amateurism and professionalism, the central feature in the history of British sport more generally. To a certain extent, cycling was leading the way as it was only in 1962 that the Gentleman-Player distinction in cricket would be abolished. Moreover, it reflected broader social change as British society began to throw off the shackles of Victorian society. Not only was deference in decline, but there was a greater awareness of global trends.

Nevertheless, any change was slow and the British tradition of the time trial did not melt away in the face of changing tastes. Instead, time trialling remained (and remains) a staple of British cycling. To a certain extent, the time trial's ongoing presence was a form of British exceptionalism and peculiarity, although time trials did take place in other countries. Looking at the winners of the Bidlake Memorial Prize, it was only in 1960 that a cyclist – Beryl Burton – was recognized for their sporting achievements in road racing.[176] Time triallists dominated the list of winners in the 1940s and 1950s and included Ken Joy, Eileen Sheridan and Ray Booty. Most of the winners were also amateur, which reflected the sport's marginal status more broadly. Of course, the actual name of the prize was synonymous with the time trial and so there was perhaps an inherent bias in who won the award. Domestic time triallists, with a low public profile, continued to win the Bidlake in the twenty-first century in the face of competition from a plethora of Olympic and World Champions and Grand Tour winners. In a sense, it highlighted the continuing esteem with which the time trial was held within the British cycling community.

CHAPTER 6

Women, modernity and cycling

In 1936 the BBC broadcast the play *Louisa Wants a Bicycle*. It had little to do with cycling. Instead, more accurate to the play's spirit and theme was its subtitle: 'The Fight for Woman's Freedom'. Ambitious and groundbreaking, it was about the rights of women spoken through the words of numerous campaigners throughout history, from Mary Wollstonecraft, Florence Nightingale, Elizabeth Garrett and Millicent Fawcett. The bicycle itself had been seen as a symbol of female emancipation in the nineteenth century. With women over 21 having gained the vote in 1928, the play – and its association with cycling – captured a sense of a woman's changing status in Britain. One example that symbolized both the new status of women and female cycling during the interwar years came in 1938. In that year, a typist, Billie Dovey (née Fleming), aged 24, cycled a record 29,603.4 miles in a calendar year for a woman; it was broken only in 2015. As much as an expression of female independence, her feats and motivations were an example of how women were increasingly seen as citizens. A member of the all-female Southern Ladies' Road Club, she had taken up cycling at the age of 18 after meeting a boy at a local youth club. She became inspired by the emerging health and fitness movement, and in particular the Women's League of Health and Beauty principles of moderate daily exercise – although there seemed little moderate about cycling an average of 81 miles a day. Her motivations were threefold. First, she just loved cycling. Second, she 'wanted to do something to encourage more women to ride bicycles as a simple and easy means of keeping fit, and also to see women's cycling in a more flourishing and respected position'.[1] In her self-appointed role as 'the national advocate for women to cycle for health and fitness',[2] she became a celebrity and her exploits received nationwide media attention. Third, she was also a professional cyclist and was known as the 'Rudge-Whitworth Keep-Fit Girl' as it was their bike she rode and hence advertised. She also received sponsorship from Cadbury's in the form of 5 lbs of chocolate a month.[3] It was a radical departure from the image of Edwardian female cyclists, but by the 1930s women cycling long distances, and in shorts, had become part of the cycling scene.

One technological innovation that highlighted a growing demand for women's cycling was the lightweight bicycle.[4] Manufacturers, for reasons of mass production, had initially continued to concentrate on producing standard roadsters. However, there was increasing pressure to build bicycles that incorporated design features which made cycling pleasurable in an attempt to revive cycling as a pastime, including for women. At first, there was a focus on racing, but 'lightweight' roadster machines, which incorporated new ideas and components began to appear.[5]

Cycling's popularity among women reflected and reinforced both this creeping female emancipation and its modern tendencies. Selina Todd has argued the First World War accelerated the evolution of a new modern woman. The period between the 1920s and 1950s was one in which 'leisure, and financial autonomy became a general characteristic of young women's lifestyles'.[6] Changes in the nature of the workforce were the primary reasons for this development. Domestic service, as an occupation, declined and instead there was an expansion in shop, factory and office employment for women. As a consequence, similar to men, leisure time for many women was increasingly structured around an industrialized working day. This greater autonomy had important cultural consequences, especially in terms of female leisure consumption. Leisure consumption for young women was not new to the 1920s. But as wage earners there was a now greater sense within families that women were entitled to more leisure time, which relieved them of some household tasks, thus marking a distinctive difference from previous generations. Indeed, Todd has further argued young women were at times more prominent leisure consumers then men, and 'pioneers in the development of working-class youth culture'.[7] Cycling had been part of a wider expansion in female physical culture during the interwar years. It appealed not only to the newly independent young women but also to married and older women from the middle and working classes.[8] As a form of bodily freedom and independence for women, it also gave a sense of personal mobility.[9] Moreover, as Zweiniger-Bargielowska has argued, the body was an important site for the construction of femininity as women began to free themselves from the constraints of the Victorian age. 'A modern, actively cultivated body was yet another aspect of women's liberation along with political emancipation, greater gender equality, along with expanding employment opportunities after 1918.'[10]

Before the First World War, cycling had remained a popular activity for both upper- and middle-class women and girls.[11] For those who enjoyed a privileged upbringing, cycling was one of a number of activities girls did in different locations for a wide variety of reasons. When she was a teenager, bicycling was Mrs Fleetwood Hesketh's 'chief pleasure'. 'We had rather a large garden with lots of paths, so we used to whizz about and play bicycle polo,' she recalled.¹² Mrs Hill-Wood claimed that she once defied social convention when 'coasting all down' the road from Hove into Brighton,¹³ while Mrs Hawkins (born 1899) regularly cycled to school in Withington in Greater Manchester.¹⁴ Joyce Mathews (born 1906) was given her first bike during the First World War. She rode it day and night, once riding home when there was a black out.¹⁵ Miss Johnson was another keen cyclist. A boarder at a school in Settrington, in North Yorkshire, she once cycled the 25 miles to Scarborough to watch the annual cricket festival, and then cycled the 25 miles back. 'Thought nothing of it. And we could do it with perfect safety,' she remembered. She continued to cycle when she was an undergraduate at Cambridge.¹⁶ The bicycle continued to serve different functions. Mrs V. Mason (born 1899) had been a keen cyclist, although she would have preferred a horse as a girl. With her father she attended the local hunts, following the hounds on their bicycles. 'He was very knowledgeable and he always seemed know which way they were going so we could get there first and see them,' she added.¹⁷ Mrs D. Lloyd's (born 1911) father became an MP in 1918 and later chancellor of the exchequer. She recounted how her mother used her bicycle a lot for her work in the constituency.¹⁸ Riding a bicycle though was also subject to parental surveillance. V. Mason's mother, for example, was not so keen on her cycling with the chauffeur's son.¹⁹ Enid Linden had learned to ride a friend's bicycle, and very much hoped that her parents would buy her one for her birthday. Instead they felt cycling was far too dangerous and bought her a brooch.²⁰

More women further down the social hierarchy were also riding a bicycle, both for practical and for leisure purposes before the First World War. In April 1914 some women undertaking seasonal work in the Fens were pictured in the *Daily Mirror* riding their bicycles. Despite earning half-a-crown per day, all of them owned a bicycle, which they had acquired on hire purchase.²¹ Women were 'the hidden workforce of Edwardian Britain'²² and a growing number of them took up cycling to get to work, especially domestic servants and governesses. Mr D. Mallet, for example, remembered that his grandmother employed a servant, Agnes, who cycled 2 miles every morning to their home.²³ Zeta Lambert, the daughter of car manufacturer Herbert Austin, recalled how her governess travelled daily from Birmingham by train and then cycled 2 miles to the Austin mansion and back again, while she also noticed that their servants had bicycles.²⁴

By 1916, almost half the workforce was made up of women due to the rapid growth in industrial activity and then the imposition of military conscription that year. The bicycle made a not insignificant contribution to the war effort on the home front as an increasing number of working women rode one to get to work. In the Southampton area, for example, female munitions workers cycled to the factories. And once women had a bicycle they could have days out in the New Forest with workmates, breathing fresh air rather than the toxic fumes of the munitions factory.²⁵

Other than munitions, it was the non-industrial sector, such as services – banking, finance and commerce – that saw the biggest increase in female workers.[26] It was probably in London where these structural changes in the workforce were most noticeable and was subsequently seen in the increased visibility of women's cycling.

The social benefits of the war for women were both mixed and not immediate. A minority experienced an 'emancipation culture' but it did not dislodge deep-seated male prejudices, while after the war most women returned to a life of 'hearth and home'.[27] There was subsequently some residual antipathy towards women cycling. Many cycling clubs had barred women while others had split over the issue of female membership. Some male cyclists had felt that women were too interested in the social side of cycling and not enough in the 'serious business' of sport and would break up the bonds of male sociability. In 1921 a jury had decided that a woman, aged 59, should not be allowed to ride a bicycle. A 'sentiment preserved from the early Victorian era than a common-sense utterance of a more enlightened day' was *Cycling*'s stern verdict.[28] While attitudes varied from club to club, male prejudices never entirely disappeared as some male members viewed clubs as masculine republics. In 1922, for example, Watford CC admitted women after 'a close vote'.[29] By contrast, in 1944 the Manchester Road Racing Club, which was affiliated to the BLRC, forced two women out of the club, just because they were women. Joyce Renshaw and Lillian Rea had been among the first members of this relatively new club. Typically, they undertook many of its administrative duties. The majority of male members 'did not mind females in the club', but a handful called a meeting to vote on an all-male club. The vote initially went in favour of the women, but then the men in question threatened to resign from the club and the majority of the members caved in, forcing the women to leave.[30] It was a rare event and not well received in cycling ranks with the club's condemned in a strongly worded editorial in *The Bicycle*.[31]

While men may have wanted a return to the status quo in terms of gender relations, the First World War had emboldened many women and one outcome was the increase in both the number and the visibility of female cyclists during the interwar years. In February 1918 at the CTC's Metropolitan District Association Annual Dinner a toast was made 'to the ladies'. It was added, 'The ladies ... had been most active in all departments of war work, they were indispensable in the CTC, and now that they had the vote they would be more important than ever', while, it had been the presence of 'lady members' that had maintained the DA's weekly runs.[32] In July that year the 2nd Ladies' Run to Brighton and back also took place.[33] The post-war growth of female cyclists was not lost on cycling's establishment. It was noted that '[t]hey are riding faster, farther, and better than before and it scarcely requires a prophet to foresee the day when the speed and stamina of wheelwomen will be tested in competition'.[34] As with cyclists more generally, it is difficult to gauge the number of women riding bicycles during this period, but in 1923 a *Cycling* editorial observed, 'One of the striking features of the present season is the great increase in the numbers of ladies among the cyclists on the road. The increase is largely disproportionately to the general advance of the pastime this year, and it is a matter for particular satisfaction.'[35] Typical of *Cycling*'s paternalistic and educational sensibilities, to supplement this increasing popularity among women, the journal published some articles for beginners.

London led the way largely due to the efforts of one woman, Mabel Hodgson. Hodgson was a 'busy-body', someone who had a great flair for getting things done. Before her unfortunate and untimely early death in 1921, Hodgson was cycling's 'most outstanding feminine figure' who brought great energy to her role in the CTC.[36] A daughter of a bicycle agent from suburban Wimbledon, she had joined the CTC's Metropolitan DA in 1909. While working as a nurse during the war, she became the DA's temporary secretary before being elected both its secretary and treasurer in 1918. Later, she became the only female member of the CTC national council and the only woman on the Road Improvement Committee.[37] Hodgson was also a modernizer. She promoted rational dress among female cyclists (as discussed further) and wrote a column in *Cycling*, providing a female perspective on the pleasures of cycling and touring. However, her most significant achievement was the 'Ladies' Cyclists' Rally'. It was first run in May 1916 and organized under the auspices of the CTC's Metropolitan DA. It was run in the same year as the first Old-Timers' Rally, and had the aim of keeping the activity of cycling alive and in the public eye during the war. The Ladies' Rally became an annual event, which attracted ever-increasing numbers. In 1921 it was estimated that there were 1,000 riders (men were welcome as long they were accompanied by a female cyclist). The rally continued to grow after Hodgson's death, so much so that in 1925 *Cycling* called for men to be excluded because there were too many of them. Men, it was estimated, made up one-third of the rally. It was argued that men and women now rode on equal terms and the presence of men in the rally gave the impression that women could not do without their support.[38]

The London 'Ladies' Rally' spawned imitators, which prioritized the social side of cycling. In Lancashire the Bolton section of the CTC's Manchester DA organized a Northern Ladies' Rally from 1922. The following year the programme consisted of 'a leisurely run to Belmont where tea will be served at Mitten's farm at 4.30 pm, followed by some competitions'. Gentlemen, again, were only eligible if accompanied by a woman.[39] In the same year, another 'Ladies' Day' was organized by the CTC in Leicestershire.[40] In the north-east the Northumberland and Durham DA formed a ladies section in 1924. The following year it organized special runs 'with the object of encouraging a stronger feminine interest in the club by providing less strenuous rides than the usual weekly excursions'.[41] Female-only rallies continued into the thirties. One was held in Essex in 1933, while the CTC's West Metropolitan DA organized a Ladies' Day at scenic Burnham Beeches in Buckinghamshire in July 1938, which was attended by leading female cycling figures, Billie Dovey and the journalist, 'Petronella'.[42]

By 1936 there was clear evidence of a growth in female cyclists. It was estimated that more than 10 per cent of the CTC's 38,000 members were women, while out of the NCU's 50,000 members nearly 20 per cent were women. Highlighting how their stock had risen, four out of the 23 members on the CTC council were female.[43] In addition, youth became increasingly established as a life-stage for young women, and in 1949 cycling, either for sport or for sociability, was cited as a major leisure interest for 18 per cent of London girls.[44] Like cycling more generally, there was some social stratification among female cyclists. While cycling was taken up by working-class and lower-middle-class females, it was increasingly shunned by the upper-middle classes. In a study of women's sports and activities depicted in advertisements featured in *Tatler*, the magazine aimed at the upper-middle classes, not one featured cycling during the interwar years.[45] Moreover, more women from the upper-middle classes had access to a car, either through their husbands or driving one themselves.

The increasing visibility of women's cycling was reflected by a growing number of female journalists in the cycling press. Mabel Hodgson was an early writer, while in 1930 a column devoted to female cycling was started in *Cycling*, titled 'Femina's Page'.[46] In the same year, *CTC Gazette* started a new regular 'Ladies Page', which was written under the pen name of Petronella.[47] Other female cyclists also put their names to articles. In December 1938 long-distance cyclist Billie Dovey featured on 'In Town To-night', talking about her feats on BBC national radio.[48] On 15 June 1938 *Cycling* devoted an entire issue to female cycling. Images and reports of women on bicycles were regularly featured in the cycling press and, occasionally, in the national papers. One peculiar example was Miss Zetta Hills who briefly achieved fame by riding a water bicycle. She was a mixture of entrepreneur and performer, rather than cyclist. Presaging the exploits of Marguerite Wilson and Billy Dovey, as well as highlighting the ubiquity of the bicycle, Hills's brief notoriety had been part of a publicity drive to promote the 'Zetta Hills Water-Cycle', which was manufactured by Wells-Forde Ltd.[49] The venture literally sunk. In August 1920 she had set out to cross the English Channel on her machine. Starting from Calais at 7.15 am on 16 August, she was only 4 miles off the English coast before her machine collapsed at about 10.30 pm. The waves from a ship from Ostend had swamped her and she was picked up by the motor boat that had supported her attempt. Hills had been cycling for 15 hours and because of tides had actually cycled over 40 miles.[50] In an attempt to generate more publicity, the following month she water cycled 15 miles down the Thames from Richmond to Temple Pier.[51] British Pathé captured the carefully choreographed event.[52] Hills and her machine were 'launched' with a bottle of champagne by the mayor of Richmond. Then, playing the patriotic card, a solider tied a union jack to her water cycle. In the next clip Hills is seen confidently using the machine on the Thames, wearing a bathing costume of the day. There was a further demonstration on the Thames, which involved a race against the champion breaststroke swimmer, Perry.[53] In 1933 Hills attempted a crossing of the Thames between Sheerness and Southend on a water cycle, but it capsized.[54]

Debates over the appropriateness of women's cycling continued throughout the period. How far should they ride, what should they wear and how should they ride were still central questions for some men and women, but mainly men. In general, though, these debates increasingly challenged and defied implicit Victorian notions about both a woman's medical limits and femininity and a woman's role in society. Feats of female riding, as well as tours, were regularly reported in the cycling press. In 1924 a Miss L. F. Kemp of Kensall Rise in London had cycled 6,200 miles, while Mrs du Heaume, a CTC member from Great Missenden, had nearly doubled that total at 12,094 miles.[55] These reports were usually tinged with more than a hint of a patronizing tone. In 1923 two women, with three men, were part of the 'Optimists' who rode in a 100-mile utility team-ride' under the auspices of the Liverpool Time-Trial Cycling Association. Under the headline 'Good Rides by Two Ladies', the two cyclists were members of both the Birmingham CTC and the NCU. It was noted that '[b]oth ladies rode splendidly throughout, never faltering ... a really meritorious ride; particularly as they rode the ordinary ladies' heavyweight'. It was also added that '[b]oth ladies are exceptionally enthusiastic cyclists and have performed many other long-distance rides including two all-night rides in North Wales.'[56] In 1927 the Bolton section of the Manchester DA had actually organized a 100-mile ride for women.[57] In 1930 one female correspondent asked, 'How far should ladies ride?' She claimed that she averaged 70 miles in a day, but had ridden up to 85. Despite not feeling tired or exhausted, she was told 'that such rides are far too long'. A doctor friend had said the same, but tellingly she had not consulted him or any other for 'many years'. It was pointed out that '[l]ady members of the club commonly ride much greater distances than those mentioned and there can be no possible harm if there is no feeling of exhaustion' and that some had ridden over 300 miles.[58] In 1937 Jessie Springall, as part of her continental tour, climbed the 8,300-foot Col du Galibier in France, a week before it was raced over during the Tour de France itself. For the secretary of the Women's Road Records' Association, climbing one of the race's steepest mountains was part of her continental tour.[59] On the ascent she noted that men were repairing the road and she was surprised 'how interested they became at the apparently rare sight of a female riding a gent's cycle, clad in shorts that showed a goodly portion of leg'.[60]

Female cycling attire

By the 1930s more female cyclists were beginning to show a goodly portion of leg. Like the men, shorts became part of the female cycling uniform, a change that was increasingly mirrored in the adverts of cycling journals over the period. Given the context, this transformation in female cycling attire was startling. At the start of the interwar years, debates over female cycling fashion had been firmly fixed within middle-class parameters with the focus on the benefits of wearing rational dress rather than skirts and dresses. By 1930 one cover of *Cycling* was adorned with six women at the seaside riding their bikes – one with her feet on the handlebars – in their bathing costumes.[61] It reflected not only a loosening of social conventions, but the popularity of cycling among working-class women and girls. Unable to afford the expensive 'uniforms' that female writers prescribed, practicality was the most important factor in what they wore.

Zweiniger-Bargielowska has outlined how shifts in interwar fashion were part of the construction of modern femininity that, along with the quest for a fit and healthy body, also included mass-produced beauty products. In the 1920s the Flapper look had been in vogue. Hemlines rose and women cut their hair short and there was a preference for a slender figure. By the 1930s a shift back to glamour brought an emphasis on broad shoulders and a return of waists – an image later personified by Marguerite Wilson (discussed further).[62] But rather than being superficial, '[t]his transformation of women's appearance went beyond adornment, and the popularity of fitness activities points towards a widespread desire among women to acquire a beautiful, healthy and fit modern body'.[63]

Much ink was spilt in cycling journals over what constituted appropriate dress for female cyclists, and hence interwar perceptions of femininity. The debate over rational dress in the late nineteenth century had in reality been short-lived and for female cyclists longer skirts remained the regular 'garb'. The origins of interwar female rational dress can be found in the First World War. During and after the war, young female cyclists had started wearing ex-service clothes similar to women land workers and members of the various auxiliary corps which comprised long coats and tight-kneed breeches.[64] These clothes were increasingly adapted to a type of rational uniform, and by 1922 'rationals' were regarded as 'an accepted and commonplace feature of modern cycling'.[65] In 1920 Mabel Hodgson had been effusive in her praise for rational dress, which was 'the most suitable attire for lady cyclists', she claimed. Hodgson, reflecting her own energetic outlook, went further to say that 'it is the only satisfactory costume for the athletic girl who desires to use her cycle for something more than mere shopping expeditions, or to ride down for a game of tennis and back'.[66] Rational dress had become so de rigueur that at the 1925 Ladies' Rally it was stated, 'The most conspicuously and unusually garbed ladies at the Rally were those who appeared in skirts'.[67]

Vestiges of Victorian puritanism were never too far away. Even for some female cyclists rationals were too modern. One 'mature' CTC member complained that 'women in rationals are not dressed as smart as they used to be'.[68] Rationals offended her sense of femininity, reflecting the persistence of Victorian discourses, among both sexes, concerning a woman's generally subordinate role in society. Fashion tastes were part of the wider package of what some people thought constituted to be a woman in interwar Britain, including attitudes to sport. One Miss S. Conabeer took offence at Hodgson's comments. For her, rational dress was 'degrading' and evidence that women were trying to 'unsex themselves'. She also disapproved of sport and believed that women should cycle in moderation. 'Surely the women of today are not out to break records! If they are they cease to be ladies and become nothing more than imitations, trying to ape men.' She continued: 'Women are naturally weaker than men, and it is unnatural and impossible in my estimation for them to apply themselves to feats of endurance and strength such as performed by men.'[69]

In 1920, *Cycling* devoted a two-page spread, consisting of readers' letters, on the subject, titled 'Is Rational Dress Unladylike?'[70] In response to Miss Conabeer's claim that rational dress was an attempt by women to 'unsex themselves', there had been 'an avalanche of protests' from all classes of readers, the journal claimed. A number of correspondents raised the issue of the role that women had played during the war and that rational dress had not prevented them from contributing to the war effort. Conabeer found an 'anti-rationals' ally, a man, J. C. Tomkins, who asked – in all seriousness – 'would every man who approves of "rationals" in the abstract prefer to see his own wife, sweetheart, or sisters so clothed when out with him?' He also knew 'scores of men who feel, like myself, that when they meet "Mrs Right" she will not be so attired'.

Whether for or against rational dress, the debate continued to be implicitly conducted within middle-class boundaries. Just as important as the attire was that women continued to be dressed respectfully, reflecting wider concerns among cycling's authorities over its position in society. One male defender of rationals, H. Collings Young, raised the issue of modesty. He compared a lady dressed in well-cut tweed coat and breeches with stockings to match, to one in a light summer dress, perpetually climbing to the knees. 'Even if the latter lady wears elastic skirt holders, the present-day length of skirt renders the "tout ensemble" less modest than the workmanlike get-up of the rationalist.' However, he reassured readers that rational riders of his club carried a light skirt during the summer. The 'rush to rationals' though was not universal and could depend on the nature of the club. As many interwar clubs were social rather than sporting, Arthur Cook noted that it was not uncommon to see 'monster club runs' from Lea Bridge to Epping Forest with 'the ladies usually wearing voluminous skirts held in decent rein, their hats often of a huge "flower-garden" variety'.[71]

Over this period, there was a literal and metaphorical loosening of female dress that expedited an increase in the participation of women in cycling. By the late 1920s, in light of the interwar dress reform movement to improve health, women were dispensing with the rational dress – even members of the CTC. In 1928 'Miss 1927' claimed that the CTC's uniform was 'very masculine' and on one occasion she rode in just her petticoat. 'I felt quite cool and refreshed, and did not care a jot what anyone thought.'[72] The practicality of shorts was also becoming increasingly evident against the stuffiness of rationals and impracticalities of wearing dresses and skirts, which flapped about in the wind and got wet in the rain. Another correspondent argued that in comparison to skirts those who wore shorts were smarter. In Liverpool they were becoming increasingly popular and 'the lady of the frills' would be considered 'antique'.[73]

Another female CTC member, 'EMAS', who modestly referred to herself as one of 'the women pioneers of cycling', was more relaxed and reflective about changes in dress code. She still wore a skirt but if she had been slim and young enough would wear shorts and a tunic in the summer for comfort. 'EMAS' foresaw the future liberalization of dress codes. She claimed that she would wear these clothes 'in the interest of health and well as of comfort'. As for modesty, 'well, we have seen a good many things that were once considered immodest accepted quite calmly when people become used to them'. She prophetically added, 'In days to come we may find both men and women exposing considerably more of their skin to the air and sunshine when taking their outdoor exercise, and everyone taking it as a matter of course.'[74]

For some of the traditionalists, whatever women wore – shorts, trousers or breeches – there was still an expectation that they should be dressed smartly. G. H. Stancer, although keen not to tell women what to wear, felt that the CTC's female members should uphold certain standards for the public image of cycling generally. Even for those who indulged in 'hard-riding' there was 'no reason why we should not be neat and clean and take a decent pride in our appearance for it gives the pastime a far better standing in the eyes of the general public'.[75] It was a 'before the flood' comment. As cycling became increasingly popular among working-class women during the 1930s, they eschewed formal dress codes on the grounds of cost and practicality, and thus for some of its administrators raised questions about respectability.

Debates over shorts and especially their appeal continued deep into the thirties, and provided insights into gender relations. Despite the pursuit of health, beauty and fitness, it further reflected a residual conservatism within British society, especially among men, which partly revolved around the issue of the amount of skin exposed. Most men – within limits – encouraged female cycling, although it was difficult pleasing all. In 1928 John Bramall complained that there was a 'woefully low standard of beauty' among the girls who cycled or rambled in the Manchester district. After giving this 'problem' a good deal of thought, he calculated that the complexion made up 75 per cent of a woman's beauty and that these were invariably below par among the 'open-air' girls and was probably due to their exposure to the breezy Derbyshire uplands.[76] For some, uncovered knees when wearing shorts brought cyclists as a class into disrepute.[77] Despite his own conversion,

Wayfarer had been more circumspect in advocating shorts for women. The position of women was rather different from men, he felt. 'A woman must have some little regard for what the public thinks ... and a woman cyclist must bear in mind the general credit of the female cycling movement,' was his belief. 'Is it too much to ask us to believe that girls need clothe themselves so scantily in order to enjoy their cycling?' Girls – 'bless 'em' – he continued, should dress so 'that they do not attract undesirable attention and hostile criticism which may tend to bring the whole cycling movement into disrepute'.[78] These fears were not without some support. In 1936 the Matlock Bath Parochial Church Council expressed the view that 'some steps should be taken to control the increasing tendency to indecent dress in the streets on the part of female cyclists and others'.[79] But in 1932 the female cycling journalist 'Femina' had declared that, rather than a passing craze, shorts were here to stay.[80] Hikers who increasingly converted to cycling wore shorts, for example, while the fact remained that most female cyclists were either unwilling or unable to purchase a tailor-made cycling uniform. Essentially, any debates over the necessity of a cycling uniform was confined to a small sector of the middle-class cycling community and the status of a cycling as a mass activity had de facto invalidated the debate.

Cycling and gender relations

During the interwar years, cycling was instrumental in loosening up sexual conventions. It acted as a way for men and women not only to meet members of the opposite sex but also to escape parental surveillance. Ken Foster recalled how his mother went cycling in the 1930s as it was a good way to meet boys.[81] A 'magic carpet of a carless age, transporting me to … boys' had been Eileen Palmer's reason for taking up cycling in the late 1930s. In fact, her courting revolved around men who had bikes. The first boy she had been smitten with owned a bike, which had been a reward for passing his 11-plus. A grammar schoolgirl herself, she forged her father's signature and laid down a deposit of '10 bob' to buy a 'bright blue, fixed gear Carlton'. During the holidays and at weekends they went on trips into the countryside, 'out of sight of censorious mum'. A later boyfriend was a geographer, who rode a black Humber, while another was a potholer. It was her cycling rather than her relationships that would benefit most. After the war she married a cyclist and they bought a tandem plus four lightweights, and she 'finally got down to the serious love of my life – cycling'.[82] For reasons other than courting, a German POW, Martin Wein, would cycle into the Cotswolds with his English girlfriend, who he would later marry.[83] Arthur Cook recalled how, with reference to North and East London, most of the Eastern road clubs would end up at a very popular cyclists' haunt, 'Guy's Retreat', on Sunday evenings. Riding home provided the opportunity to strike up relationships. Cook added, 'I hesitate to attempt counting up the number of weddings which resulted from these meetings at Guy's and those rides home.'[84] *Awheel*, Solihull CC's magazine, even carried a column under 'Club News' of marriages, engagements and births in relation to its club members.[85] Jack and Joan Bare first met at a cycling club. They later married in August 1939 and were still together in 2019 as Britain's longest married couple.[86]

While cycling acted as a form of female emancipation, it could also be a site for tensions regarding sexual relations. The increase in women cycling brought with it ethical dilemmas, which challenged some social conventions concerning male-female relationships. In 1924, a letter from 'Twenty-Two' (presumably her age) appeared in the *Cycling* letters pages asking for advice from her 'sister-cyclists' on the question whether she should join her fiancé on a fortnight-long cycling tour. Her friends and family had told her that it was not quite 'the thing'. She felt sure 'that it is done among keen cycling couples and yet I do not want to do a thing which a "nice" girl would not do'.[87] In a pre-Agony Aunt era, *Cycling* devoted a whole page of letters to the topic, titled 'The Wheelwoman's Viewpoint: Cycle Touring for Mixed Couples'.[88] The overwhelming verdict of correspondents was that it was 'correct' for 'Twenty-Two' to tour with her fiancé. Implicit in her letter was the issue of sex before marriage. Jeffrey Weeks has argued that while there was a new mood over conjugal sex during the 1920s and 1930s, there was no relenting over the perception of the immorality of non-marital or non-heterosexual sex. Instead marriage remained the cornerstone of sexual relations. The evidence tended to suggest that premarital sex among women was increasing. In one survey, some 19 per cent of married women, born before 1904, had had premarital sex; for those born between 1904 and 1914, this figure had risen to 36 per cent; and had risen to 39 per cent for those born in the 1915–24 period.[89] Yet these figures still constituted a minority. Historians know little about the cultures of courtship and, instead, 'many couples developed pragmatic personal codes of morality, which determined the behavioural choices they made'. To have sex or not was framed 'by a set of gendered and class-dependent codes'.[90] Nevertheless, it is likely that cycling played a not insignificant part in a loosening of the conventions of relationships purely due to the opportunity to escape into the countryside for a few days or even a few hours; something which from the 1920s was taking place on a greater scale than ever before.

The emergence of women's cycling as a sport

In 1934 the Women's Road Records' Association (WRRA) was formed. It marked an important moment in the development of the sport of women's cycling in Britain. Like its men's equivalent, the RRA, it gave an official stamp of approval to record attempts, which were largely based on men's distance records.[91] The association itself was dominated by journalists. Its first president was Mrs H. W. Parkes aka Petronella, while Jessie Springall of Gospell Oak CC was elected secretary and treasurer.[92] By 1940 the WRRA had 15 affiliated clubs with three all-female clubs and the committee was largely composed of prominent female cyclists.[93]

While the Victorian period had witnessed a brief boom in women's racing, this period more generally witnessed a rapid growth of women's sport. Sport had been one of the most visible expressions of female modernity during the interwar years. An increasing number of women took up sport, reflecting the growth in physical culture more generally. Whereas women's sport in the pre-1914 period was largely confined to the middle classes in the south, after 1918 this expansion was across the classes and throughout the country. In cricket the southern-dominated and middle-class Women's Cricket Association was established in 1926, while the English Women's Cricket Federation – an amalgamation of the Yorkshire and Lancashire Women's Cricket Federations – was formed in 1934 and catered for working-class women in the north.[94] Other female sporting bodies also emerged, such as the Women's Amateur Athletic Association in 1921, which within four years had 25,000 members with over 500 clubs. The most spectacular example – albeit briefly – of the growth in women's sport during and after the war was football among the working classes. Around 150 teams emerged out of the factories across the country, the most famous being Dick, Kerr's Ladies from Preston. In 1921 the Football Association banned women from playing on affiliated grounds. Part of the reason given was it was felt 'that the game of football is quite unsuitable for female and ought not to be encouraged'.[95] These attitudes towards female participation in sport, a combination of medical ideas of moderation and social conventions, persisted throughout the interwar years.

Women's sport, however, became another space for the jostling between modern notions of femininity and traditional perceptions of a woman's place in society. In particular, racing meant making strenuous effort – the antithesis of Victorian womanhood. In 1919, 'Atalanta' had pointed out that it was contradictory to oppose women racing on bicycles on ethical, medical or aesthetic grounds when at the same time they were being encouraged to competitively swim and play golf and tennis, 'in which both the nervous and muscular strain is very severe'. This view was just an extension of the prejudice that once existed against women riding at all, she reflected.[96] During the 1920s there was 'a changing cultural image of femininity ... to subvert the old idea that athleticism was desexing women'.[97] In the pages of *Cycling* in the early 1920s, for example, there were regular images of European women both racing and wearing racing attire. While it was another example of Europe as 'the other' – who did things differently over there – it planted the idea that racing was not an alien activity for women.[98] Following the Great War, the shift towards athleticism and the idea of sporting competition crept into women's cycling in a number of forms, both formal and informal. In 1919, for example, it was reported that a group of men and women had held a 25-mile time trial in the north.[99] In addition, in 1921 it was noted that clubs were introducing specific female events; one Mrs W. H. Clee won the Versatile CC's 5-mile race for ladies, for example.[100] In that same year, 'without telling her parents', 'Paddy Radclyffe' was the only girl in a '25' mile time-trial handicap.[101]

Despite persistent medical opinion morphing into 'public fact', that women could cycle long distances was beyond dispute. From the late nineteenth century the Yorkshire Road Club had set fixed time standards for female members in 12-hour rides.[102] In 1908, Nellie Rodgers completed 356 miles in 24 hours, a few weeks after leaving hospital following a serious operation. In that same year, Kate Green twice rode over 300 miles in 24 hours. A member of the Leeds Road Club, she rode regularly against men in club events. Stancer – a long-time supporter of female cycling – had actually been a helper for Green and after riding over 300 miles he noted that she showed no signs of distress, which was a common complaint and justification to oppose women undertaking vigorous exercise.[103] To a certain extent, these Yorkshire pioneers reflected different attitudes to women's sport in the country, where attitudes in the south were more reflective of middle-class perceptions of femininity.[104]

On the back of her successful Ladies' Rally, in 1921 Mabel Hodgson organized a 106-mile all-female run from London to Findon near the Sussex coast. The 28 'hard-riding' 'feminine space-eaters', all 'rationally attired', set off from the Royal Albert Hall at 7.00 am, and aimed to return 12 hours later; the youngest member of the party was 17. While many women had previously achieved 'a century' this was the first open event organized for them on a large scale. Effectively, it was a race against the clock, not dissimilar to twenty-first-century sportives. Twenty-five out of the twenty-eight riders finished the run within 12 hours and received a certificate to acknowledge their achievement. The ride garnered some positive publicity. A photograph of the party made the cover of *Cycling*, giving further proof that women could organize such an event. It was noted the party was 'capably led by feminine marshals' who were ahead of schedule throughout and they finished as 'a compact group, showing no signs of having indulged in anything other than an enjoyable ride' and completed the ride.[105] That the run was favourably reported in *Cycling* was perhaps unsurprising. First, it was a CTC event, which gave it a certain respectability, and it was a body in which women had been members since its early days.

Reaction to women racing as opposed to long-distance journeys ridden at a relatively sedate pace was mixed. In 1925 the NCU had permitted track racing for women racing (they did not of course govern road racing), but it did not meet with universal approval. Track racing placed an emphasis on speed and hence a greater danger and chance of accidents. Even for the usually supportive *Cycling* – or at least its editor – the prospect of women injured when racing was a step too far. As much as what constituted the breaching of notions of feminine behaviour, it was perhaps the possibility of damage to cycling's wider reputation from images and reports of women riders injured while racing that shaped attitudes. To minimize risk, it advocated only three women racing in a heat instead of the usual four for men.[106] The prospect of men and women competing against each other in time trials provoked further conflicting views. Some men were for and some women against mixed racing; views which were largely based on ideas of assumed physiological differences between men and women. One correspondent, 'LTM', was more concerned that female road racing would grow and the publicity from it would kill off road racing altogether. 'Keep the finest of all sports English, and not like the French style,' he added.[107]

In general, however, many men were supportive – and perhaps many did not care either way. In sport more generally, men played a significant role in promoting and supporting women's sport. In particular, many fathers, brothers, boyfriends and husbands were the reason why many women took up cycling. Stancer and Bidlake, arguably the two most influential figures in cycling during this period, were enthusiastic supporters of all types of female cycling. A *Cycling* editorial on the 1921 London-Findon event had predicted that it 'furnishes material for the opening of a new page of cycling history' and the future acceptance of regular sporting competition for female cyclists.[108] The prospect of this growth in women racing, however, did not meet with universal approval among female cyclists. Writing in the early 1920s, 'Cora', 'an experienced lady rider of proved speed abilities', was adamantly opposed. Women racing was 'absurd' – 'cheapening womanhood' – as '[e]very natural instinct is against girls taking up racing' while girls should only be competitive in the field of protecting the weak from injury. She gladly admitted she was writing from a Victorian perspective, as someone who abhorred the prospect of open-mouthed women with 'foam-flecked lips' and perspiring bodies. Rather than cultivate speed, consistent riding should be the aim for women, reflecting wider ideas of moderation. It was as much a generational response, as one based on middle-class amateur sensibilities.[109] Similarly, in 1936, 'the well-known international sporting journalist' Stella Bloch, declared – based on a mixture of racial theory and eugenics – that '[e]nforced speed trials, whether on track or road, represent an excrescence on the fair face of our sport'. Racing was a 'crowd tickler' while touring represented 'one of the most delightful and health-giving of all pastimes' with attraction of discovering the countryside, she continued, 'For women that should be its definite purpose and end.'[110]

Some men continued to oppose women cycling for sport both on medical grounds and as regards what constituted ideas of femininity and hence their role in society. In 1938 Albert Lusty, a veteran official, after hearing Stancer speaking at the North Road Club dinner, had disagreed with his views on allowing women to participate in the sport. Lusty claimed that he would feel ashamed to allow his daughter to 'participate in any sport to such as extent as to reduce her to a state of utter collapse from physical exhaustion such as I have myself been on many occasions'.[111] Yet the wider social and medical context was changing and for younger female cyclists, these objections were becoming increasingly irrelevant as ideas of competition, health and fitness were more in keeping with ideas of modern womanhood.

Rosslyn Ladies' Cycling Club and other female pioneers

The most striking sporting example of the early post-war period was the formation of a female-only road racing club, Rosslyn Ladies' Cycling Club in 1922.[112] Typical of male banter (and prejudice), they were subjected to rumours about their sexuality (lesbians) or their sexual appetites (man-eaters) and their politics (anarchists).[113] The truth was more prosaic – something that reflected cycling's growing popularity among women at the time. While the club's first president was Lady de Freece, better known as the music-hall star Vesta Tilley, its members were mainly from working-class parts of North and East London, such as Forest Gate, Tottenham, Hackney and West Ham. They were described by Arthur Cook as 'a well-run band of real tough ladies who could do the miles and sometimes the speed of a good many male cyclists'. He was well qualified to give an opinion as he later married one of these 'hard-riding bunch of girls', Nellie Kimmance.[114] The exact motivations behind the club's formation are not known, but as many clubs did not accept women, an all-female club would have met the growing demand for not only cycling but also female sport. Its membership stabilized around 50 during the interwar years.[115] Other all-female clubs followed, but they were few in number. In 1933 another London club was formed, Ross Wheelers Ladies' CC, later followed by, Southern Ladies' Road Club.[116] In the following year, it was reported that an all-female club had been formed in Torquay, while another women-only club established in Birmingham had been inspired by Rosslyn Ladies.[117] The Heatherbell Ladies' CC of Dundee was formed 1929 with seven members. By 1934 it had 60, including three-times Scottish champion Mary Stewart, while Rosslyn Ladies only had 44. The 'Bells' had been quite indignant on hearing that Rosslyn Ladies had laid claim to be the only female-run cycling club in Britain. They also claimed that their activities – track racing, road racing, touring and social functions – 'excel in enthusiasm, execution and reputation, to no small degree, that of several men's clubs in Scotland'.[118]

Sport was at the heart of 'Rosslyn' from its origins and it held both open and closed time trials. By 1942 there were club records for 10, 25, 30, 50 and 100 miles, plus 12 hours for a single bicycle and 12 hours for a tandem. The club's annual open 12-hour time trial became a de facto English women's championship. In 1929 it was won by W. Stansell for a distance of 195 miles and 6 furlongs, and was described in a full-page report as a 'neck and neck struggle between the first three'.[119] The race, its times and locations had been advertised in the daily newspapers. It not only reflected a certain curiosity among the lay press about women's sport, but also drew criticism because of unwanted publicity for time trials and the damage that it may have caused to cycling more generally.[120] Club members raced across the country, including Ireland, and on the track. Nellie Kimmance won a silver teaspoon as a prize at Herne Hill in a Ladies Only track race, which she and Arthur were still using in the 1980s. But the social side was also important – the club had both racing and social secretaries – especially club runs on the weekends, which started from the Wilfred Lawson Temperance Hotel in Woodford. It also had its own camp in the village of Ugley in Essex on the A11, near to where it started its time trials.[121] Unsurprisingly perhaps as the membership of Rosslyn Ladies hardly changed, the number of married women increased. In 1942 around 60 per cent of the members were married, increasing to 75 per cent five years later.[122]

By 1930 it was noted that in general 'racing girls are increasing in number with great rapidity'.[123] A clutch of record-breaking female cyclists also emerged whose feats received a great deal of press coverage. Moreover, there were also four professional cyclists by 1938.[124] Their media profile represented a stark contrast from that of women cyclists in the early 1920s. These cyclists epitomized modern women. They were described in various terms as athletic and were frequently pictured in sporting outfits and typical cycle racing poses, which emphasized their sporting prowess. Moreover, in purely commercial terms, it highlighted the growth in the women's bicycle market. The first professional was Lillian Dredge. In 1935 she attempted the Land's End to John O'Groats record. Riding (and advertising) a Claud Butler bike, in 1936 she set a new 24-hour record at 342 miles. In 1934 she had taken part in an international massed-start race over 54.5 miles on Belgium *pavé*, but was forced to retire after falling off on a number of occasions.[125]

The formation of the WRRA, with its emphasis on record breaking, was part of this wider development. Stancer gave it his blessing[126] while Harry England, *Cycling*'s editor, thought it 'an enterprising move'. He urged, if in a slightly patronizing way, that the WRRA 'be run entirely by women' as '[t]hey understand the peculiarities and weaknesses of their own sex, and embarrassment, distress and resultant public indignation will be avoided if the new sport ... is run ... without the intrusion of the inconvenient male.'[127] To a large extent it was a southern-dominated organization with only two of its original members clubs outside the south.

From a medical perspective, with women's growing participation in sport symptomatic of the development of modernity, the female body was a central focus. In the early 1920s there was still a body of opinion that deemed female bodies unsuited for strenuous and competitive sport due to the strain it put upon them and how this may damage their main function in society to reproduce as well as removing feminine traits of grace and charm. Nevertheless, there was a gradual changing of medical opinion by the end of the 1930s, mainly due to the number of women now playing sport. One notable critic had been Adolphe Abrahams, a pioneer in sports medicine and later author of *The Human Machine* (1956).[128] He had initially opposed all forms of violent exercise for women and instead advocated sports such as golf, tennis and swimming, which characterized 'grace, lightness and rhythmicity'. Moreover, serious competition induced aggressiveness at the expense of a woman's 'softness and ductility'.[129] Yet by 1938, writing in *Cycling* on women's athletics, his tone had changed. He still opposed violent exercise for women, but he was now of the opinion that competitive cycling 'was not harmful to the nervous system'. Furthermore, highlighting how female cyclists were being perceived as serious athletes, Abrahams' article was illustrated with photographs of Jessie Springall in a two-piece bathing costume, so that Abrahams could examine her.[130] Two months later he wrote another article, this time on Lillian Dredge, following her End-to-End record, also dressed in her underwear. This time he compared her record (3 days, 20 hours 54 minutes) with Sam Ferris (2 days, 6 hours, 33 minutes) by giving a physiological explanation for the difference in times. He found that there was nothing amiss with her following her exertions.[131]

In 1939 Marguerite Wilson (1918–72) broke the female record for cycling from Land's End to John O'Groats. She covered the 870-mile 'End-to-End' route in 2 days 22 hours 52 minutes. Between 1938 and 1941 she held all 16 bicycle records of the Women's Road Records Association.[132] In 1939 she became a full-time professional with the Hercules Cycle and Motor Company, at the time the largest bicycle manufacturer in the world. She was one of six riders on its books.[133] They aimed to set new long-distance records in order to promote the company's bikes, usually as the fastest on the road. Moreover, Wilson was used for other publicity stunts to encourage more women to take up cycling.

In 1940 Wilson switched to another bicycle manufacturer, Claud Butler, highlighting that she knew her commercial value. She continued to set new records during the summer of 1940 and later received the Bidlake Memorial Prize for her achievements, becoming the first female cyclist to do so. Given the imaginative sobriquet, 'the Blonde Bombshell', it was perhaps unsurprising that bicycle companies exploited her striking appearance. As Zweiniger-Bargielowska points out there had been a shift towards glamour during the 1930s and Wilson personified a modern England of fashion- and health-conscious young women workers.[134] During the interwar years there was an increase in the use of female athletes in advertisements. More generally, the use of athletes by advertisers reflected the close link between sport and modernity. By employing a professional rider to advertise their products, Hercules were capitalizing on the growth in numbers of women cyclists. Wilson fitted the dominant image used by advertisers, which was 'without exception one of a young, attractive, fashionably dressed and feminine woman located within a modern setting'.[135] Inevitably perhaps a growing acceptance of the athletic merits of female cyclists was mixed with less modern male views. On the 1941 BBC programme *The Health Value of Cycling*, Alex Josey (KMD) claimed, 'As for cycling causing girls to have fat or round shoulders, or muscular legs – well it's not so. Look at Marguerite Wilson, the fastest girl cyclist in the country. She holds the 1,000 mile and other records and can even beat some of the men. But she is essentially feminine and I can tell you she has some very shapely legs.'[136]

Nevertheless, as a professional athlete, Wilson was subject to a strict training regime. Frank Southall, now the Hercules team manager, established a training camp at a hotel in Kingston-upon-Thames. At the camp Wilson spent around 4 to 5 hours on her bicycle, typically riding 75 miles a day. When the weather was inclement, she and fellow Hercules riders used rollers for indoor training. Her attempt on the Land's End to John O'Groats record was carefully planned. She was supported by two coaches, her team mate Harry 'Shake' Earnshaw, a doctor and a chef with a mobile canteen as well as a caravan, which she used for rest. While she stopped for meals, she was also handed food while still on her bike. She was also accompanied throughout by a film crew along with WRRA officials. Along the way, as per tradition, she was assisted by local cycling clubs whose presence was designed to boost her morale, although they were not allowed to pace her. In 1938 Lillian Dredge had set the End-to-End record at 3 days, 20 hours and 54 minutes, Wilson's time was 2 days 20 hours and 52 minutes. She then went on to complete the 1,000 miles in 3 days 11 hours and 44 minutes.[137]

Wilson's post-war successor was Eileen Sheridan (née Shaw). In 1954 she held all 21 professional cycling records on the books of the WRRA from 25 to 1,000 miles. The early post-war period was a time of success for British sportswomen more generally. In the four Olympics from 1948 to 1960, for example, women made up less than 15 per cent of the British team, but won 30 per cent of the medals. Moreover, the achievements of the likes of Anita Lonsbrough, Dorothy Hyman and Pat Smythe were recognized by the public through various annual awards. One such award was the BBC TV Sports Personality of the Year award, which was launched in 1954 and reflected a changing media landscape.[138] Rather than Sheridan's form of cycling, this new medium was more suited to other sports, such as athletics, tennis and swimming, which was reshaping and reinforcing a new and more modern sporting experience for spectators, that is, television viewers.

At half an inch under 5 feet, weighing 8 stones, Sheridan was known as 'the Mighty Atom' and had started cycling during the war, encouraged by her husband Ken. She later joined the CTC and Coventry Cycling Club. It was after the birth of her first son, Clive, in 1946, that she took up competitive cycling.[139] In 1949 and 1950 she won the women's BAR, which had been inaugurated in 1948.[140] Women competed at events over distances of 25,

50 and 100 miles and her average speed for 1949 was 21.827 mph.[141] She had an office job with a Coventry car dealership, but in 1951 she quit after winning the Bidlake Memorial Prize. By 1954 she had moved to Isleworth in Middlesex and, like Marguerite Wilson, she was trained by Frank Southall. At the time Sheridan was the only female member of the Hercules team of seven professional riders, but she was its main star.[142] Her annus mirabilis was 1954. In setting new End-to-End and '1,000' records of 2 days 11 hours 7 minutes and 3 days 1 hour, respectively, she beat the '1,000' time the legendary Australian Hubert Opperman had set in 1934.[143]

If Wilson represented a version of interwar modern femininity and glamour, then Sheridan's record breaking was conflated with post-war domesticity. In one British Pathé news item from 1956, titled 'Housewife Cyclist', emphasis was given to her having a family and her household duties, and combining these with training. The male presenter also made reference to how she had to win races in order to get back in time to do the housework.[144] Moreover, in the foreword to her autobiography, Frank Southall believed that 'an extra reason for the Hercules Company to sign Eileen on was her charming personality and petite feminine appearance'. He added that '[e]ven on her "End to End" ride, when any girl could be excused from appearing somewhat rough, her helpers remarked that through those three gruelling days she never lost her femininity'.[145] It's likely that Sheridan, as with most female athletes, paid little or no attention to media representations and male stereotypes, and instead just 'got on with the job'.[146]

Sheridan's achievements elicited different reactions. While her achievement was heralded in the cycling press, it received minimal attention from the national papers, highlighting more generally how cycling was a minority sport. In the *Daily Mirror* it appeared in 'Sport in Brief' and underneath an article about a men's record-breaking time trial.[147] Nevertheless, she became a marketable figure through her achievements and especially her eternally cheery demeanour. In addition to advertising Hercules bikes, she advertised other products such as Ribena.[148] Later, because she was professional and unable to return to the amateur ranks, she was paid for writing (or putting her name to) a column in *Cycling*.[149]

While full of praise for her achievements, Stancer was quick to point out that two of her professional records were not as fast as the amateur ones.[150] In addition, media reports represented traditional ideas of patriarchy. Her trainer, Frank Southall, was described as 'essentially a man's man' and 'can be ruthless' but 'his care for his little protégé and his management of that extra emotional something in a woman which to man is usually unpredictable, showed a sound psychological knowledge of Mrs Sheridan'.[151] Nevertheless, as a mother, Sheridan was further challenging notions of a woman's physical limitations. Further evidence of the changing medical debate around women's sport had been provided in a report on the 1952 Olympics, 'Sports in the Cultural Pattern of the World'. It found that sportswomen were stronger and more physiologically able to cope with physical exercise than had previously been thought. It concluded that even competitive exercise did not affect the menstrual cycles of trained athletes. Like Springall and Dredge, Abrahams carried out an examination of Sheridan (before her attempt at the End-to-End record), complete with photos of her posing in a swimming costume. This time he made no reference to the impact of strenuous competitive sport on the physiology of women's bodies. Instead, he outlined some of the psychological qualities necessary, which would have been anathema to proponents of femininity in the 1920s. These were 'patience to rise superior to monotony; courage to endure fatigue, hunger, thirst, heat, cold, discomfort of all kinds; resolution to push on and resist the clamant impulse to rest'. Abrahams uncharacteristically concluded, 'When all of these are associated with an exceptionally gifted physique, we have ... the mighty atom.'[152]

In 1958 the first world cycling championships for women took place in Reims in France. In a sporting sense it represented a shift to modernity, albeit a slow one when compared to that of the men, as the first world championships were held in 1893. Although at the sport's periphery, women had been one of the driving forces behind cycling's boom from the First World War up to the mid-1950s. Just as in the late nineteenth century, the bicycle acted as an emancipatory technology for women, but after 1918, instead of being confined to a small group of the middle classes, cycling was an activity for women of all classes. During this period, women had become key consumers, thus providing insights into ideas of gender, class and age in the formation of social identities.[153] The lifestyles and status of young women had increasingly changed between the years 1918 and 1950. Through their employment in greater in numbers, it gave them greater independence. It also gave them a greater sense of citizenship as they began to play a more prominent role in public life because they had more time and money to devote to their chosen lifestyles. To a certain extent, riding a bicycle reflected and reinforced these broader patterns.

CHAPTER 7

Cycling in the age of motoring

In an early scene from the 1960 film *Saturday Night and Sunday Morning*, the main character, Arthur Seaton, is riding home on his bike – a racer – along with many of his fellow workers, after finishing his shift at the Raleigh factory in Nottingham. It was a typical image of twentieth-century British working-class life. The film, based on Alan Sillitoe's 1958 novel, was part of the new wave of the British film industry, which brought to prominence working-class characters. Seaton was from an archetypal working-class background. He lived with his parents in a terraced house on cobbled stone streets, which he cycled over on his way to and from work. In the twenty-first century, bicycle races across the pavé of Flanders and France have been romanticized and lauded by the cycling cognoscenti, but for many working-class people the bone-jarring ride across cobbles was a fact of everyday life. Britain in the 1950s was still riven with class differences; however, the film shows that change was afoot in terms of the place of the bicycle in society. While Seaton, who represented the 'rough' working class, rode a bicycle, the husband of Seaton's lover – a member of the 'respectable' and socially aspiring working class – was riding a motorcycle. In addition, although the bicycle was the main form of transport, there were increasing numbers of cars on the road. However, there was a greater indicator of modernity and consumerism when Arthur arrived home. Here he finds his father rapt watching the television and is unable to distract him from the 'gogglebox'.

Television created a revolution in household leisure habits and not far behind was the car. This had a dramatic impact on cycling. Its place in British society was transformed, although for many this was not a positive development. By 1975 the cycling historian Andrew Ritchie was lamenting:

> [O]ur Ministry of Transport remains blind to the existence of bicycles ... there is not one indication that anybody in central government is

interested in them. ... Far from being accepted as a valuable contribution to economy, safety and tranquillity on the roads, bicycle-riders are the most disadvantaged group of road users.[1]

There was no doubting where he felt the blame lay. 'Where there should be initiative and action on the part of the authorities there is only ignorance and inertia. Cyclists go on being killed and nearly all of them are killed by cars.'[2] It was during this period – from the mid-1950s to the early 1970s – that there was a significant shift in cycling's status. From a mass activity, it became increasingly marginalized within society and culture more generally. In particular, cycling became subject to the forces of modernity and consumerism in post-war Britain which had 'never had it so good' and in which 'automobility' was central.

With reference to the period from 1951 to 1970, Brian Harrison has gone so far as to state, 'Cycling went into marked decline, and for a time seemed likely to fade out altogether.'[3] It is difficult to underestimate the car's impact on cycling, not only as a form of transport, but also as regards the change in psyche it engendered. Cars not only brought ideas of comfort and freedom, but also, more importantly and with greater long-term consequences, danger and risk for cyclists. However, cycling – in its various forms, as a recreation and as a sport – did not fade away, but instead there were vigorous attempts by various cycling bodies and organizations to adapt to this new environment. There was a shift away from cycling as a mass form of transport for adults to more specialist and niche pursuits and activities among particular markets and social groups with a greater attention on young people in particular due to the emergence of an assertive youth culture.

Motoring context

Cycling's adaptation to the growth of motoring was a necessary response to post-war consumerism. Between 1950 and 1973 the British economy grew at an average of 3 per cent per year as the purchasing power of average annual incomes doubled. 'The people of Britain had more money to spend, and more things to spend it on, than ever before.'[4] While in percentage terms spending on food and clothes fell, consumer expenditure increased on the home, especially in the form of consumer durables, and transport, that is, motor cars. Importantly, from 1957 credit on more favourable terms via hire purchase was made more widely available for skilled workers, fuelling the consumer boom. The proportion of cars bought using hire purchase increased from 9 per cent in 1953 to 25 per cent by 1969.[5]

It was from the mid-1950s to the mid-1970s that a motoring revolution took place. Vehicle and car ownership grew from 4.4 million and 2.3

million, respectively, in 1950 to 15 million and 11.5 million, respectively, by 1970 – a fivefold increase in cars alone in 20 years. In 1950, 16 per cent of households had cars; this rose to 52 per cent in 1971 and 65 per cent in 1990.[6] Cyclists were also now car owners and for many the car replaced the bicycle as a mode of transport. In 1963 in a survey of its members, the CTC found that 26 per cent owned a motor vehicle, which for some was changing the nature of recreational cycling. 'Cyclists Special' rail excursions ended in 1960, for example, while there was a growing number of cars with roof racks for bicycles.[7]

In some ways, these levels of car ownership highlighted how many people did not actually own a car. However, there was now an uncritical acceptance of the car as central to the economy and culture, which brought a shift in the national psyche. For many the late 1950s represented the beginning of a motor revolution due to the onset of mass car ownership and the role of the car as a transformative social agent. John Urry has regarded automobility as 'a way of life, an entire culture', which has had far-reaching consequences for the urban layout of cities, the industrial economy, mass consumption and the nature of life more generally.[8] Simon Gunn has offered a more nuanced interpretation of 'automobility'. Without denying its transformative qualities, he has argued that new technological innovations, such as the car, 'often operate alongside older practices rather than immediately replacing them, and tend likewise to be integrated with pre-existing social and institutional arrangements rather than overturning them'.[9] With reference to cycling's place in society it could be argued that this transformation was a much faster process.

The growth in motoring's economic significance was reflected in the visible changes in the British landscape. In 1958 for the first time the motor industry was producing one million cars per year and it also employed over half a million workers. As a consequence, successive governments underwrote heavy motorway building programmes. Britain's first motorway was also opened in 1958, the 8-mile long Preston bypass. The idea of the motorway had been present since 1920, but what made this new motorway different – and symbolic – was that it was for the 'exclusive' use of motor vehicles.[10] Ironically, cycling bodies had been calling for the building of such highways in the 1920s. Their building was in response to consumer demand and by 1973 Britain had over 1,000 miles of motorway, although less than West Germany, Italy or France.[11]

Rising levels of consumption, changing rhythms in the economy and the workforce were reshaping the routine of daily life, including leisure patterns, for millions of people. Football attendances, for example, began to decline as men devoted more time to leisure in the home, which could mean DIY activities or watching television – the main agency in the changing post-war leisure habits. The nature of tourism was changing. Caravanning in Britain and Europe was increasingly popular, while cheaper flights saw an exponential rise in holidays taken abroad. Structural changes in the workforce – with a decline in the traditional industries offset by a rise in employment in the service occupations – were both a product and an agency of consumerism.[12] Changes in work patterns, combined with those in leisure, were reshaping social attitudes more generally. In 1941 J. B. Priestley had argued that leisure activities should be worthy,[13] but this appeal to the values of Victorian rational recreation was now being increasingly lost in the surge to a greater democratization of leisure choices. In his 1962 seminal work, *Anatomy of Britain*, Anthony Sampson observed, 'The old non-conformist ethos, the sense of work being itself virtuous and self-improving, is being undermined by the new prosperity.'[14]

There was also a literal changing of the guard within the cycling fraternity as members of its establishment, who had been associated with halcyon days of the Victorian age and the interwar period, passed on. In 1956 both 'Wayfarer', William Robinson, aged 78 and Frank Urry, aged 77, died. Urry, known as 'The Nomad' had written for the *CTC Gazette* on his cycling tours and had been awarded an MBE for his services on the Ministry of Transport Advisory Council.[15] In 1962 – 'the last of the great Victorian cyclists' – George Herbert Stancer passed away. The previous year, Harry England, the long-time editor of *Cycling* (1929–59) died, aged 67, signalling a new direction in its style.[16]

By 1960 Britain itself was throwing off the shackles of Victorianism. A raft of legislation, which included the legalization of abortion and homosexuality as well as the abolition of the death penalty, pointed towards a more liberal society. As Philip Larkin said, 'Sex was invented in 1963. ... Between the end of the "Chatterley" ban; And the Beatles' first LP.' Larkin himself had been a keen cyclist in the interwar years and had spent much of his leisure time in Belfast and Hull cycling in the nearby countryside. But by 1964 even he had ditched his bike and symbolically bought his first car that same year.[17] One Larkin critic, Alvarez, prophetically perhaps, argued that his 1955 poem 'Church Going' had offered an 'image of post-war Welfare State Englishman: shabby and not concerned with his appearance; poor – he has a bike (who in the poem takes off 'My cycle clips in awkward reverence') not a car; gauche but full of agnostic piety; underfed, underpaid, overtaxed, hopeless, bored wry'.[18] Whatever the poem's literary merits, it highlighted how the bicycle was now part of a foreign country where they did things differently. As a result, cycling became increasingly seen as a quirky and niche activity, seemingly out of step with the modern world.

More individual choice brought greater individualism, and automobility was an index to this new affluence with the car a key agent in this process. As an icon of mobility, it became a marker for freedom and affluence. Instead of travelling to holiday coastal resorts by train or coach, for example, now people drove in their cars. More pertinently for workers, the car was – or pre-congestion, at least – represented a faster and more comfortable journey to work. Moreover, as places of work were located further away from residential areas, the bicycle as a mode of transport was increasingly impractical. While driving a car became associated with modernity, the bicycle retained a cloth cap and proletarian image. Ironically, by the late sixties, the only people who seemed to regularly ride a bike were Oxbridge students and left-wing intellectuals, such as Stuart Hall, perhaps to symbolize their support for the working classes. Paradoxically, this was at a time when the vast majority of the masses were giving up their bikes as a result of their growing taste for material goods. 'Affluence did not eliminate class differences: but it significantly reduced them. What the middle classes had, the working classes wanted, and often got,' according to Jim Obelkevich.[19]

Cycling in New Jerusalem

In the Victorian period cycling bodies had been at the forefront of improving the condition of roads and in the interwar years there had been a sustained and high-profile political campaign against cycle paths. Underlining its diminishing status, however, cycling was not an integral part of the vision for a New Jerusalem in post-war Britain. The early post-war period was a golden age for planning. Under the title 'building a better Britain', planning was seen as the answer to reconstruction and the built environment. The establishment of the welfare state and changes to the urban landscape reflected a continuity of thinking from the interwar years as much as a rapid departure after 1945.[20]

In 1941 many were already looking forward to post-war reconstruction, something that was exemplified by the *Picture Post*'s famous 4 January 1941 edition. A precursor of the Beveridge Report, its writers briefly outlined their post-war visions for education, the health service, work, agriculture and leisure. In his article on leisure J. B. Priestley promoted cycling in the countryside as a form of rational recreation, while on page 11 there was a picture of workers (men and women) leaving their factory, many on their bicycles. However, the bicycle was not part of this future. Maxwell Fry, later a leading modernist architect, called for greater integrated thinking and planning regarding the urban environment in his article 'The New Britain Must Be Planned'. While he criticized traffic congestion in towns and cities, his solution was for new straight and wide roads with a ring road for heavy traffic. The implication here was that cycling would not be part of this New Britain.

This was perhaps unsurprising as by the 1960s the idea of a 'car-owning democracy' was beginning to take hold in the public discourse. In April 1960 the Labour MP Patrick Gordon, for example, believed that '[w]ith much greater vigour, we must rebuild our whole environment of working and living in terms of the motor car'.[21] By the early sixties, cars were 'ceasing to be simply about transport, convenience, and social status; they were becoming structured deeply into the fabric of everyday life'.[22] The uncritical acceptance of the car's primary role in modern life necessitated – in the minds of planners – a separation of 'pedestrian movement from road traffic and the separation of housing, commercial and industrial into dedicated estates'.[23]

By the early 1960s the motoring revolution and the policies of successive governments to feed consumer desires to own a car led to the reshaping of the urban environment. The Beeching Report of 1963 had aided this process. In closing down many railway lines, it ultimately placed more emphasis on road transport and building roads. At the centre of urban planning rhetoric was how to make cities more accessible to the motor car. The period between 1965 and 1975 witnessed a major phase of motorway building plus urban motorways, such as the London Ringway scheme, the Aston Expressway and Spaghetti Junction in Birmingham and the Glasgow Inner Ring Road.[24] During the same period, the Coventry ring road was built. Previously the home of the bicycle, but now a major car manufacturing centre, the city ring road was not built with cycling in mind, but instead the flow of motor traffic. The primacy of the car though continued to be uncritically presumed with other forms of transport, such as walking and the bicycle, seen as adjuncts rather than alternatives to the car. This phenomenon was not unique to Britain. By the early 1970s the bicycle was even disappearing from traditional cycling hotspots like Amsterdam and Copenhagen.[25]

The political context to the changing urban landscape could be traced back to Colin Buchanan's 1963 report, *Traffic in Towns*, which according to Simon Gunn, reflected two competing tensions: modernism and traditional British conservationism.[26] The Buchanan Report was essentially concerned with the damage unregulated car use would do to the British landscape and environment, but its solution was modernist in its vision. It recommended a radical reconstruction of the urban landscape to cope with rising traffic levels, including 'streets in the sky', which was a vertical separation of traffic and pedestrian walkways. Moreover, the report was later criticized for how it prioritized the accessibility of vehicles in urban areas over the mobility of pedestrians.[27] The report was never implemented and its aim to regulate urban traffic in some form was cast aside by successive governments in thrall to not only Britain's now deeply embedded car culture and the now economically crucial motor industry, but also the road lobby. Road building continued apace without any coherent strategy.[28] Nevertheless, as Gunn has argued, the Buchanan Report put the issue of the environment on the political agenda (see Chapter 8) as the 'attempt to solve the problem of traffic congestion in the early 1960s brought environmental concerns in the form of noise, visual blight, pollution, and destruction of the historic fabric to the forefront of public and policy attention'.[29]

Furthermore, by the end of the 1960s, the destruction and redevelopment of city centres created a backlash and a nostalgia for the urban and industrial past. Planners had failed to take into consideration local factors. Instead, they had assumed all urban dwellers would need good housing and services and all policy initiatives would converge in creating a modern society.[30] For cycling the impact of post-war planning initiatives for the urban environment had important consequences. In particular, it reinforced and institutionalized its marginal role and separate status as a leisure and transport activity; for local and central government officials the discourse of planning was now overwhelmingly dominated by meeting the needs of an exponentially increasing car-owing population.

Nevertheless, while this emphasis on faster, mechanized transport, embodied by the individualism of the car, represented the general thrust of post-war British planning, cycling was not completely absent. Indeed, the new towns of Stevenage and Harlow had cycle tracks incorporated into their design. A product of the 1946 New Towns Act, new towns, according to Helen Meller, were the most original of all town planning ventures post 1945. Between 1946 and 1976 30 new towns were built beginning with Stevenage, Harlow and Basildon and culminating in Milton Keynes. By the twenty-first century over 2 million people lived in new towns. Incorporating the ideal of Ebenezer Howard's Garden Cities, new towns were part of post-war policy to create a more democratic and socially integrated nation. The new town ideal represented another modern vision of post-war Britain, based on the ideas of Patrick Abercrombie. At the centre of new town policy was the domestic ideal, a belief in home and community life. Yet this new approach to urbanism was to be based on 'the ease of movement of the motorcar' as post-war transport planners had assumed that the circulation of traffic via arterial roads was vital to the nation's economic health.[31] Ultimately, the emphasis on the private car would undermine attempts in establishing a new local, urban and community-based culture in the new towns and instead among residents there was a preference for and consolidation of suburbia.[32]

The journey to work was essential to the new town environment. Initially, it was perceived in the form of four options, each dependent on the length of the journey: first, walking, then cycling, next public transport and failing that the private motor car as the ideal – and idealized – option.[33] Reflecting modernist tendencies, the smooth movement of traffic was to lead to a separation of its different forms: pedestrian, cycling and motor transport. As a result, this notion of segregation established the principle that cyclists should be separated from roads used by cars, not just in new towns but also in future cycle traffic projects. The cycle paths built during the 1930s had been opposed by the cycling lobby on the basis that it would marginalize cycling. Opposition to cycle paths had grown less voluble from cycling authorities after 1945. Instead there was a grudging acceptance of them, ironically though an intensive period of building new paths for cyclists did not take place until the 1970s.

Stevenage acquired a cycle track network largely through the efforts of Eric Claxton, its engineer for new town planning. Claxton's professional interest in cycling dated back to the 1930s when he had been a junior engineer at the Ministry of Transport, and had worked on the London cycle paths, which the cycling lobby had vehemently opposed. He had been unimpressed with the campaign, but equally unimpressed with the paths' quality and the lack of safety. Stevenage, therefore, offered an opportunity for him to rectify these errors. Work on Stevenage's cycling network began in 1955, the same time as the town's primary road network. It eventually extended to 40 kilometres around the town. Claxton had modelled his cycleways on those in the Netherlands. He was a keen cyclist himself and had witnessed the high volume of traffic on Dutch cycle tracks. Segregation was at the core of the design. The cycleways were 12 feet wide with 7-foot-wide footways separated by grass strips and the system included cycle and pedestrian bridges and Dutch-style underpasses. Cyclists were also provided with their own segregated junction as the road had been elevated by two metres and the cycleway lowered by 1 metre. The design therefore allowed for a safer cycling experience.[34]

One of Claxton's aims in designing a holistic transport system was to actually speed up the motor traffic, which in 1968 averaged 20 mph in central Stevenage, although he claimed that cycling journeys were still quicker.[35] However, his ambition for Stevenage to adopt a Dutch cycling culture did not materialize in the face of a now well-established car culture. In 1975 it was claimed that out of the town's population of 69,000, 15,130 owned cars with 14,030 owning bicycles; 12,540 cars were used for the daily commute to work, but only 4,200 bicycles were ridden on the daily journey to work or school.[36] The Stevenage cycle tracks, therefore, unintentionally reinforced the growing marginalization of cycling in contrast to the growing cultural and economic power of the car. New roads were primarily designed for the use of cars; cyclists would just have to adapt to this new reality, either get off the road or accept the potential dangers.

As a consequence, the utility of cycling declined dramatically during this period. In 1949 over a quarter of Britain's population over 16 used a bicycle, and of these more than two-thirds used it more than once a week.[37] In 1952 cyclists accounted for more than a tenth of all passenger miles (14.3 billion miles), but by 1972 this figure – 2.5 billion miles – had declined to 1 per cent. By contrast, over the same period, journeys on motorized vehicles (cars, taxis and motor cycles) had increased nearly sevenfold, from 33.6 billion to 202.6 billion miles.[38] Between 1952 and 1955 there had been a slight drop in the popularity of cycling among all classes, but this decline would be more dramatic due to the increase of traffic on the road.[39] The impact on the governing bodies was even more dramatic, especially touring. In 1961 membership of the CTC had dropped to 24,000.[40] By 1970 it stood at 18,000.[41] In 1966, due to rising costs, it symbolically moved its headquarters out of London to Godalming in Surrey.[42] At its first AGM, the British Cycling Federation recorded that its membership was 20,918, noting solemnly that the post-war decline had continued and that this figure compared with a total of 66,528 for the NCU alone in 1950.[43] Membership continued to steadily fall. In 1971, with the total now at 10,369, it was commented that there had been no increase in BCF membership for 21 years. During the seventies the membership actually climbed to reach 17,535 in 1980 before again falling back to 14,350 in the mid-1980s.[44]

Club life was also affected drastically. At the Comet Cycling Club, for example, where club runs had previously been the fulcrum of club life, during the fifties there was a shift away from pleasure cycling and towards more emphasis on sport, which was accelerated due to the growing risks associated with cycling on the roads. Arthur Cook felt, 'If it could be said that in earlier days the body of cycling clubs was the runs side and racing merely the tail-end, by 1960 it was the tail that was wagging the cycling body.' As pleasure cycling itself declined, many cycling cafes closed down as a result, which meant that there was even less incentive to organize club runs. Cook added, 'There were still plenty of cyclists still touring and riding their bikes for the sheer hell of it but the golden days of large friendly groups riding together had passed.'[45] The CTC, to encourage more people to join, had submitted to the desire for sport among its membership. In 1965 it eventually established a BAR for CTC time triallists, something it had rejected as far back as the 1920s.[46] It was another small chipping away at the façade of Victorianism and even cycling's conservative bodies were having to adapt to modern tastes and values.

Rethinking cycling

The industry and cycling bodies were not unaware of these wider social and economic changes. At the BCF's first AGM, it was stated that 'this long term trend [decline in membership] is likely to continue unless everybody interested in the sport and pastime of cycling does their best to spread its popularity'.[47] Sales in bicycles also fell consistently during this period. The industry was weakened and marked by mergers. Even in 1960, Raleigh, then the largest manufacturer of British bikes, lost its independence when it was taken over by TI. Because of these economic pressures, marketing began to be accepted and the market research industry rapidly expanded. Instead of selling what they produced, as happened in the past because cycling was a mass activity, bicycle companies now had to find out who their customers were and what they actually wanted.[48] This new approach ultimately intensified a process of fragmentation in the bicycle and cycling market.

The British Cycle and Motor Cycle Industries Association, which represented the cycling's industry's interests, embarked on a number of publicity schemes and initiatives in order to turn sales around. Between 1956 and 1961, the association created a National Bicycle Publicity Scheme, before reviving it in 1964, while in 1960 a sub-committee on cycle sport was set up with the object of stimulating interest in sport and touring.[49] As a consequence, usually through a levy on bicycle sales, these committees and schemes financed numerous public relations and marketing initiatives, thus embracing modernity in an attempt to transform cycling's cloth cap image.[50] Public relations itself was a relatively new profession. Its emergence in Britain has been associated with Stephen Tallents during the interwar years, and in 1948 he was elected the first president of the Institute for Public Relations.[51] Public relations was essentially concerned with the controlled and organized flow of information through media channels. During the 1955–75 period, the media changed radically as television gradually displaced newspapers as the main advertising medium. Cycling had not been absent from television screens (see also Chapter 10). As early as July 1956 ITV broadcast the Junior Cyclists Competition. It was made in partnership with the CTC and gave young cyclists the opportunity to win a cycling tour of France. In 1957 Eileen Sheridan fronted ITV's Junior Cycling League. It ran for four episodes in the summer and as the forces of affluence had yet to reshape ideas of childhood and youth, it was educational in tone, with 'young viewers invited to join the League and to learn how to make the most of this popular sport'.[52]

Cycling public relations initiatives had included the industry's sponsorship of the CTC York Rally in August 1960, used to mark the British Cycle and Motor Cycle Industries Association's golden anniversary. It was attended by around 20,000 to 30,000 people with attractions that included a 'Golden Girl of Cycling Competition'; a children's fancy dress competition; and a road race between Coventry – the home of the association – and York.[53] Despite the attempts to modernize, remnants of Victorianism still remained within cycling. To gain more publicity for the rally, it was intended to broadcast the religious service from York Minster that any cyclists could attend, but it was eventually decreed that 'it was not correct to secure publicity through the medium of a church service'.[54] Despite its investment in marketing, the chairman of the Joint Bicycle Publicity Committee expressed a desire to 'see some fireworks'. However, sales were still sluggish as cycling still struggled to adapt to its new environment.[55]

In 1965 the association hired a PR company, Planned Public Relations Limited, to undertake a National Publicity Campaign. The following year the British Cycling Bureau – set up to deal with cycling's media profile – was launched at a London restaurant with much fanfare, and included Mary Rand, Larry Adler and Joe Loss, plus Miss World riding a bike.[56] The chairman of the Joint Bicycle Publicity Committee, Victor Davies, the managing director of Viking Cycles Ltd., announced that the 'stage was set for a dramatic reappraisal of the bicycle'.[57] He would be proved correct in this prediction, but not in the way he wanted. The following year Viking went into receivership and Davies was forced to resign from the association.[58]

In 1962 the BCF appointed local public relations officers. It believed that '[t]he key to the lack of publicity is the need for hard, continuous, but patient work by local PROs who understand how to find and put over a story', along with a closer relationship with newspapers. In particular, it was insisted that '[r]iders must become personalities' in order to heighten the sport's profile. In addition, careful attention should be paid to the televising of cycling, selecting suitable venues at suitable times, with more road racing taking place on street circuits on Saturdays to maximize audiences. There was even the suggestion of approaching Football League clubs to stage cyclo-cross races.[59]

Three years later in 1965, the BCF stated that 'in an age of increasing leisure, when there is a professional attitude to the presentation of entertainment and recreation, the BCF must take steps to present itself to clubs and the public in general'. As a result, it appointed the Bureau of Commercial Information Ltd. to carry out publicity.[60] During the 1950s and 1960s, the youth market had been the main target group in an attempt to arrest the decline in sales, as it was 'believed at present that teenagers offer the best hope of a substantial market recovery, particularly if cycling can be given a new image'.[61] In its attempt to reach young people, the industry embraced television advertising. In 1960 for one commercial it adopted the jingle, 'Bike it, you'll like it' with 'an attractive girl's voice speaking ... in an engaging and convincing manner' then followed by bicycle bells with teenagers cycling in the background.[62] In 1969 another proposed initiative to capture the 'junior end of the market' was a schoolboy relay ride from Land's End to John O'Groats under the aegis of the English Schools Cycling Association.[63]

Even the normally conservative CTC was targeting the youth market. In 1959 it appointed a special Recruitment Committee to use methods of propaganda and publicity in order to arrest declining membership numbers.[64] In 1963, as part of a wider package of proposed reforms, it was proposed to change the name of the club's journal, the *CTC Gazette*, (eventually) to *Cycletouring*, in a bid 'to attract the new reader and get away from the "Victorian image"'.[65] It later included in a revamped Memorandum of Association a clause 'to stimulate by all means interest and participation of young persons in cycling'. The CTC later admitted failure. A 1965 report on its future policy concluded that there was no large potential field of new cyclists in the waiting, while younger riders were not interested in touring.[66]

Unsurprisingly, there was a major problem in this desire for youth: cycling's image had particularly suffered among young people. Britain's post-war youth culture had partly been a product of changing tastes and attitudes towards leisure. The emergence of youth cultures, in the form of mods and rockers, both reflected and reinforced a post-war decline in deference, which was further highlighted by a rejection of the bicycle for motor bikes and scooters. In his 1966 study of adolescent boys of East London, Peter Willmott found that one of their main activities revolved not around bicycles, but instead around motor bikes and scooters, in terms of riding, repairing and talking about.[67] In her 1967 study of Scottish boys and girls, aged 15–19, Pearl Jephcott found that this group of teenagers had different leisure habits to the ones she had studied in 1950. There were few references to cycling, and instead, there was a growth in home-based leisure through watching television and listening to music, especially pop, while other popular activities included cinema going, dancing and café. Only two-thirds of the group belonged to any formal leisure groups, and it was noted membership of cycling clubs was low.[68] Tellingly, in Sampson's study of British leisure habits in 1962, there was no reference to cycling, and along with ten-pin bowling and bingo, motor racing was identified as one of the growing pursuits.[69] Nevertheless, despite these competing pressures and its image problem, for many children learning to ride a bicycle was seen as a rite of passage, and cycling continued to have a presence in British society.

In addition to attempts at changing its proletarian image and at appealing to new markets, the cycling industry was forced into rethinking the design of the bicycle itself. One such new innovation was the Moulton bicycle, which was invented by Alex Moulton and launched in the winter of 1962. Bruce Epperson has argued that 'the greatest achievement of the Moulton was not its engineering, but its success in helping England's bicycle industry transition from a pre-war emphasis on standardization, simplicity, functionality, and utility into a new consumerist era of youth, allure, glamour and fund'.[70] In this sense, the Moulton would come to symbolize how the cycling industry aimed to adapt to the car's cultural supremacy through the need to reinvent itself.

The Moulton was a small-wheeled utility bicycle with a suspension, but without the diamond frame. It was claimed, from an engineering perspective, that it was the most radical design since the invention of the safety bicycle. Moulton, a member of the gentry, came from a family of engineers and had initially made his mark in inventing a new suspension for the Morris Minor, and it was actually in the automobile industry where his engineering skills were most widely applied. He also enjoyed riding a bike and adapted the principles of suspension to the bicycle. He had been impressed with the success of the Mini and set out to reinvent the bicycle as the Mini had redefined the image of the car.[71] The Moulton's wheels were 16 inches in diameter, whereas a regular road bicycle was around 26 to 27 inches, and weighed 22 to 32 pounds depending on the model. It was designed to give a lower centre of gravity, which would make the bicycle safer for the rider.[72] To give this 'funny little bike' credibility and to prove the worthiness of the design, in December 1962 a Moulton, ridden by John Woodburn, broke the Road Records Association's Cardiff to London record. He covered the 162 miles in 6 hours and 43 minutes. In ensuing advertisements, it was stated, 'All Moulton bicycles have the identical frame and suspension system.'

By 1964 Moulton had established itself as the second largest frame builder and manufacturer in the country and was producing up to 1,000 new bicycles a week.[73] Raleigh later made their own small-wheel bicycles. Despite their inferior quality compared to the Moulton, they proved to be a boon for the domestic market. In 1967 total sales had been 587,580 of which small-wheeled bikes accounted for 108,141; the following year the respective figures were 624,377 and 223,910, with the small-wheel bicycles almost outselling conventional adult ones (229,705), and mainly accounting for the 10 per cent increase in sales.[74]

Reynar Banham, both a critical advocate of and an enthusiast for pop art and culture, particularly appreciated the modernist tendencies of this designer bike. 'A historian of the immediate future', he was not only a pioneering architectural and design critic, but also regarded 'Pop' as 'the basic cultural stream of mechanized urban culture'.[75] For him the Moulton – the mini-bike – was comparable with the other sixties classic design, the Mini-Minor, and captured, through technological innovation, the aesthetic of modern pop culture. One of its innovative design features, he identified, had created a minor cultural revolution – a ring of polythene on the chainwheel, which kept oil off clothes. It meant that businessmen could ride the Moulton in a suit without trouser clips – previously a 'badge of public shame'. As a consequence, it signalled the disappearance of the working-class cyclist, and this 'thinking man's vehicle for central London' would usher in cycling for 'middle class urban radicals who would eventually come to rely on advanced-technology bicycles to meet their transport needs'.[76] Banham's prophesy was not fulfilled, but it pointed to how people would begin to think differently about cycling later in the twentieth century.

Cycling's appropriation of pop culture as a way of adapting to the new environment was further highlighted with the invention of the Raleigh Chopper. As a response to the growth of motoring, manufacturers, such as Raleigh, increasingly looked upon – and marketed – bicycles as consumer goods rather than a form of personal transportation. The development of the Raleigh Chopper in 1970 epitomized this cultural shift. The Chopper, with its small front wheel and high handlebars, had been designed in response to a craze for American dirt-track roadster bikes that emerged in the late 1960s, and was partly inspired by the Harley Davidson motorbikes in the film, *Easy Rider* (1969).[77] To a certain extent, the invention of the Chopper also reflected the changing relationship between adults and children. Children's behaviour to and relationship with their parents differed as the previous dictum of 'children should be seen and not heard' was replaced with children who found it easier to talk to parents. In addition, while the teenage consumer was not specific to the post-war period, more teenagers had more pocket money to spend.[78] From the late 1960s, an increasingly aggressive consumer culture ousted a traditionally participatory and self-improving culture, which resulted in a decline in deference. Through marketing and the media, especially television, the children's market was targeted with ever more sophistication and determination. Marketing messages aimed at children promoted ideas of individualism and freedom, with an emphasis on style and fashion, which the Chopper represented. This development marked a break from a childhood marshalled by the adult voice, one in which, argues Gary Cross, even 'toys had been instruments to train children to be adults', but now became objects – such as bicycles – that 'gave vent to a world of children's imagination in which adults had no real place'.[79]

The National Cycling Proficiency Scheme

The establishment of the National Cycling Proficiency Scheme (NCPS) in 1958 was a further indication of the changing place of children in post-war society. By 1975 three million children had passed its test.[80] The success of the NCPS highlighted how cycling was still a popular leisure pastime among children, and learning to ride a bike continued to be a rite of passage for kids, as well as how cycling responded to post-war society's modernizing and consumerist impulses. By the end of the 1960s, cycling, previously something associated with adults, was increasingly perceived as a leisure activity for children with the bicycle as a fun, leisure product. The NCPS was also a classic example of large-scale citizenship during the era of the post-war consensus. It expressed a social-democratic patriotism through a cross-class culture of activism. Voluntary organizations, such as the NCPS, reflected a broader urge among planners to make citizens participants rather spectators and in this case, through the message of safety, 'to promote recreational citizenship' through a particular educational scheme. Nevertheless, these efforts to forge 'a modern code of belonging' were complicated by affluence and modernity.[81]

Due to fears over the safety of children, the NCPS was also a product of contemporary ideas regarding welfarism. Similar concerns had not been restricted to cycling. Boxing, for example, was later banned in schools in light of contemporary medical debates over the sport's safety.[82] Just as boxing became perpetually linked with danger due to medical debates over brain damage, cycling was becoming increasingly associated with danger on the roads. It was this assumption, above all others, that directed policy towards cycling with one outcome being the establishment of the NCPS.

The NCPS, therefore, reflected broader interventions in the lives of children from the mid-twentieth century. Laura King has argued that from the 1930s through to the 1950s there was an increasing use of political rhetoric in which children were seen as future citizens.[83] State interventions were further accelerated as a product of changing post-war demographics due to the baby boomer generation. It was predicted that casualty rates would increase as it was expected that this generation would soon be taking up cycling.[84] In addition, the NCPS highlighted changing ideas of childhood in the post-1945 period. Mathew Thomson has argued, 'From the Second World War to the 1970s saw much of the groundwork for a segregation of the child from the outside world, particularly, the urban world.'[85] In a number of ways the NCPS reflected the paternalism of the post-war settlement with its emphasis on education, 'the inculcation of responsibility' and how it 'managed freedom'.[86] Not only did this period see an increased concern over the safety of children, but there was also an idealization of home and family and also new initiatives for the provision of child-specific environments.

Fears over the safety of children were not new. Concerns over walking and cycling on the roads had stretched back to the First World War. In 1917 London 'Safety First' Council launched its first campaign to educate children about road safety.[87] Cycling bodies and manufacturers – mainly for commercial reasons – had begun to pay more attention to children's cycling during the interwar years as it grew in popularity. In 1929, for example, some school children could ride bicycles purchased under an educational grant scheme.[88] For the cycling bodies and manufacturers this shift in perception created a conundrum because, as Thomson has argued, during the post-war years the danger and fear of traffic was one of the factors that had begun to limit children's freedom.[89] As a result, there was a tension between encouraging children to cycle and a growing concern over their safety on roads.

These anxieties also need to be set against a prevailing discourse in which it was now incumbent on cyclists to make themselves safer on roads despite cycling becoming increasingly dangerous due to the driving of motorists. Even during the interwar year there had been attempts to ban children from cycling. In 1929 the *CTC Gazette* argued that concerns expressed over children under the age of 12 riding bicycles was just the latest 'anti-cycling' scare found in the national press.[90] In 1931 the first edition of the *Highway Code* had included a section on children, to warn them 'of the dangers of the road and teach them how to avoid them',[91] while two years later the National Safety Congress recommended cycling lessons for children.[92] Despite its title, cycling bodies strongly believed that the National Safety Congress was a pro-motoring front due to the make-up of its membership, policies and statements over safety, which put the onus of accidents on non-motoring forms of transport instead of on the drivers of cars who were causing the accidents. In 1935 there had also been complaints over the safety risks in carrying children on bicycles, although at the time neither the Home Office nor the Ministry of Transport saw it necessary to prevent children being carried on a bicycle in basket.[93]

Nevertheless, there was growing state interest, both at national and at local levels, in regulating children cycling. 'Instruction of school children in Road Safety Matters' was one of the items in the House of Lords' 1938 Alness Report on the prevention of road accidents. A year earlier, a Children's Safety Committee, appointed by the minister of transport, had recommended that children under seven years of age should be prohibited from cycling on public roads. The cycling lobby – both press and trade – vigorously opposed the recommendation.[94] Local education authorities also began to take a more proactive role in regulating children cycling. Some attempted to introduce mandatory cycle permits for children, who in order to enable them to cycle to and from school would have to pass an examination to gain a licence.[95] The NCU was more favourable to educational initiatives. In 1938, on examining a booklet by the London County Council, titled, 'Road Safety and the London Child', its general committee considered that the best method of teaching road sense and achieving road safety was 'to educate children in the correct use of the road', but not to attempt to prevent them from cycling to school, as in some local education authorities such as Essex, Blackpool and Hendon. Instead the cycling authorities, in association with the National Safety First Association, aimed to develop further initiatives regarding road safety among school children.[96]

The assumptions on the need to educate and train child cyclists grew after 1945. In 1946, for example, it was reported that Whitby schoolchildren would not be allowed to cycle unless they passed a test.[97] In 1951 there had even been an (unsuccessful) government proposal to ban children (along with anyone over 70) from cycling on the roads.[98] A year later accident levels were at their worst in 10 years with an increase from 15,000 to 216,493. In December alone 3,000 cyclists had been victims with 404 of them children under the age of 15.[99] Later, in 1954 the police were given powers to inspect and test cycle brakes and it was an offence to permit a child to use a cycle with inefficient brakes,[100] while a year later, an MoT sub-committee on child cyclists was seriously considering some form of compulsory testing for child cyclists.[101]

These initiatives and proposals regarding schoolchildren reflected a prevailing mood among the middle classes. In 1953 a *Guardian* editorial, in typically paternalistic terms, had fully endorsed these schemes, highlighting the dangers of children cycling on the roads. It pointed out how a boy [there was no mention of a girl] who owns a bicycle is 30 times more likely to be killed in a road accident than one who does not. The *Guardian* also supported the idea that children should be prevented from riding a bike to school until they had passed the test, while further advocating compulsory testing for children under the age of 18 who, like learner drivers, should display L-plates.[102] In 1953 Dr W. P. Alexander, the secretary of the Association of Education Committees, told the National Safety Congress – in hyperbolic terms – that 'it was criminally irresponsible for parents to allow their children to ride their cycles without training'.[103] In the following year, at the Royal Society for the Prevention of Accidents' (RoSPA) previously (the National Safety First Association) annual conference, Dr Eric James, high master of Manchester Grammar School, declared that by buying their children a bicycle parents were putting a lethal weapon in their hands.[104]

Before the NCPS, there had been earlier safety training initiatives. Soon after the war, road safety became a permanent item on the agendas of cycling bodies and they began working with road safety groups. Faced with the changing climate, the cycling bodies had little option to accommodate, if not embrace, the now deeply embedded assumption that cycling on increasingly congested roads was a dangerous practice for children. Whatever their misgivings and sense of injustice, in order to gain respectability from public opinion makers they needed to encourage the education of young cyclists. In 1947 the NCU organized a road safety competition for school children, which took place at the Eastbourne cycling rally in collaboration with the local Road Safety Campaign Committee.[105] Manufacturers also became increasingly proactive in supporting local road safety schemes and competitions, including offering free bicycles.[106] In 1955 Raleigh had run a fortnight cycling course for children in Birmingham, which was repeated in Slough. The firm had provided training equipment and technical instructors in bicycle maintenance, while the CTC provided instruction in riding.[107]

The main force behind cycling safety for children was RoSPA itself. In 1947 RoSPA, with financial support from the MoT, introduced its first national training scheme 'in roadmanship for young cyclists'. It consisted of a Cycling Safety League and a cycling proficiency test. To qualify for a badge and certificate of proficiency children had to pass tests in road safety and courtesy, mastery over the machine, riding proficiency and ability to adjust the cycle to a good riding position and maintain it in good order.[108] In 1952 membership of the Cycling Safety League stood at 56,400. By 1955 100,000 children had passed the cycling proficiency test with over 500 local authorities running cycling schemes for schoolchildren.[109] In 1956 the MoT, in collaboration with the RoSPA, launched 'Mind the Child', a three-month national awareness campaign. It had three main aims: (1) to start more training schemes for child cyclists and step up road safety training for children; (2) to impress on parents their responsibility for bringing up their children to behave sensibly on the roads; and (3) to persuade other road users to show more consideration for children. However, it still did not prevent the relevant government minister ruling out the possibility of an age limit on child cyclists.[110] In 1957, a booklet, *Safe Cycling*, was produced, which was the first attempt by the government to give advice on the technique of safe cycling, such as right turns.[111] In 1959 Lancashire County Council appointed its first road safety officer. He had been earlier praised for introducing the safe cycling rally for school children, which had been widely copied.[112]

While the provision of the scheme was shared between schools and local authorities, it was permissive. The minister of transport, however, had wanted a scheme to cover the entire country. As a consequence, the NCPS was launched in 1958. The NCPS had been the product of a working party set up by the MoT, which included representatives from the Association of Education Committees, the National Union of Teachers, RoSPA, the Standing Joint Committee on Cycling and the British Cycle Industries Association.[113] A ministry grant enabled RoSPA to pay for 11 training officers who promoted the scheme on a national basis. Fears for the safety of children over traffic more generally were complemented by the growth of Tufty Clubs, which were created by RoSPA.[114] The Tufty Club was formally launched in 1961 and was dedicated to training school children about road safety more generally. In 1959 road safety had been included in a Ministry of Education handbook for primary school teachers. During the sixties and seventies, the club ran television campaigns on this theme. By 1962 more than 60,000 children had joined with 2,000 clubs formed by 1966. In 1972 there were two million members and 10,000 clubs by the following year.[115]

How did the cycling establishment react to the NCPS? Harry England, the editor of *Cycling and Mopeds*, a defender of the rights of cyclists from the interwar period, declared it as 'the greatest opportunity ever for cycling clubs' and the various cycling bodies. It was a pragmatic statement, reflecting the change in cycling's status. He added that 'the organized cyclists of the country should be leaders in this training and testing campaign'.[116] 1958 was declared the 'Child Cyclist's Year', and in its first edition of that year, *Cycling and Mopeds* cover picture showed the RAF 'Safe Cycling League' from Tern Hill, Shropshire. It was claimed that 'the local village children are also anxious to join the league and win efficiency certificates'.[117] Bicycle shops also signed up as the 4,000 shops that displayed the scheme's red triangle offered free bike check-ups.[118]

The manufacturers had provided financial support for safety campaigns and were part of various committees, although there was an ulterior motive behind this due to falling sales. As far as the industry was concerned, young people were now a major market and in encouraging them to participate in the NCPS they could 'direct the publicity into keeping them as cycle users for as long as possible'.[119] In order to maintain this momentum, by the mid-1960s the RoSPA National Safe Cycling Committee was proposing advanced testing for children between the ages of 12 and 15.[120] In addition, a competitive element was introduced into the training. In 1966 RoSPA sent a British team of children to Rome for the European Children's Cycling Proficiency finals. It gave cycling some publicity in the press and on television, especially as the British team finished second and their 'specially designed uniforms' had drawn many favourable comments.[121]

RoSPA's message of safety had also been relayed through film. After 1945, film was an increasingly popular medium that not only buttressed the road safety message, but also further reinforced the trope of safety concerning the relationship between children and cycling. Cycling bodies were at the centre of spreading the message. In 1946 and 1947, for example, the NCU, which had been in close contact with local Road Safety Committees, applied to both Odeon and Gaumont to show 'special road safety films for children.[122] Interestingly, these films changed in style to reflect contemporary tastes, while still attempting to get across the message of safety to children. In 1954, two RoSPA films were released. One, *Chain of Events*, was criticized because it was too much like a documentary film, which would 'meet with a lot of passive resistance from the public who are rather hardened to these [films]'. *Someone Else's Child*, however, was described as a modern thriller, which 'gripped the viewer's attention from the start and succeeds in its primary task of getting the audience to think about road safety'.[123]

By 1962, the first year that road accidents had fallen since 1952, it was estimated that nearly a quarter of million children had seen a cycle safety film in the cinema. Yet the growing levels of traffic continued to be matched by concerns over the safety of children cycling on the roads. In 1969 industry officials had noted that there was growing parental pressure to discourage children riding bicycles and that also some head teachers had banned pupils from riding their bicycles to school.[124] By 1970, therefore, 'the danger of traffic was largely accepted as part of the landscape of the child'.[125] As a consequence, it was in the interests of both cycling bodies and the manufacturers to reconcile the decline in cycling and the need to present it as a safe activity for children. Even in Peterborough, a town with nationally very high cycling levels, many headteachers of junior schools had forbidden pupils cycling to school by 1973.[126]

The NCPS typically produced films to promote their programme. One was released in 1964, the other in 1973, and both reflected changing social attitudes towards cycling more generally. First, although schools were used as the settings in both, there were differences. *No Short Cut* (1964)[127] was set in quiet, leafy, suburban England, which owed more to the 1950s than 1964, while *Wheels of Chance* (1973) – probably a reference to H. G. Wells's novel of the same title[128] – was filmed in Scotland, in working-class Dumbarton. The English children – boys and girls – wore uniforms and probably went to a grammar school, while their Scottish counterparts, wearing 'civvies', did not. The bicycles themselves both illuminated changing tastes. In *No Short Cut* they rode functional and relatively standard roadsters with few nods to modernity: by contrast there is a mixture in *Wheels of Chance*, including racers and a Chopper. Second, whereas in *No Short Cut* the setting is relatively traffic free, in *Wheels of Chance* fast-moving urban traffic was heavily featured. As a consequence, the message of safety was transformed. In *No Short Cut* the emphasis was as much about the cyclist developing skills, such as the proper action for pedalling, and road sense in combination with the NCPS's test. An awareness of the dangers of traffic was not absent, but in *Wheels of Chance* there was a greater emphasis on the dangers of traffic.

The start of both films began with an accident but whereas in the first film the accident only saw the bicycle – the film was filmed from the perspective of the bike – in *Wheels of Chance* we see a young boy, Mark, who has been knocked down and has been bloodied. Figures were later given and graphics used for both children's cycling accidents and fatalities to reinforce the point, which unconsciously accepted the dangers posed by traffic for cyclists. Even the notion of luck – the clue is in title – was introduced when cycling on the roads, highlighting the growing levels of traffic congestion by this time. 'Cycling is fun as long as it's safe,' it proclaims, but it also mentions that accidents can still happen and the young cyclist needed to be prepared as much as possible, via the NCPS, to lessen the odds of it happening.

Both films shared a similarity through the filming of the training and preparation of the children for the test – the films' main purpose – although there were subtle differences in how the message was relayed, which hinted at changing notions of childhood. The narrator for *No Short Cut* shared parallels with other public information films of that period. He was anonymous and projected a paternalistic persona through a Home Counties accent, as the film promoted educational values, a sense of fair play, moderation and warned of the perils of speed and selfishness. In contrast to this paternalistic approach, the narrator of *Wheels of Chance* was Formula One motor-racing driver and three-times world champion Jackie Stewart. Using Jackie Stewart in this role was not as contradictory as it may have initially seemed. While images of racing cars, speed and noise feature heavily in the film, giving it a touch of glamour, Stewart was in fact the leading figure in the drive for greater safety in Formula One, following the deaths of a number of his friends and rivals in the 1960s. In addition to this celebrity-driven approach, Stewart adopted the persona of a father figure and/or male role model as he explains to Mark the importance of safety on roads and the necessity of the NCPS, drawing on parallels of his own experiences and applying them to cycling.

In Britain's rush to post-war modernity and affluence, the utility and image of cycling had been transformed and marginalized. In the age of motoring, cycling became increasingly linked with danger, especially on evermore congested roads. This was particularly important as children were an increasingly important market for an industry coming to terms with cycling's changing nature, and at the same time had to deal with the changing place of the child in society. To a certain extent, the marginalization of cycling was symbolic of post-war affluent Britain, as it signalled a shift away from its Victorian past represented by the bicycle, to a more modern looking future, which the car now embodied. Of course, this process had not been limited to the post-1945 period. Cycling had been under political and legal pressure in Britain ever since it was invented and the continuation of these pressures was also a product of the nation's political culture. Unlike the Netherlands and Denmark, cycling in Britain did not enjoy the same status and as a consequence, the benefits from public planning like its European neighbours. As a reflection of Britain's strong liberal-voluntary tradition, cycling bodies had been keen to separate themselves from the state, while a powerful car and road lobby had been able to ingratiate itself into government thinking and ultimately state planning projects. That Britain had a capitalist economy arguably meant that any potential intervention would have been futile due to the primacy of economic interests. However, as outlined in Chapter 8, the motor car's omnipotence would lead to a backlash and growing concerns over the environment, which would see a revival of the bicycle.

CHAPTER 8

Cycling, politics and environmentalism

On 27 July 2012 Bradley Wiggins, fresh from being the first British winner of the Tour de France, rang the Olympic bell to herald the start of London 2012. Almost at the same time as Wiggins was ringing the bell, only a few miles from the Olympic stadium in Stratford, a different cycling scenario was unfolding. Critical Mass, the cycling activist group, was holding its regular monthly ride when its 182 members were stopped, 'kettled' and arrested near Bow in East London. The cyclists, including a 13-year-old boy, were locked up in a police cell overnight.[1] It was claimed that some of the arrests were violent and that at one stage mace spray was used. The cyclists were bailed under 'Olympic-conditions'. Whatever the arguments around this cycle ride, it continued to point to the ubiquity of cycling as an activity, one which could encompass both elite sport and grassroots politics.

One of the themes of this book has been that the riding of a bicycle – mostly unconsciously – is a political act. However, this chapter is concerned with how the bicycle emerged as an explicit instrument and symbol for political and cultural change through both activism and the emergence of environmentalism as a political creed. Moreover, the bicycle not only became increasingly associated with an anti-modernist critique of post-industrial society, but was also seen as part of the solution. Motoring had been subject to a backlash almost as soon as it was invented. From the 1960s, however, the exponential rise in the number of cars on the road was matched by an increasingly vehement criticism of motoring due to concerns over safety, pollution and especially congestion on roads that were becoming unable to cope.[2] Opposition to road building was growing among a normally pliant middle class, who had been both the main recipients of modernity's benefits and classic NIMBYs. This opposition, exemplified through protests against roads, such as the one organized by Earth First concerning the A3 expansion at Twyford Down in the 1990s, reflected a growing consciousness among the population of environmental issues.[3] Ben Elton's 1991 novel, *Gridlock*, also drew attention to the issue of traffic congestion, while J. G. Ballard's *Crash* (1973) offered a satirical comment, using sex as a metaphor, on the status of the car in modern life. Moreover, cycling as leisure activity began to change as cyclists felt that they were being pushed off the roads both literally and metaphorically. Out of this tension emerged the mountain bike. It initially combined the spirit of the counterculture and an innovative design, which enabled the bicycle to be adapted to both urban and rural locations.

The environmental turn

The rise of the issue of the environment up the political agenda mirrored one of the most visible shifts in British politics during the latter part of the twentieth-century. Whereas for much of the twentieth century politics had been based around ideas over production and was mirrored in the dominance of the main two political parties, there was an increasing emphasis on the politics of consumption, which incorporated social movements that could be cross-class and bipartisan in political terms. Underpinning this shift was the emergence of two competing liberal ideologies from the 1970s. Paul Addison has argued that instead of socialism and Toryism, the most enduring ideas have been those of free-market economic liberalism and social liberalism. Liberal ideas had their roots in various movements, which included the Chicago school of economics, the civil rights movement and, importantly for cycling, the libertarian countercultures of San Francisco. In broad terms, social liberals tended to be on the left and on the right were economic liberals. However, by the end of the twentieth century there was a gradual, if unconscious, acceptance of both ideals across the spectrum of society and politics. 'Economic liberalism, like social liberalism, had become an almost unexamined faith, accepted as one of the facts of life against which it was pointless to protest.'[4] Robinson et al. have similarly argued that during the seventies a 'popular individualism' emerged that was both a product of and an agent in the reshaping of the political landscape. While accepting that 'popular individualism' was eventually hijacked by the political right, that is, Thatcherism, the spread of this 'popular aspirational form of individualism', it is argued, was formed during the 1970s. Importantly, these values were also embraced on the left due to a rejection of a technocratic and modernist vision of society. Environmentalism was both at the centre of this rejection of post-materialist values and the embrace of a new orientation towards life in which many 'new individualists' based their lives around 'strong ethical attachments'.[5]

From the 1970s, cycling was increasingly associated with these values, which was reflected not only in new lifestyles, but also in changing bicycle technology. As a consequence, by the late 1980s environmentalism had come to occupy a place at the top of the political agenda in the UK. It has been claimed that Margaret Thatcher once said, 'A man who, beyond the age of 26, finds himself on a bus can count himself as a failure.' While her sobriquet the Iron Lady could have made an appropriate name for a nineteenth-century bicycle, her thoughts on cycling are not known. Given the free-market policies and neoliberal ideology of her governments, they were unlikely to be complementary and the road lobby found willing listeners in her administrations.⁶ Nevertheless, in 1988 Thatcher was declaring her green credentials. Many critics argued it was a cynical political act of being seen to be aware of the problem and to promise action, but actually delivering very little.⁷ However, whatever the lack of action, it brought the issue of the environment and climate change to the wider public and into the political discourse. Moreover, with her fall from power in 1990, some of her main supporters such as Nicholas Ridley and Cecil Parkinson also left government. For them the motor car had been the great symbol of personal freedom while ever-increasing car ownership was seen as a valuable indicator of national well-being.⁸

Cycling's growing political importance by the end of the twentieth century was partly a consequence of how the bicycle had become central to environmental politics, achieving a symbolic and iconic status, which made it immune from 'eco-criticism'. According to Horton, 'this vehicle takes centre stage in the virtuous materialities of environmentalism and, among environmental activists, cycling as a practice clearly embodies and performs environmental concern and commitment'.⁹ This had not been an inevitable process and instead owed something to the changing nature of political culture in late-twentieth-century Britain. Over this period, voter turnout at general elections decreased and trade union membership declined. However, there was a commensurate rise in the voluntary sector and non-governmental organizations around one-issue social movements. Matthew Hilton has persuasively argued that this was a form of 'ordinary politics', which constituted 'a form of politics [in] which largely non-materialist, yet still everyday concerns have been expressed in the formal political arena'.¹⁰ Environmentalism was an example of this 'new' politics, which was in evidence across the entire political spectrum and undertaken by people with a wide range of motivations.

Concern for the environment was not new. It had been present since the early nineteenth century through the link between the idea of Englishness and that of the countryside in light of industrialization and urbanization, and had been projected through the work of bodies such as the National Trust, formed in 1895. There was as much continuity as change associated with this shift in political culture as the significance and lobbying efforts of voluntary groups had been a consistent feature of civil society over the twentieth century, including matters of the environment and conservation.[11] The 1956 Clean Air Act, for example, had been a product of the lobbying of the Coal Smoke Abatement Society and the Smoke Abatement League.[12] To a certain extent there was a shift in the nature of lobbying. In the Victorian period, social status was a marker in the effectiveness of a lobby group. The recruitment of members of the establishment was key for lobbying purposes as they usually moved in the same social circles as (male) members of the government. By the late twentieth century lobbying had become increasingly professionalized with expertise a more important factor in a technocratic society. Yet those members of the higher echelons of society continued to be sought by lobby groups as figureheads. Therefore, rather than a clean break from old styles of activism, environmental politics in general was a combination of the emergence of new groups, like Friends of the Earth, and the continuation of older forms of voluntary activity, exemplified by older NGOs like the National Trust.

What changed, in terms of the debate over the environment, from the late 1960s and early 1970s was the nature and increasing intensity of political engagement.[13] Instead of concerns focussed on the protection of particular sites and species there was now a 'more explicit critique of specific environmentally damaging practices', particularly motoring.[14] There had been a growing public awareness – importantly now amplified by television – of man-made environmental pollution and catastrophe, such as the Torrey Canyon disaster. This first-generation super oil tanker ran aground on rocks between Land's End and the Scilly Isles in March 1967. Over 100,000 tonnes of crude oil was spilled, much of it washing up on beaches in England, the Channel Islands and France with thousands of sea birds dying from its effects. It remains Britain's worst ever one-off environmental disaster and its legacy continues to the present, especially in Guernsey. As a result of 'Torrey Canyon' the British government created the world's first department of environment in 1970.[15] Awareness of the effects of environmental pollution had been rising across the Western world. On 22 April 1970 the first 'Earth Day' was held across the United States. Earth Day had been the creation of Senator Gaylord Nelson of Wisconsin and it was estimated that, in conjunction with cross-party support, 20 million Americans demonstrated for a cleaner environment.[16]

A further response was the formation of non-governmental organizations and voluntary groups based around the issue of the environment. In 1970, Friends of the Earth was formed in Britain and a year later Greenpeace was established. A key moment in the development of the new environmental movement, Friends of the Earth adopted an explicitly anti-modernist stance. One early member, Thomas L. Blair, a sociologist at the Polytechnic of Central London, declared, 'The man-made environmental crisis which exists on this planet is only now being recognized as the ultimate threat to Man's survival. ... Action is required to replace the throw-away consumer philosophy with a way of life based on sound ecological principles.'[17]

Greenpeace and Friends of the Earth's formation had had its roots in the 1950s when the New Left had attempted to transform left-wing politics through '"a movement of ordinary people into politics" via a number of progressive social movements'.[18] The Campaign for Nuclear Disarmament, formed in 1958, was one such early example, while from the 1960s the environment would increasingly become a focus for left-leaning and liberal minded groups who had been politically influenced by the counterculture. However, the issue of the environment was also taken up by more mainstream and 'ordinary' bodies, and between 1970 and 2000 the NGO with the largest membership remained the National Trust.[19]

Environmentalism took hold across society. In 1973, pre-dating the activism of Greta Thunberg, the Schools Eco-Action Group – affiliated to Friends of the Earth and the Conservation Society – was formed and consisted of 'pupils in schools throughout the country working within their own areas for the survival of mankind through the creation of a stable society'.[20] One successful environmental campaign had been CLEAR – Campaign for Lead Free Air. This pressure group, led by well-known campaigner Des Wilson, was established in 1982 and through its media campaign was able to highlight mounting evidence that small quantities of lead in the air could harm children. Despite the lobbying of the oil industry, the publication of a report from the Royal Commission on Environmental Pollution the following year confirmed CLEAR's findings. As a consequence, the government caved in and supported the elimination of lead from petrol.[21] In 1990 the Environmental Transport Association, a broad-based lobby group, was founded with the objective of campaigning for the most environmentally friendly forms of transport.[22]

Where did cycling fit into this new movement? Initially the bicycle was only a small part of the Friends of the Earth's wider campaign. In *The Environmental Handbook*, published in 1971, there was only a brief reference to riding a bike as a way to alleviate the damage that the car had caused to the environment, while there were other essays on issues such as population growth, Concorde and farming.[23] Motorization had actually left a political and cultural vacuum within the cycling world. The club run, which had symbolized the traditional cycling culture through its sheer visibility, had been in itself a political act, and its gradual disappearance from the roads had reshaped the public's psychological evaluation of cycling and its subsequent diminished place in British society. It was in this context that cycling was thrust into the environment debate and the bicycle emerged as an icon of environmentalism.

By the early seventies, especially after the 1973 Oil Crisis, a growing discourse emerged over the benefits of cycling as an alternative form of transport. With cars also stigmatized as pushing affluent societies towards an environmental catastrophe, the bicycle was increasingly identified as part of the solution by ecological campaigners.[24] In 1971 Peter Hall was calling for 'Equal Rights for Bikes' in view of growing transport issues and at the same time he proposed a rent-a-bike service for London tourists.[25] Other commentators reiterated not only the environmental benefits of cycling but also how it was the most efficient form of transport – albeit an argument common since the nineteenth century.[26] In *Pedal Power*, a 1974 BBC 2 programme, Reyner Banham (riding a Moulton), demonstrated the difficulty navigating Hyde Park Corner, and advocated a bicycle network through London's royal parks, while Eric Claxton explained his thinking behind segregating the car from the bicycle in Stevenage, although it was very much from the perspective of keeping motor traffic flowing. In the same programme, though, it was claimed that the bicycle was 'the most single dangerous product in the American home', highlighting the hegemony of motoring.[27]

The emerging environmental discourse was accompanied by a growing cycling activism. In 1981 Friends of the Earth staged a 'Reclaim the Road' event with 7,000 cyclists taking over Whitehall in what was then London's biggest cycle demonstration.[28] At the same time, while the newly emergent environmental activism symbolized by Friends of the Earth catalysed the link between cycling and the environment, these ideas were complemented by those of existing groups, especially the CTC, which had their own particular environmental concerns as well as different social make-ups.[29] Indeed, some groups, formed mainly at a local level, combined both Friends of the Earth and CTC members and interests. Don Mathew, the CTC policy adviser from 1989 to 2001, for example, had been the editor of the Friends of the Earth's *Bicycles Bulletin*.[30] Yet although bicycle sales may have increased during the 1973 oil crisis once it had abated, traffic levels soon went back to growing and bicycle mileage, in terms of a form of transport, flatlined.

The rise in awareness of environmental issues among the public and the realization of the bicycle's worth in relieving traffic congestion led to the combination of new bike-friendly lobby groups, fresh initiatives and some interest from local government. Moreover, the nascent environmental movement was both buttressed by and reflected the growing technocratic ethos that had permeated post-war British society. Previously the authority of experts had emanated from ideological affinities and grassroots support, but increasingly authority came from expertise. Now 'a whole host of professions sought to position their expertise as independent of both the political and the social, of both state and society'. In the immediate post-war period, the emphasis on planning the welfare state had attracted technocrats. Later, experts became vital to the shaping of environmental debates through their association with NGOs.[31]

At local government level, there was a gamut of nationwide initiatives, which aimed to ease traffic congestion and encourage more people to cycle. In 1974 a Greater London Council report noted that there was 'a growing literature produced by local authorities, pressure groups and research organizations, the Press and other interested parties discussing the advantages of cycling as a mode of transport and looking particularly at the concept of reserved tracks or bikeways'.[32] By 1975 around 20 local councils, following the lead of Stevenage, had shown an interest in catering for cyclists in urban areas.[33] In 1973 a feasibility study, 'Cycleways for Greater Peterborough', was produced by a team of engineers and planners from the town's development corporation. It unsurprisingly concluded that 'much more can and should be done for cyclists' in the area, especially through the provision of separate cycle paths. An experimental cycle route opened five years later.[34] That same year Middlesbrough borough council had built its own 'cycling route system' in an attempt to encourage more people to cycle. In addition to a route through some residential areas, it also provided links to secondary schools.[35] In 1973 a Cambridge Transportation Plan was drawn up, which included a 'park and pedal scheme', while in Cheltenham a cycleway development throughout the town was being considered. Nearly 6 miles of cycleways and five subways were built in Daventry, following a visit to Stevenage, and Harlow was planning on extending its 7.2-mile cycleway system. Meanwhile, Thamesmead had plans for 5 miles of cycling paths.[36]

Nevertheless, these local government initiatives were patchy and were later affected by the Thatcher cuts in local authority budgets. Philip Brachi commented that rather than town planners it was the engineers and surveyors of local government who were anti-diluvian in their attitudes to cycling. Because their background and training revolved around catering for motor vehicles, he argued that they were unable to appreciate the benefits of cycling. In *The Principles and Practices of Town and Country Planning*, he noted that cycle tracks were barely mentioned in its 400 pages and that the bicycle was rated as an irritant.[37] Moreover, by 1989 there was no Friends of the Earth staff member whose job it was to campaign for cycling or coordinate cycling pressure groups. Instead, the pressure group had switched its focus to its Cities for People campaign, which was concerned with the urban environment as a whole, and by 1992 its national policy was more focussed on reducing urban traffic.[38]

By the early nineties the level of cycling provision in urban areas was still mixed; but it could have been worse. It was claimed that without the efforts of campaign groups there was every chance that cyclists 'would have been bullied off urban roads in the same way as in most of southern Europe and the US'. Some local authorities were not prepared to invest in reducing traffic levels for political and commercial reasons, while others adopted a so-called common sense attitude as they feared promoting cycling would lead to a rise in accidents. Liverpool was named as the worst cycling city while York was the most cycle friendly. The main political factor across the entire range was the permissive attitudes and levels of commitment among individual councils. Although budgets were not generally large for cycling, some authorities were more prepared than others to invest in cycling as a mode of transport.[39] Ironically, Cambridge, which had just been voted the second-best British city for cycling, banned bikes from its centre in 1992 – along with other forms of traffic.[40] As sign of things to come, in 1992 bike loan schemes sprang up in some English towns. Dacorum borough council in Hertfordshire set up a Green Bike scheme to provide community bicycles for Hemel Hempstead, Berkhamsted and Tring. Interestingly, at the same time a cycle hire service in Vienna was set up with 4,000 bikes at 100 hire sites.[41]

From the seventies, the cycling lobby emerged as a highly technocratic and sophisticated, if disparate, group. Aided by the expansion in desktop publishing, numerous publications and reports were produced to support cycling's merits.[42] However, cycling's national profile on a political front remained low and on occasions some cycling lobby groups resorted to publicity stunts. In 1982 Cyclebag (discussed further), invoking the spirit of Kinder Scout, staged an illegal ride across common land called the Downs, near Bristol, where bye-laws had prohibited cycling. Two years later a cycle path was built. Campaigns to increase media profile were also increasingly sophisticated. The Bristol Urban Cycle Campaign, for example, blocked a city centre roundabout for a short time during the morning rush with the help of 300 cyclists. In 1993 it staged a similar demonstration with 100 cyclists fanning across the city's ring road to draw attention to the need for a 20 mph speed limit for traffic. Other groups used a combination of mass rides and cooperation. Pushbikes, a Birmingham-based campaign organized events like the Great Midland Bike Ride, arguing that this was as much a political statement as any protest, as well as developing personal relations with local government and other bodies.[43]

In 1995 the first monthly Critical Mass (CM) ride in London took place. Critical Mass had been formed in 1992 in San Francisco.[44] It was a grassroots social movement and by 2000 around 100 CM groups had popped up in cities around the world. Rides all over the world take place on the last Friday of each month, hence the incident during the 2012 London Olympics. It was an urban bicycle and sustainability movement and shared similar anxieties regarding the environment and transport as other groups. CM offered a new form of activism. It was informal and its message was powered by the internet and so not subject to the frictions of distance. The World Trade Organization protests in Seattle in 1998 had been one of the earliest examples of how the web was used to organize a campaign. CM had one universal message, 'We are the traffic'. The bike rides had no predetermined route, but they started from the same place and at the same time. It was also deigned that all participants were equal leaders.[45]

Cycling conditions in the UK contrasted with those in other European nations. In a 1988 survey it was concluded that they were worst in the UK, except Belgium, whereas the best conditions were to be found in Denmark, the Netherlands, Sweden and Switzerland. According to the survey, riding a bike in the UK was the least fun and cyclists were given the least respect by other road users with UK cyclists having the least amount of priority over motor traffic.[46] However, like Britain, European countries had not been unaffected by modernizing impulses and the lure of the car. It highlighted how government policies regarding cycling were as much a political choice as a product of cycling tradition. Oldenziel has argued that Amsterdam became the cycling capital of the world by accident. Holland, and Amsterdam, had traditionally been seen as the leading cycling nation. Yet in 1971 bicycles had been banned from Amsterdam city centre. A few years later though this policy was reversed due to the pressure of the city's counterculture and its preservationist movement, which resisted motorization.[47] In 1988 the Dutch transport minister announced that it planned to cut motor traffic from 8 million to 3.5 million over the next 20 years in a bid to reduce air pollution. No new roads were to be built and taxes were to add 50 per cent on to the costs of buying and running a car while four years later cars were banned from Amsterdam's city centre.[48] By 2016, 87 per cent of trips of less than 4 kilometres were made by bicycle.[49] Cycling was similarly seen as an integral part of Denmark's transport system. This was perhaps unsurprising as 75 per cent of Denmark's population owned a bicycle as against 1.6 million car owners. Cycling had been integrated into its transport infrastructure since 1912 when Copenhagen had laid 50 kilometres of cycle paths. By the early nineties plans for the construction of 1,150 kilometres of cycle paths nationwide had been approved, while Odense, Denmark's third city, had over 250 kilometres of cycle paths. At the centre of this construction was the government strategy of reducing traffic and increasing pedestrianization.[50]

The road to the National Cycling Strategy

In Britain the efforts at a local level and the activism of voluntary groups were instrumental in a change to central government attitudes towards cycling by the 1990s. The change culminated in 1996 when the transport secretary George Younger, a keen cyclist himself, launched the government's National Cycling Strategy. A strategy as opposed to an aspiration, it aimed to double cycling by 2002, then double it again by 2012. It marked an important moment in the history of cycling as both a mode of transport and a leisure practice. The *Guardian* commented that it completed 'a revolution in attitudes towards cycling'. As late as 1991 the government had openly discouraged cycling due to safety concerns. Now the bicycle's role was seen as crucial in reducing pollution and congestion.[51] With the National Cycling Strategy in place, cycling moved up the political agenda. Increasingly, cycling groups were integrated into both local and central government policies.

It would be stretching the argument to say that the 1996 National Cycling Strategy marked a complete volte face in terms of the government's overall transport policy. Government attitudes had only changed slowly towards cycling as a serious form of conveyance. There had been growing public opposition over the plans to build or widen roads in London, forcing the Department of Transport to abandon many projected schemes. In 1982 the proposal of the Cycling Project Team of the Greater London Council for a network of 1,000 miles of safe cycle routes in the capital had been welcomed but there was no substantial progress. By 1989 the target for 1,000 miles had received formal, if reluctant, approval from the Department of Transport, although it was not directly funded from central government and instead put in the hands of local authorities.[52] In 1991 the first ever session of the House of Common Select Committee on Transport was held devoted to cycling. But even here fundamental differences were still apparent with Neville Rees, the head of traffic policy at the Department of Transport, insisting that there was no suppressed demand for cycling, before stating that cycling in London was not a safe activity.[53] In other words, it was the actions of the drivers of motor vehicles keeping cyclists off the roads; it was an attitude that underscored Tory ideology over the free market and notions of individualism.

Moreover, by the early 1990s the roads of Britain were being used as never before. In 1993 Barker and Gerhold posed the question, 'Are the number of vehicles on some of Britain's roads, especially in towns and cities, already reaching their ultimate limit?'[54] Since 1970 the number of licensed vehicles in Britain had risen from 13 to 28 million in 2000 with two-thirds of families owning a car, while nearly a quarter had more than one.[55] Passenger mileage increased from 259 billion in 1972 to 410 billion in 1990. The figure for the bicycle had remained at around 3 billion during this period, while the mileage for cars, taxis and motor bikes had increased from 202 billion to 353 billion.[56] The ever-growing emphasis on the car was accompanied by an expansion in the motorway network. In 1989 it was estimated that road traffic would grow annually by 5 to 6 per cent.[57] That year, to accommodate this predicted growth, the then transport secretary Paul Channon declared that the government was to launch 'the greatest road-building programme since the Romans'. A White Paper, *Roads to Prosperity*, was published to announce the £12 billion programme of road building – an increase from £5 billion – to cater for an estimated increase in road traffic of between 83 to 142 per cent above the then 23 million vehicles in use.[58] The proposals were mostly directed at the major motorways and included the widening of the entire 107 miles of the M25 into an American-style eight-lane motorway with a 145-mile stretch of the M1 also having four lanes on each carriageway, while the reintroduction of toll roads was proposed.[59] Naturally the proposed programme was welcomed by the road lobby following a 10-year lobbying campaign, but equally opposed by environmental groups. Editorials in *The Times* and the *Guardian* both gave Channon's plans a cautious welcome reflecting an uncritical acceptance among political elites more generally that the only solution to cater for the growth in traffic was to build more roads.[60]

By 1995, however, Don Mathew, a CTC policy adviser and early Friends of the Earth advocate, stated that the government's 1989 proposed road-building programme 'was in full retreat as the financial and environmental costs of this became fully apparent'.[61] How did this turnaround take place? One factor was the changing context of political lobbying regarding transport. Nicholas Robinson has identified a shift, albeit a qualified one, in the lobbying process from the Thatcher administrations to the Major government. The Thatcher administrations had been ideologically opposed to any dealings with organized interests and even traditionally powerful lobby groups, such as the BMA, took on the status as 'outsiders'.[62] Groups like the road lobby had benefitted from a 'predict and provide orthodoxy', which dominated government policy and conferred on them an 'insider' status. In the Major era though both the scope and the breadth of the opposition to the roads programme increased significantly. Traditional transport groups with a long history of transport campaigning, such as Transport 2000 and ALARM UK, were joined by the direct action movement, highlighted by the protest over Twyford Down, along with moderate, mass membership organizations such as the Royal Society for the Protection of Birds and the National Trust. However, the anti-road lobby was never particularly cohesive due to differences in core beliefs between groups, and this had negative implications for cycling initiatives gaining support across a broad spectrum of lobbying groups.[63]

Nevertheless, the opposition to the building of roads did allow for cycling to enjoy greater visibility in the media and more access to government. Up until the 1990s the Department of Transport's attitude to the cycling had revolved around the issue of safety. Rather than promoting cycling as a mode of transport it chose instead to highlight its dangers over the responsibility of drivers of motor vehicles. Moves to make the wearing of bicycle helmets compulsory, for example, had been criticized by the cycling lobby, because it put the onus on cyclists and shifted responsibility away from the behaviour of drivers. In 1988, for example, Greater Manchester Police launched a unilateral helmet campaign for local primary schoolchildren, which was aimed especially at the parents.[64] Three years later the UCI made the wearing of hard shell helmets compulsory for professional cyclists, which acted as form of legitimation for those authorities who were keen for it to be compulsory at all levels of cycling.[65]

The focus on safety was perhaps unsurprising given the strength of the road lobby. Perhaps more revealing was that in 1991 it was estimated that the Department of Transport had 13,000 people dealing with cars and roads with fewer than 100 concerned with railways and none for cycling.[66] In 1988 Peter Bottomley, the minister for roads and traffic, commenting on the rise in bicycling casualties among children, blamed everyone but motor vehicles. He said that '[p]arent and teachers need to act urgently to try and put this right and ensure that children know how to cycle safely on our roads.'[67] He later admitted that it was not the role of the government to encourage people to cycle 'that must be a matter of personal choice'. The rhetoric of choice of course was bound up with the ethos of Thatcherism and in this case proved a useful and enduring smokescreen to promote and defend the car industry and road lobby. Bottomley was equally as ambivalent on the economic and transport benefits of cycling and instead stated that 'making it safer must be a high priority' as a safer environment 'may lead indirectly to more cycling'. In addition, he urged a change of culture among cyclists and that they 'must act sensibly *and* within the framework of road traffic law'. While also pointing out the responsibility of motorists, Bottomley was also clear that 'irrespective of whose fault it was, the cyclist is infinitely more likely to be killed or hurt'.[68] In a 1992 survey of MPs, there was a sense of inevitability among Conservative members over the growth in traffic and a need to accommodate it rather than find other solutions to congestion and pollution, although a large majority of MPs were in favour of greater cycling provision.[69] These sentiments were nothing new, but it further reinforced government and Whitehall assumptions about the place of cycling in society, and highlighted the screeching U-turn that had taken place by 1996.

As much as transport concerns, perhaps the most important report to push cycling up the British political agenda was the British Medical Association's (BMA) *Cycling towards Health and Safety*, published in 1992.[70] Written by Mayer Hillman, a prominent activist for sustainable transport, the report was key in changing the nature of the debate over cycling on two accounts. First, it was produced by the BMA, which was a conservative body that (again) carried more influence in government circles and among the general public than emerging environmental lobby groups, which were perceived as left-wing and the ideological polar opposites to the Tory government. Second, the report accepted that there were some safety issues over cycling, but it pointed out that this cost was heavily outweighed by the public health gains through improvements in fitness and quality of life, and as a consequence it could help reduce spending on the NHS, which was now rising in real terms, following cuts to the budget during the 1980s.[71] While the link between cycling and health was hardly new, the report shifted debates over the benefits of cycling as a form of transport to one concerning public health. Unsurprisingly perhaps the report did not immediately find favour in government circles and its impact was tempered by its publication shortly before the 1992 general election.[72] However, the report's findings offered an opportunity to mitigate the growing health bill, which was much greater than government spending on transport.

Cycling and New Labour

New Labour administrations continued to promote cycling both as a form of sustainable transport and for its health benefits. Moreover, following its election in 1997 the voluntary sector experienced the development of the 'third sector' – what became known as the 'third way' regarding public policy planning. Cycling became a beneficiary of this new approach to policy formulation and implementation. Essentially, the third way aimed to capture a rejection of public service policy planning that relied primarily on the state or the market. While the mixing of a reliance on state and market forces was not new, there was now an enhanced role for voluntary action. The third way was buttressed through the establishment of institutions within government, such as the Office of the Third Sector in 2006, that provided sites for policy development. While voluntary bodies and agencies were potentially sites for state intervention, they also had shared interest in promoting the third sector, especially through the increased funding available to them.[73] As a result, the National Cycling Strategy was coordinated between government, the private sector and road user groups via a National Cycling Forum.[74]

In addition to the incorporation of organizations such as Sustrans into government policy, New Labour also created a quango called Cycling England.[75] Cycling England had replaced the National Cycling Strategy Board, established in 2005, and was supported and funded by the Department of Transport with the aim of getting 'more people cycling, more safely, more often'. The board was a typical New Labour mixture of people from business, public health, the environment, transport as well as cycling.[76] The initial chair had been Sustrans' John Grimshaw, but he was later succeeded by Philip Darnton, a former management consultant with Unilever plc. It was given an initial 3-year budget of £5 million rising to £140 million from 2008 to 2011.[77]

Armed with this funding, Cycling England promoted two flagship projects. The first was a Cycling Demonstration Towns programme, which aimed to bring levels of investments equivalent to the best European cycling cities.[78] Initially, between 2005 and 2008 six towns – Aylesbury, Brighton, Darlington, Derby, Exeter and Lancaster – were selected in an attempt to raise cycling levels to 4 per cent. In 2008 it named Bristol as England's first cycling city with another 11 named cycling towns. The initial six towns had been chosen for their relatively low levels of cycle use. Then 2 per cent of all journeys in the UK were made by bicycle; in places like Darlington it was 1 per cent.[79] It was believed that 4 per cent was a 'tipping point', which would not only see an increase in cycle use but more significantly produce a change in cultural perceptions regarding cycling.[80] The second major initiative was Bikeability. Beginning in 2007, it was termed 'cycling proficiency' for the twenty-first century and was aimed at children who it was felt were a lost generation regarding training.[81] In many ways, it reflected persistent fears over safety – and which had been at the core of the original cycling proficiency scheme in the 1950s. In the twenty-first century the discourse of safety on the road remained the main factor in preventing people cycling.

The benefits for the health of the nation were now a major aspect of the discourse in the promotion of cycling. While this was as an age-old argument, since the late twentieth century the promotion of cycling was increasingly linked to broader shifts in public health policy which moved away from a stress on medical intervention to an emphasis on health education, with a particular accent on individual lifestyles. The McKeown thesis – the idea that the health of the population was dependent on dietary requirements and overall standards of living rather than on medical intervention – became influential in the thinking of policy makers. Virginia Berridge has identified how during the eighties and nineties this argument had been appropriated by neoliberals to justify policies of 'cost containment, of restriction of medical autonomy and a focus on lower cost forms of health provision'.[82] The popular individualism that had emerged in the 1970s, arrogated by the radical right in the eighties, also prospered under New Labour. As a result, demands for increased patient power and incipient consumerism became redefined; patients' rights were now interpreted in the context of them as consumers of health services. Instead of a democratic or collectivist approach of popular participation the rhetoric of 'patients as consumers' was used to reduce the power of health care providers with the ultimate goal of reducing costs.[83]

One wide-ranging government initiative was the 'Cycle to Work' scheme. Introduced in the 1999 Finance Act, it allowed employers to buy bicycles and safety equipment – up to £1,000 – and hire it to their employees as a tax-exempt benefit for the purpose of cycling to work. By 2012 over 500,000 people had taken advantage of the scheme with 2,200 approved bicycle retailers and 32,000 companies signed up. Cycle to Work, in aiming to change the behaviour of society, was in many ways a typical New Labour project. It mixed public initiatives with private finance, reflecting the then chancellor of the exchequer Gordon Brown's promotion of tax-free allowances for companies.[84] A Cycle to Work Alliance was formed and made up of a group of leading providers of the cycle to work scheme, and included Cyclescheme, Cycle Solutions, Evans Cycles and Halfords. At the same time as trying to promote a greener lifestyle, the scheme became a valuable source of revenue for cycle retailers. In terms of the cycling industry its main benefit was to encourage more people to purchase more expensive bicycles and accessories.[85]

Sustrans: From grassroots activism to corporatism

At the heart of the rise of cycling's political profile had been the emergence of a thriving grassroots activism. The most influential British cycling activism group has been Sustrans (Sustainable Transport). Its story has also been an insight into the development of the voluntary sector in late-twentieth-century Britain as it went from a grassroots organization to one that became part of New Labour's third way. Originally formed in 1977, it emerged out of the Bristol cycle group 'Cyclebag' (Channel Your Calf and Leg Energy Bristol Action Group). During the summer of 1979 volunteers from

'Cyclebag' built a bike path along 8 kilometres of a disused rail line between Bath and Britton (halfway to Bristol).[86] Not only was it a seminal moment in the changing climate of cycling activism; it also pointed towards a greater incorporated approach of cycling organizations in building partnerships with public and state bodies. The Bath-to-Britton line had been leased by British Rail to Avon county council who in turn gave Cyclebag a licence to construct and maintain the path. For Friends of the Earth the benefits of bike paths were obvious. It had been calculated that not only would they provide work at a time of record unemployment levels, but the cost of materials and design worked out at £7,000 per kilometre, £7 million for 1,000 kilometres. In comparison, £7 million then equated to 3 miles of motorway.[87]

Other 'Cyclebag' schemes followed and their initiatives found favour, although not funding, with the government. In 1980 a report commissioned by the Department of Transport on disused railways concluded with ways to promote 'Railway Bike Paths' and stressed their potential for encouraging cycling. Other groups and bodies were galvanized into action, including local authorities, bike groups, individuals and British Rail's regional boards.[88] After the Bristol to Bath project, Sustrans became responsible for 180 miles of cycle paths across the UK with hundreds more built by councils on the initiative of the charity. By 1989 one such project was a Trans Pennine Trail from Hull and York to Liverpool and Southport via Barnsley. Designed in conjunction with Barnsley Council, the route utilized disused railway lines and canal towpaths. An even more ambitious Sustrans project was a 1,000-mile cycle network of railway paths, forest tracks and minor roads linking Inverness to Dover.[89] Disused railway lines of course had been a result of the Beeching Report and the state's drive towards motorization. Old lines had fallen into a state of disrepair and were used by motor cyclists, as well as being sites for illegal tipping. In 1982 it was calculated that there was over 11,000 kilometres of disused lines since 1923, with half completely unused, in addition to old tramways and canal towpaths. By 1989 there was a growing number of cycle paths nationwide, which included county schemes such as a 450-kilometre route in Cumbria, plus off-road routes utilizing disused railways.[90]

From its modest beginnings, Sustrans developed into an important agency for the development of cycle paths, the promotion of sustainable transport more generally and the enhancement of cycling's status. In 1988 Sustrans converted to a limited company status. Frustrated at the lack of organized protest by cyclists about the dearth of provision for them, it made the decision to become a campaigning organization and lobby on transport policies that affected cyclists and pedestrians. It also acquired sponsors including Task Force, the Countryside Commission, British Rail, Scottish Development Agency and the house builder Taylor Woodrow.[91] Highlighting how organizations from the voluntary sector provided specialist services for the state, in the 1980s Sustrans had benefitted from cooperation with the state through labour provided by Manpower Services – albeit a mechanism for the Conservative government to water down unemployment figures.[92] Later, in the 1990s a greater cooperation with government led to more support for volunteering. However, this dialogue only gained substance with the start of the National Lottery in 1994 under the Conservative government. Sustrans, along with the Royal Opera House (£55 million), was one of the early large beneficiaries of lottery funding. In 1995 Sustrans was awarded an initial £42 million of National Lottery funding to build a 6,000-mile National Cycle Network (NCN) across the country.[93] By 1997 the NCN, in partnership with local authorities, 'Safe Routes to School' and other organizations, had opened more than 1,400 miles of paths.[94] In 2000 the NCN had extended to 5,000 miles at a cost of £200 million, funded by a combination of lottery money, 400 local authorities and money from the private sector.[95]

Sustrans continued to expand into the new millennium and its scope widened. In addition to infrastructure projects, its remit now included projects to encourage cycling and fitness-related initiatives, in conjunction with other providers, such as Active Travel Consortium. In 2011 Sustrans worked with 340,000 pupils in 1,400 schools to encourage more children to cycle to work. As a result, there was an 80 per cent increase among participating schools. It also provided travel information to many households around the country. In Ipswich there was a 31 per cent increase in cycling while car use fell by 11 per cent. That year it also began the largest personalized travel planning programme in the UK. It aimed to reach 100,000 Welsh households over four years, and began with 63,000 houses in Cardiff. The announcement of an Active Travel (Wales) Bill placed the onus of providing walking and cycling routes and, hence, consulting Sustrans for its services on Welsh local authorities.[96]

Another major Sustrans project was Connect2. Initially, it was one of the projects competing for a single £50 million grant from the Big Lottery's 'Living Landmarks: The People's Millions'. Typically, given the nature of how audience participation had become a growing feature of television, Connect2 won a public vote on ITV's 'The People's £50 Million Lottery Giveaway' in 2007. The project aimed to create new routes for walking and cycling with crossings and bridges created over railway lines, rivers and roads in 79 communities throughout the UK.[97] Sustrans generated impressive numbers. By 2012 14,000 miles had been completed, with a third of the route traffic free and 60 per cent of the population living within 1 mile of the NCN.[98] In 2011 it was calculated that 484 million journeys had been made on the NCN by 3.3 million people – an increase of 15 per cent on 2010.[99]

Yet despite its success Sustrans attracted criticism.[100] It was perceived in some quarters that the charity had moved away from its grassroots, democratic origins and now exhibited the characteristics of a corporation and had become unaccountable despite being in receipt of large public funds. To a certain extent, these criticisms reflected wider tensions regarding the third way, due to the increasing integration of some voluntary bodies into the state planning process. Indeed, Sustrans had shifted its position away from advocacy to one of service provider. In 2008 Sustrans' founder and later chief executive officer, John Grimshaw, left the charity. By then Sustrans was run by a board of 11 trustees, complete with senior management team, but this made it democratically unaccountable as it only had supporters rather than members. In 2012 it employed over 400 people with 187 full-time staff. Despite the development of the NCN through central funding, Sustrans delivery was 'localized' due to the different groups it had to negotiate with. These included not only local authorities but also local landowners, central government and local community groups. Instead, because of a lack of direct central government funding, the NCN has been to a certain extent a piecemeal project. Sustrans had to bid for funding when it became available and much of the maintenance of the NCN has been carried out by local volunteers, who have looked after a particular stretch of the route.[101] Cycling continued to hold a low priority for central government.

Cycling activism in London

The focus of many cycling developments and early activism had been in London. In 1978 the London Cycling Campaign was launched and by 1987 it had 4,000 members.[102] It was a campaigning body and in 1981 it had two representatives on Greater London Council's Cycling Co-ordination Group. Other representatives included Friends of the Earth, CTC, Transport 2000 and London Amenity and Transport Association.[103] During the 1980s, London developed into a global financial behemoth while the north and Midlands suffered from economic recession; the capital if not recaptured, then consolidated its position as the centre of cycling in Britain. A metropolitan middle class – now more mobile as well as university educated – was attracted to London's booming financial services industry. It was also one increasingly aware of environmental issues and hence critical of London traffic. Riding a bicycle to work was both a solution to congestion and a way to keep fit when the long hours in the office prevented other opportunities for physical activity. By 2002, there were 650,000 Londoners who cycled at least once a week.[104] While national cycling levels remained stubbornly low at 2 per cent, in gentrified Hackney it was 9 per cent in 2015, reflecting how cycling had become a marker of affluence.[105]

The cultural shift in attitudes towards cycling in London was both a reflection of and a response to a greater political interest in cycling as a form of transport in the capital. In particular, transport was one policy area that came under the remit of the new London mayor's office, which was created in 2000. The new mayor though had limited autonomy as Parliament had curbed the powers of the new office and that of the newly formed Greater

London Assembly (GLA). The mayor had no tax-raising powers and continued to be reliant on central government and private sector funding. The GLA's areas of responsibility for which the mayor set policies included transport, environment, sport and policing, but not key local services such as education, housing or social care.[106]

Transport was the central issue of the first London mayoral election in 2000. Steve Norris, the Conservative candidate, had been an important figure behind the National Cycling Strategy, and had won praise from environmental groups like Transport 2000.[107] However, he was defeated by Ken Livingstone, then standing as an independent candidate.[108] Livingstone, despite his socialist credentials, would foster a positive relationship with business while managing to combine a commitment to social issues, in working to build and project London as a global city. It was this approach that proved effective in London's successful bid to host the 2012 Olympics. His main selling point as mayoral candidate was a congestion charge for traffic entering central London. While London's traffic problems dated back to Victorian times, by 2000 congestion had been identified by Londoners and its business community as the capital's main problem and a congestion charge was eventually introduced in 2003.[109] Bicycles were not included in the charge and cycling was openly encouraged.

Under Livingstone, Transport for London (TfL) established a Cycling Centre of Excellence, which was headed by Rose Ades, who also acted as chief cycling adviser to the mayor. Ades, later a member of the Green Party, had been one of the original founders of the feminist magazine *Spare Rib*. She had previously been a prominent activist as a member of the Cyclists' Public Affairs Group and her appointment reflected the growing influence of green and left-wing ideas – based around notions of sustainability – on mainstream transport policies.[110] Reflecting the lack of mayoral powers, Ades's role involved negotiating with local authorities within the capital to improve cycling routes and parking facilities. By 2004 TfL could claim that the number of cyclists on London's roads had increased by 23 per cent over the previous 12 months.[111] One initiative to further encourage cycling was the construction of bicycle parks throughout the capital, such as at London Bridge station. In 2008 TfL built a large bicycle park at Finsbury Park station. Not only did it have space for 130 bikes, but also 24-hour CCTV in order to combat rising levels of bicycle theft that had accompanied cycling's growing popularity.[112] Ades also developed the Cyclesafer Challenge aimed at developing an awareness of cycling safety among primary schoolchildren.[113]

Livingstone also endorsed the idea of a bicycle-hire scheme that had been used in other cities, which would come to fruition under his Conservative successor, Boris Johnson. 'Boris Bikes' were launched in 2010 and would later become part of the lexicon. By November 2010, 5,000 bikes were available at 344 docking stations with over 8,000 docking points.[114]

Johnson himself had ambitious plans to increase cycling in the capital. In summer 2008, he committed £55 million to cycling, a figure that was doubled the following year. He also hired his own cycling czar, former journalist Andrew Gilligan, and promoted a number of projects, including a Cycle Superhighways scheme, which was based on Livingstone's attempt to establish a cycle commuter network. In 2010 the first of 16 planned Superhighways – a fast commuting route from Outer and Inner London to Central London – was launched.[115] The most ambitious London project was perhaps the 'mini-Holland' scheme, which was initiated during Johnson's second term as mayor. Three boroughs – Waltham Forest, Enfield and Kingston – were awarded 'mini-Holland' status in an attempt to change the culture of mobility in London. Each area was pedestrianized to encourage more cycling and walking and awarded £30 million to invest in cycling infrastructure. Initially, there were tensions with local businesses, but the schemes did produce increases in cycling and walking levels.[116] Where London led, there rest of the country usually followed. In October 2012, the City of Nottingham launched a bike scheme similar to the Barclays Cycle Hire initiative in London, with up to 250 cycles available to hire. A new £6.9 million cycling scheme was launched in the city of Coventry in a bid to provide extensive new cycle paths, maps and training to boost cycling in the city from 2015.[117] Later, in 2017, former Olympic champion, Chris Boardman was appointed Manchester's cycling and walking commissioner, charged with the same task in the capital, to get people out of their cars.

The environment and changing bicycle design

At the same time as the bicycle was both complementing and reinforcing its status as an icon of environmentalism, the nature and appeal of cycling began to change. In particular, by the early 1990s the mountain bike (MTB) became the pre-eminent bicycle. In the seventies the 10-speed road bike – a 'racer' – had been regarded as the archetypal bicycle design, but, at a time when on-road cycling had become increasingly unpleasant and dangerous, the mountain bike was crucial in changing the image of cycling as a leisure activity. The mountain bike represented both a conscious and an unconscious response to the environmental impact of motoring; there was a shift in ideas regarding not only bicycle's function, especially for leisure, but also bicycle design. The practice of off-road cycling became increasingly widespread as an escape from car-cluttered roads. As a sign of the wider cycling community's acceptance of the MTB, by 1990 it was claimed that when the off-roaders nodded to the 'deeaichters' (cyclists riding bikes with dropped handlebars) they would now nod back.[118]

To a certain extent, the MTB captured the changing mood regarding cycling. It was most evident among those on the political left who were keen to promote cycling's environmental benefits. One prominent early cycling activist was Richard Ballantine. Ballantine, an American publisher (for Friends of the Earth) who had moved to London, not only promoted the pleasures of cycling but, like Reynar Banham, was an early advocate for urban cycling where he saw cycling as an 'antidote to the horrors of consumerism'.[119] His eponymous 1972 *Richard's Bicycle Book* sold over one million copies. His obituarist and friend Richard Grant claimed that for Ballantine, 'riding a bicycle was a defence against the alienation of modern life and the dehumanising effects of cars'.[120] He took a particular interest in the idea of human powered vehicles (HPV) and especially recumbent tricycles (discussed further). Ballantine claimed that not only were there economic, health and convenience benefits to riding a bicycle in a city, but more importantly cycling would enhance your life and its quality, building your consciousness and identity. Through cycling,

> consciousness, self-awareness and development are the prerequisites for a life worth living. Now look at what happens to you on a bicycle. It's immediate and direct. *You* pedal. *You* make decisions. *You* experience the tang of the air and the surge of power as you bite into the road. You're vitalized. As you hum along you fully and gloriously experience the day, the sunshine, the clouds, the breezes. You're alive! You are going some place, and it is *you* who are doing it. Awareness increases and each day becomes a little more important to you.[121]

Without ignoring Ballantine's criticism of modern life, his advocacy and promotion of cycling had more than a few echoes of its great interwar supporters, Wayfarer and Kuklos. On one summer ride in Dorset, riding an old 1935 BSA, Ballantine waxed lyrical about how '[t]he countryside was England at its most brilliant; lovely, soft green fields dotted with thatched cottages. I wove the old bike from side to side in sheer joy as we rolled along the lanes.'[122] Nevertheless, Ballantine was more in tune with modern forms of activism due to his ideological critique of the environmental damage caused by the car. He used his column in the journal *New Cyclist* to promote this critique and the benefits of cycling. However, his forecasts were usually overly optimistic. In 1992 he asked if the bicycle was now at last overtaking the car.[123] His instinct that people now thought cars did not work was not realized as car ownership continued to grow, reaching 27.2 million by 2000.

Ballantine had declared that the mountain bike's emergence was 'the sunrise of a new age in cycling – the return of bicycles by and for the people'.[124] In 1989 Geoff Apps claimed that 'the arrival of the mountain bike, ATB, cross-country cycle – call it what you will – appears to have shifted the image of cycling in remarkable ways. It has increased public interest in bicycles no end.'[125] Three years later Tom Bogdanowiz, an off-road enthusiast, could observe,

> Mountain bikes have given cycling a new lease of life and … they may bring healthy living back to our cities as well. Environmental awareness

is no longer an eccentricity. ... Mountain bikes, with their high profile in the media and on the roads, have changed the image of cycling. No longer just a means of transport, cycling is now perceived as a healthy and inexpensive leisure pursuit.[126]

Bogdanowiz was being slightly disingenuous about the cost of a new mountain bike. Increasingly, it was the middle classes who were becoming associated with cycling. As Bogdanowiz points out himself, MPs, bankers, newscasters, lawyers and stockbrokers were now to be seen on a bike.

Not only did the mountain bike emerge as the most popular model, but it became a multipurpose machine with its popularity extending to both off-road and on-road cycling, while it was also cross-generational in its appeal. In 1988 mountain bikes accounted for 15 per cent of the 2.2 million cycles sold in Britain; over the next 12 months that figure had risen by 600,000. By the following year mountain bikes accounted for 50–60 per cent of all bicycles sold.[127] Another indication of a mountain bike's popularity was that it had become a prime target for thieves.[128] The late eighties and early nineties were a period of fertile innovation in terms of the design of bicycles. (For BMX, see Chapter 9). Other new models emerged out of the MTB, such as the hybrid, which was a cross between a mountain bike and a road bike and could be used for all types of terrain.[129]

The story of the mountain bike's origins is well known. However, it is still worth recounting as it can be argued that the mountain bike has been the single most significant innovation in bicycle design and technology since the nineteenth century. The mountain bike was essentially developed from the grassroots. Rather than large bicycle manufacturers, similar to bicycle design and manufacture in the nineteenth century, it was a group of individuals instead who were entrepreneurs. Buenstorf has argued that it was an example of consumer-led, demand innovation,[130] while according to Rosen 'their emergence and their rising popularity provide an outstanding example of the serendipity of sociotechnical change, which cannot be predicted or easily directed towards particular desired objectives'.[131] Because of its origins in early 1970s California, the mountain bike was initially associated with the hippie-led counterculture. It was alleged that for early races winners received envelopes containing marijuana. There were at first around 20 to 30 people who would gather in Marin County on Pine Mountain and ride down steep, unpaved mountain tracks – the most famous of which was known as the 'Repack' – on bikes known as 'clunkers'. To withstand the pounding the bikes were taking they were subject to continual innovation. Component innovations included motorcycle brake levers, drum brakes, five speed gears, large knobbly tyres and tubular forks. One of the pioneers, Gary Fisher, introduced thumb shifters for changing gears. In this sense, the mountain bike shared similarities with the early history of the bicycle. Racing and the need for speed were important factors in shaping the design among a small group of racers, which in the nineteenth century led to the development of the ordinary. Initially a subculture in California, it was not until in 1982 that the clunker group's MTBs first came to the wider public's attention in the United States.

The practice of off-road cycling was not new. In Britain there was a tradition of 'rough riding', while Wayfarer's famous accounts of his journeys over the Welsh mountains were essentially off-road adventures. In the 1950s a Rough Stuff Fellowship had been founded, which largely catered for touring cyclists. Yet this culture of cycling was in stark contrast to the emergence of mountain biking. While the MTB was an American invention, there was a brief, parallel British 'clunker culture'. Geoff Apps, a graphic artist and an ex-moto-cross rider, designed the first British MTB in 1979. Before the advent of the American mountain bike, David Wrath-Sharman set out to design a 'bridleway bike'. He later developed literally his own cottage industry, designing and making custom-built bicycles in a rural retreat in Wales. Rather than a designer, Wrath-Sharman considered himself a sculptor. Instead of the 'rugged individualism' that the American mountain bike symbolized, Wrath-Sharman's bicycles epitomized a traditional British rural ideal regarding its use. He made bicycles for people who wanted to use it on a nature reserve and wanted to go from point A to point B fast and silently in summer and winter and to go long-distance touring. He thought that this type of cycling was 'legitimate' whereas the cyclist that 'wants to go yomping all over the countryside, riding at breakneck speed down bridleways is not legitimate, that is not appropriate use at all'.[132] This particular cycling ideal though contrasted with the growing American influences within British society. Moreover, British designs were poorly marketed and only built for off-road use whereas the US models were more adaptable to the urban environment, which was a major factor in their later success.

The sudden increase in MTB sales was due to various factors. One bike shop owner felt that their success was because they reflected the customers' needs and desires rather than because of their design qualities. Another felt that 'the mountain bike provides people with what they want rather than what they can be persuaded to need'. It meant that for reasons of practicality more people bought them to commute than as a fashion accessory. On the leisure side, mountain bikes cornered the cheap touring bike market. As opposed to bikes with drop handlebars, with its upright riding position and perceived ease of riding and safety MTBs had a less fussy image. This was important for the over-30s market who may not have cycled for a number of years and were driving the consumer boom (see Chapter 9).[133] The absence of design rules for mountain bikes led to more changes in frame design during the early nineties than there had been in the previous four decades. However, its macho image – through advertising its ability to go fast down steep hills – was probably off-putting to many women, but it was ideal for urban use: flat handlebars, chunky tyres, lots of gears, not too heavy and strong brakes.[134] Indeed, it was noted that in London the mountain bike was the main choice of machine for bicycle messengers at the time.[135]

By the 1990s the mountain bike fulfilled the criteria of a renewed middle-class interest in cycling and because of its versatility and durability, it opened up a new wave of cycling tourism. Bicycle tourism had been given a boost in the Countryside Act of 1968 when the right cyclists of to ride on bridleways was legalized, despite opposition from a powerful landowner lobby.[136] In 1988 'Avon Valley Cyclery' was offering a 'Dirty Weekend' with off-road bike hire. The range of cycling holidays increased with more people interested in starting up their own cycling tourism business. One Scottish businessman claimed that in the off season he received a phone call a week from such budding entrepreneurs.[137]

The bicycle industry in Britain more generally was undergoing major change. By 2000 Raleigh, its flag bearer, and formerly the world's biggest manufacturer of cycles, stopped volume production of bicycle frames.[138] The industry underwent profound change not just in Britain but also in Europe in face of global competition. As a result, there was more choice and design diversity within the bicycle leisure market. Film director Richard Longcraine, for example, built a 'velochino' in his workshop, which was designed to be carried in the boots of cars and for use in the city.[139] Peter Cox has attributed some of these developments as part of wider change in the UK cycling industry through a combination of environmental activism and technological innovation.[140] In 1990 Clive Sinclair, famous as a pioneer of home computers and infamous for his eponymous C5, brought out his own electric bicycle, the Zike. Battery powered – pedal power could also be used – it had a top speed of 12 mph and could climb a 1-in-10 hill, weighed 24 lbs and cost less than a penny to recharge.[141] In commenting on criticism about Sinclair's design, Jim McGurn, invoked the spirit of innovation and environmentalism, arguing that it was an alternative form of transport, and that any idea could only be judged over time. The Zike did not live up to these expectations.[142]

In addition, the recumbent made a brief comeback. Recumbent tricycles had been popular during the interwar years. As HPV they were faster and more efficient than the classic diamond-framed bicycles. In 1933 Francis Faure broke the world hour record on a recumbent, but in 1938 the UCI excluded them from sporting competition, removing the financial incentive for further technological development and mass production.[143] As a result, any developments were pioneered outside the mainstream cycle industry, mostly by innovators working on their own.[144] In 1975 the International Human Powered Vehicle Association was formed with the aim of creating technologies that would produce environmentally friendly vehicles capable of replacing the combustion engine. Richard Ballantine had been one of the recumbent's most enthusiastic advocates. He claimed that these types of vehicles were more efficient than other forms of transport and more dubiously that they were safer than two wheelers because they were more visible.[145]

Recumbents were custom built by specialist cycle makers and hence very expensive. One such design was the Peer Gynt, which in 1989 had a number of variations. There was the classical recumbent that cost at least £1,250 and the duet wheelchair tandem, which was designed a wheelchair user for £2,000.¹⁴⁶ This particular cycling machine was sold from the Lees Stables in Coldstream on the England-Scotland border. It was also the site for the office of the *New Cyclist* magazine, which promoted an anti-modernist critique through cycling. Importantly, the location acted as a commune for two families who had become disillusioned with city life and 'decided to get away to find a saner way of life and to be closer to nature' and have a 'greener lifestyle'. The group included Nancy Woodhead and her partner, Graham Bell, and Jim McGurn, author and editor of *New Cyclist*, and his wife; there were also their seven children. Their 'vision was of an activity centre which would show practical working alternatives in both lifestyle and personal transport'.¹⁴⁷ All were also heavily involved in permaculture, which aimed at creating sustainable lifestyles through nature. Woodhead was a bicycle mechanic, while Bell, with a background in marketing was the one who saw a market for cycles not available in the regular shops. The Lees Stables were also converted into a venue for cycling holidays and activities.¹⁴⁸ Cox argues that it was examples such as these that highlighted how cyclists themselves were active agents in shaping cycling cultures as well as reshaping the industry.¹⁴⁹

The popularity of the mountain bike embodied cycling's transformation since the 1960s when it had been overlooked in the rush to modernity. Again, cycling had adapted to changing circumstances, in this case political and cultural changes, to eke out a new role. In terms of politics, its profile had never been higher due to the incorporation of cycling into a multitude of local and central government policies and initiatives. It had (re-)established its health-giving properties in combination with its newly endorsed green credentials. This new status had broadly been a product of an increasing political pluralism founded on values that the relationship between the bicycle and environmentalism encapsulated. In addition, it was supplemented by a cycling consumer boom (see Chapter 9). In reality, however, Britain's car culture had remained undiminished, even stronger, during this period. Whatever the environmental impact, it was still difficult to persuade people to give up their cars. In a number of ways, this issue returned to the issue of how the values of individualism, a legacy of Thatcherism, continued to trump those of collective action. Without (unpopular) government legislation, it would be difficult for a culture of change to take place.

CHAPTER 9

Cycling in post-industrial Britain

In October 2013 a Londoner rode up Mount Ventoux on his bicycle. There was nothing unusual about this. Mount Ventoux was, and is, seen as a legendary climb on the Tour de France, and for British riders it had increasingly become something of a pilgrimage and shrine as it was where Tom Simpson had died in 1967. Now hundreds climbed up the mountain to acknowledge and 'pay their respects' to Simpson's memorial located at the site about a kilometre from the summit. What made this particular ride up the Ventoux unusual was that it was achieved on a 'Boris Bike', a 3-speed, 23-kilogram machine that belonged to the London bicycle-hire scheme. It was part of a challenge as a result of a conversation between friends to pick up the bike from a South London docking station, drive hundreds of kilometres to the foot of the mountain in Provence, before an ascent of the mountain. The group of three men involved then had to return the bike to London within 24 hours to avoid a £150 fine. They made it with less than a minute to spare. It was Rob Holden who rode the 22 kilometres to the top in 3 hours and was trying to raise money for charity following the death of his father from cancer.[1]

Beyond this example of British quirkiness and ingenuity, the challenge highlighted the changing characteristics of cycling as an activity in the twenty-first century. It combined attempts to encourage cycling in London through a public bicycle-hire scheme with a new found fascination about the Tour de France and the history of cycling, especially among middle-aged, middle-class men, as well as the entire episode being posted on YouTube.[2] In many ways cycling had turned full circle from its nineteenth-century origins. It experienced another boom in popularity, one which was dominated by middle-class men, who adopted cycling as a lifestyle choice, leading to the invention of a new acronym – MAMIL (Middle-Aged Men In Lycra). In addition to its conspicuous consumption, and on the back of its links with environmentalism, the cycling boom was accompanied with messages of health and well-being, which had barely changed since the 1800s.

From the 1970s, cycling as an activity underwent a revival, which by the early years of the twenty-first century had turned into another boom.[3] Those who actually owned a bicycle ranged from around 15 to 18 million in the 1970s, but activity levels were low.[4] By 1990 it was found that cycling was the fourth most popular sport and physical activity among both men and women.[5] Exact figures though were still difficult to ascertain as any increase was both relatively small and not unilinear. Neither did the number of cyclists and the number of bicycles equate to levels of cycling, as it was estimated that 25 million people owned a bicycle in 2013[6] while in the same year it was claimed that the total number of cyclists – those who actually rode their bikes – was 13 million, with a million starting to cycle that year.[7] According to Sport England's Active People's Survey, levels of cycling among adults over 16 years of age had increased by 28 per cent between 2005 (1.63 million) and 2014 (2.07 million).[8] The levels in the UK, however, continued to lag behind those in most European Union countries. In 1992, it was estimated that there were 3 million active cyclists in Britain, compared to 10 million in France.[9] By 2013 only 4 per cent of British people said that they cycled every day; 10 per cent, a few times a week; 17 per cent, a few times a month or less often, with 69 per cent saying that they never cycled. The majority of other EU countries had much higher levels of cycling, especially the Netherlands with figures of 43 per cent, 28 per cent and 16 per cent, respectively; and only 13 per cent said they never cycled. Interestingly though France – a nation renowned for its cycling – had levels not dissimilar to the UK: 5 per cent, 13 per cent, 26 per cent, respectively, and 56 per cent said they never cycled.[10]

Despite the rise in the number of bicycles and cyclists – and the host of initiatives plus the rise of cycling activism – cycling's decline as a form of passenger transport continued into the twenty-first century. In 1952, cycling accounted for 11 per cent of all journeys. By 1973 this total had dropped to 1 per cent and flatlined thereafter. By 2001, cycling's share of people travelling to work stood at 2.8 per cent, and this remained the same in 2011, equating to 741,000 working adults. Cycling was more popular in urban areas. In 1975–6 around 8 per cent of those living in towns of up to 250,000 used a bicycle at least once a week with cycling accounting for about 5 per cent of all trips. Two-fifths of all cycle trips were made to and from work, though only 6 per cent of all these work trips were made by bicycle.[11]

Membership of cycling organizations provided an indication of cycling's popularity and status. In 1971 membership of the BCF had dropped to 10,369 from its 1950 peak of over 66,000.[12] In 1980 it reached 17,000 before dropping away again in the early eighties due to the economic recession, which had an impact on working-class cyclists.[13] However, it retained some public visibility when Britain staged the 1970 and 1982 world championships at Leicester with both televised.[14] In 1999 there were still only 13,119 BCF members, a fall of 5 per cent on the previous year. By 2006 this figure had risen to 20,028.[15] In 2010 only 2 per cent of respondents agreed that sporting success had 'inspired me to take up cycling'.[16] But this almost certainly began to change due to the later success of the likes Wiggins, Mark Cavendish and Victoria Pendleton. At the end of 2012, following the London Olympics, membership had increased to 63,000. After Wiggins won the Tour de France 13,000 people joined up, with 250 per day joining up during the Games.[17] Four years later, membership had doubled to 125,000 with 2,200 registered clubs.[18] Cycling continued to appeal to a wide spectrum of the population. Touring was still popular and in 2012 the CTC had around 70,000 members.[19]

The latest cycling boom had emerged out of a post-industrial landscape, which shaped the make-up of the cycling population. As the post-1945 political consensus was eroded, it was replaced by a neoliberal ethos, which included rolling back the state and an emphasis on the deregulation of financial markets. From the 1979–97 Tory governments through to the New Labour administrations, greater social and regional inequalities emerged as the occupational structure shifted away from primary industries 'to a service-based, knowledge-oriented and computer-centred economy where non-manual labour dominated'.[20] Between 1971 and 1990 changes in the British workforce's occupational structure had pointed to a growing middle class with a small but significant rise in the number of people working as professional, employers or managers. For men the combined percentage had increased from 20 per cent to 26 per cent; for women it increased from 18 per cent to 24 per cent.[21] By 2010 90 per cent of all employed women and 70 per cent of all employed men worked in service-sector industries such as insurance, banking and transport, while 44 per cent alone held professional, technical and managerial jobs. There had also been a shift in the pattern of work; from standard full-time, secure work – 'a job for life' – to more flexible, insecure forms of work, bringing with it more part-time working and temporary contracts as well as more career changes. The job market was increasingly insecure, reliant on a flexible workforce and more polarized. At the top end of the labour market there were 'iMacJobs' with 'McJobs' at the bottom. A divide opened up between, at one end, a growing university-educated middle class and, at the other, a 'precariat', a section of society characterized by poverty, inequality and a lack of social mobility.[22]

With the growth in car ownership, over the 1975–90 period there were correlating changes in the social and economic make-up of cyclists. In 1991 the newly published magazine *New Cyclist* claimed that it was serving a new social group – one that was a high-spending audience of educated, affluent regular cyclists interested in all aspects of cycling, not just sport.[23] Since 1970 a persistent feature of sporting participation more generally had been how professional and managerial groups were almost three times as likely to have participated in sport as unskilled workers.[24] In one 1977 survey the breakdown of occupational groups who cycled was as follows: professional and managers, 11 per cent; other non-manual, 37 per cent; skilled manual, 19 per cent; semi and unskilled, 18 per cent; and others, 15 per cent.[25] By comparison, the traditionally middle-class sport of golf was noted as having exceptionally high participation rates among the professional and managers group: 37 per cent (professional and managers); 28 per cent (other non-manual); 21 per cent (skilled manual); 7 per cent (semi and unskilled); and 7 per cent (others) respectively. Typically, soccer was one of the few activities where the skilled manual group was the most predominant (36 per cent).[26] A 1978 Countryside Commission survey revealed that the professional class accounted for 7 per cent of bicycle owners, while the intermediate class comprised 19 per cent with the skilled non-manual sector at 22 per cent and at 28 per cent, the skilled manual group, the two largest classes. The lowest two were semi- and unskilled workers at 15 and 10 per cent, respectively.[27] However, this survey perhaps indicated that while many members of the working classes owned a bicycle and had previously used it as a form of transport, they were now increasingly leaving it at home and instead driving to work. By 1990 the General Household Survey had indicated that there had been some changes to levels of participation.[28] It was found that of those who had participated in cycling four weeks previously, professionals were the highest socioeconomic group at 13 per cent with employers and managers accounting for 8 per cent and 9 per cent for intermediate and junior non-manual workers. The figures for golf were not dissimilar: 13 per cent; 10 per cent; and 4 per cent; mirroring cycling's drift towards a middle-class activity.[29] Moreover, cyclists were now invariably drivers. In 1990 *New Cyclist* found that over 90 per cent of its readers held a driving licence,[30] while in 2015 90 per cent of British Cycling members owned a car.[31] This development had broader cultural and economic implications as it reinforced the image of the bicycle as both a minor mode of transport and a form of leisure.

This drift of the middle classes cycling in greater numbers and more often than other social groups continued into the twenty-first century. In 2005, the market research company Mintel produced five typologies of cyclists, which confirmed both the social divisions within cycling and the markets companies were trying to capture. The group most sought after by retailers and manufacturers were tagged 'regular riding fanatics', who were most likely to read a broadsheet, use the internet, shop at Waitrose and Sainsbury's, but watched little commercial TV. By contrast, 'hard targets', that is, the social group most difficult to sell bicycles to, were deemed to read popular tabloids and were avid watchers of satellite television. The groups in between included 'safety cyclists' who were broadsheet newspapers readers, Waitrose shoppers, but didn't watch much commercial television; 'recreational riders' similarly watched little commercial TV, but were viewers of satellite television used the internet and were heavy users of mobile phones as well as shopping at Marks & Spencer; the 'occasionally fit' were readers of the 'red top' tabloids.³² In 2008 it was further claimed that those cyclists who held the most positive attitudes towards cycling belonged to the ABC socioeconomic group, resided in households with an income of over £50,000 and were *Guardian* readers.³³ A 2011 survey confirmed that London cyclists were more likely to come from affluent social groups. Cyclists living in households earning under £15,000 per annum accounted for on average 1.5 per cent of cyclists in the capital; for those in households earning over £35,000, the figure was 2.2 per cent.³⁴

Despite its democratic appeal, cycling was increasingly seen as an aspiration activity, highlighting an increasing social divide in cycling. One signifier of this change was Mintel's growing interest in cycling.³⁵ Sport and leisure has been crucial to middle-class identities since the nineteenth century. However, by the late twentieth century the values of the middle classes, especially men, had begun to shift, which in turn had shaped the nature of their leisure activities. Whereas previously joining organizations like the Freemasons, a Rotary club or the local rugby union club cemented the status of middle-class men, identity was increasingly becoming formed around ideas of lifestyle. The importance of leading a fit and healthy life was one such male middle-class aspiration. Where he may have previously purchased an expensive motorbike or a car, or a set of golf clubs, now buying an expensive bicycle became a lifestyle accessory.

By 2012 many London commuters were busy professionals who used cycling as an opportunity to fit in some form of physical activity into their daily routines.³⁶ One product of these shifting attitudes to cycling in the capital was the 'Hipster Spice Route'. During the rush hour, Clerkenwell Road – a major east-west artery road – became jammed, full of cyclists commuting from the eastern boroughs into the centre of town and back again. In addition, the King's Road and Embankment brought in bankers from the south-west of London, while a feature of the mainline stations at rush hour was hundreds of commuters from the Home Counties unfolding their Brompton bikes before pedalling to work. Popular weekend cycling destinations included Regent's Park and Richmond Park on the edges of West London. There was no one type of London cyclist, ranging from the slow and law abiding, to kids riding around town centres in groups, to the kamikaze. There was no typical London bicycle either as they could include track bikes, Pashley princesses, 'tourers' and 'roadies'.³⁷

Cycling and diversity

How socially diverse was cycling in post-industrial Britain? In 2006, Matt Seaton observed that there were now generally two types of cyclists who could be divided up by class: 'One is white, middle-class, educated, and probably liberal in their politics; they have good-quality, new-ish bikes, with the right accessories. The other is either poor or teenaged, often non-white, and has whatever bike comes to hand – old and ill-maintained or cheap from Halfords.'[38] Thus, there was no monolithic cycling culture and instead a range of subcultures existed. Yet, cycling remained an overwhelmingly white and male-dominated activity. There has been an increasing number of female cyclists and a growing visibility of their presence due to sporting success, but there has traditionally been a male bias. In 1989, for example, over 95 per cent of *Cycling Weekly* readers were male while bicycle shops were perceived as intimidating places for women.[39] Cycling had a long tradition associated with people with disabilities, stretching back to interwar years. If anything, this relationship became stronger across the disability spectrum. In 1988, for example, the Spastics Society organized a 'Cycling for the Disabled' weekend, which included those with specially adapted bikes.[40] Moreover, the Paralympics would later act as a beacon of inspiration for people with disabilities, both physical and learning.

In multicultural Britain, ethnic minorities remained under-represented in cycling. Even in London, the UK's most ethnically diverse city where more than one in three residents belonged to a minority ethnic group, in 2011 cycling was declared 'disproportionately an activity of affluent, white men'. It was found that 86 per cent of male cyclists and 94 per cent of female cyclists identified themselves as white.[41] While ethnic minorities have made up a disproportionately higher number of people from lower income groups, the lack of cyclists from a minority ethnic background cannot be explained by class alone. Certainly, racism has not been absent from the sport. Back in 1976 Maurice Burton claimed that he was denied a place in the men's Olympic pursuit team on account of his skin colour.[42] In 2017 Kevin Hylton noted that his cycling group of all black riders had attracted racist comments from passing motorists.[43] Yet it seems that the image of cycling has been an important factor. Cycling's decline as a mode of transport coincided with the mass migration from the 1950s and the relative rise of the car as a signifier of social status. This was not the case for everyone. Jaiprakash Chudasama was one of many Ugandan migrants who eventually settled in Leicester in 1972 after being thrown out by Idi Amin. Because of his irregular shift patterns, the lack of suitable public transport and initially being unable to afford a car, he began riding a bike to work in 1981 and continued riding to the same place of work up to his retirement in 2019.[44]

Despite cycling organizations usually pleading for all the members they could get, this tolerance did not reach as far as the gay community on occasions. In 1981 an application had been rejected from the Gay Outdoor Club for an advertisement – 'Gay Outdoor Club for gay people who enjoy the outdoor life' – to be placed in the CTC's magazine *Cycletouring*. No reason was given by the CTC committee. Two years later Ben Stout had similarly wanted to advertise in the magazine's companions' column with: 'Lesbian and Gay Friends wanted to share social activities and riders with a view to setting up a national group'. Initially, it was rebuffed, accompanied by a vague reply and no particular reason, as it stated that the entry was 'unacceptable for publication' and that '[t]his is no new attitude for CTC, but is a question of Council followed by successive editors of *Cycletouring*'. At the next council meeting though the matter was raised by Derek Roberts, and it became increasingly vexed. One council member, Bob Carmichael-Riddell, referred to the gay community as perverts who were contagious, but he 'reasoned', according to Roberts, 'it must be better for them to be out in the open where they could be left to indulge in their sinful activities without our pure and righteous members getting contaminated'. Other council members felt that the CTC would actually lose members if the club was associated with the gay community in any way. The CTC secretary later claimed that he had received 'shoals of letters' from members asking why the advert had been published.[45] To what extent the whole of cycling held similar homophobic tendencies is unknown. Certainly, the CTC had an image as a conservative body, but as cycling was as a democratic activity, it was as likely to reflect contemporary social attitudes as any other. Moreover, other CTC members had supported the groups in protesting against their treatment.

Cycling and consumerism

Cycling's changing image and social profile provided the background to its subsequent consumer boom in the twenty-first century. Over the same period, sport and leisure emerged as an important industry. By 1997 sport and leisure accounted for around £10 billion annually of consumer expenditure as well as employing 750,000 workers and paying £3.5 billion per year in tax revenues. Sport was Britain's eleventh largest industry and one that expanded quickly.[46] Just as importantly a powerful sports lobby developed, which gave any proposed cycling projects a greater sense of legitimacy. The leisure industry had been growing since the 1960s and was partly a product of political responses to changing employment patterns. While the much-vaunted 'leisure society', as predicted by thinkers such as John Maynard Keynes, did not materialize, changes in employment patterns contributed to post-war Britain's social and cultural transformation.[47] From the 1950s increasing political attention had been paid to workers' growing time off work, highlighted by a series number of reports and political party pamphlets. In Labour's 1959 policy statement, *Leisure for Living*, emphasis was put on how leisure was as much a right as work, its importance and uses in light of changes in the nature of work and as part of the party's wider aims for a planned society. Later in 1980 the Trades Union Congress outlined its concerns about low levels of participation regarding recreations, especially among the working class, the women, the elderly and those among the working class living in inner-city areas.

Earlier the 1960 Wolfenden Report on sport had been ostensibly concerned with elite sport and matters such as amateurism and professionalism, but it also took an interest in sport for the masses, advocating the establishment of a centrally funded Sports Council.[48] In 1965 the Sports Council was eventually created, and by 1972 it had adopted the European-led campaign of 'Sport for All'. In addition, local authorities came to regard leisure as an important area of policy, which was reflected in the exponential rise of sports centres. In 1964 there had been no such facilities, by 1979 there were over 400, fulfilling the growing demand for municipal facilities from a population with greater flexible working hours, more affluent and wider car ownership. Initially, cycling did not feature heavily in the plans for local authorities. One of the few exceptions to this investment in sporting facilities was at Leicester, where a new track was built at Saffron Lane to host the 1970 world championships.

As a form of consumption, cycling was neither politically nor culturally neutral. Hilton has identified certain 'goods' – semi-luxuries or comforts – that have been 'crucial in shaping the social and political environment of the latter half of the twentieth century'. It could be argued that in the early twenty-first century the bicycle became one of these goods. With its links to public health, the environment and sporting activity, the bicycle had become 'central to modern notions of citizenship and the good life'.[49] Similarly, in his study of late-twentieth-century consumption and masculinities, Frank Mort has shown how consumerism has not been monolithic but instead is continually shaped and reshaped by complex interrelationships including a diverse range of non-economic factors, such as culture, politics and business.[50] While the growth in cycling partly reflected a world of privatized leisure where many cyclists chose to invest their energies and aspirations, it was also a world that collective social action – in its broadest terms – continued to thrive, buttressed by changing technology and attitudes towards environment and especially health.

How did these changes reveal themselves in the consumption of cycling? Following a dip in the sale of bicycles in the 1960s, there was a marked increase by the early seventies. In 1957 one million bicycles had been sold. By 1969 sales had dropped by nearly 50 per cent to 563,000, before recovering to the one million figure again in 1974. There was now a distinct shift in age profile of those buying a bike. Out of the million bikes purchased in 1974 595,000 had been adult machines, representing a 100 per cent increase on the previous year, while bicycles for children had dropped 27 per cent to 405,000.[51] Over the final quarter of the twentieth century, total annual sales of bicycles in the UK rose from around 1 million to 2.7 million.[52] The market though was subject to fluctuations and fashions. In the early 1980s the industry had received a fillip through the BMX craze with 800,000 sold each year at its height. In 1983 a total of 2.3 million bicycles had been sold in Britain, but this fell to 1.5 million after the BMX bubble burst due to a saturation of the market.[53]. They were also regarded as a kid's bike as well as unconducive to mass road use due to being too low geared and too heavy.[54] By 2010 the cycling industry was worth £2.9 billion a year. In that year, 3.7 million bicycles had been sold, an increase of 28 per cent on the previous year, while more than £1.5 billion was spent on bicycles with another £850 million more on accessories.[55] Sporting success had a short-term impact. Following Wiggins' 2012 Tour de France victory and Olympic success, Halfords, the UK's largest bicycle retailer reported an 18 per cent increase in sales of bikes and related equipment in that week.[56]

By contrast, over a similar period, the car industry maintained its position as a pillar of the British economy. The manufacturing of motor vehicles was worth £8.4 billion to the UK economy and accounted for 6 per cent of UK manufacturing and 0.6 per cent of the whole UK economy. By 2016 these figures had increased to £15.8 billion, 9.4 per cent and 0.9 per cent, respectively. In 2015 the motor-vehicle industry employed 155,000 people across Britain; 23,000 by contrast worked in cycling in 2010.[57]

In terms of the type of bicycles, the mountain bike's popularity endured into the twenty-first century. MTBs (40 per cent), regarding bikes ridden, were still the most popular in 2014. With the growth of cycle commuting, the hybrid (18 per cent) was the second most popular, while the traditional roadster accounted for 15 per cent. Road bikes accounted for 15 per cent of the most-ridden type of bicycle, but it was the one where there had been the most growth in sales and by 2012 there was a trend towards premium-priced road bikes. These bikes were sold at significantly higher prices than other types increasingly becoming the bicycle of choice for the growing number of middle-class cyclists. They were more likely to be more serious, riding more than once or twice a week, either commuting or training for a race or sportive, leading to the emergence of the 'Weekend Warrior'. It was this particular group of consumers that became the most attractive to cycling retailers.[58]

In addition to bicycles, there was a growing demand for specialist cycling accessories and clothing, especially among young men from the high-earning AB socioeconomic group.[59] Rather than high-street retailers like Halfords, this group was more likely to buy at independent and specialist cycling shops.[60] Accessories such as lights and clothing had been an early and essential aspect of the cycling subculture. By the twenty-first century, however, there was a greater demand for items such as sun glasses and even food supplements. In 2014 it was calculated that the UK market for bicycle parts, accessories and clothing was valued at £1.2 billion, an increase of 27.6 per cent from 2010. The most popular parts were locks and lights while the most popular items of clothing were the helmet and hi-vis jackets, reflecting concerns over safety.[61] Unsurprisingly, sales of bike racks for cars boomed, reflecting the changing nature of cycling with an increasing emphasis on its leisure market.[62] Bicycle locks were another accessory growing in popularity, albeit because there was an increase in bike theft.[63]

What they wore on a bike had been important to cyclists since the nineteenth century. By the twenty-first century cycling fashions mirrored wider cultural tastes, especially the liking for sports gear, even for non-competitive cyclists. Whereas British cyclists were once obsessed with cycling gear from Europe, top British fashion houses were now incorporating the cycling 'look' into their designs. Paul Smith was one such fashion designer. He was also a cycling fan who later developed a friendship with, among others, Mark Cavendish. To a certain extent, wearing cycling gear was both a reflection and a rejection of the free-market values of late-twentieth-century Britain. The sharp functional elegance of cycling gear contrasted with both the homogenous and faceless business suit of yuppies that symbolized Thatcherism and the fashions of the seventies, which included long hair and flared trousers; in wearing cycling gear young men were clipped and smart, as per business executive, but also fashionable as well as having street cred. It was also a fashion that was European in origin, illustrating Britain's increasingly closer political and cultural ties with the continent after it joined the European Economic Community.

The rise of the clothing brand Rapha was a product of this growing demand. Founded in 2004 by Simon Mottram, a former branding consultant, Rapha was built around the idea of 'passion marketing'. In tapping into the affluent over-30 male cycling market it sold a romantic view of cycling, including the cycle messenger lifestyle who were used to test and promote Rapha products. As a result of this strategy, Rapha's products were not cheap. Embrocation creams, for example, were priced at £20 while its Soho shop stocked the latest hi-tech gear, such as high-performance jerseys at £195 as well as offering bespoke cycling holidays in the Alps. There were also 9,000 members of the Rapha riding club at £135 per year.[64] As a brand it concentrated on how potential customers saw themselves, who they wanted to be – a lifestyle – through the 'timeless appeal of classical design, the nostalgia of vintage racing'.[65] But for some cycling aficionados Rapha (named after a defunct French cycling team from the 1950s) represented a form of elitism. Yet the selling of nostalgia was an increasing feature of the growth in cycling's popularity.

Cycling nostalgia was also reflected in the re-emergence of traditional bicycles, such as the hand-built Pashley Princess. The company had started in 1926 and in 2010 it was reporting that its orders had doubled. Accessories such as helmets also took on a retro style, while Bobbin Bicycles, established in 2008, supplied classic bicycles. Reaching further back into cycling nostalgia was the Tweed Run. Set up in 2009, it attracted 300 tweed-clad – including plus fours – participants for a cycle-through-London run, before establishing other Tweed Runs around the globe.[66] Going even further back, the penny farthing was also making a comeback. A number of companies began to manufacture 'Pennies', while the 2013 Smithfield Nocturne featured a criterium race of penny farthings.[67] Another type of bicycle that came back into fashion was the 'fixie'. Used mainly by cycle messengers, single, fixed-gear bikes achieved a cult status in London among some city cyclists and commuters due to the different and more challenging cycling experience they offered.[68]

By 2012 cyclo-sportives had become an important factor behind the growth in sales of road bikes.[69] Mass bicycle rides were not a new idea, but a growth in mass bike rides had been further evidence of cycling's growing popularity in the 1980s, as well as highlighting a shifting dynamic in cycling participation. These events owed something to the earlier boom in marathons, which attracted thousands of participants, and jogging more generally. At the 1989 Great Northern Bike Ride there were 6,000 cyclists, for example. Like marathons, bike rides not only acted as a form of mass participation, but gained respectability for their reputation for raising money for charity. In 1976 the London to Brighton ride was revived with 36 riders. By 1991 it was part of a series run by Bike Events, which in total organized 11 charity rides with a total of 30,000 cyclists.[70] Another 30,000 riders on the Historic Churches Trust's sponsored cycle rides in 1991 raised nearly £900,000 for the trust.[71] In June and July 1992, for these types of events, it was claimed that over 100,000 cyclists would be on British roads, raising the profile of cycling more generally. For these rides an emphasis was put on 'fun' and creating a carnivalesque atmosphere, which contrasted with the traditionally staid attitudes of the cycling fraternity.[72] In 1993 the CTC admitted that it still struggled to shake off its stereotypical image of the elderly gent 'pedalling a cherished British hand-built touring bike with mudguards and CTC sticker, clad in plus fours, Argyle socks and black leather touring shoes, with the black cotton duck saddle bag'.[73]

In 1992, to celebrate its twenty-first anniversary, Friends of the Earth launched its 'Bike to the Future' with four massed rides with around 20,000 riders at venues around the country. It also acted as a fund-raising campaign for Friends of the Earth issues on transport, air pollution and ozone depletion.[74] By the twenty-first century, sportives were regular events. Aping the l'Etape du Tour de France in which thousands of cyclists rode one stage of the Tour, its popularity in Britain led to the Etape Caledonia, the Etape Pennines and the Etape Mercia, which were held on closed roads. The Etape Mercia was based at the Oulton Park motor-racing circuit, which could accommodate over 2,000 riders, and was run by IMG which also ran two other events catering to 8,000 riders. Others included the Etape du Dales, the Dartmoor Classic and the Circuit of the Cotswolds. The biggest sportive though was Ride London. Inaugurated in 2013, it developed into a weekend of cycle events, culminating in a 100-mile closed-roads sportive. The route covered the one used for the London 2012 Olympics and attracted 27,000 participants, mainly enthusiasts. However, there were also other events designed to reflect the diverse character of cyclists. Freecycle, held the day before on an 8-mile route through central London, attracted

70,000 people, especially families, and was designed to promote cycling more generally.[75] Naturally, the cycling industry was involved. One of the leading retailers, Evans Cycles sponsored 16 sportives under the 'RideIt' series, as well as 14 mountain bike rides. UK Cycling Events organized 38 sportives that year, sponsored by *Cycling Weekly* and the online retailer Wiggle.

Performance and how to measure it became an integral part of the new cycling subculture. Filling in a mileage chart – *Cycling* would provide a copy for readers at the start of each new year – had been a common feature among dedicated cyclists during the interwar years. By the 1990s, however, digital accessories, to measure speed, mileage and cadence were starting to become popular.[76] In 2008 Strava, a San Francisco-based website as well as a mobile software application, was invented. These 'apps' enabled both riders and joggers to track their athletic activity via the global positioning system (GPS) on a mobile phone. By 2015 there was a growing number of cycling apps available either for measuring performance or as a route planner.[77] People recorded their runs or bike rides, which then provided them with data on their performance. This has included heart rate and power-output information as well as highlighted sections of a ride, especially climbs. Reflecting web 2.0 developments and the digital revolution, Strava styled itself as the social network for athletes as it allowed weekend warriors to share their data with friends, who could then also comment on social media about their performance.

To a certain extent, Strava and other digital products reflected changes and continuities in the new cycling subculture. In 2010 it was claimed that the typical cycling enthusiast was 'an AB, internet-savvy adult'.[78] The use of this new technology pointed to an increasingly middle-class, technocratic society in which the notion of performance was being applied to all aspects of life, even commuting. Moreover, it reflected the changing values of the middle classes. Through a prevailing Thatcherite ethos, work was increasingly framed around ideas of performance and competition, such as in the form of league tables. In their quest for fitness, the ability to measure performance, in the form of a cycling run, through this new technology was for many an essential part of the new cycling subculture. At the sharper end of this particular wedge was the use of performance-enhancing drugs in amateur cycling. In 2017 a BBC poll of 1,000 athletes found that 14 per cent of cyclists had taken anabolic steroids with 45 per cent claiming that they knew someone who had taken steroids. In the wider survey those aged between 18 and 34 were more likely to use PEDs than any other age groups; there was little difference between genders. The motivations though were not confined to performance enhancement with some taking them for pain relief while others for reasons of body image.[79]

Given cycling's myriad of motivations and meanings, its changing image and growing consumer culture was not welcomed by everyone. In 1992 Jim McGurn, responding to how sport promoted values of individualism, decried the increasing use of the word 'performance' and instead claimed that there was need to keep cycle sport in perspective. He argued that

> if it becomes nothing more than a voyeuristic glamour activity, it could take cycling as a whole into a cultural cul-de-sac. Any social activity which comes to be viewed by the public as a mere sport, and an exclusive one at that, loses prestige as a socially useful and practical activity.[80]

For others, it was simple: cycling was becoming too expensive. In 1990 one veteran cyclist claimed the costs were too high and that 'it's no longer a poor man's sport. It has developed into a middle-class sport'; even cycling magazines were becoming too expensive.[81] Despite cycling's democratic appeal, therefore, consumerism and its growing association with the middle classes opened the fractures among social classes. Riding a bike increasingly symbolized affluence, partly in terms of the expense of machines and the accompanying accessories purchased by those members of the middle classes who were keen cyclists, but the ability to ride a bicycle represented a form of freedom that was out of reach to some members of the community.

Cycling and cultural legitimacy

During the twenty-first century, cycling achieved a cultural legitimacy within the media, which would have seemed highly unlikely a few decades previously. While it was not universal, during the 1980s the image of cycling began to change. Cycling has from its beginnings attracted many writers and artists and it regained popularity among performers both in comedy and in popular music and hence credibility among the general public. It was claimed, for example, that comedian Billy Connelly was a cycling addict who cycled 20 miles around Richmond Park every day. He also worked cycling into his stage act with references to 'penile numbness'. Popular music groups such as the Style Council, Kraftwerk, Madness and Queen incorporated cycling into their songs and videos.

However, another perception was that cycling remained a marginal and quirky activity. In 1989, 'Me and My Bike', shown as part of the BBC documentary series *40 Minutes*, offered a more traditional British perspective on cycling, even nostalgic, with its mixture of touring, recreational cycling and sport. This panoply of cycling included an elderly couple riding a tandem, and a family riding a tandem 'trike', followed by a feature on the specialist cycle maker who constructed the machine. Josie Dew was briefly seen on her 'meals on wheels' machine while cycling antiquarian John Pinkerton and his wife displayed their collection of machines, including an ordinary, and memorabilia. Rather than the more modern road racing, there was a feature on the 'End to

End' record attempt (cycling from Land's End to John O'Groats) by John Woodburn. The Eureka tea rooms, in Two Mills, Cheshire, a traditional club run destination was also featured. It evoked memories of the thirties and fifties precisely because many of these cafes had closed down due to the impact of motoring. A West Yorkshire couple, members of Holme Valley Wheelers, who were planning a round-the-world trip by bicycle, invoked a sense of rejection of eighties' materialism in search of a greater sense of independence, which cycling could offer.[82] But with reference to the contrast between its new found chic and British quirkiness, in many ways that was the point of cycling; its sheer diversity and ubiquity meant it was difficult to pinpoint what it meant, instead it continued to mean different things to different people at different times. This impression was confirmed to a certain extent two years later with the BBC's six-part series, *The Bicycle*. A series on its global appeal, part one featured the Tour de France as well as its American imitator, the short-lived Tour de Trump.

After the millennium there was an exponential rise in cycling literature that led to the creation of a British cycling literati, albeit a largely male one. This literature took numerous forms. In particular, there were books on the history of the sport, especially of the Tour de France, biographies and autobiographies of cycling greats and famous British riders.[83] In addition, there were books by cycling enthusiasts on their experiences of riding a bike, on touring and what it meant to them. To a certain extent, the emergence of this literature mirrored wider literary trends around confessional memoirs during the late twentieth century. According to Christopher Lasch, there had been a growing loss of faith in political authority and society, which environmentalism had reflected, as 'the old certainties' were being broken down. There was a subsequent retreat into the 'inner self', which fostered the rise of confessionalism and narcissism. Moreover, confessional writing had been a product of the second-wave of feminism. It had spearheaded the rise of identity politics, feeding into other social groups, which later included men, writing and talking more about their emotions.[84] One cycling *flaneur*, Ken Worpole, a writer on the arts and urban policy, invoked Wittgenstein's philosophy of 'being in the world'; it wasn't so much about where you go as the sheer range of experience that cycling brings to the journey. In 1992, in reference to his commute through London, he cogitated on how cycling was

> an intensely physical form of transport, and brings into play nearly all the senses. This makes cycling the ideal way of travelling in a city like London that is itself kaleidoscopic and in a process of continual change and transformation. A back street route from Hackney to King's Cross can be partly derelict one year and gentrified or radically cosmopolitan the next; the demolition of an old cinema can suddenly transform an urban panorama. Yesterday's office block suddenly becomes today's archaeological dig.[85]

Taking four books from this genre, they reveal a number of similarities in each author's cycling 'journey'. First, like many other cycling writers, they were from middle-class, university-educated backgrounds – all journalists in this case. In the case of Ned Boulting, now the main cycling commentator on ITV, he was also representative of the books' target audience, as like many middle-class cyclists he came late to the sport. In his witty account of how he initially came to work on the Tour de France, he admitted, 'I am not the only one to have made this progression. The chapters to come are for anyone who has made a similar journey in following this extraordinary sport. They reflect … my transition from novice to devotee.'[86] By contrast, as a cyclist with vast experience, Tim's Hilton's sweeping memoir offered a nostalgia-tinged account of the British club scene when cycling was at its peak with relatively little traffic on the roads in the 1950s as well as bringing a European perspective to the reader, especially through famous riders such as Fausto Coppi. The literature also reflected a continuity with cycling of the past with its stories of cycling tours and how cycling could put the rider back in touch with nature. Matt Seaton's collection of his wide-ranging articles for the *Guardian* catered for cycling's growing metropolitan 'peloton'. In addition to his notes on cycling in the city, Seaton wrote on 'rural rides' to replenish both physical and mental health as well as how cycling in London was developing as a form of mobility. One of the main confessional aspects of this literature is what cycling has meant to the writer, or what it has come to mean. Of course, 'sensory' relationships between a cyclist and their bike were not new. Robert Penn expressed these emotions through an account of the building of his 'dream bike'. Penn had already cycled round the world and had owned many bicycles; however, his motivation for having this particular bicycle built offered the idea that a bicycle became an extension not only of a rider's body but also of their personality. He reasoned,

> Anyone who rides a bike regularly and has even the faintest feeling of respect or affection for their own steed will know this hankering – I want *my* bike.
> I need a talismanic machine that somehow reflects my cycling history and carries my cycling aspirations. I want craftsmanship, not technology; I want the bike to be man-made; I want a bike that will never be last year's model. I want a bike that shows my appreciation of the tradition, lore and beauty of bicycles. The French nickname for the bicycle is La Petite Reine – I want my own 'little queen'.[87]

To a certain extent, the growth of cycling literature mirrored similar developments in football following the publication of Nick Hornby's *Fever Pitch* in 1992. *Fever Pitch* gave football both respectability among the intelligentsia and greater coverage in broadsheet newspapers. If British cycling literature had a 'Fever Pitch' moment, it might have been the publication of William Fotheringham's 2002 biography of Tom Simpson,

In Search of Tom Simpson.[88] As a former professional cyclist and the *Guardian*'s cycling journalist, Fotheringham had the credentials to appeal to cycling's bourgeoning middle-class audience and would become one of the beneficiaries of its literary boom. In addition to the book being published when there was a growing interest in the sport, it came at an important time in the sport's history. The book was written when cycling was still coming to terms with the 1998 Festina drugs scandal, reinforcing cycling's reputation as a sport associated with doping – and one that has continued. Moreover, Simpson's reputation since his death on Mount Ventoux had been tainted because of its connection with performance-enhancing drugs. In 2001 *Cycling Weekly* readers ranked Simpson only second in a poll of the best British cyclists of all time. A debate later ensued in the magazine's pages over the choice of Chris Boardman as the winner in which the main issue revolved around Simpson's association with doping. One contributor who had voted for Simpson posed the question, 'Why not Tom?', answering it rhetorically, 'We know why, don't we?'[89]

Fotheringham's book not only revived interest in Simpson, but also placed his career in a wider light without becoming hagiographical (see also Chapter 10). The issue of doping was confronted head on by Fotheringham. He brought out its complexities out into the open in the context of Simpson's career in the tough world of professional cycling. He avoided a simplistic 'good versus evil' trope, which was how doping was usually portrayed within the media.[90] More pertinently, what was the impact on the cycling audience? To a certain extent, the book acted as a forum for debate and allowed for a justification for Simpson's life and career and for cycling's doping past to be been discussed in a different light. This 'humane' portrait of Simpson was further enhanced by a 2005 BBC documentary, *Death on the Mountain: The Story of Tom Simpson*. It might also be speculated that Fotheringham's book further boosted interest in the Tour de France itself and its mystique with its accounts of heroism and suffering of its riders. In the video of him riding up Mount Ventoux, Rob Holden 'tips' his helmet to acknowledge the Simpson memorial. He claimed that he had read a number of books on Simpson, although he does not mention his doping past, highlighting this shift in popular attitudes towards him. Whereas before it was doping that had framed his image in the eyes of the public, now there was greater acknowledgement and acceptance of his ability and achievements.

Newspapers, largely the broadsheets, gave greater coverage to cycling, especially as a leisure activity. As a consequence, it gave cycling more kudos among the political class and social elites. In particular *The Times*' interest in cycling was catalysed after one of its journalists was knocked off her bicycle and severely injured while commuting in London. The paper launched a safety campaign, 'Cities Fit for Cycling', in February 2012. After the issue of cycling safety was debated in Westminster Hall, it gained support of all three political parties, the House of Commons Transport Select Committee and provided the impetus for the parliamentary inquiry, 'Get Britain Cycling'.[91]

While the campaign raised awareness of cycling, it also further reinforced the discourse of safety, still regarded as the main impediment to raising levels of cycling.

Not all newspapers were as supportive. The *Daily Mail*, a right-wing tabloid, was not anti-cycling, but believed that some forms of cycling were more preferable than others. In particular, some of its articles reflected an urban–rural divide, which mirrored the paper's political stance more generally. For example, the paper promoted cycling as a leisure pastime in rural areas and on the Sustrans National Cycle Network, but due to a growing association between urban cycling and left-wing politics, it was more critical of the behaviour of cyclists in cities.[92] In 1997, under the headline 'Beastly Cyclists Are Such a Menace', John Edwards, in a sustained critical article on London cyclists, which was akin to a moral panic, argued, 'In the hands of some lame-brain teenagers the bike has become a missile. It is the new worry in the shopping precinct and rates close to bag snatching as a threat.'[93] A year later, the *Daily Mail* labelled some cyclists in London as 'Lycra Louts' causing a danger to pedestrians and motorists alike. The newspaper's motoring correspondent – unsurprisingly perhaps – claimed, 'Many motorists have also fallen foul of aggressively militant Lycra-clad cyclists who believe that all cars should be driven off the road.'[94] To a certain extent, these articles echoed the *Daily Mail*'s historically divergent attitudes, stretching back to the 1930s, over the merits between motoring and cycling when it had promoted motoring from the outset as a symbol of freedom and independence.

Cycling subcultures, such as downhill mountain biking and BMX, were themselves legitimized by their own niche publications. In 2004, for example, *Mountain Biking UK*, reflecting the then popularity of MTB had the highest circulation of 45,772 while the second most popular was *Mountain Bike Rider* with 37,333. The long-established *Cycling Weekly* only had 26,429 readers.[95] Later a number of high-quality print titles emerged, which targeted the growing middle-class market. *Conquista*, for example, was a quarterly publication, which placed an emphasis on high-quality journalism and photography with behind-the-scenes articles, mainly on road racing. By the twentieth-first century, however, more cycling enthusiasts were consuming their particular subculture through the internet and a growing range of websites. In 2005, the biggest UK-based site was singletrackworld.com, which in July that year attracted nearly 200,000 single visitors. Some sites were adjuncts of print titles, but others were now internet only.[96] Social media brought further fragmentation and new forms of consumption. Some sports developed their own dedicated YouTube channels, while on Twitter and Facebook individual cyclists were able to build up their own followings through videos. Martyn Ashton, for example, had been a successful downhill mountain bike racer before an accident had left him paralysed from the waist down. However, he was later filmed tackling the Fort William downhill course on an adapted bike.[97]

The BMX Bubble: A case study in cycling consumerism

At the 2008 Olympics Britain won gold in the men's team sprint at the track cycling. Two out of its three members had begun their cycling careers riding a BMX – Jamie Staff and Chris Hoy.[98] At those Beijing Olympics, BMX was actually included as a sport for the first time. It marked a growing 'Americanized' shift in Olympic sports. Mark Dyreson has argued that for Americans, 'sport is not a plastic cultural form that adapts to the world's diverse plurality of cultures but rather a uniquely national form of culture that carries and replicates the indelible strains of a specific nation's cultural patterns, literally a cultural "DNA".'[99] BMX was just one part of a long-term American vision of sport to Americanize the globe's cultures, stretching back to the 1920s. Moreover, it highlighted not only an example of cycling's consumerism but also how cycling was increasingly fragmented as an activity as it increasingly appealed to different parts of the population. In the case of BMX, it appealed initially to children.

BMX in Britain was an early 1980s craze. It was exported from America and created a whole new cycling subculture, not dissimilar to the cycle speedway craze after the Second World War. Like cycle speedway, its popularity was short-lived, but the sport endured. BMX came with its own fashion, style and language, such as being 'rad'. It also highlighted the development of sports more generally which could be considered marginal, especially in terms of the need of voluntary efforts of enthusiasts in combination with commercial interests. Nor was it accepted by the cycling establishment. The BCF initially described the young up-start as 'not a cycling sport'.[100]

It is widely acknowledged that the sport of BMX was born in California in the late 1960s with two strands later emerging: racing and freestyle.[101] Initially the bikes – single low gears with motorcycle handlebars and handle grips – were popular with teenagers who began to arrange unorganized races in Los Angeles dirt fields.

It had evolved out of the European-imported motocross where kids not old enough to ride a motorcycle began to imitate motocross on bicycles they had specially adapted.

One of the earlier pioneers was Scot Breithaupt, a motocross rider. In 1970, then aged 13, he organized one of the first organized BMX races at his own track, called BUMS in Long Beach. BUMS (Bicycle United Motocross Society) would later become the first BMX riders' body. Another major influence on BMX was the 1971 Oscar-nominated film *On Any Sunday*, starring Steve McQueen. Ironically, it was about motocross, but at the start it showed kids trying to emulate their motocross heroes by racing on bicycles.[102]

British BMX itself both challenged and confirmed some of the narratives regarding cycling during this period in a number of ways. Most strikingly it was a sport from its outset that was dominated by children, both boys and girls, although mainly teenage boys. It reflected how at this time cycling was as much an activity for children as it was for adults, especially by those within the cycling industry. Rather than being part of a youth culture, it was a kids' culture, although one in which adults had a major role in shaping. It was a dangerous activity where injuries were common and since the Second World War there was increasing concern from parents over the safety of children, including riding their bicycles on the road. Despite its dangers, BMXing was more akin to a playground where the play of children could be closely monitored and controlled by adults, with the wearing of protective clothing and helmets compulsory and where health and safety procedures were put in place through St. John Ambulance, as well as the presence of parents themselves.[103] Moreover, it was sport that came from the suburbs and was funded by the 'bank of mum and dad'. Without parental support and especially the driving of their children around the country, the sport would have failed to have taken off, although for children whose parents did not have cars, they were unable to fully participate. Chris Hoy's parents were one example of this commitment.[104]

BMX's early development in Britain was a product of a DIY and grassroots movement when it first appeared during the late 1970s. Ironically, given how motoring and motor sports had originated from cycling, a number of BMX's early enthusiasts had ridden in motocross, but BMX was cheaper. Advertisements for BMX from America began appearing in motocross publications, which raised awareness of the sport and some people began to build their own bikes. Like High Beech in Essex, where speedway began in Britain in 1928, early races took place on hastily arranged tracks, usually grass and mud, if it rained. One early pioneer was Jay Hardy who with his friends built their own track in local woods while Alan Woods was an early enthusiast in the north-west. He had been a motocross rider but switched to BMX, building a track at Little Lever near Bolton in 1980, then at Wigan. His father owned a car garage, who later began to sell BMX bikes and also built a track after hiring a JCB digger. Other people across the country had similar ideas and led to a fledgling BMX scene. In 1982 Arnold Higginson built a racing track on the former Morecambe band arena made up of car tyres. With agreement from the holidays firm Pontins, a race track was built at nearby Middleton, which hosted the UK championships in 1983.

In 1980 the first official BMX race, and the start of organized BMX in Britain, took place in Redditch in the West Midlands. The location was crucial as this was the town where Halfords had its head office. Halfords funded the building of a dedicated BMX track and the man behind this initiative was David Duffield. Duffield, later a cycling commentator on Eurosport, worked in marketing for Halfords and had earlier publicized the Moulton bike, while he also set a Land's End to John O'Groats record riding a tricycle.[105] Halfords then imported some BMX bikes, which local kids used in a demonstration race, as well as arranging for some Dutch riders to race at Redditch as the Netherlands was an early European BMX pioneer.

BMX would not have flourished or survived as a sport without the establishment of a national governing body, although in Britain there were two – the UKBMX, formed in 1981 with its headquarters in Wigan, and the NBMXA (changed to BBMXA in 1988), which was largely based in the south. They amalgamated in 1989, as a condition for funding from the Sports Council.[106] UKBMX divided up the riders into age divisions. In 1981, the top division was for those aged 16 or over. The other divisions included children aged 14, 11, 7, and 6 and under. Ranking points were awarded at 'mains' competition, which were run throughout the season, where the winner was awarded 10, the second 9 and so on. Double points were awarded at the 'Nationals'. Those who topped the rankings at the end of the season had the honour of wearing the Number 1 plate for the next year.

By 1983 there were three colour BMX magazines, which had been vital to the sport's development. Sport and the media have historically enjoyed a symbiotic relationship, and the one between BMX and its media was especially close, mainly because it was intimately connected with the interests of the trade. Wade Nelson has argued that through magazines the history of the sport has been linked inextricably to the history of the mediation of BMX culture and that while BMX 'may have existed in some form prior to mediation', it was only 'post-mediation' when it reached a large public audience.[107] Importantly, these magazines provided the early oxygen of publicity for companies and their bikes. In this sense, BMX provides a fascinating example of how the relationship between sport and entrepreneurship can develop from the grassroots.[108] In the mid-1980s, for example, *BMX Weekly*, sold 46,000 copies per edition. In order to maximize coverage of their products a number of companies formed their own BMX teams. It meant that the riders, mainly children, were paid with some earning substantial sums of money. The first one set up in Britain was Team Ace, by Don Smith, an ex-motorcycle trials rider, and Richard Barrington. Barrington had set up a shop in 1980 and sponsored some local riders, who would include Andy Ruffell. A transfer market developed. Ruffell in particular earned not inconsiderable sums as a teenager. He was the sport's first superstar in Britain and proved to be a telegenic ambassador for the sport. BMX received not inconsiderable television coverage. In 1984 Channel 4 broadcast the Kellogg's BMX Championships, a made-for-television weekly tournament between different teams, including American and French riders. David Duffield was the commentator and its main presenter was sports broadcaster, Mick Brown. However, the series acted as a vehicle for Ruffell who was interviewed before and after every race as well as giving some racing tips. Initially, Ruffell rode for Ammaco Mongoose, run by a husband-and-wife team, Michael and Sue Jarvis. In 1984, it was claimed that Ruffell, aged 18, earned £20,000 in that year. He later joined the Raleigh team, Britain's main bicycle manufacturer, and an indication of BMX's importance. Ruffell's main rival, Tim March, had his own sponsors, including Lee Cooper jeans and in 1985 he persuaded the supermarket chain VG to sponsor his team, March Racing Developments. Many of the teams though were smaller and were set up by bike shops and importers or with manufacturers to help out local riders.[109]

By 1987 the bubble had deflated as magazine circulation fell, along with rider numbers. In 1987 the average rider numbers at meetings for both bodies were between 1,000 and 1,100, but the following year they had dropped to between 500 and 600 while the BBMXA could no longer afford to pay prize money. Like the track cycling bubble at the turn of the twentieth century, BMX's commercialization ran out of steam. The sport of BMX did continue with teams now running mainly on voluntary and altruistic means and continuing to attract a loyal following.

While the sport of BMX racing declined, another sport, BMX Freestyle, began to flourish. To a certain extent, Freestyle resonated with the early values of BMX. For many BMX was more than a sport, if a sport at all. Instead riding a BMX bike, unlike racer bikes at the time, offered the opportunity to have fun on your own, or with friends, by messing around learning tricks and building jumps on spare land, in car parks or local woods. You didn't necessarily have to race or belong to a club. There was much here that reflected the allure of American culture. On first riding his BMX bike with his friends, Jay Hardy recalled how he had felt like an outsider:

> In our minds we lived the Californian lifestyle that inspired us and we paid a price for it. In England at that time there was a mod revival, short hair, loafers, preferably burgundy and of course what every football loving sixteen-year-old saw as a rite of passage, the moped or scooter. We on the other hand had long hair, wore vans, rector skate shorts and rode around on those stupid kids' bikes. In early 1980 the UK was not a BMXer friendly place.[110]

Riding a BMX was a lifestyle choice, an alternative that marked a contrast with other British sports and their relatively conservative values. BMX Freestyle became a lifestyle sport, which had its roots in the 1960s' counterculture. Wheaton points out that many lifestyle sports had 'characteristics that are different to the traditional rule-bound, competitive and masculinized, "dominant" institutionalized, western "achievement" sport cultures'.[111] These sports, such as skateboarding and snowboarding, were for 'adrenaline junkies' who embraced risk and danger, but in a non-aggressive manner. There was no bodily contact and instead the focus was on personal challenges rather than competing against other.[112] Ironically, perhaps this lifestyle choice itself would morph into lifestyle sports, subject to the constraints of sporting competition. The X Games – for extreme sports – began in 1995, and such was their appeal that a number of them were increasingly included in the programme at the Summer and Winter Olympics.[113]

Riding a BMX and practising tricks also became associated with an urban culture. One unusual grassroots event had been the Tour d'Elephant. It was staged in 1991 to celebrate urban cycling through a festival hosted in the shopping centre at the Elephant and Castle; it came under the umbrella of the London Cycling Campaign. The location of the Elephant and Castle could be interpreted as an ironic response to the urban blight caused by post-war planning, which had been centred around motoring and had largely ignored cycling. The event had a number of features. There was the 'Challenge', for which 1,500 riders had entered and turned this urban environment of 1960s shopping precincts, concrete ramps and subways into a sporting arena. The competition attracted teams from all around the world and there were also stalls and stunts and other related entertainments.[114] Some urban locations later became appropriated by riders. One such location was the South Bank Undercroft, near the Royal Festival Hall. Although mostly populated by skateboarders, it was also at one point used by BMX riders.[115]

In his classic article, 'Bowling Alone' Robert Putnam argued that in late-twentieth-century America (and by extension the Western world) there had been a decline of 'social capital' due to a reduction in civic engagement, especially at the associational level.[116] Through the consumption of a fragmented media, an increasingly transient and insecure labour market and a commensurate decline in the collective, on the face of it BMX, and Freestyle in particular, reflected this shift. It was an activity that venerated the values of individualism and an expression of 'self-identity'. However, Putnam's thesis discounts the ability of groups to interact by adapting to a changing environment, both socially and technologically. In the early twenty-first century the community of BMX in Britain was revived precisely because of the consumption of this media landscape. Social media allowed people who had been interested in the sport in its early days to reconnect with one another. Internet forums were established, old videos were posted on YouTube and Facebook pages set up that reinvigorated this interest. It led to reunions in the form of a series of nationwide annual weekend 'ride-outs'. In reality, these events were informal and were mainly 'booze cruises' with the riders stopping off at pubs along a fixed route. One such annual trip was 'Radbury', a ride from Bury to Radcliffe in Lancashire.[117] Other venues included Cleethorpes where the attendance in the early 2010s jumped from around 90 to 300.[118] It gave people the opportunity to watch or even perform some 'freestyle' tricks and moves in front of a crowd, display their bikes, share memories and information on BMX, as well as mix with some of the star riders who also attended, including Eddie Fiola from America.[119]

In 2019 the membership of British Cycling reached 145,000. Cycling UK, formerly the Cyclist's Touring Club, had over 65,000 members. These figures when combined were unprecedented, even surpassing those of the early 1950s and indicating the popularity of cycling. Of course, membership of cycling bodies only represented a fraction of cyclists, yet they can give some insights into the changing cycling landscape. In post-industrial Britain cycling was no longer a mass form of transport, although, as per Chapter 8, this was still a long-term aim of many people. Instead, it had found a niche in an expanding sport and leisure market, which was a product of Britain's neoliberal service-dominated economy. As a result, clearly defined cycling identities were formed. Among the expanding middle classes, the bicycle came to represent a lifestyle choice built round the values of health and environmentalism, as well as notions of performance and competition. For children riding a BMX it was – or had been – a way to separate themselves from adults. Yet if cycling was a marker of social status, it also highlighted increasing social and regional differences.

CHAPTER 10

Elite cycling and British society

On 16 September 2000 Britain's Jason Queally won the gold medal for the Kilometre TT at the Sydney Olympics. Starting 13th out of 16 riders, he broke the Olympic record and then watched on nervously as his remaining three rivals were unable to beat his time. Four years earlier Britain had won one gold during the entire Games; Queally's was on the first day of competition. It was only Britain's second cycling gold medal since 1908. It was this achievement perhaps more than any other that signalled a resurgence in the sport of cycling in Britain. Queally's reaction to his victory unconsciously captured both Britain's past record and future success. He said, 'I just cannot believe it, I'm speechless – I came here thinking a potential medal, maybe a bronze, but it all depends on what happens on the day – something strange happened.'[1] While a gold medal represented the pinnacle of his sport, Queally's success highlighted a new direction in British sport more generally, largely due to an influx of funding from the National Lottery. Brian Cookson, then chairman of British Cycling, later commented, 'It took 61.609 seconds [Queally's winning time] for the perception of this place [the Manchester velodrome] to change from white elephant to gold medal factory.'[2] By 2012, cycling was Britain's most successful Olympic sport and one of the country's most visible from a media perspective due to a combination of this funding, the application of modern coaching and sports science, plus the luck of a group of talented cyclists emerging at the same time. This chapter examines how the sport of cycling moved from the margins of Britain's sporting landscape to its centre. Cycling in Britain eventually shook off the mud of amateurism from its cleats to fully embrace a professional and technocratic ethos, and, later through Team Sky, a form of hyper-commercialization. From its status as a marginal player that celebrated occasional triumphs, Britain became the dominant cycling nation.

Underpinning this makeover was the transformation of sport itself. As Tony Collins has argued, 'By the dawn of the twenty-first century, the value of sport could be measured in tens of billions of dollars, its popularity was truly global and it once more offered a metaphor for life in a world in which the capitalist market reigned supreme.'[3] A neoliberal ideology pervaded societies across the globe, witnessed by the decline of trade unions, an erosion of the welfare state and a decay of social democratic values, along with the break-up of the Soviet Union. At the same time, the emergence of satellite broadcasting signalled a technological breakthrough, which ushered in a transnational and global market for sport. Access to elite, high-performance sport was unrestricted and generated vast wealth for these sports and their athletes who cut across national boundaries.

To a certain extent, the increase in cycling's profile reflected Britain's shifting sporting landscape. While football remained the behemoth that overshadowed all other sports in terms of its reach among all social classes, its media profile and the sheer number of participants and spectators, there were changes taking place elsewhere. Cricket, for example, once a national sport, had denied itself the oxygen of terrestrial television after the heights it reached during the 2005 Ashes contest. It virtually vanished from the national conversation, restricted like many other niche sports to coverage on satellite channels, as the sport's marketing people strove to capture the lucrative ABC1 audiences. By contrast, rugby union's stock rose. After it turned professional in 1995, it eschewed (some of its) amateur ideals and embraced the Thatcherite ethos of competition. It proved particularly attractive to those professional middle classes who attended private schools and now held similar values. Importantly, rugby union struck the right balance between coverage on terrestrial and satellite television, enabling itself to increase its profile while at the same time profiting from satellite's largesse. In 1995 rugby league took a more radical step and transformed itself into a summer sport on the promise of a vast contract from Sky television.

The change in cycling's status was in no small part due to the unprecedented sporting success of British cyclists. Not only did Bradley Wiggins win the Tour de France in 2012, but at the Beijing and then London Olympics the British cycling team dominated the medal table. These sporting achievements not only elevated the public profile of the sport and other cyclists such as Chris Hoy, Victoria Pendleton and Nicole Cooke, but conferred the activity of cycling more generally with a greater cultural legitimacy, which was further reinforced with the vastly increased media coverage the sport received. Wiggins' Tour victory for instance was the lead story on that evening's BBC late news programme. He also won the BBC Sports Personality of the Year that year, following Mark Cavendish the previous year and Chris Hoy in 2008. In addition, cycling's new status was further underpinned through the bestowing of knighthoods on Hoy, Wiggins and Dave Brailsford, while numerous other cyclists were awarded various honours.

Before the successes of the twenty-first century, in the 1960s British cycling had remained a minority sport. It lagged behind the cycling heartlands of Europe in terms of prestige and – like most other sports – was in the shadow of football in terms of visibility. It was still characterized by voluntarism and amateurism, mainly because there was a lack of demand for professional cycling in Britain. There had traditionally been few professional riders in Britain with only five in 1964. In 1966 this figure jumped to 77 after the Independent class of riders had been abolished, but as a consequence, the Tour of Britain aka the Milk Race became a race for amateurs.[4] In 1970 there were 62 professional cyclists in Britain; by 1995 there were still only 70.[5] Some of them earned their living on European teams, while others worked for trade teams in Britain.[6] Cycling's status as a minority sport was confirmed in 1989; in a list of sports most enjoyed on television in Britain, cycling did not make the top twenty.[7] Cycling still had a relatively strong racing culture at club level. In 1959 there were around 6,500 riders registered for racing at BCF events, although dropping to below 5,000 by 1969.[8] Membership of the BCF picked up but it was nowhere near its heights of the late forties and early fifties (see Chapter 9). Some clubs also went into decline. In 1971 the once influential Anfield Bicycle Club held no club events 'due to a lack of interest'.[9]

In terms of the racing culture, the contest between the time trial and road racing as the most popular form of sport had tipped in the balance of the latter. In 1964 Geoffrey Nicholson claimed, 'The dynamic unmistakeably belongs to the racing men.'[10] Membership of clubs affiliated to the Road Time Trials Council fell from 1,046 in 1959 to 701 by 1970, while those who qualified for a certificate in the BAR also declined, reflecting a lack of interest among elite British riders. More symbolically, in 1964 the RTTC moved its annual end-of-year Gala Ball from the Royal Albert Hall to the more modest Rainbow Room in London, which held about 1,000 compared to 5,000. Nevertheless, time trialling was hardly moribund and in 1967 it was reported that over 15,000 club and open time trials had been staged. The time trial would continue to form an essential part of club life in Britain. Restrictions though were gradually lifted on riders allowed to participate in road racing. In 1963 the number of riders allowed to race in the Tour of Britain, as a special case, was increased to 84 through an amendment to the 1963 Cycle Racing and Highways Act. Another 24 races were allowed up to 60 riders, with the remaining races restricted to fields of 40.[11]

Beryl Burton

No one symbolized British cycling's amateur-voluntary and time-trial culture better than Beryl Burton (nee Charnock) (1937–96), arguably Britain's greatest ever cyclist. As Dave Russell states, '[N]o other British woman has ever dominated her sport as she dominated cycling from the late 1950s to the mid-1980s.'[12] Burton was world champion seven times, five times in the individual pursuit and twice on the road. In 1967 she not only broke the women's world record for a 12-hour time trial, but at the same time broke the British men's record, recording 277.25 miles. In the same race, the second-placed also broke the men's record. While the men's record was beaten two years later, her women's record stood until 2017. Perhaps even more remarkably, in terms of her levels of consistency, mental fortitude and a lack of injuries, she won the British Women's BAR 25 years in a row from 1959 to 1983. In addition, she won a further 24 national titles – 12 road races and 12 pursuit titles as well as setting around 50 national time-trial records between 10 and 100 miles. In recognition of her achievements, she was awarded the sport's highest honour in Britain, the Bidlake Memorial an unprecedented three times. In the broader context of women's sport, she was an exception to broader trends as during her career, women's cycling declined in popularity and standards. In 1960, for example, 38 women had qualified for their BAR RTTC certificate by recording an average speed on 21 mph, by 1964, this number for 21 mph had dropped to 22, and led to a relaxation of the standard to 20 mph.

Like many girls and women, she had been introduced to cycling in 1954 by her then boyfriend, Charlie Burton. They married in 1955 when she was 18. Despite her national and international success, Burton was embedded in the local Yorkshire cycling scene. Her loyalties were to her clubs, first Morley CC, then to later Knaresborough, with whom she went on club runs. Initially she struggled but within a couple of years it was the men who were unable to keep up with her. For many in the sport she was 'Our Beryl' because despite her success, she was modest and down to earth and someone who represented the sport's grassroots and democratic values at club level. Burton, like other high-profile Yorkshire female athletes, such as Anita Lonsbrough and Dorothy Hyman, from similar lower-middle and working-class backgrounds, combined training and competing with paid employment. In Burton's case, at one time she worked as a labourer at a Morley rhubarb farm. Moreover, she was also a working mother; her daughter, Denise was born in 1956. Victorian attitudes regarding the perception of a woman's place in society continued into the 1960s, although Burton was allowed some flexibility within this context to pursue her sporting ambitions.[13]

In 1960 Burton, like her predecessors Marguerite Wilson and Eileen Sheridan, was offered a professional contract by a bicycle manufacturer, Raleigh. She turned it down. Burton felt that at the end of the proposed three-year contract, she would have been little better off when compared to her then present employment (in machine accounting) and that she would also lose her amateur status, meaning she would be no longer able to race.[14] In some ways, it was also a statement on the development of women's cycling. Whereas in the early post-First World War period, debates around women's cycling revolved around ideas of femininity, which concerned the style in which women rode, what clothes they should wear and the impact that cycling might have on their bodies, here the focus was mainly on business and sport.

Cycling and creeping commercialization

In the post-1945 period, cycling's long-standing amateur tradition came under pressure from commercial and broader social forces. During the 1960s British sport in general was undergoing a process of modernization. In cricket, the one-day game began in 1963 ushering a new commercial era, a year after the abolition of the gentleman–amateur distinction. Football, always a professional game, became increasingly commercialized after the ending of the maximum wage in 1961 and then the modification of the retain-and-transfer system in 1963. In 1966 England won the World Cup in front of an estimated television audience of 30 million, highlighting the potential of the symbiotic relationship between sport and television.

Nevertheless, amateur–professional tensions continued to characterize cycling. These tensions had materialized in a dispute between the RTTC, an avowedly amateur body, and the BCF over clothing as prizes for amateurs in 1960.[15] Following a referendum, RTTC members eventually agreed with the BCF ruling to permit the award of clothing to amateurs as prizes.[16] In 1962 the BCF also endorsed sponsorship for clubs. Rather than pay riders salaries the sponsorship was used to provide services which varied from the provision of facilities at clubs to transport and payment of expenses for racing or for training, including the provision of clothing. By 1979 there were 74 sponsored clubs, which equated to over 10 per cent of the total affiliated to the BCF, compared to 60 in the previous year.[17]

The sports' public profile was reflected through its sporadic coverage on the new medium of television. During the 1950s, cycling was featured on ITV's *Cavalcade of Sport*, a magazine type programme. In May 1956, for example, it covered professional cycling at the Reg Harris Stadium in Manchester. Cycling was guaranteed coverage every two years at the Olympic and Commonwealth Games as both these events were listed events, deemed to be of national importance that they had to be televised. By contrast, reflecting more modern tastes, there was more coverage of motor sport on television. It was not until the sixties that ownership of television sets reached levels of over 90 per cent. One cycling event that did attract not inconsiderable BBC television coverage was the International Six-Day Race held in September 1967. Sponsored by the brewer Skol, it was part of the Cycle Show at the Earls Court Exhibition. The track cost nearly £30,000 to assemble and international riders were given appearance money.[18] Naturally it was also supported by the manufacturers' association, and so the main purpose of the race was to sell bicycles. Over the six days it was intended to promote the race with various publicity gimmicks such as a display by 'Biking Belles' and trick cycling.[19] In 1970 Britain hosted the world championships for the first time since 1922. Their staging pointed towards both changes and continuities in the place of cycling in the sporting landscape. When compared to football, the championships received minimal press coverage, for example. However, the event did raise the sport's profile through the media coverage it received, both by the press and importantly on television. Over 100,000 people attended the final event of the week, the men's road race, although BBC coverage was mainly confined to late-night highlights during the week. However, for the men's road race there was live coverage on *Grandstand* and some special programmes.[20]

During the 1980s, cycling gained a more regular television presence on Channel 4. To a certain extent, coverage of cycling reflected the new channel's edgy brief when it began broadcasting in 1982. From its outset, Channel 4 had aimed to cover alternative subjects, not just in sport, and cycling as well as American football were part of its early programming policy. In 1983 the inaugural Kellogg's' City Centre Races – a series of Kermesse-type races in Britain, and later Ireland – were televised. The series included mainly domestic cyclists, but were sometimes supplemented with high-profile riders. The channel also played an important role in promoting the new cycling sport of BMX (see Chapter 9). In 1986 it took the step of televising the Tour de France, thus bringing a daily highlights programme of the race to British screens for the first time. It was perhaps fortunate that in three out of its first four broadcasts it covered some of the Tour's most memorable editions. There was British interest in the form of the Scot Robert Millar as well Sean Kelly and 1987 winner, Stephen Roche from Ireland. In addition to his success at the tours of Italy and Spain, Millar won three stages and the King of the Mountains classification in 1984. Millar was later the subject of a 1985 ITV documentary, *The High Life*, and also endorsed Kellogg's cereals. Coverage of cycling was given a further boost when from 1989 Eurosport began to cover the sport, although it remained limited to an audience largely made up of enthusiasts.

Tom Simpson – pioneer and legacy

Interest in international cycling in Britain had actually been growing since the mid-sixties. In 1966, for example, the BBC first covered the Tour de France, as well as the Tour of Britain, while coverage began to increase markedly on ITV from 1969. That they did so was almost certainly due to the achievements of one cyclist, Tom Simpson. Simpson symbolized British cycling's first phase of post-war modernity and the shift from its amateur-voluntary roots to a more professional and commercial future. While he came up through the ranks of club cycling, Simpson was a trailblazer for British cycling in Europe. There had been other pioneering British riders, such as Brian Robinson, but it was Simpson who later inspired the likes of Barry Hoban and Vin Denson to compete in the sport's European heartlands.[21] Simpson's biographer, William Fotheringham, speaking in 2005, stated that 'he achieved a depth of public recognition that no cyclist has achieved since'.[22]

To a certain extent, Simpson was an exemplar of the increasingly assertive and confident working classes. A miner's son from Durham, who later moved to Nottinghamshire, Simpson was a 'character' who regularly played up his Englishness to the press, albeit mainly on the continent where he enjoyed a greater profile where he lived and rode full-time. He also wanted to enjoy the consumer boom and was prone to buying expensive cars for example.[23] While Simpson was a bigger star on the continent, his successes were not ignored in Britain. In 1965 he had given cycling's national profile a major boost when he became the first British man to win the World Road Race Championship. Importantly, the event was televised and was probably the key factor in Simpson winning that year's BBC Sports Personality of the Year in addition to two other national awards. As an indication of the marginal status of cycling, in his victory speech Simpson was quick to acknowledge that his BBC award was a big honour for himself and cycling. Even before his triumph that September he had come to public prominence after being featured in 'The World of Tom Simpson' on the BBC 2 programme, *Time Out*, presented by Ludovic Kennedy.[24] This attention had been sparked by Simpson's triumphs on the roads of Europe. In 1961 he won the Tour of Flanders, becoming the first Briton in 80 years to win one of the major classic races. The following year he became the first Briton to wear the yellow jersey at the Tour de France. He also added three other major one-day classics to his 'palmares' – the 1963 Bordeaux-Paris race; Milan-San Remo the year after; and then the Tour of Lombardy in 1965, wearing the rainbow-striped jersey as world champion.

Simpson's death in 1967 on Mount Ventoux unsurprisingly attracted headline news back in Britain. It is arguably the most documented and controversial moment in the history of British cycling. The episode has since taken on a life of its own, mythologized, written about, debated and continually reinterpreted up to the present day. Simpson's career reflected the commercial pressures and rewards of professional cycling, which he had to leave Britain to pursue. During the fateful 1967 Tour he already had fallen ill, but continued to ride on, against the advice of his team. He had been motivated by the prospect of a lucrative new contract with the Italian Salvarani team for the following year where the size of his retainer was dependent on his final position on the Tour.[25] That his death was televised represented a darker side of modern cycling and in many ways prefigured the sport's future, especially its association with doping and the media. His death, partly through taking amphetamines, was a product of an increasingly competitive, commercialized and unhealthy sporting landscape in which athletes were pushing their bodies to the limits in the quest for great rewards.[26]

Despite the death of Simpson and the negative publicity it brought, in 1974 Britain hosted its first ever stage of the Tour de France. The actual staging of the Tour was a bizarre moment not only in the history of British cycling but also in the Tour's history. The staging of the race in Plymouth had been partly a result of Brittany's 'Artichoke War'.[27] That year's Tour had been designated to start in Brittany with two stages, a third in Britain, before the peloton again crossed the Channel for another stage in the Breton region. All the stages had been designed to publicize Brittany's most famous agricultural product as well as the newly opened Roscoff-Plymouth ferry, a development that reflected Britain's recent membership of the European Economic Community.[28] The Breton organizers had bid an unusually high sum of £180,000 to hold the opening stages, while the contribution of the local authorities in Plymouth was £40,000. During the British leg of the race the Tour's travelling caravan bombarded bewildered spectators with artichokes, who were unfamiliar with the delicacy. It had been hoped that the race would improve Plymouth's tourism, especially with the presence of Eddy Merckx in the field. In addition, with the arrival on British shores of the world's greatest bicycle race, it was, to a certain extent, the fulfilment of the growing interest in massed-start racing in Britain that had been growing since the 1930s.

The stage itself was a qualified success at best. Estimates of the crowd present ranged from 15,000 to 30,000, which contrasted with an expected 200,000. There was also a lack of television coverage. There was a British presence in the race, especially in the shape of Barry Hoban, but the event only served to highlight how professional cycling in Britain was at a low ebb. While there were over 120 riders in the Tour, there were fewer than 40 active professionals in Britain, and only 6 of those received enough money from sponsors and prizes not to need another job.[29] The race itself lacked the spectacle associated with the Tour. It was essentially a 100-mile circuit race that comprised 14 laps of a stretch of the A38 on the Plympton by-pass. The race was won by the unheralded Dutchman, Henk Poppe, but due to the lack of action it was not well received by the watching public, many of whom retreated to the various beer tents round the course. *The Times*' Norman Fox felt that unless 'Plymouth, or any other town, can persuade the police and Government to allow the use of "real roads" with real hills and sections where riders can escape from the bunch ... then Britain will always have synthetic versions of the authentic Continental stage'.[30] In truth, the French organizers had chosen the route, to minimize the disruption of the Tour criss-crossing the Channel. In hosting the Tour, the stage – run on a by-pass – was also symbolic of cycling's marginal place in British society more generally. But by this time the age of cycling as an activity based around the club run along quiet country lanes had disappeared. It was now reflecting and adapting to a more consumer-based society. Hence, the staging of the Tour – the acme of cycling – enhanced the image of cycling in Britain as a brash, modern sport.

Cycling and the state

One of the major developments in British sport from the final quarter of the twentieth century was its increasingly close relationship with the state. In particular, British cycling and sport more generally in the twenty-first century was a beneficiary of significant state funding, which was highlighted by the medal hauls at successive Olympic Games from 2000. Yet it is perhaps unrecognized that state funding has also been a precursor for the growth in the commercial arm of the sport. Not dissimilar to a form of welfarism, state funding for cycling has provided a solid foundation in terms of the development of professional cyclists and just as importantly a pool of highly qualified and experienced coaches and sport scientists.

It was during the 1960s that cycling first began to benefit from the state's growing, albeit limited, involvement in sport. Because of the growth of a global media and commercial interests as well as an increasing political awareness of the 'leisure society', sport was becoming impossible to ignore for political parties and was seen as a form of soft power. Moreover, during the 1950s Britain's sporting stock had declined. This decline can mainly be attributed to the rest of world catching up with the pioneers of modern sport, but this universal truth notwithstanding sporting failure still elicited criticism from the popular press. British sport was still largely organized on an amateur and voluntary basis and at the Olympics British competitors were now competing against both de facto state-sponsored professional athletes from the countries behind the Iron Curtain and American athletes who enjoyed college scholarships and the modern facilities of its universities. Even in football, English clubs had been overtaken by their European rivals. The 1960 Wolfenden Report had signalled a change in political discourse towards sport and physical culture more generally, but it was only when 1964 Labour government came to power that there was a decisive shift in favour of state intervention in sport. In that year, it established the Sports Council, which – eventually – would act as the main quango in the development of British sport.

Some state funding for sport had been available from various government departments in the immediate post-war period.[31] The BCF benefitted from these pots in its quests to improve its coaching infrastructure. In 1961 a coaching scheme – an indicator of modernity more generally – was established. Initially, the national coach, Tommy Godwin had operated in an honorary capacity, but funding from the Ministry of Education and the

Central Council for Physical Recreation – a legacy of the 1937 Physical Training and Recreation Act – made it a salaried position from 1964.[32] It also enabled the BCF to expand their coaching portfolio by hosting conferences and establishing training courses for prospective coaches.[33] Cycling greatly benefitted from state backing when it hosted the 1970 world championships in Leicester. The Championships were given the royal seal of approval with the attendance of the Duke of Edinburgh and were officially opened by the Conservative prime minister Edward Heath.[34] However, it had been the energy of the previous Labour minister for sport, Denis Howell, and the support of Harold Wilson as prime minister that had made it possible. Between 1963–64 and 1970–1, direct grants for sport had doubled to £2.5 million while the success of the 1966 soccer World Cup provided a template for hosting major championships.[35] Britain was awarded the Championships in 1968, following the backing of state funds of £60,000. Leicester was then Britain's only international-standard track (albeit outdoors) at 333.33 metres, which had been completed in 1966.[36] In addition, the city council contributed £90,000 to the refurbishment of the stadium's facilities.[37]

At the performance level, however, Britain continued to lag at international sport more generally as a result of the Cold War-inspired US–USSR rivalry. This rivalry, as well as the growing importance attached to sport by national governments, stimulated an increase of state funding for sport that Britain could not match. While French and West German athletes benefitted from more funding than Britain's, it was East Germany that took this relationship to a new level in terms of investment in infrastructure, talent identification schemes and sports science (and later state-sponsored doping programmes). By contrast, every four years the British Olympic Association launched a public appeal for funds to send competitors to the Games, a legacy of British sport's amateur-voluntary tradition.

The seeds of Olympic track success and later success on the road were sown in the government's changing attitudes towards sport during the 1990s. Criticism of a perceived failure of British sport at international level was a regular source of media analysis. In 1995 John Major's government responded through the report *Raising the Game*, and then more significantly through a new source of the funding, the National Lottery, which was established in 1994. In general, the greater state intervention in sport gained cross-party support and has been continued ever since. Importantly, sporting success at international level was also seen as a way to encourage more people to participate and improve the health of the population. Later the 2002 report, *Game Plan*, a typical New Labour initiative, aimed to marry increasing participation and sporting success with other political objectives. These included – naturally – improving health, improving educational outcomes, reducing crime and greater social cohesion, plus creating 'a feel-good factor' through British sporting success. Interestingly, no clear link was established between international sporting success and these political objectives. However, it did not prevent the recommendation for a greater emphasis on high-performance sport and a systematic talent identification scheme with funding apportioned to a select number of sports.[38] Nevertheless, the report highlighted how sport would be used to underpin wider political aims. Finance was at the centre of cycling's transformation. In the first distribution of lottery funding the BCF was awarded £2.5 million in 1999 to prepare for the Olympics.[39] In 2002, British Cycling[40] received £8 million of Olympic funding, increasing to £24.7 million (2008 Olympics) and £32 million (2012 Olympics).[41]

How did cycling take advantage of this new climate? A no-compromise philosophy was introduced, which would eventually be extended to other Olympic sports. Essentially, a small group of elite riders were selected and were supported by a large number of support staff, such as coaches, masseurs, sports scientists, psychologists, who were leading practitioners in their field. At the 2007 World Track Championships, for example, there were 28 support staff to 18 riders.[42] Early elite cyclists, such as Chris Hoy and Craig MacLean, were awarded £12,000 a year, allowing them to give up work and become full-time athletes, solely devoting their time to training and resting.[43] By 2008, elite riders were receiving £25,000 per annum.[44] Just as important was the building of the Manchester velodrome, a product of Manchester's failed bid to host the 2000 Olympics. It was opened in 1996 and would act as the new home of British Cycling. The new no-compromise approach revolved specifically around the four-year Olympic cycle. Funding became largely dependent on the number of medals won at previous games. Moreover, the extra funding allowed governing bodies to make greater investment in sports science and coaching.

The science of cycling

At the centre of British cycling's transformation was its embrace of sport science. Cycling's adoption of new techniques had not been a linear process. In the post-war period the increasingly intense sporting competition during the Cold War had stimulated the development of sports science and sports medicine as academic disciplines. A paradigm shift took place in coaching and training methods that led to the application of physiological principles to understand and enhance athletic performance.[45] Initially, there was resistance in cycling to these innovations as older and popular ideas of training persisted. Some of the preparation and training of professional cyclists, for example, had been in the hands of cyclists themselves and soigneurs. Soigneurs, before the employment of team doctors, offered advice, massage and secret home-made remedies (that included stimulants). They relied on experience-based methods, and their trade secrets were handed down through the generations by word of mouth. Their home-spun ideas continued right through until the 1980s.[46] The Irish rider Sean Kelly recounted how during his career, he basically trained and coached himself, while there was no specialist preparation for the Tour de France. Instead, teams were selected just 10 days before it began. By contrast, by the 2010s riders prepared for certain races months beforehand.[47]

Yet by the 1980s attitudes were changing as cyclists began to engage doctors and trained scientists. One early exponent of these new techniques was the Italian Francesco Moser. In 1984 he broke the world one-hour record in Mexico City. Not only was he assisted by the altitude, but he was also supported by a team of doctors.[48] In the vanguard of this shift regarding British cycling was the sports scientist Peter Keen. Given the subsequent transformation in British sporting fortunes, Keen has arguably been one of the most influential coaches in the history of British sport, not just cycling. He had initially graduated with a degree in sports studies from the University of Chichester (then Chichester College, Brighton) in 1985 before taking a Master of Philosophy in Human Biology at Loughborough University in 1989, while continuing to work as a lecturer at Chichester College. Between 1989 and 1992 he was the BCF's national coach, albeit on an unpaid basis, which necessitated him working in academia. In 1997 he was appointed the BCF's performance director, a role he continued in until 2003. It was Keen who brought in the no-compromise philosophy which was later extended to all sports. After British Cycling he joined UK Sport as first a performance adviser, before becoming its performance director between 2008 and 2012.

A cyclist himself – in 1980 he had won the schools' 10-mile time-trial championship – his first 'project' was working as a sports physiologist for Britain's former pursuit world champion, Tony Doyle. Doyle earned his living mainly from the lucrative European Six-Day circuit and as well as engaging Keen as a sports physiologist, his team consisted of a psychologist, a doctor, a mechanic and a soigneur, plus employing someone to video his riding for analysis.[49] However, Keen was not part of his inner circle and was unable to persuade Doyle to adapt to his methods. It was Keen's later association with Chris Boardman that would enhance both their careers and provide a template for British cycling's future success. Boardman and Keen had first met in 1987 at Chichester College where he was carrying out tests on cyclists, which would then be translated into a rational training programme. At the 1992 Olympics, Boardman won the gold medal in the 4,000 metres pursuit in spectacular fashion. It was Britain's first cycling gold medal since 1908.

When in 1989 Keen was appointed the BCF's national coach, he implemented a nationwide training programme at national centres of excellence. Initially, he aimed to establish an individual training programme for each cyclist using the Kingcycle Performance Potential Test. It was designed for four levels of intensity with the aim to determine a cyclist's maximum heart rate (MHR) at each level and hence their capabilities at the time. To further refine 'the numbers' from MHR tests and bring greater accuracy to training schedules, power meters were used to gauge a cyclist's output. Just as important as the design and implementation of these training programmes was their absorption and understanding by the riders themselves. Boardman was one of the earliest cyclists to 'engage with the process'. With these ingredients, it allowed coaches more control as they could break down athletic performance in ever smaller details.[50] This was the reason why Britain at first – successfully – focussed on timed track Olympic events, rather than road racing, viewed by many as the pinnacle of the sport. Another factor Keen later admitted was road racing's ingrained doping culture.[51] Moreover, he was under pressure to win medals in order to justify and maintain funding levels, and there were more medals to be won on the track than the road – hence the no-compromise approach. It was a formula that was later shared with sports such as rowing and canoeing, which also allowed coaches a high-degree of control over the athletes. At British Cycling, Keen put in place a World Class Performance Plan, which would be the basis for Britain's future success. It began in 1998 and was in effect a business plan for the sport in which each rider's performance was analysed over a 12-month period, based on scientific principles.[52] The British system had echoes of the former East Germany in terms of how athletes were both prepared and how talented younger riders were selected. In 1998, for example, a 'playground to podium' talent pathway was put in place, which later identified future world champions Ed Clancy and Lizzie Armitstead.[53] Later, Grand Tour winners Geraint Thomas and Simon Yates came through the British Cycling programme.

Following his departure from British Cycling in 2003, Keen was succeeded by his assistant, Dave Brailsford. Brailsford, who had a background in both business and cycling, had joined British Cycling in 1997, and built on and improved Keen's initial vision, as evident by the growing medal hauls at successive Olympics. He devised a four-person senior management team, which included himself, Shane Sutton, Steve Peters and Chris Boardman. To a certain extent, Sutton was an 'old school' coach. A former professional cyclist, he was promoted to performance manager, after being the coach for the sprinters, and dealt with man-management issues and acted on the behalf of the cyclists. Peters brought his expertise as a forensic psychiatrist who had worked in high-security hospitals, and worked on the mental preparation of cyclists.[54] In addition, British Cycling, due to its growing funds from UK Sport, was now able to recruit some of the best sports scientists and coaches. The Australian Scott Gardner, for an example, had been a sports scientist with the Australian cycling squad, while the German Jan van Eijden, the 2000 world sprint champion, was employed as the sprint coach. Later another German, Heiko Salzwedel, was appointed the coach of the endurance team. In the recruitment of global coaching talent, British Cycling was merely reflecting trends in other sports like football. At the centre of Brailsford's philosophy, as perhaps befits someone with an MBA, was some management-speak in the form of phrases such as 'compassionate-ruthlessness' and notably the doctrine of the 'aggregation of marginal gains'. Based on the Japanese business theory of 'kaizen', it was essentially the search for small improvements – 1 per cent according to Brailsford – that added up to a decisive advantage. It was an approach that had been adopted by companies such as Toyota, Ford and Lockheed Martin. Later Brailsford advised the civil service on how to improve the running of the NHS.[55]

In addition to developments in sports science, by the late twentieth century technology played an increasingly important role in professional cycling. Cyclists had long had a reputation for an attention to the design and capability of a bicycle. Moreover, it had been the sport of cycling that had driven improvements in the design of the bicycle from its birth. Cyclists gained a reputation as 'techies', forever fiddling about with their bikes, whether it was gears or saddles. In the film *A Sunday in Hell*, before the start of Paris-Roubaix in 1976, Eddy Merckx is featured making last-minute changes to his saddle height, which was one of his idiosyncrasies. The moment when the importance of technological innovation in modern cycling was fully realized – or at least the moment when it was most amplified – came at the 1989 Tour de France. In the final 24.5 kilometres time trial Greg Le Mond set off 50 seconds behind leader Laurent Fignon on General Classification, but would win the Tour by 8 seconds. For the time trial Le Mond had used aerodynamic handlebars, wore a similarly aerodynamic teardrop helmet and used a rear disc wheel. Fignon by contrast opted to use two disc wheels, but no helmet and ordinary handlebars. Fignon later criticized Le Mond's use of the handlebars, something he would take with him to an early grave.

Technological innovation had not been absent in British cycling. Until the twenty-first century, however, because of the lack of funding and a professional team, any innovations were usually the property of one-off inventors. What had made Chris Boardman's 1992 Olympic success headline grabbing was his bicycle, a Lotus Windcheetah.[56] It was a monocoque (one-piece) frame, which had been designed by Mike Burrows. Rather than gluing sections of carbon fibre tubes together, similar to a steel frame, the Lotus Windcheetah was the first bike to use and exploit the properties of composite materials. The bike's aerodynamic qualities stemmed from its one-fork blade, which reduced the frontal area helping the air to flow smoothly around the front wheel.[57] Burrows himself was not particularly a fan of sport, and one of his prototype monocoques was actually banned from the 1985 British National Track Championships.[58] Burrows was fascinated by the possibilities and potential of the bicycle, but instead was more influenced by the principles of HPV; the sport was a means to an end for him.[59] In 1991 he admitted that the bike would be difficult to be commercially viable as manufacturers had wanted bikes that had previously won medals and something that was immediately commercially viable.[60] After 1992 the possibilities for the monocoque for cycling more generally seemed to be endless. Richard Ballantine hailed it as one of the most significant bicycle designs in history, up there with the Rover Safety and the Moulton small wheeler and embraced how the pursuit of better performance was central to the cutting edge of design. He even went as far to predict that by the 2000 Olympics there would be specific bicycle design classes as in sailing and that the monocoque composite bicycle would be mass produced.[61] The bicycle manufacturers, however, continued to focus on mountain bikes and racers.

At the same time, a rival of Boardman emerged. Graham Obree was very much an individualist in how he approached his cycling, although it was a method perhaps forged as much out of necessity than desire. Unlike Boardman, who despite being an amateur until 1994, drew on the support of Peter Keen, Obree relied on scraping together enough money and sponsorship from where he could. Nevertheless, he was a thinker and scientifically minded about cycling – he did begin a design-engineering degree at Glasgow University but had to drop out in the first year – and how he could improve his own performance, especially when it came to aerodynamics. One of his first innovations was his riding style. Because he used flat handlebars, they enabled him to adopt a tuck position, like a downhill skier, which as result of keeping his arms tucked in reduced the air flow, thus improving his aerodynamic position. In 1994, one hour before the start of the defence of his world pursuit title, the UCI deemed his handlebars illegal and disqualified him. The following year he invented another style, the Superman position, which was aerodynamically more efficient and one that Boardman copied.

Obree was just as renowned for his bike, 'Old Faithful', which he built himself in 1993. He would later use a Burrows bike, but preferred his own.[62] Obree eschewed the classical diamond frame and instead made one with only a centre beam – using BMX tubing – because he had wanted his legs closer together when he pedalled, which reduced the frontal area and his legs would not be impaired by a top tube. As consequence, the bike had to have a custom-made bottom bracket for which he used ball bearings from a washing machine. When he went to the world championships in 1993 'Old Faithful', with its very large gear and his unconventional style, had caused some sniggering among opposing teams – until he began riding and won.[63] In some ways Obree was a throwback to the nineteenth century when early professional cyclists built and improved their own machines in the pursuit of performance, which was to benefit in the long term the cycling industry.

Both Boardman and Obree were both world champions at 4,000 metres pursuit, but perhaps more significantly they would break the one-hour record, an achievement appreciated more in Europe than in Britain, beyond its small cycling community.[64] This was ironic given the history of cycling in Britain, and how it had traditionally been based around racing against the clock and timed record attempts over distance. The lack of reception for Boardman's and Obree's one-hour records perhaps also indicated the cultural shift among the general public in how road racing was now regarded as the main form of cycling sport; so while also technologically oriented, Boardman and Obree were both hewn from this British tradition of the time trial.

By the twenty-first century, British Cycling had the resources to indulge in the pursuit of marginal gains through technological innovation. As a member of its senior management team, from 2004 until 2013 Chris Boardman was put in charge of research and development, what became known as the 'Secret Squirrel Club' that acted as an equipment bunker where technical innovations were stored. It was so secret that Dave Brailsford was banned from its meetings due to his self-proclaimed propensity for talking too much and hence giving away its secrets; there was a certain amount of subterfuge involved in which other teams participated. Built on the policy of marginal gains, the main innovations revolved around making cyclists' kit, in the form of more aerodynamic skinsuits, helmets and bicycles. Importantly, Boardman was unafraid to go outside of cycling for advice on technological information and thus help change the mindset of him and his team.

He stated:

> All the big ideas came from the non-biking industry. We visited the military, F1 [Formula 1 motor racing], academia, aviation .... When we first went to McLaren, they knew nothing about cycling. And because they didn't know, they always asked, 'Why do you do that'? And we replied, 'We don't know.' You suddenly realize how restricted by tradition you are. ... A mix of ignorance and expertise is the ideal marriage for breaking boundaries.[65]

However, Boardman did not feel any loyalty towards these people. Once their ideas had come to fruition, he would be looking for new ideas from someone else. The bicycle that Chris Hoy rode to win the Kilometre TT at the 2004 Athens Olympics was designed by Dimitris Katsanis. A former member of the Greek national cycling team, he worked for Advanced Composites Group, which was a Derbyshire firm that made components for Formula One and the aerospace industry. Research into the bike's aerodynamics was carried out by the Sheffield University Sports Engineering Research Group.[66] For helmet design an expert, Rob Lewis, from Totalsim, which specialized in computational fluid dynamics, was hired.[67] In the design of skinsuits, a fashion designer Sally Cowan was employed and at one stage they looked at skinsuits complete with sequins to see how wind flow was affected.[68]

The growth of female cyclists

In 1996 the sudden death of Beryl Burton received little attention from the mainstream media. Obituaries were published in the broadsheets while tributes in the cycling press to her were plentiful, but it could be argued that it was only in death that she was brought back into the public consciousness. Later, in 2012 the actor Maxine Peake wrote and starred as Burton in a BBC

Radio 4 drama *Beryl: A Love Story on Two Wheels* (later a stage play) after admitting she had not known her story.[69] There had been hardly any professional female cyclists since Eileen Sheridan, and none who raced for a living. Instead, the sports of athletics, tennis and golf were the leading professional female sports, while in the 1990s there was an exponential growth in women's football.

By the twenty-first century, the profile of British female cyclists had never been higher. Not only had some become household names because of their sporting success, but they were also now part of celebrity culture. In 2016 the marriage of Olympians Jason Kenny and Laura Trott made the main television news, while another Olympian, Rebecca James, appeared as a guest on the BBC's *Great British Bake Off: An Extra Slice*. Success at sport was reflected in the increase in the number of women cycling more generally, although it still lagged behind that of men.[70] By 2014, it was calculated that of those people who cycled once a week, around 525,000 (27 per cent) were women. Out of the 1.2 million who cycled once a month, women made up 33 per cent, while the number of female commuters cycling had risen 40 per cent from 2008. At the same time British Cycling aimed for 1.5 million women to cycle every week by 2020.[71]

Historically, cycling had been a leisure activity where the boundaries between men and women were blurred, becoming almost non-existent. However, attitudes to cycling as a sport for women reflected those of women's sport more generally, and it was considered a marginal activity and received little encouragement from the cycling authorities. On the international front, the women's world cycling championships were first staged in 1958. However, it was not until 1984 that women's cycling became part of the Olympic programme – and only then a road race. It was only in 2012 when there was parity in the number of Olympic events between men and women. In 1984 a women's Tour de France was staged, but after a few editions the race fell into abeyance. In 1990 there were no female professional cyclists in Britain and just 146 senior and 23 junior women BCF licence holders. By comparison the figures for male riders were 4,574 and 1,037, respectively. The average field for woman's road races was 35, which was short of the 60 allowed and needed by promoters to break even.[72]

By the late nineties, women were gaining a higher profile in society generally. The new intake of MPs in 1997 comprised a record number of women, the vast majority from the Labour Party. More women graduated from university than men and in some professions such as medicine, female graduates now markedly outnumbered men. At the start of the twenty-first century, cyclists were part of the new breed of professional female athletes in Britain. Lottery funding was crucial to this development, which allowed athletes to train and compete on a full-time basis, aided by access to sports medicine and sports science services. Lottery funding was also an important step in the drive for equality for female athletes, albeit an unconscious one as now a women's Olympic medal was worth just as much as a male athlete's. Some female cyclists were also able to capitalize on their success through sponsorship and endorsements.

One professional female cyclist from this new breed was Victoria Pendleton. Pendleton won gold medals at the 2008 and 2012 Olympics in addition to six world individual sprint titles.[73] Like many female cyclists, she was born into a cycling family. Her father Max was a member of Nomads (Hitchin) Cycling Club and had a national reputation for hill climbing.[74] She later attended Northumbria University, graduating with a degree in sports science. It was Pendleton who raised and changed the media profile of female cycling more than anyone else. In addition to her sporting prowess, she cultivated an image in the media as someone unafraid to express and project her femininity and sexuality. As Boyle and Haynes argue, one way for female athletes to increase their earning capacity was managing their media profile and playing the image game.[75] Pendleton appeared on the front cover of 'lads' mag' *FHM* as well as riding a bike naked on the cover of the *Observer Sport Monthly*.[76] Pendleton later capitalized on her increased profile to enter the mainstream media, becoming a summarizer on BBC.[77] Polley has argued that sport has been a location for 'the display and negotiation of gender politics' and to a certain extent, Pendleton's actions both reinforced and challenged the masculine republic of sport.[78] While it could be argued that they were an example of female empowerment, it was also an indication of an enduring patriarchy in how men continued to sexualize women more generally and at the same marginalize their sporting achievements. Pendleton's success and subsequent profile raised familiar questions over female athletes and body image. Pendleton herself was not unaware of these debates and believed that '[b]ody consciousness has kept a lot of women out of the sport'. Masculine traits even extended to some of her female competitors, she claimed. It was her intention, however, 'to retain and celebrate her femininity' while training and competing.[79] To what extent a changing of the sporting landscape, where women competed on equal terms in terms of media exposure and prize money, would reshape the gender politics of sport remains unclear, because, as an act of empowerment, female athletes could still exploit their body image.

Team Sky, the globalization of cycling and doping

In 2010 Team Sky was formed. Funded by the media corporation and headed by Dave Brailsford as its 'Directeur Sportif', Brailsford boldly announced that it would win the Tour de France with a British rider within five years. Bradley Wiggins won the race two years later. The 'aggregation of marginal gains' ethos honed at British Cycling was now brought to road racing, aided by substantial funds, which allowed Sky to buy some of the best riders.⁸⁰ Success subsequently followed success, but by 2016, Team Sky was under increasing scrutiny over allegations of doping. To a certain extent, the rise of Team Sky reflected cycling's increasing globalization as a sport. Globalization reflected a new form of interconnectedness, especially in the West. Eric Reed writes,

> The rise of novel regimes of mass consumption and leisure, growing economic interdependence, ever-more-complex, voluminous, and intertwined networks of economic and cultural interaction, and the maturation of new technologies such as airline travel, telecommunications, and the internet sparked this sea change.⁸¹

Given that it was largely a European sport, cycling was well-placed to exploit this new conjuncture of forces. The transformation of European cycling was an uneven process, however, and was subject to the characteristics of individual countries in terms of their sporting traditions and regulation of the media.⁸²

Initially, Eurosport was cycling's main satellite broadcaster. Launched in 1989 as a pan-European channel at the start of the satellite revolution, it covered numerous minority sports. Traditionally, sponsors of European professional teams had been bicycle manufacturers, but from the 1960s this began to change as other companies looked to tap in to the commercial potential that cycling offered through its growing coverage on television. Companies from industries as diverse as insurance, motoring, the media (Discovery), a chain of food health stores (La Vie Claire) and an espresso machine manufacturer (Faema) all sponsored cycling teams. With the later digital revolution in television, there was more space to fill and hence more opportunities to televise more sports and more opportunities for sponsors to advertise their products. Moreover, further digitization and the internet fragmented the media market, meaning that watching television was becoming less important as the main medium to consume sport. That a major media corporation like Sky became involved in British cycling is perhaps instructive to the development of a sports-media complex. Moreover, road racing had been the sport's most lucrative form due to sponsorship and later television. In 1989 it was reported that that year's Tour de France winner, Greg Le Mond, earned a salary of $5.5 million on a three-year contract.

Cycling's global profile had been further enhanced by Lance Armstrong. Until his eventual downfall in 2013, following his confession to doping, Armstrong was the sport's biggest star. However, he was never really accepted in France, despite – or because of – winning the Tour de France for seven consecutive years, 1999 to 2005, mainly due to suspicions that he was 'taking something'.⁸³ Nevertheless, he helped to transform the sport from a European-centred one to one that was increasingly global in its popularity. It was perhaps Armstrong, as a charismatic American, who more than anyone helped shift the sport's lingua franca from French to English – the language of business – thus attracting international sponsors and television. Armstrong transcended the sport not just because of his seven successive Tour de France victories, but also through his 'against all the odds', 'inspiring' backstory. He became world champion in 1993 but shortly after was diagnosed with cancer. He returned to cycling following surgery and chemotherapy to compete and win the Tour in 1999. Armstrong's story gave a fillip to the sport following the previous year's race, which had been disrupted by the Festina doping scandal. He later set up his own very successful charity, 'Livestrong', which spawned a charity wristband and his 2000 book *It's Not About the Bike* was an international bestseller. In 2003, following his fifth Tour de France victory, he was named BBC Overseas Sports Personality, highlighting the extent of his celebrity. Rumours over doping had not been absent during his career,[84] but they were largely ignored by the general public. Indeed, it could be argued that complicit in the avoidance of this issue were the UCI, sponsors, broadcasters and many journalists, all of whom had invested too much in Armstrong's success.[85]

As the world's biggest annual sporting event, the Tour adapted to the new globalized realities of sport. In effect, the Tour transformed itself into a global made-for-television spectacle, which provided more publicity for its corporate sponsors. However, at the same time the French character of the race was retained, if not amplified, through regular camera shots of the French countryside and famous buildings, making broadcasts half sporting events and half tourist advertisements for the country. Moreover, the race's standards regarding the rules and commercialization were emulated in other national tours across the globe.[86]

The establishment and later dominance of Team Sky marked another fundamental shift in the perceptions of British cycling, not only among the British public, but also in other countries. Despite being bankrolled by an American company, Team Sky was seen as a British team, and at first it shared its headquarters in Manchester with British Cycling.[87] While it had initially been set up to develop British road racing talent, Sky acted more like a Premier League football team, buying up the best talent available. British riders were in a minority, but this was unsurprising because as in football, cycling teams operated in a global market with few barriers on whom they could sign. Dave Brailsford, as the team's successful Directeur Sportif – a kind of general manager figure – represented a new kind of Britishness, offering a stark contrast with the traditional image of the gentleman–amateur. Whereas the values of the gentleman–amateur were based on fair play and modesty, British sport had adopted an obsession with performance and winning. Brailsford was technocratically minded, highly educated with a professional and business background and was someone who was very focussed and performance oriented. He could be ruthless and single-minded in the pursuit of success and in this sense – his persona was not dissimilar to football managers like Alex Ferguson or Arsène Wenger. Before the 2012 Olympics he selected Jason Kenny for the Men's Sprint ahead of defending champion Chris Hoy, while the following year, he dropped the 2012 Tour de France winner, Bradley Wiggins, from the Sky team, in favour of Chris Froome. Yet the dominance of Sky would backfire among cycling fans and aficionados. Like Armstrong, its riders, especially Chris Froome, faced criticism and scepticism from France and French cycling fans. The team's methodical style of racing through setting a fast tempo at the front to deter attacks did not endear it to those who felt that they were not winning with panache and not being true to the history and traditions of cycling. Sky's image was also not helped by its black uniform, which gave a sense of foreboding, although mainly for the other teams.

Because of Team Sky's dominance and style, it drew comparisons with Armstrong's US Postal Team and all the implications that came with it due to Armstrong's later confession of doping. In 2018, in its findings, a House of Commons Select Committee criticized Sky for crossing an ethical line in legally using performance-enhancing drugs.[88] It was claimed – but not proved – that in 2011 Bradley Wiggins was given a PED, triamcinolone, under the Therapeutic Exemption Use protocol, in order to increase his power-to-weight ratio rather than as a medicine to treat his asthma, and that this constituted a cynical abuse of the system. When Brailsford set up Team Sky he had declared that it would have a 'zero tolerance' attitude towards doping. Ensuing revelations would bring into disrepute this stated aim, although no actual evidence of doping was found. Doping (and anti-doping) had become the great moral sporting issue of its time. Like amateurism in the nineteenth century, it was underpinned by a set of values in which ideas of cheating were socially and culturally constructed. The use of science to determine what constituted doping was not neutral either, but instead an arbitrary process, based on a similar set of values. Ultimately, looking beyond Sky's desire to manage its image, what the Wiggins's incident and others did reveal was that Sky was little different to most other professional sports team – one that would push the rules to their limits to win.

In 2018 Simon Yates won the Vuelta a España. He was the third British cyclist to win a Grand Tour that year, the others being Chris Froome, the Giro d'Italia and Geraint Thomas, the Tour de France. It was unprecedented for one country to supply three different winners of these races and possibly marked the highpoint in the history of the sport in Britain. By the following year there were signs that British dominance was coming to an end with Thomas runner-up in the Tour to his teammate, the Colombian Egan Bernal. Yet it was a mark of British dominance over the previous decade that Thomas's second place was met with a muted response in the media with the focus on his perceived failure. Ten years previously this achievement would have been lauded, given the paucity of past British success. This response highlighted the transformation that British cycling had undertaken during the previous forty years. Like other minor British sports, cycling had moved decisively away from its amateur roots to embrace a fully professional and technocratic direction. The influx of state funding had provided not only the catalyst for Olympic medals but also a boost to the commercial arm of the sport in Britain. Cycling successes had boosted the profile of cycling as a leisure activity more generally as well as catapulting some cyclists into the realms of celebrity culture. While cycling remained dominated by men, it was increasingly a sport where women were gaining a higher profile. Nevertheless, despite all these developments and successes cycling has remained in the shadow of traditionally popular British sports. As a sport, cycling has also been characterized by a certain dislocation. Although the Tour of Britain had been revived and gained in popularity during the twenty-first century, it has lacked the unifying cultural power of the Tour de France and the Belgian classic races. There is a sense, therefore, that its current popularity in Britain is transient, lacking the deep roots of European nations, especially Belgium, and it remains to be seen if British cycling's popularity will be maintained when its successes almost inevitably dry up.

Conclusion

At Glastonbury 2019, Stormzy became the first British rapper to headline the Pyramid Stage. It was declared 'a glorious victory lap for black British culture', marking a fusion between Britain's growing urban ethnic populations and Glastonbury's traditional white middle-class audience.[1] Midway through his song 'Vossi Bop', two teenagers appeared on the stage performing 'wheelies' on their bikes. Groups of teenagers riding their bikes around British town and city centres pulling wheelies of their own are a relatively common sight, and in this case it was a nod to the artist's South London roots. Once the preserve of the prosperous and striving Victorian middle classes, by the twenty-first century the bicycle had morphed into a symbol of urban Britain's energetic but disaffected youth. Moreover, the performance highlighted one of this book's main themes: how cycling has been a source of politics and pleasure as the riding of bicycles for fun was a political act in itself, which in this case asserted an urban identity. Now a symbol of urban culture, this performance also highlighted the ubiquity and versatility of the bicycle and how cycling has continually adapted to broader societal change.

This book has examined cycling from a variety of perspectives from the nineteenth century up to and including the twenty-first century. It has attempted to understand cycling history as a form of transport, a leisure activity, a sport and as a technology, one that has been subject to broader contexts – in terms of consumption, culture, the social make-up of cyclists, technology and politics – which have shaped and continually reshaped its legal, economic and cultural status. One of the book's main arguments has been that to understand the history of cycling in Britain it is difficult to disentangle the politics from the pleasures of riding a bicycle and vice versa. In this sense, the role of the state has been ever pervasive, depending on how you judge the depth and intensity of its involvement. Thus, while British sport in general has been rooted in a voluntary and associational culture, cycling has been shaped by broader political and legal factors, more than most other sports. In addition, cycling political activism has benefitted from a consumer boom, something which has been partly due to growing environmental concerns. The history of cycling in Britain has not produced a dominant narrative; there has been no one cycling identity, but instead a myriad of cycling identities. Cycling's history has been characterized by a series of ebbs and flows in regards to its popularity and status. The peaks or booms have comprised three specific periods: the 1890s; the 1930s to the mid-1950s; and the early twenty-first century. However, just as interesting for the historian are the troughs especially the mid-twentieth century. Indeed, at one stage during the twentieth century there were serious doubts as to its survival as a form of transport. The most marked characteristic of cycling's history, therefore, has been those sporadic periods of adaptation to historical changes and continuities.

At the centre of this social and cultural history has been the bicycle itself: a persistent presence in British life. By 2018, it was found that 42 per cent of people in England, amounting to around 20 million people, either owned or had access to a bicycle.[2] However, the nature of this presence was never fixed or inevitable. Like other forms of technology, such as the VCR, which were once the height of fashion, but have now become moribund or extinct, the bicycle has been subject to the whims of markets and the changing tastes of consumers. Technological change has acted as the headless horseman of history – a disruptive force in reshaping social relations. In referring to the car, O'Connell has argued that '[s]ociety's choices between possible technological developments are highly indicative of patterns of political, social and economic power'. The same can be said of the bicycle. It was not a one-way process as social relations shaped bicycle design and uses. Bicycle designs, from the safety to the mountain bike, in turn reshaped the cycling population as they capitalized on and reflected changing consumer tastes and demand. As attitudes to motoring change, particularly in urban centres, it may be that bicycle technology will adapt to these circumstances. During the 2010s, there has been steady increase in electric bicycles, which may increase the appeal of cycling among those groups of the population who basically find riding a bike too hard.

Riding a bicycle, therefore, has appealed to different sections of society at different times, although at one time for a large number of workers it was as much a necessity as a luxury. Moreover, this appeal was never monolithic as, except briefly in the 1890s, it has never appealed to the entire population at the same time. At the heart of the book has been that riding a bicycle in all its different ways is also an individual experience, which can give meaning to people's lives. It is just that these meanings have mutated over the period in light of changing historical forces. Even this very individualistic appeal was subject to context. Thus, in the nineteenth century cycling in the countryside for some middle-class tourists could represent a reaction against modernity and a re-engagement with a rural Britain being rapidly swallowed up by industrialization and urbanization. The sport of cycling on the other hand was the embodiment of modernity with its emphasis on the values of competition, records and speed. By the late twentieth century, cycling had a greater association with urban Britain due to a growing awareness of environmental issues, while for the expanding professional middle classes cycling had become a lifestyle choice which required 'having all the gear'.

Middle-class consumption has been at the heart of cycling's ebbs and flows. Initially it was the middle classes who catalysed its consumption before shaping its direction and the discourses around cycling. By the interwar years, they had started to abandon the bicycle for the motor car due its increasing usefulness as transport for work as more lived in the expanding suburbs and for its social status, something the bicycle could no longer offer. The middle classes were never a monolithic group. Instead, they constantly evolved in light of social and economic circumstances as well as due to generational change. Until the mid-twentieth century the gentleman–amateur continued to provide a model for middle-class men, but by the end of the century this has been replaced by one based around notions of competition. At the same time, cycling's late twentieth-century renaissance was based on different set of middle-class values, which reflected changing attitudes to health and the environment. For women, cycling was initially a symbol of emancipation, but it was mainly restricted to those who enjoyed relatively affluent middle-class lifestyles. It was only during the interwar years that the bicycle was seen in relatively equal terms for men and women. After the mid-1950s, cycling returned largely to a male-dominated activity with women increasingly discouraged by the growing fears over safety on the roads.[3]

Another of the main themes of the book has been the relationship between cycling and motoring, or more specifically the car. Of course, this became a particularly one-sided relationship as the twentieth century progressed. The bicycle, once a symbol of nineteenth-century modernity, became a victim of it in the second half of the twentieth century as the importance of the car, politically, economically and culturally, became embedded in the British psyche. The shaping of the relationship between cycling and the car had taken place in the 1930s, largely due to the efforts of the road lobby and the assistance of an accommodating media. Importantly, a discourse of safety, promoted by technical experts and planners, created a sense of danger regarding riding on the roads, which has dominated transport policy ever since. Legislative restrictions on motoring were limited and a segregation of road users, including cyclists, was encouraged. Growing road casualties were regarded as a price worth paying in the pursuit of economic interests. A combination of commercial and middle-class interests, therefore, formed the context for transport politics in the latter part of the twentieth century where transport policies in the UK have become much more contested by both cycling activists and organizations than in countries like the Netherlands and Denmark.

In comparison to these countries, cycling in Britain has not reached the same or similar levels and range of cycle use; the bicycle only makes up 1 per cent of traffic on British roads. Cycling in Britain is largely a recreational activity for young people rather than the population as a whole.[4] Nevertheless, there have been considerable efforts to 'Europeanize' urban areas through mini-Hollands, Cycle Superhighways and bicycle-hire schemes. To a certain extent, these developments have revealed fractures within British society, based around the forces of social liberalism and economic liberalism. Whereas in general these cycling initiatives have been supported by social liberals, they have been opposed by social conservatives. In urban areas especially, for some, especially professional working-class drivers, the growing number of cyclists have come to represent not just a nuisance, but a challenge to their authority and perceived right on the road. These tensions can also be found among pedestrians as some cyclists, in asserting their supposed right to cycle, have been deemed aggressive and anti-social. It was ever thus. Back in the nineteenth century, the bicycle had struggled to gain legal status as a conveyance of the road. The bicycle in this sense reflected broader historical changes and continuities, something likely to continue into the future.

NOTES

Introduction

1 Harry Oosterhuis, 'Cycling, Modernity and National Culture', *Social History*, vol. 41, no. 3 (2016), pp. 233–48.
2 Ibid., p. 240.
3 Hugh Dauncey, *French Cycling: A Social and Cultural History* (Liverpool: Liverpool University Press, 2012), pp. 1–4.
4 For Italy, see Simon Martin, *Sport Italia: The Italian Love Affair with Sport* (London: IB Tauris, 2011); John Foot, *Pedalare! Pedalare! A History of Italian Cycling* (London: Bloomsbury, 2011).
5 Stijn Knuts, 'Converging and Competing Courses of Identity Construction: Shaping and Imagining Society through Cycling and Bicycle Racing in Belgium before World War Two' (Unpublished PhD: University of Leuven, 2014).
6 Oosterhuis, 'Cycling, Modernity and National Culture', p. 246.
7 Harold Perkin, The Third Revolution: Professional Elites in the Modern World (London: Routledge, 1996), chapter 3.
8 David Cannadine, *Class in Britain* (London: Penguin, 1998), Conclusion.
9 Lawrence James, *The Middle Class: A History* (London: Little, Brown, 2006), p. 1.
10 Jeffrey Hill, '"What Shall We Do with Them When They're Not Working?": Leisure and Historians in Britain', in B. Bebber (ed.), *Leisure and Cultural Conflict in Twentieth-Century Britain* (Manchester: Manchester University Press, 2012), p. 22.
11 Eric Zuelow, *A History of Modern Tourism* (Basingstoke: Palgrave, 2016), p. 11.
12 Jose Harris, *Private Lives, Public Spirit: Britain 1870-1914* (London: Penguin 1993), p. 36.
13 Andrew Denning, *Skiing into Modernity: A Cultural and Environmental History* (Oakland: University of California Press, 2014), p. 10.
14 For research on women's cycling, see: http://www.sheilahanlon.com; Clare Simpson, 'A Social History of Women and Cycling in Late-Nineteenth Century New Zealand' (Unpublished PhD: Lincoln University, New Zealand, 1998); Fiona Kinsey, 'Reading Photographic Portraits of Australian Women Cyclists in the 1890s: From Costume and Cycle Choices to Constructions of Feminine Identity', *International Journal of the History of Sport*, vol. 28, no. 8–9 (2011), pp. 1121–37; Fiona Kinsey, 'Stamina, Speed and Adventure: Australian Women

and Competitive Cycling in the 1890s', *International Journal of the History of Sport*, vol. 28, no. 10 (2011), pp. 1375–87; Dave Russell, 'Mum's the Word: The Cycling Career of Beryl Burton, 1956–1986', *Women's History Review*, vol. 17, no. 5 (2008), pp. 787–806.

15 Viscount Bury and G. Lacy Hillier, *Cycling, 2nd Edition* (London: Longmans, Green and Co., 1889).

16 For example, Frederick Alderson, *Bicycling: A History* (Newton Abbot: David & Charles, 1972). The prolific work of Derek Roberts can be found at the University of Warwick's Modern Record Centre in the file MSS.328/N7; Andrew Ritchie, *King of the Road: An Illustrated History of Cycling* (London: Wildwood, 1975); *Quest for Speed: A History of Early Bicycle Racing 1868-1903* (Self-published, 2011).

17 David Rubenstein, 'Cycling in the 1890s', *Victorian Studies* (Autumn 1977), pp. 47–71.

18 Brian Griffin, *Cycling in Victorian Ireland* (Dublin: Nonsuch, 2006); William Manners, *Revolution: How the Bicycle Reinvented Modern Britain* (London: Duckworth, 2018).

19 One notable exception is Peter Cox, '"A Denial of our boasted Civilisation": Cyclists' Views on Conflicts over Road Use in Britain, 1926–1935', *Transfers*, vol. 2, no. 3 (Winter 2012), pp. 4–30.

20 The first International Cycling History Conference took place in Glasgow in 1990.

21 David Horton, Paul Rosen and Peter Cox (eds), *Cycling and Society* (Aldershot: Ashgate, 2007).

22 Rachel Aldred, 'The Role of Advocacy and Activism', in J. Parkin (ed.), *Cycling and Sustainability* (Bingley: Emerald Group Publishing Limited, 2012); Rachel Aldred, '"On the outside": Constructing Cycling Citizenship', *Social & Cultural Geography*, vol. 11, no. 1 (2010), pp. 35–52; Rachel Aldred, 'Incompetent or Too Competent? Negotiating Everyday Cycling Identities in a Motor Dominated Society', *Mobilities*, vol. 2, no. 8 (2013), pp. 252–71; Peter Cox, 'Activism and Market Innovation: Changing Patterns in the Cycle Trade', Paper presented at 4th CSRG Symposium, CTC Guildford, 7 September 2007; Peter Cox, 'Social Movement Activism, Social Change and Bicycling in the UK', Paper presented at The Future of Mobilities: Flows, Transport and Communication. T2M/ Cosmobilities joint conference, Caserta, Italy, 2–15 September; Dave Horton, 'Fear of Cycling', in David Horton, Paul Rosen and Peter Cox (eds), *Cycling and Society* (Aldershot: Ashgate, 2007), pp. 133–52.

23 Peter Cox, *Cycling: A Sociology of Vélomobility* (London: Routledge, 2019).

24 David Herlihy, *Bicycle: The History* (New Haven: Yale University Press, 2004).

25 Paul Rosen, Framing Production: Technology, Culture, and Change in the British Bicycle Industry (Cambridge, MA: MIT Press, 2002); Wiebe Bijker, Of Bicycles, Bakelites and Bulbs: Towards a Theory of Socio-technical Change (London: MIT Press, 1995).

26 Roger Lloyd-Jones and M. J. Lewis with Mark Eason, *Raleigh and the British Bicycle Industry: An Economic and Business History, 1870-1960* (Aldershot:

Ashgate, 2000); Andrew Millward, 'Factors Contributing to the Success of the UK Cycle Industry, 1870-1939' (Unpublished PhD: University of Birmingham, 1999).
27 Herlihy, *Bicycle*, chapters 4–5.
28 *Spectator*, 22 May 1869.
29 Andrew Ritchie, 'The Origins of Bicycle Racing in England: Technology, Entertainment, Sponsorship and Advertising in the Early History of the Sport', *Journal of Sport History*, vol. 26, no. 3 (Fall 1999), pp. 490–2.
30 Ibid.
31 Later derogatorily referred to as the Penny Farthing.
32 Ritchie, 'The Origins of Bicycle Racing in England', p. 499.
33 Aldred, 'The Role of Advocacy and Activism', p. 84. See also Aldred, '"On the Outside"', pp. 35–52.
34 Richard Holt, *Sport and the British: A Modern History* (Oxford: Clarendon Press, 1989), p. 3.
35 Joe Robinson, *Tommy Turnbull: A Miner's Life* (Newcastle upon Tyne: TUPS Books, 1996), p. 213. I am grateful to Rob Colls for this reference.
36 Ibid., pp. 219–20.
37 The Raleigh archive at Nottingham was not consulted, but further highlights the extent of archival material on cycling. There is also a bourgeoning collection of cycling archives deposited at local record offices.

Chapter 1

1 Modern Records Centre, University of Warwick, MSS.328/N7/1/23, Derek Roberts Archive, London-Brighton Race, *Cycling*, 24 August 1916, pp. 333–4; *National Cyclists' Union Review*, January 1914, p. 4; *Bicycling News*, 24 August 1939, p. 172, MSS.328/N7/1/152, Derek Roberts Archive, Rowley B Turner.
2 John Lowerson, *Sport and the English Middle Classes 1870-1914* (Manchester: Manchester University Press, 1993), p. 1.
3 Richard Holt, 'The Amateur Body and the Middle-Class Man: Work, Health and Style in Victorian Britain', *Sport in History*, vol. 26, no. 3 (2006), pp. 366–7.
4 Neil Carter, *Medicine, Sport and the Body: A Historical Perspective* (London: Bloomsbury Academic, 2012), chapter 1.
5 Ina Zweiniger-Bargielowska, *Managing the Body: Beauty, Health, and Fitness in Britain, 1880-1939* (Oxford: Oxford University Press 2010), chapter 1.
6 *The Tricyclist*, 4 January 1884, p. 368.
7 *Daily Mail*, 25 March 1899, p. 5.
8 MSS.328/C/6/3/1, Edinburgh Amateur Bicycle Club, Minute Books, 9 August 1876.

9. Marine Bellégo, 'Bicycles and Bodies in Britain at the Fin-de-Siècle' (Unpublished MPhil: Cambridge University, 2013), p. 21.
10. MSS.328/C/4, *Cyclists' Touring Club Gazette*, March 1884, pp. 71–2 (hereafter, *CTC Gazette*).
11. *Daily Mail*, 25 March 1899, p. 5.
12. *The Tricyclist*, 4 January 1884, p. 368.
13. Rubenstein, 'Cycling in the 1890s', p. 51.
14. Ibid.
15. http://www.sheilahanlon.com/?p=1889 (accessed 16 January 2018).
16. Ritchie, *Quest for Speed*, pp. 152–3.
17. Richard Holt, 'The Bicycle, the Bourgeoisie and the Discovery of Rural France, 1880-1914', *British Journal of Sports History*, vol. 2, no. 2 (1985), p. 128. In 1898 the cycle tax was paid on 483,414 machines in France. *Daily Mail*, 12 September 1899, p. 6.
18. Ritchie, *King of the Road*, p. 72.
19. Bury and Hillier, *Cycling*, p. 130.
20. Irvine Loudon, 'Doctors and their Transport, 1750-1914', *Medical History*, vol. 45 (2001), pp. 185–206.
21. In 1851 for the first time urban dwellers exceeded the rural population.
22. MSS.328/N7/1/47, End to End, 'End to End in 1880', n.d.; 'A History of the Cycling Record', n.d. It was also suggested that in 1869 a party of 24 riders set off from Land's End to John O'Groats with only 3 arriving three weeks later. Ibid.
23. Both bodies now allowed people with tricycles and sociables to join.
24. *Daily Mail*, 21 July 1899, p. 6. CTC members joined directly while for the NCU, the vast majority of cyclists were members via the affiliation of their club.
25. Harold Perkin, *The Rise of Professional Society: England since 1880* (London: Routledge, 1989), pp. 79–80.
26. Michael Heller, 'London Clerical Workers 1880-1919: The Search for Stability', (Unpublished PhD: University College London, University of London, 2003), Appendix 2, p. 382.
27. Tony Mason, *Association Football and English Society 1863-1915* (Brighton: Harvester Press, 1980), pp. 30, 52–3 n. 44, 45.
28. *Cycling*, 30 March 1934, p. 202. Shaw wrote about their rides into the country in his letters to Ellen Terry.
29. Alicia Rix, '"Henry's Bicycle": Cycling and Figurations of Exposure in "The Papers"', *The Henry James Review*, vol. 39, no. 1 (2018), pp. 23–36.
30. Ritchie, *King of the Road*, pp. 72–3.
31. Ibid., p. 97, 113.
32. *Spectator*, 22 May 1869.
33. Rubenstein, 'Cycling in the 1890s', p. 49.

34 *Manchester Courier*, 20 April 1895, Supplement, p. 4. Balfour continued in the role until the 1920s.
35 *Daily Mail*, 25 March, p. 6; 16 June 1899, p. 6.
36 *Daily Mail*, 3 January 1899, p 6.
37 *Daily Mail*, 13 June 1899, p 6.
38 *CTC Gazette*, April 1904, p. 159.
39 Holt, *Sport and the British*, p. 116.
40 Mike Huggins, *The Victorians and Sport* (London: Hambledon and London, 2004), pp. 52.
41 Ibid., p. 54.
42 Peter Borsay, *A History of Leisure: The British Experience since 1500* (Basingstoke: Palgrave, 2006), pp. 113–14.
43 Jeffrey Hill, *Sport, Leisure and Culture in Twentieth Century Britain* (Basingstoke: Palgrave, 2002), pp. 130–1; Simon Gunn, *The Public Culture of the Victorian Middle Class: Ritual and Authority in the English Industrial City 1840-1914* (Manchester: Manchester University Press, 2000), p. 4, 15; J. Garrard and V. Parrott, 'Craft, Professional and Middle-Class Identity', in Alan Kidd and David Nicholls (eds), *The Making of the British Middle Class? Studies of Regional and Cultural Diversity since the Eighteenth Century* (Stroud: Sutton Publishing, 1998), p. 149.
44 Gunn, *Public Culture*, p. 15, 84; Rob Ensor, '"The Champion Club of the Midland Counties": A Social Study of the Nottingham Chess Club, 1829 – c.1904' (Unpublished MA Dissertation: De Montfort University, 2016); Garrard and Parrott, 'Craft, Professional and Middle-Class Identity', p. 166.
45 Ritchie, *Quest for Speed*, p. 63, 76, 368; S. H. Moxham, *Fifty Years of Road Riding (1885-1935): A History of the North Road Cycling Club, Ltd.* (Bedford: Diemer & Reynolds, 1935), p. 1.
46 Ritchie, *Quest for Speed*, p. 376, Table 9B.
47 Bury and Hillier, *Cycling*, p. 261.
48 Griffin, *Cycling in Victorian Ireland*, pp. 33–5.
49 http://www.classiclightweights.co.uk/clubs-reminiscences.html (accessed 19 February 2015).
50 Jeremy Crump, 'Amusements of the People: The Provision of Recreation in Leicester, 1850-1914' (Unpublished PhD: University of Warwick, 1985), p. 256.
51 Peter Radford, *1866 and All that ...: The Story of the World's First National Athletics Championships* (Birmingham: England Athletics, 2016), pp. 25–6.
52 MSS.328/C/10/2/2, Rules of Amateur Bicycle Club, c. 1872.
53 MSS.328/C/6/3/1, Rules of Edinburgh Amateur Bicycle Club, 1882.
54 Catherine Budd, 'The Growth of an Urban Sporting Culture – Middlesbrough, c.1870-1914' (Unpublished PhD: De Montfort University, 2012), pp. 81–3.
55 MSS.328 C/10/2/2, Amateur Bicycle Club, *Bicycling News*, 2 February 1877, p. 34.

56 *The Tricyclist*, 4 August 1882, p. 63.
57 Geraldine Biddle-Perry, 'Fashioning Suburban Aspiration: Awheel with the Catford Cycling Club, 1886-1900', *London Journal*, vol. 39, no. 3 (November 2014), p. 189.
58 MSS.328/N7/1/29, Clarion Club, *passim*.
59 Tony Mason, 'Veitch, Colin Campbell McKechnie (1881–1938)', *Oxford Dictionary of National Biography* (Oxford University Press, 2004). http://www.oxforddnb.com/view/article/64560 (accessed 9 May 2013).
60 Denis Pye, *Fellowship Is Life: The Story of the National Clarion Cycling Club* (Bolton: National Clarion Publishing, 2014), pp. 27–33.
61 Dick Geary, '"Beer and Skittles?" Workers and Culture in Early Twentieth-Century Germany', *Australian Journal of Politics and History*, vol. 46, no. 3 (2000), pp. 388–9.
62 Ross McKibbin, 'Why Was There No Marxism in Great Britain?' *English Historical Review*, vol. 99, no. 391 (April 1984), pp. 297–331.
63 Chris Waters, *British Socialists and the Politics of Popular Culture 1884-1914* (Stanford: Stanford University Press, 1990), pp. 1–9.
64 McKibbin, 'Why Was There No Marxism in Great Britain?', pp. 297–331.
65 Ibid., p. 309.
66 Diana Sheets, 'British Conservatism and the Primrose League: The Changing Character of Popular Politics, 1883-1901' (Unpublished PhD: Colombia University, 1986).
67 Rohan McWilliam, *Popular Politics in Nineteenth Century England* (London: Routledge, 1998), p. 94.
68 *Pall Mall Gazette*, 6 December 1899, p. 5.
69 McWilliam, *Popular Politics*, p. 94.
70 Zuelow, *A History of Modern Tourism*, p. 114.
71 Ibid., p. 76.
72 William Oakley, *Winged Wheel: The History of the First Hundred Years of the Cyclists' Touring Club* (Godalming: Cyclists' Touring Club, 1977), p. 5.
73 In January 1899, it was reported that membership of the French touring club was 70,892, while in 1910 the membership of the German Cycling Federation was 46,206. *Daily Mail*, 27 January 1899, p. 6; *Cycling*, 17 August 1910, p. 160.
74 *CTC Gazette*, June 1884, pp. 193–4.
75 *CTC Gazette*, March 1884, pp. 92–4.
76 During the same period the geographical spread was as follows: England and Wales 439 council members; Scotland, 90; Ireland, 76; and 'Foreign Countries', 43. *CTC Gazette*, January 1900, p. 7.
77 *CTC Gazette*, January 1897, p. 22.
78 *CTC Gazette*, February 1897, p. 68.
79 *CTC Gazette*, June 1897, p. 256.

80   Borsay, *A History of Leisure*, p. 57.
81   MSS.328/C/4/BIT, *Bicycle Touring Gazette Monthly Circular*, October 1880, p. 5.
82   For example, MSS.328/C/4/BIT, *Bicycle Touring Gazette Monthly Circular*, March 1880, p. 168.
83   *CTC Gazette*, March 1889, pp. 47–9.
84   MSS.328/C/4/BIT, *Bicycle Touring Gazette Monthly Circular*, January 1882, p. 40.
85   *CTC Gazette*, November 1889, p. 218.
86   Lowerson, *Sport and the English Middle Classes*, p. 157.
87   *CTC Gazette*, April 1930, p. 118. Although by that time the amateur regulation had become more of an oddity. It is possible that hostility had abated in the early twentieth century when the CTC's membership rapidly declined.
88   *Bicycle Touring Gazette Monthly Circular*, July 1880, pp. 250–1, p. 589. The membership of the League of American Wheelmen had topped 100,000 during the boom of the mid-1890s, but by 1899, it had dipped to 51,756. *CTC Gazette*, November 1899, p. 589. In 1902, in a sign of the times, the LAW agreed to accept motor cyclists as members. *CTC Gazette*, September 1902, p. 424.
89   *CTC Gazette*, September 1897, pp. 373–5. Those in attendance were: the CTC; Touring Club de France; Touring Club de Belgique; Touring Club de Luxembourg; Touring Club de Suisse; Austrian Touring Club; Ligue Vélocipédique Belge; Union Vélocipédique Russe; Netherlands Cyclists' Union; and the German Cyclists' Touring Club.
90   In 1899 the bodies present were: Oesterreichischer Touring Club; Touring Club de Belgique; Ligue Vélocipédique Belge; Dansk Cycle Ring; Touring Club de France; Union Vélocipédique de France; Deutscher Radfahrer Bund; Algemeene Nederlandsche Wielrijders Bond; Touring Club Ciclistico Italiano; Touring Club Luxembourgeois; Touring Club de Russie; Svenska Turistfureningen; League of American Wheelmen. *CTC Gazette*, July 1899, pp. 362–6.
91   David Edgerton, *The Rise and Fall of the British Nation: A Twentieth-Century History* (London: Penguin, 2019), p. 9.
92   *CTC Gazette*, September 1897, p. 375.
93   MSS.328/C/6/3/1, Edinburgh Amateur Bicycle Club, Minute Books, 18 April 1874, 10 October 1874.
94   Mike Huggins, 'More Sinful Pleasures? Leisure, Respectability and the Male Middle Classes in Victorian England', *Journal of Social History*, vol. 33, no. 3 (Spring 2000), p. 587.
95   MSS.328/C/6/3/1, Edinburgh Amateur Bicycle Club, Minute Books 18 January 1884. The EABC later became the main force in the formation of the Scottish Cyclists' Union. Ibid., 1 February 1884.
96   Mike Huggins, 'Second-Class Citizens? English Middle-Class Culture and Sport: A Reconsideration', *International Journal of the History of Sport*, vol. 17, no. 1 (2000), p. 21.

97 *Daily Mail*, 23 March 1900, p. 6.
98 MSS.328/C/6/3/1, Edinburgh Amateur Bicycle Club, Minute Books, 26 November 1874.
99 MSS.328/C/6/3/1, Edinburgh Amateur Bicycle Club, Minute Books, Wednesday 26 May 1875, Special Meeting.
100 MSS.328/C/6/3/1, 'Result of Captain Colquhoun Prize', Edinburgh Amateur Bicycle Club, Minute Books, Special Meeting, 18 October 1877.
101 MSS.328/C/6/3/1, Rules of the Edinburgh Amateur Bicycle Club, 1882.
102 *Daily Mail*, 28 April 1900, p. 6.
103 Zweiniger-Bargielowska, *Managing the Body*, p. 107.
104 See Catriona Parratt, 'Little Means or Time: Working Class Women and Leisure in Late Victorian and Edwardian England', *International Journal of the History of Sport*, vol. 15, no. 2 (1998), pp. 22–53.
105 Alan Metcalfe, *Leisure and Recreation in a Victorian Mining Community: The Social Economy of Leisure in North-East England, 1820-1914* (London: Routledge, 2006), p. 164.
106 MSS.328/N7/1/143, Tandems. It had been designed by H. P. Butler from Cambridge, MA.
107 *CTC Gazette*, October 1880, p. 3.
108 Leonore Davidoff and Catherine Hall, *Family Fortunes: Men and Women of the English Middle Class, 1780-1850* (London: Routledge, 1987), p. 331.
109 *CTC Gazette*, June 1884, pp. 193–4.
110 *CTC Gazette*, 1904, *passim*.
111 See Zweiniger-Bargielowska, *Managing the Body*, chapter 3.
112 Sarah Hallenbeck, 'Riding Out of Bounds: Women Bicyclists' Embodied Medical Authority', *Rhetoric Review*, vol. 29, no. 4 (2010), pp. 327–45.
113 Carter, *Medicine, Sport and the Body*, pp. 152–5.
114 One exception is Ritchie, *King of the Road*, pp. 101–19.
115 Glen Norcliffe, 'The Technical and Social Significance of the Tricycle', in *International Cycling History Conferences Proceedings*, No. 17 (Toronto/Canada, 2006), p. 60.
116 Ibid.
117 *The Tricyclist*, 30 June 1882, p. 7.
118 James Starley died in 1881 and it was his nephew John Kemp Starley who would be credited with inventing and mass-producing the Rover Safety.
119 Ritchie, *King of the Road*, pp. 101–19.
120 *The Tricyclist*, 30 June 1882, pp. 2–3.
121 John Tosh, *A Man's Place: Masculinity and the Middle-Class Home in Victorian England* (London: Yale University Press, 1999), p. 59.
122 Ibid., p. 46.
123 *The Tricyclist*, 21 July 1882, p. 35.

124 *The Tricyclist*, 30 June 1882, pp. 2–3.
125 *The Tricyclist*, 28 December 1883, p. 357; Hilary Marland, '"Bicycle-Face" and "Lawn Tennis" Girls', *Media History*, vol. 25, no. 1 (2019), p. 71.
126 *The Tricyclist*, 7 July 1882, p. 12; 10 August 1883, p. 85.
127 *The Tricyclist*, 28 July 1882, p. 47.
128 *The Tricyclist*, 11 August 1882, p. 74.
129 *The Tricyclist*, 29 February 1884, p. 466.
130 *CTC Gazette*, March 1884, p. 82.
131 *The Tricyclist*, 14 December 1883, p. 331.
132 Ibid.
133 Ibid., pp. 323–4.
134 Ibid.
135 Ibid.
136 Holt, 'The Amateur Body', p. 363.
137 Biddle-Perry, 'Fashioning Suburban Aspiration', pp. 187–9.
138 Bellégo, 'Bicycles and Bodies', p. 9.
139 MSS.328/C/6/3/1, Edinburgh Amateur Bicycle Club, Minute Books, Wednesday 19 August 1874.
140 Robert Goodall, 'Cycling Clubs of North Yorkshire and South Durham, 1876-1914', *Bulletin of the Cleveland and Teesside Local History Society*, No. 57 (Autumn 1989), p. 20.
141 *Bicycle Touring Gazette Monthly Circular*, January 1880, pp. 127–8; August 1880, p. 15.
142 *CTC Monthly Gazette*, May 1885, p. 128.
143 James T. Lightwood, *The Cyclists' Touring Club Being The Romance of Fifty Years' Cycling* (London: The Cyclists' Touring Club, 1928), pp. 213–16.
144 Millward, 'UK Cycle Industry', p. 357. Selfridges, admittedly, did not open until 1909.
145 H. G. Wells, *The Wheels of Chance* (1896), chapter 4.
146 Geraldine Biddle-Perry, 'The Rise of "The World's Largest Sport and Athletic Outfitter": A Study of Gamage's of Holborn, 1878-1913', *Sport in History*, vol. 34, no. 2 (June 2014), p. 303.
147 *The Tricyclist*, 21 December 1883, p. 339.
148 MSS.328/N7/1/41, Derek Roberts, 'How Cyclists Used to Dress', *The Boneshaker*, August 1967, pp. 133–5.
149 *The Tricyclist*, 29 September 1882, p. 161.
150 *The Tricyclist*, 6 October 1882, p. 176.
151 For more on the relationship between cycling and female suffragettes, see http://www.sheilahanlon.com
152 *The Tricyclist*, 21 December 1883, p. 339; *CTC Gazette*, February 1884, p. 23.

153 Zweiniger-Bargielowska, *Managing the Body*, p. 107.
154 Jihang Park, 'Sport, Dress Reform and the Emancipation of Women in Victorian England: A Reappraisal', *The International Journal of the History of Sport*, vol. 6, no. 1 (May 1989), pp. 14–16.
155 Ibid., pp. 18–25.
156 For more on female cycling in this period, see http://www.sheilahanlon.com
157 *CTC Gazette*, March 1897, p. 116.
158 Zuelow, *A History of Modern Tourism*, p. 89.
159 Robert Colls, *Identity of England* (Oxford: Oxford University Press, 2002), p. 225.
160 Ibid., pp. 225–30.
161 Ibid., p. 230.
162 Ibid.
163 *CTC Gazette*, June 1903, p. 318.
164 Zuelow, *A History of Modern Tourism*, chapter 2.
165 *CTC Gazette*, November 1900, vol. 19, no. 11, p. 558.
166 Alun Howkins, 'The Discovery of Rural England', in R. Colls and P. Dodd (eds), *Englishness: Politics and Culture 1880-1920* (Breckenham: Kent, 1986), p. 62.
167 Holt, 'The Bicycle, the Bourgeoisie', pp. 135–7.
168 Ibid., p. 138.
169 *CTC Gazette*, December 1881, p. 15.
170 Sara Dominici, '"Cyclo-Photographers", Visual Modernity, and the Development of Camera Technologies, 1880s–1890s', *History of Photography*, vol. 42, no. 1 (2018), pp. 46–60.

Chapter 2

1 In 1891 the tyres were made detachable from the wheel.
2 Ritchie, *Quest for Speed*, pp. 225–36; http://thepedalclub.org/archives/william-hume/ (accessed 3 April 2019); *Athletic News*, 22 July 1889, p. 3. Between 1890 and 1892, the NCU ran both ordinary and safety championships.
3 Ritchie, *Quest for Speed*, p. 225.
4 Lloyd-Jones and Lewis, *Raleigh and the British Bicycle Industry*, chapter 2.
5 'Cyclomania', *Chambers's Journal of Popular Literature, Science and Arts*, 18 July 1896, vol. 13, no. 655, p. 458.
6 http://doc.ukdataservice.ac.uk/doc/7154/mrdoc/pdf/guide.pdf (accessed 3 April 2019).
7 All were subject to regional variations. Mason, *Association Football*, pp. 102–3.

8   Huggins, *Victorians and Sport*, pp. 14–17.
9   *CTC Gazette*, May 1885, p. 128.
10   Robert Goodall, 'Cycling in North Yorkshire and South Durham 1869-1914' (unpublished MA Dissertation: University of Teesside, 1989), p. 5.
11   Budd, 'The Growth of an Urban Sporting Culture', p. 83.
12   *Daily Mail*, 12 September 1899, p. 6.
13   Metcalfe, *Leisure and Recreation*, pp. 120–9.
14   *Shields Daily News*, 17 August 1898, p. 3.
15   MSS.328/N7/1/25, A.W. Neal, 'The Penny Four Farthing Cycle of Horsham', n.d.; Author Unknown, 'Post Office Cycles', n.d.
16   *Daily Mail*, 16 April, p. 6; 1 April 1899, p. 6. They were offered the sum of 2d per mile towards the cost and depreciation of the bike, although the concession was limited to 24 miles per day. Beyond this distance the postman had to use his bike at his own expense. Ibid.
17   *Daily Mail*, 25 August 1899, p. 6.
18   'The Cycling Epidemic', *Scottish Review*, January 1897, p. 56.
19   'Co-Operative Camps for Cyclists', *The Review of Reviews*, May 1894, p. 516.
20   *CTC Gazette*, November 1884, p. 341.
21   *Daily Mail*, 9 August 1898, p. 6.
22   *Daily Mail*, 11 November 1898, p. 6.
23   Goodall, 'Cycling in North Yorkshire and South Durham 1869-1914', p. 12.
24   *CTC Gazette*, August 1904, pp. 306–7.
25   MSS.328/N7/1/65, *passim*.
26   *CTC Gazette*, September 1884, p. 288.
27   Harold Shepstone, 'Decorated Bicycles', *Windsor Magazine*, August 1899, p. 243.
28   *Daily Mail*, 19 September 1899, p. 6.
29   *Daily Mail*, 16 June 1899, p. 6.
30   Lowerson, *Sport and the English Middle Classes*, p. 253.
31   Bury and Hillier, *Cycling*, pp. 314–16.
32   *Cycling*, 16 March 1934, p. 270.
33   David Rubenstein, 'Cycling Eighty Years Ago: A Change in Social Habits when the New Bicycle Replaced the Old Penny-Farthing', *History Today*, August 1978, p. 545.
34   Andrew Horrall, *Popular Culture in London c.1890-1918* (Manchester: Manchester University Press, 2001), pp. 54–64.
35   *The Times*, 2 September 1879, p. 4.
36   MSS.328/N7/1/3, *passim*.
37   *Daily Mail*, 3 January 1899, p. 6.
38   *Illustrated Sporting and Dramatic News*, 12 August 1899, p. 20; *Daily Mail*, 25 August 1899, p. 6; *Cycling*, 16 September 1899, p. 194.

39 HG Wells, 'A Tour of Chance', *CTC Gazette*, October 1904, pp. 367–8.
40 Dominic Sandbrook, *The Great British Dream Factory: The Strange History of Our National Imagination* (London: Penguin, 2015), p. 394.
41 *Daily Mail*, 16 April 1899, p. 6.
42 *Daily Mail*, 12 January 1900, p. 6.
43 *Daily Mail*, 14 November 1914, p. 3.
44 Ritchie, *Quest for Speed*, pp. 71–4.
45 For an overview of the historical relationship between sport and entrepreneurs, see Dilwyn Porter, 'Entrepreneurship', in John Nauright and Steve Pope (eds), *Routledge Companion to Sports History* (London: Routledge, 2012), pp. 197–215.
46 Tony Collins, *Sport in Capitalist Society: A Short History* (London: Routledge, 2013), pp. 48-59.
47 *Sporting Life*, 30 March 1878, p. 4.
48 Samantha-Jayne Oldfield, 'Running Pedestrianism in Victorian Manchester', *Sport in History*, vol. 34, no. 2 (2014), pp. 223–48.
49 Ritchie, *Quest for Speed*, p. 69.
50 MSS.328/N7/1/147, H. W. Bartleet, 'The Crystal Palace and Cycling', n.d..
51 Crump, 'Amusements of the People', p. 352.
52 Ibid., pp. 347–64.
53 Radford, *1866 and All That*, pp. 25–6.
54 Bury and Hillier, *Cycling*, p. 260; Robert Sinker, 'Ion Grant Neville Keith-Falconer (1856–1887)', rev. John Gurney, *Dictionary of National Biography* (Oxford: Oxford University Press, 2004), http://www.oxforddnb.com/view/article/15279 (accessed 9 May 2013).
55 Ritchie, *Quest for Speed*, pp. 80–3.
56 *The Times*, 18 February 1878, p. 10. It changed to the National Cyclists' Union in 1883 to allow all types of cyclists and cycling machines, for example tricycles, to join and for racing to come under its umbrella.
57 *The Sportsman*, 15 February 1878, p. 4; *The Times*, 18 February 1878, p. 10. They included the clubs from Oxford and Cambridge universities, Pickwick, London, Surrey, Temple, West Kent, Wanderers, Civil Service and Stanley.
58 *Athletic News*, 15 May 1878, p. 6.
59 Huggins, *Victorians and Sport*, pp. 36–8.
60 Bury and Hillier, *Cycling*, pp. 86–7.
61 *The Times*, 14 October 1879, p. 6.
62 Ritchie, *Quest for Speed*, p. 264.
63 Between 1885 and 1887, Hillier was the nominal editor of *Bicycling News* and the actual editor was Viscount Rothermere, later the owner of the *Daily Mail*. MSS.328/N7/1/66, George Lacey Hillier.
64 See Chris Bolsmann and Dilwyn Porter, *English Gentlemen and World Soccer: Corinthians, Amateurism and the Global Game* (London: Routledge, 2018).

65 MSS.328/N7/1/66, Walter Groves, 'The Late George Lacey Hillier', unpublished article.
66 Ibid.
67 *The Tricyclist*, 21 March 1884, p. 506.
68 *Guardian*, 10 May 1910, p. 13; 27 February 1911, p. 3; *Observer*, 10 March 1912, p. 14; *Guardian*, 27 March 1912, p. 5.
69 Collins, *Sport in Capitalist Society*, p. 34.
70 Ritchie, *Quest for Speed*, p. 327.
71 *Cycling and Moting*, 24 November 1900, p. 406.
72 Simon Inglis, *Played in London: Charting the Heritage of a City at Play* (London: English Heritage, 2014), p. 316. In France at least 110 velodromes were built between 1885 and 1900.
73 It was initially home to the Polytechnic CC and a venue for national championships, but was eventually removed in 1987. A cricket pitch now occupies the site of the cycling track. Inglis, *Played in London*, p. 34, 316.
74 Inglis, *Played in London*, pp. 314–21.
75 MSS.328/N7/1/147 Tracks, 'HW Bartleet, The Crystal Palace and Cycling', n.d.
76 *Cycling*, 27 July 1895, p. 25.
77 *Cycling*, 23 February 1895, p. 96. The track was built by McQuone from Scarborough. *Cycling*, 9 March 1895, p. 119. The Catford track was not owned by the club, but by London Sports Co. Ltd. *Cycling*, 6 August 1898, p. 83.
78 *Cycling*, 1 June 1895, p. 319.
79 *Cycling*, 16 May 1896, p. 299.
80 *Cycling*, 4 July, p. 437; 8 August 1896, p. 71.
81 *Cycling*, 7 August 1897, p. 77.
82 *Cycling*, 6 August 1898, p. 83.
83 Metcalfe, *Leisure and Recreation*, pp. 122–3.
84 *Daily Gazette* (Middlesbrough), 6 August 1875, p. 3.
85 Keith Gregson and Mike Huggins, 'Ashbrooke Whit Sports, Sunderland and Its Records: A Case Study of Amateurism in Late Victorian and Edwardian Athletic and Cycling Competition', *International Journal of the History of Sport*, vol. 31, no. 9 (2014), p. 997.
86 *Daily Mail*, 14 June 1897, p. 6.
87 *Daily Mail*, 17 February 1914, p. 5.
88 *Northern Echo* 21 June 1880.
89 *North-Eastern Daily Gazette* (Middlesbrough), 28 June 1886.
90 *York Herald*, 5, September 1887; *Northern Echo*, 19 September 1892.
91 *Northern Echo*, 16 August 1897.
92 *North-Eastern Daily Gazette* (Middlesbrough), 12 May 1898.

93 *Northern Echo*, 16 August 1897.

94 In 1901 it was recorded that the annual cycling races were run in wet weather after being postponed from the previous week. The attendance was poor due to the weather and the annual Lingdale Silver Cup had only two riders after the holder pulled out. *Sheffield Daily Telegraph*, 19 August 1901, p. 9.

95 Clare S. Simpson, 'Capitalising on Curiosity: Women's Professional Cycle Racing in the Late-Nineteenth Century', in Dave Horton, Paul Rosen and Peter Cox (eds), *Cycling and Society* (Farnham: Ashgate, 2007), p. 48.

96 Ibid., pp. 47–66.

97 https://www.sheilahanlon.com/?p=292 (accessed 16 January 2018) It was not until 1947 that Cambridge degrees were granted on equal terms for men and women.

98 David Day, 'Kinship and Community in Victorian London: The "Beckwith Frogs"', *History Workshop Journal* (Advanced Access, 25 February 2011), pp. 1–24.

99 M. Ann Hall, *Muscle on Wheels: Louise Armaindao and the High-Wheel Racers of Nineteenth-Century America* (Montreal: McGill-Queen's University Press, 2018). I am grateful to Heather Dichter for this reference.

100 Ritchie, *King of the Road*, p. 148.

101 Goodall, 'Cycling Clubs', p. 26.

102 Metcalfe, *Leisure and Recreation*, p. 123.

103 *Daily Mail*, 7 May 1896, p. 6.

104 http://www.sheilahanlon.com/?p=1556; http://www.sheilahanlon.com/?p=1889 (accessed 19 April 2018);

Simpson, 'Capitalising on Curiosity', pp 47–66.

105 *Daily Mail*, 14 June 1897, p. 6.

106 Goodall, 'Cycling Clubs', p. 26.

107 Elizabeth Robins Pennell, 'Cycling', in Beatrice Violet Greville (ed.), *Ladies in the Field: Sketches of Sport* (New York: D. Appleton and Co., 1894), pp. 245–66.

108 Theo Barker and Dorian Gerhold, *The Rise and Rise of Road Transport, 1700-1990* (Cambridge: Cambridge University Press, 1993), p. 51.

109 *Cycling*, 4 July 1896, p. 448.

110 *The Sketch*, 15 August 1906, p. 157; [Bill 214.] Committee. HC Deb 09 July 1878, vol. 241 Cc1078-83.

111 [Bill 214.] Committee. HC Deb 09 July 1878, vol. 241 Cc1078-83.

112 *Cycling*, 16 July 1953, p. 62.

113 A. F. Pollard, 'Keppel, William Coutts, Seventh Earl of Albemarle and Viscount Bury (1832-1894)', rev. H. C. G. Matthew, *Oxford Dictionary of National Biography* (Oxford: Oxford University Press, 2004), http://www.oxforddnb.com/view/article/15444 (accessed 31 May 2015).

114 *The Times*, 22 August 1888, p. 3.

115 Indeed, so close were the aims of both that there were periodic calls that they should merge into one governing body. For example, *Daily Mail*, 16 June 1899, p. 6.
116 Cox, "'A Denial of Our Boasted Civilisation'", p. 11.
117 The NCU's object was first to secure a fair and equitable administration of justice as regards the rights of bicyclists on the public roads; second, to watch the course of any legislative proposals in Parliament or elsewhere affecting the interests of the bicycling public, and to make such representations on the subject as the occasion may demand. *The Times*, 18 February 1878, p. 10.
118 MSS.328/C/4/BIT, *Bicycle Touring Gazette Monthly Circular*, August 1880, p. 15.
119 *Daily Mail*, 22 February 1913, p. 3.
120 *Daily Mail*, 28 April 1900, p. 6.
121 *Daily Mail*, 27 May 1899, p. 3.
122 *Daily Mail*, 20 September, p. 4; 9 October 1900, p. 3.
123 For example, *Daily Mail*, 17 November 1897, p. 6; 11 November 1898, p. 6; 29 November 1898, p. 6.
124 *Daily Mail*, 24 September 1907, p. 5.
125 *Daily Mail*, 3 November 1899, p. 6. There were four main points. First, better accommodation for cycles during transit by rail; second, the provision of better cloak-room accommodation for cycles; third, the rates railway companies charged for the conveyance of bicycles; and fourth, liability for any damage to bicycles. Ibid.
126 *Daily Mail*, 15 April 1897, p. 6.
127 *Daily Mail*, 22 February 1901, p. 6.
128 *CTC Gazette*, September 1889, p. 163.
129 *CTC Gazette*, August 1889, pp. 137–8.
130 *CTC Gazette*, October 1889, p. 184.
131 MSS.328/C/1/1, CTC, Minutes of Council Meeting, 8 December 1883. Permission to erect the boards was initially required from the local surveyor of highways, but was rarely refused. *CTC Gazette*, July 1884, p. 224.
132 *CTC Gazette*, December 1884, p. 362.
133 *Punch*, 16 October 1897, p. 180.
134 *CTC Gazette*, 1 December 1897, pp. 534–5.
135 Sean O'Connell, *The Car in British Society: Class, Gender and Motoring 1896-1939* (Manchester: Manchester University Press, 1998), p. 1.
136 William Plowden, *The Motor Car and Politics in Britain* (London: Penguin, 1971), Appendix C, p. 482.
137 *Daily Mail*, 21 August 1908, p. 5; *CTC Gazette*, September 1884, p. 287.
138 *Daily Mail*, 28 October 1905, p. 5.
139 *Daily News*, 4 August 1906, p. 11.

140 Cyclists were fined 10s if pleading guilty, 15s if they did not; motorists' fines were £2 and £5, respectively.
141 *Daily Mail*, 21, p. 3; 25 October 1901, p. 3.
142 *Daily Mail*, 28 January 1901, p. 6.
143 Mick Hamer, *Wheels Within Wheels: A Study of the Road Lobby* (London: Routledge & Kegan Paul, 1987), pp. 23–36; P. W. J. Bartrip, 'Jeffreys, William Rees (1871–1954)', in *Oxford Dictionary of National Biography* (Oxford: Oxford University Press, May 2013),
http://www.oxforddnb.com/view/article/98052 (accessed 21 July 2013).
144 *Daily Mail*, 8 February 1907, p. 5.
145 *Daily Mail*, 18 July 1911, p. 8.
146 Moxham, *Fifty Years of Road Riding*, p. 18; *Athletic News*, 21 February 1888, p. 4.
147 *The Tricyclist*, September 1883.
148 Ritchie, *Quest for Speed*, pp. 253–67.
149 Elizabeth Robin Pennell, 'Cycling: Past, Present, and Future', *The New Review*, vol. 4, no. 21 (February 1891), p. 177.
150 *CTC Gazette*, May 1889, p. 77.
151 Ibid.
152 Metcalfe, *Leisure and Recreation*, p. 122.
153 *Athletic News*, 21 February 1888, p. 4.
154 Moxham, *Fifty Years of Road Riding*, p. 53; *South Wales Echo*, 1 November 1897, p. 4; *Daily Mail*, 1 November 1897, p. 4. The deleting of time trial from the original proposal to 'paced record attempts' had been suggested by a Mr Owens. *Daily Mail*, 27 October 1897, p. 6.
155 Ritchie, *Quest for Speed*, pp. 295–303; Dauncey, *French Cycling*, pp. 65–71.
156 *Cycling and Moting*, 25 November 1899, p. 429.
157 Lloyd-Jones and Lewis, *Raleigh and the British Bicycle Industry*, pp. 24–31.
158 A. E. Harrison, 'Joint-Stock Company Flotation in the Cycle, Motor-Vehicle and Related Industries, 1882-1914', *Business History*, vol. 23, no. 2 (1981), p. 169.
159 Lloyd-Jones and Lewis, *Raleigh and the British Bicycle Industry*, pp. 32–3.
160 Jonathan Wood, *The British Motor Industry* (Oxford: Shire, 2012), p. 8.
161 Although the Stanley Show would go on. *Daily Mail*, 21 March 1904, p. 2.
162 *Cycling*, 14 October, p. 274; 21 October 1899, p. 287; *Cycling and Moting*, 20 January 1900, p. 31. For more details see, NA/BT 34/1025/42907, North London Cycling and Athletic Grounds Company Ltd, Liquidation 1900. *Daily Mail*, 1 December 1899, p. 6.
163 Charles Korr, *West Ham United: The Making of a Football Club* (London: Duckworth, 1986), pp. 1–13.
164 *Athletic News*, 8 September 1913, p. 7.

165   *Cycling and Moting*, 24 March 1900, p. 215.
166   Ibid.
167   *Daily Mail*, 18 July 1911, p. 8. This was an estimate as the NCU did not release total membership figures, only figures for clubs. Club membership naturally differed from club to club.
168   Tony Rennick, 'Bailey, William James (1888–1971)', in *Oxford Dictionary of National Biography* (Oxford: Oxford University Press, 2004), January 2011, http://www.oxforddnb.com/view/article/65058 (accessed 9 May 2013).
169   *Daily Mail*, 3 July 1909, p. 7. To enable the riders to race through the night 24 Empire oil lamps were used plus 115 electric arc lamps. In addition, there were searchlights and a flashing electronic scoreboard. Ibid., 2 July 1909, p. 7.
170   *Northern Whig*, 15 July 1910, p. 3.
171   Nicholas Oddy, 'The Flaneur on Wheels?' in Dave Horton, Paul Rosen and Peter Cox (eds), *Cycling in Society* (Aldershot: Ashgate, 2007), p. 111.
172   Wood, *The British Motor Industry*, p. 8.
173   Oddy, 'The Flaneur on Wheels?', pp. 106–7.

Chapter 3

1   Robert Colls, *George Orwell: English Rebel* (Oxford: Oxford University Press, 2013), p. 148.
2   In other versions it is claimed that the old maids were hiking.
3   http://www.johnmajor.co.uk/page1086.html (accessed 25 April 2018).
4   *Cycling*, 22 September 1933, p. 277. He never fully recovered from being knocked off his bicycle a few weeks earlier.
5   For example, *CTC Gazette*, October 1933, p. 327.
6   *Cycling*, 29 June 1934, pp. 640–1.
7   TNA/CAB 24/254/0/0014, Cabinet Papers, Mr. Lloyd George's Memorandum On Unemployment, Plans Submitted By The Right Hon. D. Lloyd George O.M., M.P., For Utilising The Depression To Reorganise and Develop our National Resources and to Improve National Conditions, 1935, p. 26.
8   Quoted in Juliet Gardiner, *The Thirties: An Intimate History* (London: Harper Press, 2010), p. 239.
9   David Matless, *Landscape and Englishness* (London: Reaktion Books, 1998), p. 63.
10   Ibid., p. 67.
11   Ross McKibbin, *Classes and Cultures: England 1918-1951* (Oxford: Oxford University Press, 1998), pp. 46, 49, 67–9.
12   Laura Dawkins, 'Bidlake, Frederick Thomas (1867–1933)', in *Oxford Dictionary of National Biography* (Oxford: Oxford University Press, May

2012), http://www.oxforddnb.com/view/article/103434 (accessed 9 May 2013).

13 Matthew Taylor, *The Leaguers: The Making of Professional Football in England, 1900-1939* (Liverpool: Liverpool University Press, 2005), p. 59.
14 MSS.328/N7/1/123, W. M. Robinson, *passim*.
15 *CTC Gazette*, February 1924, p. 34.
16 http://www.anfieldbc.co.uk/circulars/c_1936_oc.pdf, April 1936 (accessed 7 May 2018).
17 http://www.centuryroadclub.org.uk/history.html (accessed 16 May 2018).
18 *The Times*, 31 October 1962, p. 15; http://thepedalclub.org/archives/george-stancer/ (accessed 15 April 2016).
19 *Cycling*, 28 September 1934, p. 341.
20 *Cycling*, 14 July 1921, cover page.
21 Tim Hilton, *One More Kilometre and We're in the Showers: Memoirs of a Cyclist* (London: HarperCollins, 2004), pp. 81–6.
22 *Cycling*, 9 November 1934, p. 506.
23 Anthony Bateman, '"Guilty, M'Lud, to Fiction": Neville Cardus and the Moment of Scrutiny', *Sport in History*, vol. 29, no. 2 (2009), p. 262, 260.
24 Lightwood, *The Cyclists' Touring Club*, pp. 182–4.
25 Tom Bray, 'The Pleasure Factory and Delights of the Game: The Intersections of Health, Leisure and Environment in Interwar England' (Unpublished MA Dissertation: University of Warwick, 2013), p. 3.
26 MSS.328/N7/1/156, Wayfarer, *Anfield Circular: The Journal of the Anfield Bicycle Club*, May 1974, Bill Finn, 'Wayfarer', p. 5.
27 Cited in Bateman, '"Guilty, M'Lud, to Fiction"', p. 262.
28 MSS.328/N7/1/156, Wayfarer, *Anfield Circular: The Journal of the Anfield Bicycle Club*, May 1974, Bill Finn, 'Wayfarer', pp. 3–5.
29 *Cycling*, 20 November 1919, pp. 380–2.
30 *Cycling*, 18 April 1924, p. 322.
31 *Cycling*, 16 March 1922, p. 192.
32 *Cycling*, 29 April 1920, pp. 318–19.
33 *Cycling*, 18 January 1924, p. 49.
34 MSS.328/N7/1/156 Wayfarer, *Anfield Circular: The Journal of the Anfield Bicycle Club*, May 1974, Bill Finn, 'Wayfarer', p. 4.
35 Lucy Newlyn, 'Dorothy Wordsworth', paper presented at DMU History seminar, 28 January 2015.
36 *CTC Gazette*, 23 December 1920, p. 540.
37 *Cycling*, 6 July 1922, p. 14.
38 See Dilwyn Porter, 'Revenge of the Crouch End Vampires', *Sport in History*, vol. 26, no. 3 (2006), pp. 406–28.
39 The Bartleet Collection can still be viewed today at the Coventry Transport Museum.

40 MSS 328 N93/1, Diaries of David Allan Hamilton 1905-2001, 12 August 1923; https://mrc-catalogue.warwick.ac.uk/records/NCA/1/24; See also, https://warwickmrc.wordpress.com/2014/02/06/cycling-rambles/.
41 *Cycling*, 19 October 1919, p. 296, 299.
42 *Cycling*, 22 April 1920, p. 295.
43 Tony Collins, *A Social History of English Rugby Union* (London: Routledge, 2009), p. 65.
44 *Cycling*, 8 April 1920, p. 259.
45 *Cycling*, 20 November 1920, p. 409.
46 Richard Weight and Abigail Beach, 'Introduction', in Richard Weight and Abigail Beach (eds), *The Right to Belong: Citizenship and National Identity in Britain, 1930-1960* (London: IB Tauris, 1998), p. 3.
47 *Cycling*, 18 December 1919, p. 489.
48 MSS.328/NL/CTC/DA/MA/1, *The Northern Wheel*, 1935–38, February 1937 Vol. 2, no. 8, Memories of a Meriden 'All-Nighter', pp. 11–15.
49 *Cycling*, 14 April 1921, p. 283.
50 Bray, 'The Pleasure Factory'.
51 Matthew Taylor, 'Sport and Civilian Morale', *Journal of Contemporary History*, vol. 53, no. 2 (2016), pp. 315–38.
52 In 1942, in an abrupt change of career, Josey left Britain to take up a position as a journalist in Malaysia. In 1965 he was expelled for apparently attempting to disrupt racial harmony in Malaysia. *The Times*, 9 July, p. 10.
53 MSS.328/N10/A2, How the Cyclist is helping by Alex Josey, Home Service, Thursday 29 August 1940, 6.45–7pm.
54 MSS.328/N10/A2, The Bicycle in War by Alex Josey, Home Service, 8 September 1941.
55 Paul Donovan, 'Quigley, Janet Muriel Alexander (1902–1987)', in *Oxford Dictionary of National Biography* (Oxford: Oxford University Press, 2004). http://www.oxforddnb.com/view/article/65432 (accessed 20 Sept 2016).
56 O'Connell, *The Car in British Society*; Cox, '"A Denial of Our Boasted Civilisation"', pp. 4–30.
57 Out of this total, 38 miles were dual paths with 3 miles of single paths.
58 TNA/MT 39/127, Cycle Tracks, Proposed construction, 1926–43, Letter, Ministry of Transport to HR Watling, British Cycle and Motor Cycle Manufacturers, 20 January 1939.
59 TNA/MT 39/127, Cycle Tracks, Proposed construction, 1926–43, Report, Chief Engineer, North East Cycle Tracks, 21 February 1938.
60 Plowden, *The Motor Car*, Appendix C, p. 482.
61 Ibid., p. 269.
62 The working class were able to become car owners through various means. O'Connell, *The Car in British Society*, pp. 32–7.

63 Plowden, *The Motor Car*, p. 269.
64 Richard Trainor, 'Neither Metropolitan nor Provincial: The Inter-war Middle Class', in Alan Kidd and David Nicholls (eds), *The Making of the British Middle Class? Studies of Regional and Cultural Diversity since the Eighteenth Century* (Stroud: Sutton, 1998), p. 204, 212.
65 The Royal Automobile Club (RAC) did not keep membership records until the 1960s, but in 1938 it was estimated that it had 300,000 members. http://www.roadswerenotbuiltforcars.com/alnessreport/ (accessed 21 July 2013). The AA was formed in 1905. Its membership figures up to 1954 were: 1909, 10,000; 1914, 82,000 (50,000 motorists, 32,000 motor cyclists); 1920, 150,000; 1924, 200,000; 1926, 300,000; 1934, 500,000; 1938, 680,000; 1950, 1 million; 1954, 1.5 million. Plowden, *The Motor Car*, p. 353.
66 Cox, '"A Denial of Our Boasted Civilisation"', p. 25.
67 *Cycling*, 10 August 1934, p. 158.
68 TNA/CAB 24/254/0/0014, Cabinet Papers, Mr Lloyd George's Memorandum On Unemployment, Plans Submitted By The Right Hon. D. Lloyd George O.M., M.P., For Utilising The Depression To Reorganise and Develop our National Resources and to Improve National Conditions, 1935, p. 18.
69 Anne-Katrin Ebert, 'When Cycling Gets Political: Building Cycling Paths in Germany and the Netherlands, 1910-40', *Journal of Transport History*, vol. 33, no. 1 (June 2012), p. 117.
70 *Sunday Times* quoted in *CTC Gazette*, March 1901, p. 122.
71 *CTC Gazette*, February 1901, p. 86.
72 *CTC Gazette*, April 1922, p. 72.
73 *Cycling*, 10 April 1935, pp. 438–9.
74 *CTC Gazette*, January 1920, p. 2.
75 *CTC Gazette*, March 1920, pp. 37–8.
76 *Cycling*, 15 January 1920, p. 41.
77 *CTC Gazette*, June 1922, p. 124.
78 TNA/MT 39/127, Cycle Tracks, Proposed construction, 1926-43, Letter, Wright Miller to Minister of Transport, Cycle Tracks, 24 March 1927; Reply, Minister of Transport, 30 March 1927.
79 TNA/MT 39/127, Cycle Tracks, Proposed construction, 1926-43, Letter, CB Bird, Cycle Paths, 16 November 1932, Reply, 17 January 1933.
80 TNA/CAB 24/245/0/0033, Road Accidents, Memorandum by the Minister of Transport, November 1933, p. 21.
81 TNA/MT 39/127, Cycle Tracks, Proposed construction, 1926-43, Letter, Question to Minister, Cyclists and Footpaths, 30 November 1933.
82 Keith Robbins, 'Belisha, (Isaac) Leslie Hore-, Baron Hore-Belisha (1893–1957)', in *Oxford Dictionary of National Biography* (Oxford: Oxford University Press, 2004); online edn, January 2008, http://www.oxforddnb.com/view/article/33986 (accessed 4 April 2016).
83 Hamer, *Wheels Within Wheels*, p. 40.

84 http://www.roadswerenotbuiltforcars.com/alnessreport/ (accessed 6 May 2018).
85 *Cycling*, 21 December 1934, p. 683.
86 *Cycling*, 28 December 1934, p. 700.
87 TNA/CAB 24/254/0/0014, Cabinet Papers, Mr Lloyd George's Memorandum On Unemployment, Plans Submitted By The Right Hon. D. Lloyd George O.M., M.P., For Utilising The Depression To Reorganise and Develop our National Resources and to Improve National Conditions, 1935, p. 18.
88 Hamer, *Wheels Within Wheels*, chapters 3–4.
89 TNA/CAB 24/254/0/0014, Cabinet Papers, Mr Lloyd George's Memorandum On Unemployment, Plans Submitted By The Right Hon. D. Lloyd George O.M., M.P., For Utilising The Depression To Reorganise and Develop our National Resources and to Improve National Conditions, 1935, p. 18.
90 O'Connell, *The Car in British Society*, pp. 119–23.
91 Hamer, *Wheels Within Wheels*, p. 27.
92 O'Connell, *The Car in British Society*, pp. 134–5.
93 Cox, '"A Denial of Our Boasted Civilisation"', p. 4.
94 *Daily Mail*, 9 April 1936, p. 16.
95 O'Connell, *The Car in British Society*, p. 119.
96 Ibid., pp. 119–23.
97 *Cycling*, 14 December 1934, p. 639.
98 *Cycling*, 12 January 1934, p. 23.
99 *Cycling*, 10 August 1934, p. 158.
100 *Cycling*, 27 February 1934, p. 235.
101 *Cycling*, 6 March 1935, p. 269.
102 *Cycling*, 13 March 1935, p. 311.
103 *Cycling*, 15 April 1936, p. 499.
104 *Cycling*, 15 July 1936, p. 100. Each member received a badge bearing the letter 'C' for cyclist.
105 TNA/MT 34/131, Accidents, Order of the Road, Cyclists' Touring Club and National Cyclists' Union-Joint Committee Report.
106 The Order of the Road was established in 1928 as '[t]he first safe drivers' organisation in the world' with the aim to 'distinguish the Good Driver'. TNA/MT 34/131, Accidents, Order of the Road, Cyclists' Touring Club and National Cyclists' Union-Joint Committee Report.
107 TNA/MT 34/131, Accidents, Order of the Road, Cyclists' Touring Club and National Cyclists' Union-Joint Committee Report.
108 *Cycling*, 30 November 1934, p. 590.
109 *The Times*, 6 December 1921, p. xv.
110 *Cycling*, 12 January 1934, p. 23.
111 TNA/MT39/127, Cycle Tracks, Proposed construction, 1926-43, 'Holland, New Traffic Fund, Taxes', 1 January 1935.

112 Ebert, 'When Cycling Gets Political', pp. 115–37.
113 Ibid., pp. 120.
114 TNA/MT 39/127, Cycle Tracks, Proposed construction, 1926-43, Translated copy of *De Kampion* article, 25 January 1935.
115 http://www.roadswerenotbuiltforcars.com/alnessreport/ (accessed 21 July 2013).

Chapter 4

1 David Kynaston, *Austerity Britain 1948-51: Smoke in the Valley* (London: Bloomsbury, 2007), p. 114.
2 Richard Hoggart, *The Uses of Literacy: Aspects of Working-Class Life with Special Reference to Publications and Entertainments* (London: Penguin, 1957), pp. 329–30.
3 McKibbin, *Classes and Cultures*, p. i.
4 Ibid., p. 160, 161.
5 Ibid., pp. 67–9.
6 https://www.youtube.com/watch?v=QPkT0paGEnQ (accessed 20 June 2017).
  https://www.youtube.com/watch?v=qyz5d3entBw (accessed 20 June 2017).
  The film was part of a documentary series that began in 1949.
7 https://www.youtube.com/watch?v=QPkT0paGEnQ (accessed 20 June 2017).
8 *Guardian*, 3 April 1923, p. 6.
9 Stephen Jones, *Workers at Play: A Social and Economic History of Leisure 1918-1939* (London: Routledge and Kegan Paul, 1986), chapter 1.
10 Millward, 'UK Cycle Industry', p. 331, p. 159, Table 2.1.
11 Rosen, *Framing Production*, chapter 3.
12 See for example, *Cycling*, 26 October 1923, p. 351, Cover, p. 354, Editorial, 'The Cult of the Lightweight'.
13 Millward, 'UK Cycle Industry', p. 331.
14 MSS.328/BU/1/8, National Cyclists' Union, Minutes of Council and Annual General Meetings, November 1919 – 16 March 1935, Meeting of the General Council, 19 November 1932; MSS.204/1/1/1, British Cycle and Motor Cycle Manufacturers and Traders Union Ltd, Bicycle Manufacturers' Section Minutes, 28 April 1933.
15 *Cycling*, 7 December 1934, p. 615.
16 There were also 66 associations affiliated to the NCU not registering members. *Cycling*, 23 December 1936, p. 900.
17 MSS.328/BU/2/8, National Cyclists' Union Racing Committee, 9 April 1927; TNA/MT 34/131, Accidents, Order of the Road, Cyclists' Touring Club and National Cyclists' Union-Joint Committee Report; NCU, National Cyclists' Union Committees-MSS.328 BU 2 8-Conference of Centre Officials 20

April 1929; TNA/ED 113/74, National Fitness Council-Minutes, Papers and Reports. Voluntary Organisations, The National Cyclists' Union.
18. MSS.328/C, Cyclists' Touring Club Historical Landmarks; *Daily Mail*, 11 August 1938, p. 3.
19. Anon., *Statistical Digest of the War* (London: HMSO, 1951), Table 168, p. 191
20. *Daily Mail*, 23 March 1940, p. 4.
21. *Daily Express*, 18 November 1948.
22. MSS.328N/45, Ernest Green Papers. The membership consisted of 43,009 – Affiliated; 9,755 – Private; 13,764 – Associates.
23. Inglis, *Played in London*, pp. 336–7. 'Cycle speedway: The "skid kids" who raced bicycles on WW2 bomb sites', http://www.bbc.co.uk/news/magazine-31013387 (accessed 20 April 2015).
24. An adult was defined as someone who had left school. Another 3 per cent used a bicycle belonging to someone else. Anon., *Board of Trade Journal*, 12 January 1946, p. 24.
25. Anon., *Board of Trade Journal*, 12 January 1946, p. 24.
26. Ibid.
27. Michael Law, '"The car indispensable": The Hidden Influence of the Car in Inter-war Suburban London', *Journal of Historical Geography*, vol. 38 (2012), p. 426.
28. Peter Bailey, 'Jazz at the Spirella: Coming of Age in Coventry in the 1950s', in Becky Conekin, Frank Mort and Chris Waters (eds), *Moments of Modernity: Reconstructing Britain 1945-1964* (New York: Rivers Oram, 1999), p. 23.
29. Bruce Epperson, 'A New Class of Cyclists: Banham's Bicycle and the Two-wheeled World it didn't Create', *Mobilities*, vol. 8, no. 2 (2013), p. 241.
30. Personal information, Tony Mason.
31. Kynaston, *Austerity Britain*, p. 114.
32. Anon., *Board of Trade Journal*, 12 January 1946, p. 24. For a more detailed social and economic breakdown of cyclists, see the Wartime Survey on Cycling in 1944:
http://www.moidigital.ac.uk/reports/wartime-social-survey/wartime-social-survey-rg-23-62/idm140133747457344/ (accessed 9 November 2019). I am grateful to Matt Taylor for this reference.
33. Kynaston, *Austerity Britain*, p. 114.
34. *Daily Express*, 18 November 1948.
35. Simon Gunn, 'People and the Car: The Expansion of Automobility in Urban Britain, c.1955-70', *Social History*, vol. 38, no. 2 (2013), p. 224.
36. MSS.328/N90/10, Tom Finn Diaries, 7 May 1945 (Monday).
37. Pearl Jephcott, *Some Young People* (London: George Allen, 1954), p. 58.
38. Ibid.
39. Ibid., pp. 43–4.

40 Joanna Bourke, *Dismembering the Male: Men's Bodies, Britain and the Great War* (London: Reaktion, 1996), p. 33.
41 Ibid., p. 31.
42 *CTC Gazette*, February 1918, p. 22; March, p. 57; April, p. 61.
43 Millward, 'UK Cycle Industry', p. 312. One article featured bicycles for one-legged former soldiers. *Cycling*, 23 September 1920, p. 257.
44 For example, *Cycling*, 18 March 1920, p. 198.
45 *Cycling*, 17 June 1920, p. 450.
46 *CTC Gazette*, September 1899, p. 494.
47 *Cycling*, 7 October 1920, p. 303.
48 Greaves beat the previous record held by the Australian, Ossie Nicholson, of 43,936. On one day in June he rode 262 miles.
49 *Yorkshire Post*, 6 January 1936, p. 10. The previous year he had ridden 328 miles in 24 hours.
50 *Western Daily Press*, 31 December 1936, p. 3; http://autobus.cyclingnews.com/features/?id=2006/woodland_greaves (accessed 18 March 2018).
51 *Leeds Mercury*, 4 July 1936, p. 11.
52 *Lincolnshire Echo*, 9 October 1936, p. 8. He had been living in Lincoln for a number of months during his record attempt.
53 *Sunderland Daily Echo and Shipping News*, 7 July 1936, p. 2.
54 *Yorkshire Post*, 26 September 1936, p. 8; *Western Daily Press*, 31 December 1936, p. 3. In 1938 it was reported that another Yorkshireman, Ken Ingle, who had lost the use of his left leg, had been inspired by Greaves and was to attempt to break the record himself. *Yorkshire Evening Post*, 25 May 1938, p. 12.
55 *Cycling*, 5 January 1938, pp. 2–3.
56 Fiona Skillen, 'Fleming [née Bartram; First Married Name Dovey], Lillian Irene [Billie]' (1914–2014), in *Oxford Dictionary of National Biography*, https://doi.org/10.1093/odnb/9780198614128.013.108832 [Published online: 15 February 2018]; *Cycling*, 5 January 1938, p. 7.
57 *Sports Argus* (Birmingham), 22 May 1937, p. 5.
58 *Daily Mirror*, 7 August 1945, p. 5.
59 MSS.328/RTTC/1/1/3, Minutes of General Purposes Committee, 16 July, 20 August 1940.
60 Hill, *Sport, Leisure and Culture*, p. 140.
61 *Sports Argus* (Birmingham), 22 May 1937, p. 5.
62 MSS.328.BU/1/9, NYSD Centre 1935 Handbook.
63 *Cycling*, 23 December 1936, p. 900.
64 Jones, *Workers at Play*, p. 67.
65 MSS.328/N55/4/1, *Awheel: Official Organ of the Solihull Cycling Club*, passim.

66 MSS.328/N57/3/1/5, Cycling Memories of Arthur Cook, chapter 2.
67 Oakley, *Winged Wheel*, p. 65.
68 *CTC Gazette*, March 1918, p. 57.
69 *CTC Gazette*, April 1918, p. 70.
70 Pye, *Fellowship Is Life*, p. 70.
71 For more on the BWSF, see Stephen Jones, *Sport, Politics and the Working Class: Organised Labour and Sport in Inter-war Britain* (Manchester: Manchester University Press, 1988), chapter 4.
72 *CTC Gazette*, October 1930, pp. 370–1.
73 *CTC Gazette*, November 1930, p. 401. It was also reported that the BWSF had recently organized a road race over a 2-mile course at Hampstead.
74 Jones, *Sport, Politics and the Working Class*, p. 75.
75 Pye, *Fellowship Is Life*, p. 64.
76 Jones, *Sport, Politics and the Working Class*, p. 109.
77 Ibid., p. 149.
78 The CPGB's membership was relatively low during the interwar years. In mid-1921 it had nearly 5,000 members; by the time of the General Strike in 1926, there were 10,430 members, but it declined soon after. In the 1930s numbers began to grow, however, from 6,500 in February 1935 to 18,000 in December 1938. Thomas Lineham, *Communism in Britain, 1920-39: From the Cradle to the Grave* (Manchester: Manchester University Press, 2007), p. 93, 105, 152.
79 Lineham, *Communism in Britain*, p. 4, 146.
80 Ibid., pp. 150–2.
81 http://www.classiclightweights.co.uk/clubs-reminiscences.html (accessed 19 February 2015).
82 *Cycling*, 23 November 1938, p. 772.
83 http://www.classiclightweights.co.uk/clubs-reminiscences.html (accessed 19 February 2015).
84 *Cycling*, 23 November 1938, p. 772.
85 http://www.classiclightweights.co.uk/clubs-reminiscences.html (accessed 19 February 2015).
86 David Dee, *Sport and British Jewry: Integration, Ethnicity and Anti-semitism 1890-1970* (Manchester: Manchester University Press, 2013), p. 125.
87 MSS.328/N17/3/1/22, *Cycling and Mopeds*, 19 February 1958, p. 202.
88 Dee, *Sport and British Jewry*, p. 125.
89 MSS.328/N55/4/2, *Awheel: Official Organ of the Solihull Cycling Club*, March 1950, no. 168, p. 5; MSS.328/N55/4/1/10, *Awheel: Official Organ of the Solihull Cycling Club*, January 1962, p. 4.
90 Hilton, *One More Kilometre*, p. 8.
91 Harold Briercliffe, David Renney and Paul Stanbridge, *The Nomads (Hitchin) Cycling Club: The First 50 Years* https://simdoyle.files.wordpress.com/2013/07/hncc_50_years.pdf (accessed 23 March 2016).

92 MSS.328/N57/3/1/5, Cycling Memories of Arthur Cook, chapter 2.
93 Briercliffe, Renney and Stanbridge, *The Nomads*.
94 *Cycling*, 18 January 1951, p. 74.
95 MSS.328/N7/1/30, History of Essex Roads Cycling Club, 1953.
96 MSS.328/N57/3/1/5, Cycling Memories of Arthur Cook, p. 46.
97 *Cycling*, 30 March 1922, pp. 222–4.
98 MSS.328/NL/CTC/DA/NOM, *The Loiterer: The Official Organ of the Loiterer's Section North Metropolitan District Association CTC*, July 1938, vol. 1, no. 1, p. 3.
99 MSS.328/N99/1/2, South Lancashire Road Club, Committee Meeting, 19 December 1935.
100 MSS.328/N57/3/1/5, Cycling Memories of Arthur Cook, chapter 2.
101 Hilton, *One More Kilometre*, p. 9.
102 MSS.328/N99/5/6, South Lancashire Road Club, Golden Jubilee, 1935-1985.
103 Personal correspondence, Dilwyn Porter, 4 June 2019.
104 MSS.328/NL/CTC/DA/NOM, *The Loiterer: The Official Organ of the Loiterer's Section North Metropolitan District Association CTC*, July 1938, vol. 1, no. 1, p. 4.
105 MSS.328/NL/CTC/DA/MA/1, *The Northern Wheel*, 1935-38, August 1936, vol. 2, no. 2, pp. 11–15.
106 *CTC Gazette*, August 1928, p. 277.
107 *Cycling*, 20 November 1925, p. 454.
108 Ibid.
109 *Cycling*, 27 November 1925, p. 471; 4 December 1925, pp. 489–90; 11 December 1925, p. 511; 18 December 1925, p. 513.
110 MSS.328/N99/5/6, South Lancashire Road Club, Personal Memoir, J.E. Ford, 27 January 1985.
111 Carol Osborne, 'Gender and the Organisation of British Climbing c.1857-1955' (Unpublished PhD: University of Lancaster, 2004), p. 281.
112 MSS.328/N57/3/1/5, Cycling Memories of Arthur Cook, chapter 5.
113 *Cycling*, 16 December 1954, pp. 650–2.
114 Women were officially allowed to join in 1969 when the Comet CC amalgamated with another club, the Crescent Wheelers, to form the Lea Valley Road Club.
115 MSS.328/N57/3/1/5, Cycling Memories of Arthur Cook, chapter 11.
116 MSS.328/N57/3/1/5, Cycling Memories of Arthur Cook, chapter 5.
117 MSS.328/NL/CTC/DA/NOM, *The Loiterer: The Official Organ of the Loiterer's Section North Metropolitan District Association CTC*, July 1938, vol. 1, no. 1, p. 4.
118 Pye, *Fellowship Is Life*, pp. 42–7; pp. 60–1.

119 MSS.328/NL/CTC/DA/NOM, *The Loiterer: The Official Organ of the Loiterer's Section North Metropolitan District Association CTC*, May 1945, vol. 7, no. 68, p. 2.

120 MSS.328/NL/CTC/DA/NOM, *The Loiterer: The Official Organ of the Loiterer's Section North Metropolitan District Association CTC*, August 1945, vol. 7, no. 70, p. 3.

121 MSS.328/N99/1/2, South Lancashire Road Club, Committee Meeting, 13 August 1956.

122 Hilton, *One More Kilometre*, p. 16.

123 *Cycling*, 16 December 1954, p. 646.

124 In 1930 the NCU became affiliated to the YHA. MSS.328/BU/1/8, Minutes of Council and Annual General Meetings, November 1919–16 March 1935, Annual Meeting of the General Council, 15 March 1930.

125 *CTC Gazette*, January 1930, p. 10.

126 Michael Cunningham, 'Ethos and Politics in the Youth Hostels Association (YHA) in the 1930s', *Contemporary British History*, vol. 30, no. 2 (2016), p. 177. In 1931, initially, there had been 50 hostels after receiving an initial grant of £10,000 from the Carnegie Trust. By the end of the year 80 had been built. *Cycling*, 19 June, p. 595, 13 November 1931, p. 470.

127 *Cycling*, 6 April 1938, pp. 508–9.

128 *Cycling*, 6 March 1935, p. 271.

129 Hoggart, *The Uses of Literacy*, pp. 329–30.

130 Michael Cunningham, '"Two Wheels Bad"? The Status of Cycling in the Youth Hostels Association of England and Wales in the 1930s', *Transfers*, vol. 8, no. 2 (2018), p. 5.

131 MSS.328/NL/CTC/DA/MA,1, The Northern Wheel 1935-38, *The Northern Wheel: The Official Organ of the Manchester District Association CTC*, July 1935, vol. 1, no. 1, p. 28; August 1936, vol. 2, no. 2, pp. 11–15.

132 MSS.328/N99/1/2, South Lancashire Road Club, Minute Book 6 October 1935–10 December 1938, AGM, 10 December 1938.

133 *Cycling*, 6 March 1935, pp. 271–2.

134 *Cycling*, 6 April 1938, p. 508.

135 *Cycling and Mopeds*, 21 May 1958, p. 501.

136 Elizabeth Edwards, *The Camera as Historian: Amateur Photographers and Historical Imagination, 1885-1918* (London: Duke University Press, 2012), p. 2.

137 *Cycling*, 8 July 1920, p. 41.

138 For example, in 1919 there was an article on how to take self-portraits using a cycle lamp. *Cycling*, 20 November 1919, p. 379, 1 September 1921, pp. 180–1.

139 MSS.328/NL/CTC/DA/NOM, *The Loiterer: The Official Organ of the Loiterer's Section North Metropolitan District Association CTC*, July 1938, vol. 1, no. 1, p. 7.

140 *Cycling*, 26 September 1930, pp. 317–18.
141 Zweiniger-Bargielowska, *Managing the Body*, p. 223.
142 *Cycling*, 29 July 1920, p. 107.
143 Zweiniger-Bargielowska, *Managing the Body*, p. 223.
144 *Cycling*, 14 September 1922, p. 222; 5 October 1922, p. 279. One definition of Watney's is a clumsy or awkward male.
145 MSS.328/N57/3/1/5, Cycling Memories of Arthur Cook, p. 156.
146 Zweiniger-Bargielowska, *Managing the Body*, p. 224.
147 *Cycling*, 11 April 1924, p. 287.
148 MSS.328/N57/3/1/5, Cycling Memories of Arthur Cook, p. 158.
149 *Cycling*, 26 September 1924, p. 271.
150 MSS.328/N57/3/1/5, Cycling Memories of Arthur Cook, p. 158.
151 Geoffrey Finlayson, 'A Moving Frontier: Voluntarism and the State in British Social Welfare 1911-1949', *Twentieth Century British History*, vol. 1, no. 2 (1990), pp. 183–5.
152 Robert Snape, 'The New Leisure, Voluntarism and Social Reconstruction in Inter-War Britain', *Contemporary British History*, vol. 29, no. 1 (2015), p. 53.
153 Brad Beaven and John Griffiths, 'Creating the Exemplary Citizen: The Changing Notion of Citizenship in Britain 1870-1939', *Contemporary British History*, vol. 22, no. 2 (2008), p. 212.
154 Brad Beaven, *Leisure, Citizenship and Working-Class Men in Britain, 1850-1945* (Manchester: Manchester University Press, 2005), pp. 112–13.
155 Ibid., p. 8.
156 Millward, 'UK Cycle Industry', p. 404, 427. In 1936 a National Committee of Cycling was formed; an alliance between the manufacturers and the NCU and CTC to promote cycling and defend it in the political sphere.
157 *Cycling*, 1 March 1923, p. 141.
158 Ibid., p. 145.
159 *Cycling*, 3 May 1923, p. 325.
160 *Cycling*, 31 May 1923, p. 417.
161 Helen McCarthy, 'Associational Voluntarism in Inter-war Britain', in M. Hilton and J. McKay (eds), *The Ages of Voluntarism: How We Got to the Big Society* (London: British Academy, 2011), p. 48.
162 National Archives, NA/ED/113/74, National Fitness Council, Minutes, Papers and Reports. Voluntary Organisations: The National Cyclists' Union.
163 This was the group that was identified in the 1960 Wolfenden Report that needed the greatest attention, later known as the 'Wolfenden Gap'.
164 MSS.328/NL/CTC/DA/NOM, *The Loiterer: The Official Organ of the Loiterer's Section North Metropolitan District Association CTC*, April 1939, p. 10.
165 NA/ED/113/74, National Fitness Council, Minutes, Papers and Reports. Voluntary Organisations: The National Cyclists' Union. Holdsworth was paid a salary of £550.

166 Richard Weight, *Patriots: National Identity in Britain 1940-2000* (London: Macmillan, 2002), p. 191.
167 Becky E. Conekin, *'The Autobiography of a Nation': The 1951 Festival of Britain* (Manchester: Manchester University Press, 2003), p. 7.
168 *Cycling*, 26 April 1951, p. 443.
169 *Cycling*, 5 April 1951, p. 394.
170 MSS.328/N55/4/1, Solihull Cycling Club, *Awheel: Official Organ of the Solihull Cycling Club*, June 1951. The Festival of Cycling lost £3,000. MSS.204/1/1/23, British Cycle and Motor Cycle Manufacturers and Traders Union Ltd, 18 October 1950–5 December 1951, 4. Festival of Cycling.
171 *Cycling*, 26 April 1951, p. 447.
172 Ibid., pp. 448–9.

Chapter 5

1 Becky Conekin, Frank Mort and Chris Waters (eds), 'Introduction', in Becky Conekin, Frank Mort and Chris Waters (eds), *Moments of Modernity: Reconstructing Britain 1945-1964* (London: Rivers Oram Press, 1999), pp. 19–20.
2 Ibid.
3 *Cycling*, 14 July 1921, p. 29.
4 Ritchie, *Quest for Speed*, chapter 6.
5 Ibid.
6 Moxham, *Fifty Years of Road Riding*, p. 40.
7 For example, when Beryl Burton broke both the men's and women's British records for 12 hours in 1967 she did it on course V181, designed for the Otley CC 12-hour race. Beryl Burton, *Personal Best* (Huddersfield: Springfield Books, 1986), p. 96.
8 *Cycling*, 23 January 1935, p. 104.
9 *Cycling*, 24 June 1936, p. 377.
10 *Cycling*, 12 January 1938, p. 38.
11 MSS.328/RTTC/1/1/6, Minutes of the Road Time Trials Council, Report of the National Committee, 1942.
12 *Athletic News*, 25 January 1904, p. 7.
13 *Cycling*, 1 January 1920, pp. 10–13. The principal events considered then were Century RC – 50 miles; Catford CC – 50 miles; Anfield BC – 100 miles; Kingsdale CC – 50; Highgate CC – 50; Forest CC – 50; Yorkshire RC – 50; Bath Road – 100; East Liverpool W – 50; Anerley BC – 12 hours; Polytechnic CC – 12 hours; Anfield BC – 24 hours; Speedwell BC – 100 miles; University CC – 50 miles; North Road CC – 24 hours.
14 *Cycling*, 6 January 1921, p. 7.

15 *Cycling*, 13 May 1920, p. 349.
16 *The Times*, 12 July 1922, p. 7.
17 *Cycling*, 3 August 1922, pp. 90–1.
18 Ibid.
19 *Cycling*, 9 February 1922, p. 92.
20 While the UCI recognized the NCU as the sport's governing body in Britain, the time trial itself was organized by the Anfield BC on the NCU's behalf because the NCU no longer had responsibility for road racing; its remit only stretched to track racing.
21 *Cycling*, 27 July 1922, p. 65.
22 The winner was: D. Marsh; second, W. T. Burkill; third, C. F. Davey. The 1920 Olympic champion, Sweden's Stenquist dropped out.
23 *Cycling*, 10 August, pp. 115, 124–6.
24 Moxham, *Fifty Years of Road Riding*, p. 88. The full list was: Anerley BC (F. Maton); Anfield BC (W. P. Cook); Bath RC (J. Burden Barnes); Century RC (G. H. Stancer); Etna CC (S. E. George); Kingsdale CC (H. Farmer); Midland C & AC (F. J. Urry); North Road CC (F. T. Bidlake); Polytechnic CC (J. F. Ditchman); and Unity CC (A. Shillito).
25 *Cycling*, 24 August 1922, p. 153; 21 September 1922, p. 230.
26 Moxham, *Fifty Years of Road Riding*, p. 89.
27 MSS.328/N57/3/1/5, Cycling Memories of Arthur Cook, chapter 4.
28 Ibid.
29 MSS.328/RTTC/1/1/2, Minutes of the Road Time Trials Council, Minutes of National Committee, 1 January 1939, National Committee Report, 1938.
30 *Cycling*, 2 February 1938, p. 135.
31 MSS.328/RTTC/1/1/6, Minutes of the Road Time Trials Council, Meeting of National Council, 11 January 1948, Report of National Committee, 1947.
32 MSS.328/RTTC1/1/8, Minutes of the Road Time Trials Council, Report of the National Committee, 1949.
33 Ibid.
34 MSS.328/RTTC/1/1/9, Minutes of the Road Time Trials Council, Report of the National Committee, 1950. Riders could display an optional panel, but not exceeding four inches by 3 inches on either arm 'on which club colours or other flashes may be displayed.'
35 MSS.328/RTTC/1/1/6, Minutes of the Road Time Trials Council, Resume of a meeting between reps of RTTC and NCU Emergency Committee, 29 July 1945. Eventually, two separate events – one for professionals, one for amateurs – were organized which allowed the RTTC to send two riders for the amateur event; both crashed and the one who completed the course, finished last. Minutes of National Committee, 9 September 1945, 7 October 1945.
36 MSS.328/RTTC/1/1/7, National Committee, 1947-1948, Meeting of National Council, 11 January 1948, Report of National Committee, 1947.

37 MSS.328/RTTC/1/1/6, Minutes of the Road Time Trials Council, Resume of a meeting between reps of RTTC and NCU Emergency Committee, 29 July 1945.
38 MSS.328/RTTC/1/1/7, National Committee, 1947-1948, Meeting of National Council, 11 January 1948. Report of National Committee, 1947.
39 MSS.328/RTTC/1/1/7, National Committee, 1947-1948, Report of National Committee for the Year ended 30 September 1948.
40 From the start, the Tour de France and Giro d'Italia were both sponsored by newspapers.
41 There were around 120 to 130 designated races where times could count towards a rider's average time. *Cycling*, 17 March 1937, p. 363.
42 *Cycling*, 27 December 1929, pp. 581–2, 585.
43 Of the first 64 cyclists in the 1933 competition the geographical spread was London 23; Merseyside 15; Yorkshire 11; Midlands 6; Lancashire (excluding Liverpool) 4; North of England 2; Scotland 2; and Eastern Counties 1. *Cycling*, 13 October 1933, p. 342.
44 *Cycling*, 8 July 1932, pp. 39–40; 13 February 1935, pp. 170–1.
45 *Cycling*, 3 February 1937, p. 133; 2 February 1938, pp. 129–32.
46 *Cycling*, 3 October 1930, p. 335.
47 Originally, it had the catchy title, *Cycling's* Great Smoking Concert and Prize Distribution. In addition to the Best All-Rounder trophies, prizes were presented for second, third and fourth places, 12 Certificates of Merit and a Team Shield and team medals. *Cycling*, 10 October 1930, p. 357.
48 Dave Russell, 'Deeply Honoured: The Rise and Significance of the British Sporting Award, 1945-c.1970', *Sport in History*, vol. 29, no. 3 (September 2009), p. 491.
49 Dave Russell argues a similar point in relation to the retirement of the footballer Tom Finney. Dave Russell, *Football and the English: A Social History of Association Football in England, 1863-1995* (Preston: Carnegie, 1997), p. 154.
50 MSS.328/RTTC/1/1/8, Minutes of the Road Time Trials Council, Report of the National Committee, 1949. In 1948 the concert was held at Olympia and the following year Empress Hall (with a capacity of 6-7,000) was the venue.
51 *Cycling*, 2 February 1933, pp. 129–32. Yorkshire cyclists won 9 out of the 14 prizes that year.
52 By 1944 the RTTC had taken ownership of the BAR competition from *Cycling*. MSS.328/RTTC/1/1/6, Minutes of the Road Time Trials Council, Minutes of National Committee, 24 September 1944.
53 W. J. Mills, 'Cycling', in James Rivers (ed.), *The Sports Book 3* (London: MacDonald, 1949), p. 56.
54 Millward, 'UK Cycle Industry', p. 328 n1.
55 At the time of retirement as an amateur, Southall held world unpaced records at 1, 5, 10 and 20 miles. He also held 28 national track records, including the hour unpaced at 26.5 miles (42.65 kilometres). On the road he won 150 open

road races and every classic open event, including hill climbs and held the BAR records at 25 and 100 miles. From 1925 until he became a professional, he was never off the scratch mark in any event at any distance. He did also ride in some massed-start races and on the track. *Cycling*, 13 October 1933, p. 342; 20 October 1933, p. 387.

56 *Cycling*, 23 March 1934, p. 276.
57 *Cycling*, 26 October 1934, pp. 18–19a.
58 Because of the media coverage of his record-breaking rides, Opperman was also voted Australia's most popular sportsman, ahead of Don Bradman. *Cycling*, 30 November 1934, p. 587; 13 February 1935, p. 192.
59 *Cycling*, 11 September, p. 290; 17 July 1935, p. 68.
60 *Cycling*, 28 August 1935, p. 240.
61 *Cycling*, 31 July 1935, p. 119.
62 *Cycling*, 7 October 1936, p. 527.
63 Mills, 'Cycling', pp. 56–7.
64 *Cycling*, 2 October 1931, p. 332.
65 In the 1936 edition Frank Southall crashed within 10 minutes and broke his right arm. *Cycling*, 23 September 1936, pp. 431–3.
66 *Cycling*, 17 March 1937, pp. 352–3.
67 Dauncey, *French Cycling*, p. 45.
68 Barbara Keys, *Globalizing Sport: National Rivalry and International Community in the 1930s* (Cambridge, MA: Harvard University Press, 2006), pp. 11–12.
69 Dauncey, *French Cycling*, p. 113. The move to national teams though was underpinned by commercial factors.
70 Michael Oriard, *Reading Football: How the Popular Press Created an American Spectacle* (London: University of North Carolina Press, 1993), pp. xxii–xxiii; Christopher Thompson, *The Tour de France: A Cultural History* (Berkeley: University of California Press, 2006).
71 *CTC Gazette*, June 1930, pp. 202–3.
72 *Cycling*, 4 December, p. 449, 11 December, pp. 476–9, 18 December 1919, pp. 487–8 1919. Blake also wrote a story on road racing in France, which an English rider had entered, 'A Southern Road Race', *Cycling*, 25 December 1919, pp. 513–14.
73 *Cycling*, 4 December 1919, p. 460.
74 *CTC Gazette*, September 1923, pp. 240–3.
75 *CTC Gazette*, September 1925, p. 296.
76 *Cycling*, 11 August 1937, pp. 198–9.
77 MSS.328/N57/3/1/5, Cycling Memories of Arthur Cook, chapter 2.
78 *Cycling*, 23 March 1938, p. 403, 422.
79 *Cycling*, 24 June 1936, p. 864.

80 Wolverhampton Archives, Percy Stallard Papers, DB 45/2/2/3/2, RTTC; Letters re: 1942 Massed Start Race, Letter to Alex Josey, sec of RTTC re: MSR, 14 April 1942. Indeed, at the 1948 London Olympics, it was the NCU that had responsibility for the cycling road race, which was held on a closed circuit around Windsor Park.

81 Initially, the act allowing the roads to be free in the Isle of Man of motor-vehicle traffic was only relevant to motorcycle races. It was in the following year, 1937, when an act by the House of Keys, permitted the same conditions for massed-start cycle races. *Cycling*, 24 June 1936, p. 865.

82 *Cycling*, 27 July 1934, p. 96.

83 *Cycling*, 15 July 1936, p. 95.

84 In 1935 the race was won by Luke Youll, in 1937 the winner was D. Morrison. *Cycling*, 19 May, p. 694; 1 September 1937, p. 308. The Scottish Amateur Cycling Association was formed in 1937 (with 96 clubs), it seems as a consequence of the dispute over this race. Its main function was to control all aspects of road racing in Scotland, and this was complete when the Borders Time Trials Association joined that year. *Cycling*, 23 February 1938, p. 254.

85 *Cycling*, 16 February 1938, p. 207; 23 February 1938, p. 254.

86 Crowe had stated that, 'We shall welcome an event of the nature you have in mind. The interest in massed-start during the past few years has increased considerably and it seems to us to that provided your event can be put over on satisfactory lines it may create a precedent which would permit similar events to be held in other parts of the country.' Crowe clarified his remarks by later stating that the NCU would not grant a permit for the race unless it was not only police permitted but also police controlled. *Cycling*, 16 March 1938, p. 362.

87 *Cycling*, 30 March 1938, pp. 426–7.

88 Holland and Burl were part of a three-man British Empire team, which included a Canadian, P. Gachon. Gachon did not complete the first stage, while Burl crashed out in the first week. *Cycling*, 7 July 1937, p. 7.

89 Andre Paul of Belgium had been third but was disqualified after the UCI Bureau found he breached amateur rules. *Cycling*, 20 February 1935, p. 217; 7 October 1936, pp. 512–13.

90 *Cycling*, 23 June 1937, p. 885.

91 *Cycling*, 21 July 1937, p. 102.

92 Ibid., p. 104.

93 *Cycling*, 19 January 1938, pp. 66–7.

94 There were 10 races held at Donnington, 23 at Brooklands and one each on the Isle of Man and at Blenheim Palace. Most were 100 kilometres in distance. *Cycling*, 19 October 1938, p. 569; 13 April 1938, pp. 532–3.

95 *Cycling*, 1 June 1938, p. 799; 13 July 1938, pp. 56–7.

96 In 1951 it was noted that there had been a boom in NCU registrations for track racing men with a record 7,000 for 1950; a few years previously

registrations had numbered in the hundreds. However, on the road it was estimated that there were over 30,000 time triallists riding against the clock every Sunday morning during the season. *Cycling*, 8 February 1951, p. 159.
97 *Cycling*, 14 October 1936, p. 543, 561.
98 *Cycling*, 23 November 1938, p. 785.
99 *Cycling*, 24 August 1938, p. 273; 7 June 1938, p. 853.
100 Edmund Blunden, *Cricket Country* (London: The Imprint Society, 1945), p. 153.
101 Geoffrey Nicholson, *The Professionals* (London: Andre Deutsch, 1964), p. 107.
102 It was first published in 1946 and ceased in 1971.
103 As his parents were communists and had links to the French communist party, Hilton read it.
104 Hilton, *One More Kilometre*, pp. 96–7.
105 Ibid., pp. 59–60.
106 *Cycling*, 9 November 1938, p. 673. The top 11 was (1) Touring in Britain, 27 per cent; (2) Club riding, 24.3 per cent; (3) Lone Riding, 16.4 per cent; (4) Road Time Trial Sport, 14 per cent; (5) Cycle Camping, 6.4 per cent; (6) Massed-start Racing, 3.1 per cent; (7) Touring Abroad, 2.7 per cent; (8) Path Racing, 2.7 per cent; (9) Cycle Polo, 1.4 per cent; (10) Riding to and from work, 1.3 per cent; and (11) Record-Breaking, 1.0 per cent.
107 J. B. Priestley, 'When Work Is Over', *Picture Post*, 4 January 1941.
108 *Cycling*, 22 June 1934, p. 626.
109 MSS.328/BU/1/8, Annual Meeting of NCU General Council, 16 March 1935.
110 *Cycling*, 3 August 1934, p. 123.
111 By 1938 Josey was assistant editor of *Cycling*. He was vice-president and founder of Poole Wheelers C and AC; a member of Century RC, Polytechnic CC, Charlotteville CC, plus the CTC and NCU. *Cycling*, 24 August 1938 p. 266.
112 *Cycling*, 25 November 1936, pp. 768–9, 776.
113 Jones, *Sport, Politics and the Working Class*, pp. 142–6.
114 Taylor, 'Sport and Civilian Morale', pp. 315–38.
115 *Guardian*, 15 October 2001, p. 15.
116 *Cycling*, 19 October 1938, pp. 548–9, 569.
117 MSS.328/N17/3/1/3, British League of Racing Cyclists, *passim*. He re-joined later in the year, but only as a cyclist.
118 *Cycling*, 23 June 1933, pp. 634–7; 14 July 1933, p. 43; 18 August 1933, p. 171. Frank Southall was also in the race, but suffered a puncture.
119 *Cycling*, 22 June 1934, p. 616.
120 *Cycling*, 15 May 1935, p. 509. The others were: W. Harvell, Poole Wheelers; Charles Holland, Midland C and AC; and EV Mills, Addiscombe CC. Six countries were represented in a 100-kilometre MSR.

121 *Cycling*, 22 May 1935, p. 622. The following year he was third in the same race with Charles Holland second, and then second in 1937, which earned him a place on England's team in the amateur World Championships' team. 24 June 1936, p. 872, 875; 9 June 1937, p. 795; 18 August, pp. 229–31.
122 *Cycling*, 8 June 1938, p. 849.
123 *Cycling*, 19 October 1938, pp. 548–9, 569.
124 The RTTC remained a separate body. Previously banned/proclaimed riders who had joined the BLRC could be reinstated by the RTTC and NCU, but this was a six-part process. MSS.328/RTTC/1/1/6, Minutes of the Road Time Trials Council, Resume of a meeting between reps of RTTC and NCU Emergency Committee, 29 July 1945.
125 The founding members were M. J. Gibson; S. A. Padwick; P. T. Stallard; E. F. Ansgrave; J. E. Finn; R Jones; E. R. Hickman; G Anstee; L Plume; G Truelove; C. J. Fox; L Merrills; W. W. Greaves; E Reddish; E Thompson; R Hartley; K Swaby; S Copley; S Cooper; K Pattison; G Clark; Mrs W. W. Greaves and Miss G. A. Stiff. MSS.328/N17/3/1/22, Charles Messenger Files.
126 Fox, a company secretary, died in 1946, aged 53, following an accident during a pursuit race for the Bradford Cycling Club. *Harrogate Herald*, 29 May 1946, p. 4.
127 The business was 'Cyclists' Equipment Co. Ltd.' at 15 St. Mary's Road, Ealing Green.
128 MSS.328/N7/1/80, James Kain.
129 The clubs were: Birmingham RCC; Bradford RCC; Ealing CC; English Electric (Stafford) CC; Ensign RC; Glen CC; Halifax RCC; Leeds Wellington CC; Luton RC; Manchester RCC; Olympia RC; Sanden CC; Sheffield RCC; Southern Coureurs; Vegetarian RCC (London Branch); Vegetarian RCC (Yorkshire branch) Laycrest Manor RC; Wolverhampton RCC; Wolverhampton Wheelers; and Wrekin RCC.
130 MSS.328/RTTC/1/1/6, Minutes of the Road Time Trials Council, Minutes of National Committee, 18 June 1944.
131 MSS.328/RTTC/1/1/6, Minutes of the Road Time Trials Council, Minutes of National Committee, 24 September 1944.
132 MSS.328/RTTC/1/1/6, Minutes of the Road Time Trials Council, Minutes of National Committee, 21 January 1945.
133 By comparison, before the war the NCU's membership was 54,000. By 1940 it had dropped to 32,808. In 1941 it was 24,415; 1942, 35,192; and 1943, 32,568. MSS.328/BU/1/9, Minutes of Annual General Meeting of NCU, 14 April 1945, NCU Post-War Planning Committee Report 1945.
134 MSS.328/N17/3/1/1, British League of Racing Cyclists, Minutes of a meeting held at the Youth Hostel Association, Sherebrook Lodge, Buxton, Sunday 15 November 1942.
135 *Cycling*, 25 February 1942, p. 140.
136 *The Bicycle*, 29 December 1943, p. 6, p. 22.

137 MSS.328/N17/3/1/3, BLRC, London Section, Committee meeting, 24 May 1944.
138 *Cycling Record*, January 1947, p. 7.
139 DB 45/2/2/2/2, Tour of the Peak Amateur Road Race, 14 June 1943.
140 MSS.328/NL/BL/RC/2, *The Leaguer: Official Journal of the British League of Racing Cyclists*, February 1955, vol. 10, 8, p. 8; MSS.328/BLRC/1/1/3, BLRC NEC Minutes, 14 October 1956, Chairman's Report.
141 MSS.328/NL/BL/RC/2, *The Leaguer: Official Journal of the British League of Racing Cyclists*, August 1954, vol. 10, 2, p. 3.
142 The membership was divided up in terms of licences: 1st class – 396; 2nd class – 384; 3rd class – 2,796. There were also 1,113 Junior members; 82 Lady members; 4 Aspirants; 17 Independents plus 388 associate members. MSS.328/BLRC/1/1/3, BLRC NEC Minutes, 14 October 1956.
143 Over 5–7 August 1944 Britain's first stage race, the Southern Grand Prix, took place, and was won by Percy Stallard.
144 The BLRC's initial plan had been for a 2,000-mile race over two to three weeks. 'Round Britain on a Bike', *Sporting Chronicle*, 25 November 1944, MSS.328/N17/3/1/4.
145 Charles Messenger, *Ride and be Damned: Chas Messenger's Glory Years of the British League of Racing Cyclists* (London: Pedal Publishing, 1998), p. 71. In 1948, Katharine Dunham, the black American star of Caribbean Rhapsody, presented the yellow jersey to the winner of the first stage of the Brighton to Glasgow race. MSS.328/BLRC/1/1/3, BLRC Management Committee Minutes, 11 May 1958.
146 MSS.328/RTTC/1/1/6, Minutes of the Road Time Trials Council, Minutes of National Committee, 11 March 1945.
147 The split in cycling continued to stir emotions into the twenty-first century. See for example, http://www.britishcycling.org.uk/search/article/bc20100114-B assett-memories and accompanying comments (accessed 7 August 2014).
148 MSS.328/RTTC/1/1/6, Minutes of the Road Time Trials Council, Minutes of National Committee, 18 June 1944.
149 MSS.328/RTTC/1/1/8, RTTC, Report of the National Committee, 1949.
150 MSS.328/RTTC/1/1/7, National Committee, 1947-1948, Meeting of National Council, 11 January 1948. Report of National Committee, 1947.
151 MSS.328/N17/3/1/3, British League of Racing Cyclists, London Section Minutes, 1943-44, Committee meeting, 15 September 1943.
152 MSS.328/RTTC/1/1/10, Report on a meeting between a delegation from NCU and officials of the MoT and HO, 25 January 1952.
153 Ibid.
154 Ibid.
155 However, if two delegates had voted for MSR instead of against it at a London Centre meeting (with 213 voting) the general council vote would have been 50 (for)–19 (against).

156 MSS.328/RTTC/1/1/10, Report on a meeting between a delegation from NCU and officials of the MoT and HO, 25 January 1952.

157 Alderson, *Bicycling: A History*, p. 165. For an example of the struggle, see MSS.328/BLRC/1/1/3, BLRC 1958 AGM Agenda.

158 *Cycling*, 17 February 1943, p. 133. Instead of clubs, it was actually 13 out of 15 NCU centres who were against MSR.

159 MSS.328/M/1333, Barnesbury Cycling Club Handbook 1943-44.

160 MSS.328/N99/5/6, South Lancashire Road Club, Golden Jubilee, 1935–85. Perhaps unsurprisingly the language in this official history is more emollient on the split than that in the official minutes, although interestingly the original 'deserters' are given the prefix 'Mr'.

161 MSS.328/N99/1/3, Records of the South Lancashire Road Club, Minutes of AGM, 28 November 1948.

162 MSS.328/N99/5/6, Records of the South Lancashire Road Club, Personal Memoir, J.E. Ford, 27 January 1985.

163 MSS.328/N99/1/3, Records of the South Lancashire Road Club, Minutes of AGM, 28 November 1948.

164 MSS.328/N99/1/3, Records of the South Lancashire Road Club, Minutes of AGM, 18 December 1955.

165 MSS.328/N55/4/1/1, *Awheel: Official Organ of the Solihull Cycling Club*, November 1947. In May 1948 550 copies of the magazine were sold.

166 MSS.328/N55/4/1/1, *Awheel: Official Organ of the Solihull Cycling Club*, October 1948.

167 MSS.328/N55/4/1/1, *Awheel: Official Organ of the Solihull Cycling Club*, January 1950.

168 http://www.concordecc.org.uk/history1.htm (accessed 18 March 2017).

169 MSS.328/N55/4/1/1, *Awheel: Official Organ of the Solihull Cycling Club*, March 1950.

170 MSS.328/N55/4/1/3, *Awheel: Official Organ of the Solihull Cycling Club*, 29 June Souvenir Programme, p. 15. The 90-mile race consisted of five laps run on a 17.75-mile course, which began at Bassetts Pole, Staffordshire, and finished 1.5 miles beyond Bassetts Pole on Coleshill Road.

171 Tommy Simpson, *Cycling Is My Life* (London: Yellow Jersey Press, 2009), p. 39. Simpson was able to compete at the time under RTTC rules due to a Tripartite Agreement between the three main bodies.

172 Iain Wilton, '"A Galaxy of Sporting Events": Sport's Role and Significance in the Festival of Britain, 1951', *Sport in History*, vol. 36, no. 4 (2016), pp. 459–76.

173 *Cycling*, 22 February 1951, pp. 222–34.

174 John Foot, *Pedalare! Pedalare! A History of Italian Cycling* (London: Bloomsbury, 2011), chapter 7.

175 *Cycling*, 22 February 1951, p. 228. Coppi was a British POW in Africa during the war.

176 The Bidlake Memorial Prize was awarded to the cyclist who the panel felt – it was a subjective decision – had made an outstanding contribution to cycling that year. It was not limited to sporting cyclists but also administrators and those outside the sport. Burton had won it the previous year, but mainly for winning the individual pursuit at the World Championships. http://www.bidlakememorial.org.uk/index.htm (accessed 20 August 2019).

Chapter 6

1 *Cycling*, 15 June 1938, p. 857.
2 *Hendon and Finchley Times*, 4 March 1938, p. 10.
3 Skillen, 'Fleming, Lillian Irene [Billie]'.
4 See for example, *Cycling*, 26 October 1923, p. 351, Cover, p. 354, Editorial, 'The Cult of the Lightweight'.
5 Millward, 'UK Cycle Industry', p. 331.
6 Selina Todd, *Young Women, Work, and Family in England 1918-1950* (Oxford: Oxford University Press, 2005), p. 197.
7 Ibid., p. 198.
8 Zweiniger-Bargielowska, *Managing the Body*, p. 237.
9 Simon Szreter and Kate Fisher, *Sex before the Sexual Revolution: Intimate Life in England 1918-1963* (Cambridge: Cambridge University Press, 2010), p. 285.
10 Zweiniger-Bargielowska, *Managing the Body*, p. 237.
11 In Paul Thompson's study of middle- and upper-class families between 1870 and 1918, the subject of cycling crops up in around half of the 62 interviews undertaken. Paul Thompson, *Family Life and Work Experience before 1918: Middle and Upper Class Families in the Early 20th Century, 1870-1977 2nd Edition* (Colchester: UK Data Archive, 2008), UKDA: 5404.
12 Ibid., UKDA, 5404, int 031, Mrs Fleetwood Hesketh, p. 109.
13 Ibid., UKDA, 5404 int 003, Mrs A. Wood-Hill, p. 21.
14 Ibid., UKDA, 5404 int 004, Mrs Hawkins, p. 62.
15 Ibid., UKDA, 5404 int 045, Mrs Cadbury, p. 7. She later married Laurence John Cadbury, the chocolate maker.
16 Ibid., UKDA, 5404 int 002, Miss Johnson, p. 36.
17 Ibid., UKDA, 5404 int 007, Mrs V. Mason, p. 41, 58.
18 Ibid., UKDA, 5404 int 022, Mrs D. Lloyd, pp. 4–5.
19 Ibid., UKDA, 5404 int 007, Mrs V. Mason, p. 41, 58.
20 Ibid., UKDA, 5404 int 061, Miss Linden, p. 42.
21 *Daily Mirror*, 11 April 1914, p. 8.
22 Alan G.V. Simmonds, *Britain and World War One* (London: Routledge, 2012), p. 130.

23 Thompson, *Family Life and Work Experience*, UKDA, 5404 int 025, Mr D. Mallet, p. 7.
24 Ibid., UKDA, 5404 int 048, Mrs Zeta Lambert, p. 6, 16.
25 Angela Woollacott, *On Her Their Lives Depend: Munitions Workers in the Great War* (Berkley: University of California Press, 1994), p. 142.
26 Simmonds, *Britain and World War One*, pp. 134–5.
27 Ibid., pp. 153.
28 *Cycling*, 8 December 1921, p. 453.
29 *Cycling*, 19 January 1922, p. 44.
30 *The Bicycle*, 1 March 1944.
31 *The Bicycle*, 15 March 1944.
32 *CTC Gazette and Official Record*, February 1918, p. 23.
33 *CTC Gazette*, August 1918, p. 101.
34 *Cycling*, 2 June 1921, p. 411.
35 *Cycling*, 24 August 1923, p. 151.
36 *Cycling*, 15 September 1921, p. 218; *CTC Gazette*, October 1921, p. 194.
37 *The Times*, 14 September 1921, p. 5.
38 *Cycling*, 22 May 1925, p. 405.
39 *CTC Gazette*, April 1923, p. 95.
40 *CTC Gazette*, July 1922, p. 167.
41 *CTC Gazette*, March 1924, p. 75; March 1925, p. 79.
42 *Cycling*, 5 January 1934, p. 20; 13 July 1938, p. 52.
43 *Cycling*, 8 July 1936, pp. 68–9.
44 Claire Langhamer, *Women's Leisure in England 1920-60* (Manchester: Manchester University Press, 2000), p. 78.
45 Fiona Skillen, *Women, Sport and Modernity in Inter-War Britain* (Oxford: Peter Lang, 2013), p. 217. The study looked at the years 1925, 1930 and 1935. The top three sports were: Golf, Tennis, Swimming and Horse Racing.
46 *Cycling*, 3 January 1930, pp. 15–16.
47 *CTC Gazette*, September 1930, pp. 321–2.
48 *Cycling*, 21 December 1938, p. 914.
49 *Manchester Guardian*, 7 October 1920, p. 2.
50 *The Times*, 18 August 1920, p. 7. In the October of that year Harold Rigby actually succeeded in crossing the channel on a water cycle. *Manchester Guardian*, 16 October 1920, p. 10.
51 *Cycling*, 23 September, p. 261; 30 September 1920, p. 278.
52 http://www.britishpathe.com/video/cycling-the-thames-miss-zetta-hills (accessed 22 April 2016).
53 *Observer*, 3 October 1920, p. 14. In 1923 Hills attempted to swim the channel but gave up after 8 miles. *The Times*, 21 August 1923, p. 5. In 1929 a French woman, Mlle Pfanner, attempted to cross channel on a pedal boat.

It was stated that first person to do so was Rene Savard. *Cycling*, 1 March 1929, p. 176.
54 *Cycling*, 20 October 1933, p. 385.
55 *Cycling*, 30 January 1925, p. 86.
56 *Cycling*, 28 September 1923, p. 261.
57 *CTC Gazette*, September 1927, p. 293.
58 *CTC Gazette*, August 1930, p. 287.
59 She came across four cyclists from Yorkshire on her trip.
60 *Cycling*, 11 August 1937, pp. 198–9.
61 *Cycling*, 15 August 1930, cover page.
62 Zweiniger-Bargielowska, *Managing the Body*, p. 239.
63 Ina Zweiniger-Bargielowska, 'The Making of a Modern Female Body: Beauty, Health and Fitness in Interwar Britain', *Women's History Review*, vol. 20, no. 2 (2011), p. 300.
64 *Cycling*, 26 February 1932, p. 199.
65 *Cycling*, 2 November 1922, p. 347.
66 *Cycling*, 27 May 1920, pp. 383–4.
67 *CTC Gazette*, June 1925, p. 177.
68 *CTC Gazette*, May 1926, p. 170.
69 *Cycling*, 10 June 1920, p. 442.
70 *Cycling*, 24 June 1920, pp. 478–9.
71 MSS.328/N57/3/1/5, 'Cycling Memories of Arthur Cook', chapter 3.
72 *CTC Gazette*, April 1928, p. 120.
73 *CTC Gazette*, June 1928, p. 208.
74 *CTC Gazette*, July 1928, p. 257.
75 *CTC Gazette*, September 1928, p. 316.
76 *CTC Gazette*, July 1928, p. 256.
77 *Cycling*, 8 March 1929, p. 185.
78 *Cycling*, 26 September 1930, p. 317–18.
79 *Sheffield Independent*, 18 August 1936, p. 7; *Cycling*, 26 August 1936, p. 310; 2 September 1936, pp. 332–3, 343.
80 *Cycling*, 26 February 1932, p. 199.
81 Personal correspondence.
82 *New Cyclist*, January/February 1992, p. 42.
83 BBC Radio 4, 'World at One', date unknown.
84 MSS.328/N57/3/1/5, 'Cycling Memories of Arthur Cook', chapter 3.
85 For example, MSS.328/N55/4/1, *Awheel: Official Organ of the Solihull Cycling Club*, October 1946, no. 127.
86 https://www.mirror.co.uk/news/uk-news/britains-longest-married-couple-celebrating-18850524 (accessed 14 August 2019).

87 *Cycling*, 18 January 1924, p. 54.
88 *Cycling*, 1 February 1924, p. 88.
89 Jeffrey Weeks, *Sex Politics and Society: The Regulation of Sexuality since 1800*, Second Edition (London: Longman, 1989), pp. 206–14.
90 Szreter and Fisher, *Sex Before the Sexual Revolution*, pp. 113–15.
91 The records that they ratified were 25 miles (out and home); 50 miles; 100 miles; 12 hours; 24 hours; London to York; London to Liverpool; London to Birmingham; London to Bath and back; London to Brighton and back; London to Portsmouth and back; Land's End to London; Land's End to John O'Groats; Liverpool to Edinburgh; York to Edinburgh; 1,000 miles; London to Edinburgh; and Edinburgh to Glasgow and back.
92 *Cycling*, 12 October 1934, p. 402. Petronella later married G. H. Stancer, who was her second husband. William Mason, *Marguerite Wilson: The Story of the First Star of Women's Cycling Told in Her Own Words and those of Her Admirers* (self-published, 2014), p. 50.
93 MSS.328/N10/G/F/1, Women's Road Records Association, Year Book for 1940.
94 See Judy Threlfall-Sykes, 'A History of English Women's Cricket, 1880-1939' (Unpublished PhD: De Montfort University, 2016).
95 Carter, *Medicine, Sport and the Body*, pp. 156–8.
96 *Cycling*, 16 October 1919, pp. 309–10.
97 Carter, *Medicine, Sport and the Body*, p. 156.
98 For example, *Cycling*, 30 May 1924, p. 443.
99 *Cycling*, 16 October 1919, p. 306.
100 *Cycling*, 16 June 1921, pp. 30–1; 24 November 1921, p. 387.
101 *Cycling*, 15 December 1921, p. 466.
102 *Cycling*, 8 December 1921, p. 450; 3 July 1935, p. 231.
103 *Cycling*, 26 February 1936, p. 253.
104 *Cycling*, 9 March 1934, p. 218; 13 February 1935, p. 193.
105 *Cycling*, 16 June 1921, p. 457.
106 *Cycling*, 20 November 1925, p. 442.
107 *Cycling*, 6 November 1925, p. 414.
108 *Cycling*, 16 June 1921, p. 441, 447.
109 *Cycling*, 24 November 1921, p. 387.
110 *Cycling*, 25 March 1936, p. 392.
111 *Cycling*, 5 January 1938, p. 21.
112 *Cycling*, 4 May 1922, p. 316.
113 Hilton, *One More Kilometre*, pp. 295–6. The club was still in existence in 2005 – with thirty members – and after reading the reference about their sexuality in Hilton's book, it voiced its disapproval. *Independent on Sunday*, 28 August 2005 http://www.independent.co.uk/news/uk/this-britain/were-not-deviants-say-the-cycling-ladies-308628.html?printService=print (accessed 19 February 2015).

114 MSS.328/N57/3/1/5, 'Cycling Memories of Arthur Cook'.
115 In 1929, membership was 54; 1932, 48; 1942, 54, 1947, 47; 1955, 60. MSS.328/M/249, 'Rosslyn Ladies CC'; MSS.328/M/1333.
116 *Cycling*, 17 March 1933, p. 270.
117 *Cycling*, 2 February 1934, p. 107; *Birmingham Gazette*, 1 March 1934, p. 13.
118 *Dundee Evening Telegraph*, 23 February 1934, p. 7; *Cycling*, 9 March 1934, p. 232; 16 February 1934, p. 162. Rosslyn Ladies was run by a committee of 13 members.
119 *Cycling*, 30 August 1929, p. 192.
120 Ibid., p. 185.
121 http://www.classiclightweights.co.uk/clubs-reminiscences.html (Accessed 19 February 2015). Even in 1947 the shadow of Mrs Grundy was still evident as male visitors were only allowed on to the camp site between 7.30 pm and 9.30 pm on Saturday evenings.
122 MSS.328/M/249, 'Rosslyn Ladies CC'; MSS.328/M/1333.
123 *Cycling*, 3 January 1930, p. 16.
124 *Hendon and Finchley Times*, 30 December 1938, p. 3. These included Dovey, Lillian Dredge and Marguerite Wilson.
125 *Western Morning News*, 18 September 1934, p. 7; *Cycling*, 8 April 1936, p. 483.
126 *Cycling*, 13 February 1935, p. 193.
127 *Cycling*, 12 October 1934, p. 385.
128 Abrahams had carried out examinations of male BAR winners since 1930. *Cycling*, 1 July 1954, p. 2.
129 Quoted in Carter, *Medicine, Sport and the Body*, p. 164.
130 *Cycling*, 15 June 1938, pp. 874–6.
131 *Cycling*, 10 August 1938, pp. 208–9.
132 http://thepedalclub.org/archives/marguerite-wilson/ (accessed 15 April 2016).
133 The others were two British 'cracks' Cyril Heppleston and Harry 'Shake' Earnshaw plus three Belgian road racing professionals Richard Kemps, Celestine Riga and Jeff Moerenhout. Mason, *Marguerite Wilson*, p. 59. In 1939 there were 13 professionals in the entire country.
134 Zweiniger-Bargielowska, *Managing the Body*, pp. 239–40.
135 Skillen, *Women, Sport and Modernity*, pp. 213–14.
136 MSS.328/N10/A1, Health Magazine, The Health Value of Cycling by Alex Josey, 13 June 1941.
137 Mason, *Marguerite Wilson*, pp. 78–87.
138 Joyce Kay, 'A Window of Opportunity? Preliminary Thoughts in Women's Sport in Post-war Britain', *Sport in History*, vol. 30, no. 2 (June 2010), pp. 196–217.
139 https://www.cyclinguk.org/article/cycling-guide/eileen-sheridan (accessed 3 August 2018).

140 The women's BAR was under the control of the RTTC rather than the WRRA.
141 MSS.328/RTTC/1/1/8, RTTC, Report of the National Committee, 1949. The men competed over 50 miles, 100, miles and 12 hours.
142 The six men were Ken Joy; Dave Bedwell; Clive Parker; Den Talbot; Derek Buttle; and Fred Krebs. *Leamington Spa Courier*, 16 July 1954, p. 9; *Cycling*, 2 December 1954, cover.
143 His time for the End-to-End was 2 days, 9 hours and 1 minute; for the 1,000-mile record, it was 3d 1h 52 minutes.
144 https://www.youtube.com/watch?v=XjNzpWph-io (accessed 31 July 2018). In a 1948 British Pathé news item, Wilson is described as having a 'shapely shape'. https://www.youtube.com/watch?v=jDXgv3pcPcw (accessed 31 July 2018).
145 Eileen Sheridan, *Wonder Wheels: The Autobiography of Eileen Sheridan* (London: Nicholas Kaye, 1956), p. 10.
146 Kay, 'A Window of Opportunity?', pp. 197–8.
147 *Daily Mirror*, 12 July 1954, p. 13.
148 *The Leaguer: Official Journal of the British League of Racing Cyclists*, November 1955, vol. 10, p. 17. Reports of her record breaking usually included details of her bike. Thus, after breaking the WRRA 25-mile record, it was noted that she used gears of 81-86-91-96-102 riding her Hercules bicycle, which was fitted with Dunlop tyres, Cyclo gear, GB brakes, Renold chain and Fibrax brake blocks. *Cycling*, 28 October 1948, p. 442.
149 For example, *Cycling and Mopeds*, 16 January 1958, p. 61.
150 *Cycling*, 4 November 1954, p. 456.
151 *Cycling*, 22 July 1954, p. 82.
152 *Cycling*, 1 July 1954, pp. 2–3.
153 Todd, *Young Women, Work, and Family*, p. 225.

Chapter 7

1 Ritchie, *King of the Road*, p. 174.
2 Ibid.
3 Brian Harrison, *Seeking a Role: The United Kingdom 1951-1970* (Oxford: Oxford University Press, 2009), p. 137.
4 Jim Obelkevich and Peter Catterall, *Understanding Post-war British Society* (London: Routledge, 1994), chapter 11.
5 Plowden, *The Motor Car*, p. 326.
6 Obelkevich and Catterall, *Understanding Post-war British Society*, chapter 11.
7 Oakley, *Winged Wheel*, p.169, 186.

8   John Urry, *Mobilities* (Cambridge: Polity Press, 2007), p. 133.
9   Gunn, 'People and the Car', p. 226.
10 Harrison, *Seeking a Role*, p. 138.
11 Plowden, *The Motor Car*, p. 482; Gunn, 'People and the Car', p. 224.
12 Paul Addison, *No Turning Back: The Peacetime Revolutions of Post-War Britain* (Oxford: Oxford University Press, 2010), pp. 168–73.
13 *Picture Post*, January 1941.
14 Anthony Sampson, *Anatomy of Britain* (London: Hodder and Stoughton, 1962), p. 572.
15 Oakley, *Winged Wheel*, p. 162.
16 Ibid., p. 197.
17 James Booth, *Philip Larkin: Life, Art and Love* (London: Bloomsbury, 2015), pp. 21–2, 293.
18 Ibid., p. 206.
19 Obelkevich and Catterall, *Understanding Post-war British Society*, chapter 11.
20 Helen Meller, *Towns, Plans and Society in Modern Britain* (Cambridge: Cambridge University Press, 1997), chapter 5.
21 Quoted in Simon Gunn, 'The Buchanan Report, Environment and the Problem of Traffic in 1960s Britain', *Twentieth Century British History*, vol. 22, no. 4 (2011), pp. 527–8.
22 Gunn, 'The Buchanan Report', p. 535.
23 Anthony Alexander, *Britain's New Towns: Garden Cities to Sustainable Communities* (London: Routledge, 2009), p. 19.
24 Gunn, 'The Buchanan Report', p. 534.
25 Peter King, 'Equal Rights for Bikes', *New Society*, 12 August 1971, p. 280.
26 Gunn, 'The Buchanan Report', p. 522.
27 MSS.328/N/12, Philip Brachi, 'The Bicycle as Urban Transport', May 1973, p. 5, File: Transport.
28 Meller, *Towns, Plans and Society*, p. 82.
29 Gunn, 'The Buchanan Report', p. 542.
30 Meller, *Towns, Plans and Society*, pp. 81–4.
31 Alexander, *Britain's New Towns*, p. 7.
32 Ibid., p. 87.
33 Meller, *Towns, Plans and Society*, pp. 71–3.
34 http://www.roadswerenotbuiltforcars.com/stevenage/ (accessed 15 August 2015).
35 Eric Claxton, 'The Future of the Bicycle in a Modern Society', *Journal of the Royal Society of Arts*, vol. 16 (1968), p. 121.
36 http://www.roadswerenotbuiltforcars.com/stevenage/ (accessed 15 August 2015)

37 Harrison, *Seeking a Role*, p. 137.
38 Ibid., Barker and Gerhold, *Rise and Rise*, p. 72.
39 Hoggart, *The Uses of Literacy*, p. 368, n. p. 329.
40 *Daily Mirror*, 15 September 1961.
41 *Daily Mail*, 20 December 1973, p. 31.
42 Oakley, *Winged Wheel*, p. 179.
43 MSS.328/BCF/1/1/1, British Cycling Federation 1959-64, BCF, Annual Meeting of the National Council, 10 December 1960.
44 MSS.328/BCF/1/1/1-4, British Cycling Federation 1959-84, *passim*.
45 MSS.328/N57/3/1/5, Cycling Memories of Arthur Cook, Chapter 3.
46 Oakley, *Winged Wheel*, p.187.
47 MSS.328/BCF/1/1/1, British Cycling Federation 1959-64, BCF, Annual Meeting of the National Council, 10 December 1960.
48 Obelkevich and Catterall, *Understanding Post-War British Society*, chapter 11.
49 MSS.204/1/1/34, British Cycle and Motor Cycle Industries Association, Minutes of the Bicycle Manufacturers' Section, 17 March 1964.
50 MSS.204/1/1/37, British Cycle and Motor Cycle Industries Association, Bicycle Manufacturers' Section Minutes, 19 January 1967, p. 7182.
51 Scott Anthony, *Public Relations and the Making of Modern Britain: Stephen Tallents and the Birth of a Progressive Media Profession* (Manchester: Manchester University Press, 2010).
52 Information from British Universities Film and Video Council http://bufvc.ac.uk (accessed 20 October 2018)
53 MSS.204/1/1/30, British Cycle and Motor Cycle Industries Association Minutes of the York Rally Sub-Committee, 22 December 1959.
54 MSS.204/1/1/31, British Cycle and Motor Cycle Industries Association Minutes of the York Rally Sub-Committee, 4 August 1960.
55 MSS.204/1/1/36, British Cycle and Motor Cycle Industries Association, Minutes of the Joint Bicycle Publicity Committee, 14 April 1966.
56 MSS.204/1/1/36, British Cycle and Motor Cycle Industries Association, Minutes of the Joint Bicycle Publicity Committee, 25 November 1965.
57 *Guardian*, 17 February 1966, p. 7.
58 MSS.204/1/1/38, British Cycle and Motor Cycle Industries Association, Minutes of Bicycle Manufacturers' Section, 6 July 1967.
59 MSS.328/BCF/1/1/1, British Cycling Federation 1959-64, BCF Annual Meeting of the National Council, Executive Committee Report, 8 December 1962.
60 MSS.328/BCF/1/1/2, British Cycling Federation, 1965-71, BCF Annual Meeting of the National Council, 11 December 1965. The contract was cancelled the following year.
61 MSS.204/1/1/34, British Cycle and Motor Cycle Industries Association, Minutes of the Joint Bicycle Publicity Committee, 13 February 1964.

62 MSS.204/1/1/34, British Cycle and Motor Cycle Industries Association, Minutes of the Joint Bicycle Publicity Committee, 23 February 1960.

63 MSS.204/1/1/40, British Cycle and Motor Cycle Industries Association, Minutes of the Joint Bicycle Publicity Committee, 22 April 1969.

64 Oakley, *Winged Wheel*, p.163.

65 Ibid., pp. 165–6.

66 Ibid., p. 174, 171.

67 Peter Willmott, *Adolescent Boys of East London* (London: Routledge & Kegan Paul, 1966), p. 28.

68 Pearl Jephcott, *Time of One's Own: Leisure and Young People* (Edinburgh: Oliver & Boyd, 1967), chapter 5, p. 66, 114..

69 Sampson, *Anatomy of Britain*, pp. 572–9.

70 Epperson, 'A New Class of Cyclists', p. 239.

71 Andrew Nahum, 'Moulton, Alexander Eric [Alex] (1920–2012), Engineer and Inventor', in *Oxford Dictionary of National Biography*, https://doi.org/10.1093/ref:odnb/105896 (accessed 11 December 2018).

72 '*Cycling*, 7 November 1962, p. 11', MSS.328/N7/1/102, Moulton.

73 '*Cycling*, 23 May 1964', MSS.328/N7/1/102, Moulton. Raleigh was the first.

74 MSS.204/1/1/40, British Cycle and Motor Cycle Industries Association, Minutes of the Joint Bicycle Publicity Committee, 4 June 1969. In 1967, sales of conventional adult bikes were 269,715. For conventional juvenile bikes sales were 190,002 in 1967, dropping to 170,762 in 1968. However, this was only a blip in the downward trend. Home sales for first 3 months of 1969 were 83,740, compared with 102,810 for first 3 months in 1968.

75 See Nigel Whiteley, *Reyner Banham: Historian of the Immediate Future* (Cambridge, MA and London: MIT Press, 2002); Reyner Banham, 'The Atavism of the Short-distance Mini-cyclist', in Penny Sparke (ed.), *Design by Choice: Reyner Banham* (London: Rizzoli, 1981), p. 88.

76 Epperson, 'A New Class of Cyclists', p. 241; Reyner Banham, 'A Grid on Two Farthings', *New Statesman*, vol. 66, no. 1 (1 November 1963), p. 626; Gillian Naylor, 'The Banham Factor: The Ninth Reyner Banham Memorial Lecture', *Journal of Design History*, vol. 10, no. 3 (1997), pp. 241–52.

77 Rosen, *Framing Production*, pp. 100–2.

78 Hugh Cunningham, *The Invention of Childhood* (London: BBC Books, 2006), pp. 216–17.

79 Quoted in Dave Russell, '"Interesting and Instructive Reading"? The FA Book for Boys and the Culture of Boyhood, 1945-1973', *Journal of Sport History*, vol. 34, no. 2 (2007), p. 249.

80 In 1964 the millionth child had been trained under the now National Cycling Proficiency Scheme. In 1970 the figure was 2.5 million; 5 years later it was 3 million. In 1974 it was claimed that child cycling fatalities went below 100 for the first time since records began and since 1959 casualties had fallen by 40 per cent.

81 Weight and Beach, 'Introduction', pp. 1–17.
82 Carter, *Medicine, Sport and the Body*, p. 188.
83 Laura King, 'Future Citizens: Cultural and Political Conceptions of Children in Britain, 1930s-1950s', *Twentieth Century British History* (Advance Access published 31 May 2016), pp. 1–23.
84 *Guardian*, 26 March 1957, p. 4.
85 Mathew Thomson, *Lost Freedom: The Landscape of the Child and the British Post-war Settlement* (Oxford: Oxford University Press, 2013), p. 1.
86 Ibid., p. 152.
87 Ibid., p. 141. In 1923 the London Safety First Council affiliated to the National Safety First Association, which itself was renamed the Royal Society for the Prevention of Accidents (RoSPA) in 1941.
88 *Cycling*, 17 May 1929, pp. 397–8.
89 The other was fear of strangers. See Thomson, *Lost Freedom*.
90 *CTC Gazette*, November 1929, p. 390.
91 *Cycling*, 17 April 1931, p. 365.
92 *Cycling*, 2 June 1933, p. 548.
93 MSS.328/BU/1/9, General Council Minutes, Report of the General Committee, 16 November 1935; MSS.328/BU/1/8, Annual Meeting of General Council, 16 March 1935.
94 MSS.204/1/1/14, British Cycle and Motor Cycle Manufacturers and Traders Union Ltd, Bicycle Manufacturers' Section Minutes, 7 October 1937, p. 2557.
95 MSS.328/BU/1/9, NCU, Ordinary Meeting of General Council, 20 November 1937.
96 MSS.328/BU/1/9, Minutes of the Annual Meeting of the General Council, 18 March 1939, Report of General Committee, 18 March 1939, p. 147.
97 MSS.328/N17/3/1/3, *The Cyclist*, June 1946, p. 67.
98 *Cycling*, 8 February 1951, p. 168, 183.
99 *Cycling*, 28 February 1952, p. 199.
100 *Cycling*, 5 August 1954, p. 149.
101 MSS.204/1/1/26, British Cycle and Motor Cycle Manufacturers and Traders Union Ltd, Bicycle Manufacturers' Section Minutes, 20 January 1955, p. 4937.
102 *Guardian*, 16 October 1953, p. 6.
103 Ibid., p. 5.
104 *Guardian*, 3 November 1954, p. 3.
105 MSS.328/BU/1/9, NCU General Council Minutes, Annual Meeting of the General Council, 22 March 1947; Meeting of General Council, 5 July 1947; General Council Minutes, Legal and Parliamentary Committee – Report 1947.
106 MSS.204/1/1/26, British Cycle and Motor Cycle Manufacturers and Traders Union Ltd, Bicycle Manufacturers' Section Minutes, Bicycle Manufacturers' Section Minutes, 20 January 1955, p. 4937, 25 August 1954, p. 4866.

107 *Observer*, 16 September 1956, p. 5.
108 *Guardian*, 24 September 1947, p. 8. By 1951 12,000 children had gained a certificate for 'safe cycling'. *Guardian*, 6 October 1951, p. 2.
109 *Guardian*, 5 September 1956, p. 1.
110 Ibid.
111 *Guardian*, 26 March 1957, p. 4.
112 *Guardian*, 7 January 1959, p. 14.
113 *Observer*, 16 September 1956, p. 5.
114 The club was based on a RoSPA cartoon character, Tufty Fluffytail, a red squirrel, which was created by Elsie Mills in 1953.
115 https://www.rospa.com/about/history/tufty/ (accessed 28 October 2017).
116 MSS.328/N17/3/122, *Cycle and Mopeds*, 22 October 1958, p. 299.
117 *Cycling and Mopeds*, 2 January 1958, p. 3.
118 *Guardian*, 6 August 1960, p. 2.
119 MSS.204/1/1/37, British Cycle and Motor Cycle Industries Association, Bicycle Manufacturers' Section Minutes, 19 January 1967.
120 The notion of cycling safety tests was even broached for adults by the Solihull CC. It does not seem to have been taken seriously. MSS.328/N55/4/1/8, January 1960, p. 1.
121 MSS.204/1/1/37, British Cycle and Motor Cycle Industries Association, Bicycle Manufacturers' Section Minutes, 19 January 1967; MSS.204/1/1/38, British Cycle and Motor Cycle Industries Association Minutes of Bicycle Manufacturers' Section, 6 July 1967.
122 MSS.328/BU/1/9, NCU General Council Minutes, Minutes of a Meeting of the General Council of NCU, 16 November 1946; Annual Meeting of the General Council, 22 March 1947.
123 *Cycling*, 12 August 1954, p. 185.
124 MSS.204/1/1/40, British Cycle and Motor Cycle Industries Association, Minutes of the Joint Bicycle Publicity Committee, 3 September, 22 October 1969.
125 Thomson, *Lost Freedom*, p. 152.
126 MSS.328/N/12, 'Cycleways for Peterborough', File: TRRL – Transport and Road Research Laboratory.
127 https://www.youtube.com/watch?v=JlEm4tEodhU (accessed 15 July 2018).
128 https://www.youtube.com/watch?v=-lEnGQxP8zs (accessed 15 July 2018).

Chapter 8

1 *Observer*, 29 July 2012. I am grateful to Martin Polley for this reference. https://netpol.org/2012/07/28/mass-arrests-of-critical-mass-cyclists/ (accessed 27 October 2016).
2 Hamer, *Wheels Within Wheels*, pp. 58–9.

3 See Nicholas Robinson, 'Major Government, Minor Change: The Politics of Transport, 1990-1997' (Unpublished PhD: University of Warwick, 1998). Members of cycling campaigns also joined the protests. *New Cyclist*, April 1992, p. 10.
4 Addison, *No Turning Back*, pp. 409–10.
5 Emily Robinson, Camilla Schofield, Florence Sutcliffe-Braithwaite and Natalie Thomlinson, 'Telling Stories about Post-war Britain: Popular Individualism and the "Crisis" of the 1970s', *Twentieth Century British History*, vol. 28, no. 2 (2017), pp. 268–304.
6 Hamer, *Wheels Within Wheels*, chapter 11.
7 *Guardian*, 14 October 1988, p. 23; 20 February 1989, p. 20; 9 November 1989, p. 20.
8 *New Cyclist*, March/April 1991, p. 57.
9 Dave Horton, 'Environmentalism and the Bicycle', in Dave Horton, Paul Rosen and Peter Cox (eds), *Cycling and Society* (Aldershot: Ashgate, 2007), pp. 43–4.
10 Matthew Hilton, 'Politics Is Ordinary: Non-governmental Organisations and Political Participation in Contemporary Britain', *Twentieth Century British History*, vol. 22, no. 2 (2011), p. 235.
11 Ibid., p. 232.
12 Matthew Hilton, James McKay, Nicholas Crowson and Jean-Francois Mouhot, '"The Big Society": Civic Participation and the State in Modern Britain',
http://www.historyandpolicy.org/papers/policy-paper-103.html (accessed 23 June 2010).
13 Hilton, 'Politics Is Ordinary', p. 232.
14 Horton, 'Environmentalism and the Bicycle', p. 43.
15 https://www.theguardian.com/environment/2017/mar/18/torrey-canyon-disaster-uk-worst-ever-oil-spill-50tha-anniversary (accessed 18 March 2017).
16 *Guardian*, 24 April 1970, p. 2; http://www.earthday.org/about/the-history-of-earth-day/ (accessed 3 April 2017).
17 Thomas L. Blair, 'Friends of the Earth', in John Barr (ed.), *The Environmental Handbook: Action guide for the UK* (London: Friends of the Earth, 1971), p. 325.
18 Hilton, 'Politics Is Ordinary', p. 231.
19 Ibid., p. 239, Figure 3.
20 MSS.328/N/12, Letter from Schools Eco-Action Group to Claxton, 2 July 1973, Schools Eco-Action Group Manifesto, File: Transport.
21 *The Economist*, 13 August 1994, p. 50.
22 *New Cyclist*, Summer 1990, p. 61.
23 Barr (ed.), *The Environmental Handbook*, p. 221.
24 Horton, 'Environmentalism and the Bicycle', pp. 43–4.
25 King, 'Equal Rights for Bikes', pp. 280–2.

26 For example, MSS.328/N/12, Philip Brachi, 'The Bicycle as Urban Transport', May 1973, File: Transport.
27 MSS.328/N/12, *Daily Telegraph*, 5 February 1974, File: Transport; https://www.youtube.com/watch?v=QXT83ne4fHM (accessed 18 December 2018).
28 *New Cyclist*, June 1992, p. 75.
29 In 1993 its membership stood at around 40,000. *New Cyclist*, January 1993, p. 22.
30 MSS.328/N107/1, Don Mathew.
31 Hilton, 'Politics Is Ordinary', pp. 253–6.
32 MSS.328/N/12, 'Bikeways in Urban Areas', *London Topics*, March 1974, File: Transport.
33 Terence Bendixson, 'The Return of the Bicycle', *New Society*, 12 June 1975, p. 652.
34 MSS.328/N/12, 'Cycleways for Peterborough', File: TRRL – Transport and Road Research Laboratory.
35 MSS.328/N/12, 'The Way to Cycle: Middlesbrough Cycleways', File: TRRL – Transport and Road Research Laboratory.
36 MSS.328/N/12, H. F. Wallis, 'Has the Age of the Bicycle Returned?', *Municipal Review*, December 1973, File: Transport.
37 MSS.328/N/12, Philip Brachi, 'The Bicycle as Urban Transport', May 1973, p. 5, File: Transport.
38 *New Cyclist*, Spring 1989, p. 50; June 1992, p. 75.
39 *New Cyclist*, March 1992, pp. 49–55; May 1992, p. 33.
40 *New Cyclist*, August 1992, pp. 8–9.
41 *New Cyclist*, January 1993, p. 38.
42 For example, MSS.328/NL/FOTE, Friends of the Earth, 'Bike Path Special', *Bicycles Bulletin*, September/ October 1982; 'The GLC Cycle Project Team', *Bicycles Bulletin*, April/May/June 1985; MSS.328/N107/3, 'Government launches National Cycling Strategy', *Cycle-Wise*, Summer 1996, no. 9. Cycle-Wise was first published in 1994 and acted as an information service for local authorities by the Bicycle Association.
43 *New Cyclist*, July/August 1991, pp. 52–3; February 1993, p. 11.
44 See Susan Blickstein and Susan Hanson, 'Critical Mass: Forging a Politics of Sustainable Mobility in the Information Age', *Transportation*, vol. 28 (2001), pp. 347–62.
45 https://www.cyclinguk.org/local-campaigners/ctc-local-campaigners-information-kit/campaigning-skills-and-tactics/tactics-an-11 (accessed 21 February 2019).
46 *New Cyclist*, Summer 1988, p. 52. The interim report was produced by the European Cyclists' Federation and titled, *A comparison and evaluation of policy provision for cyclists in Europe*.
47 *Guardian*, 26 November 2016. https://www.theguardian.com/uk-news/davehillblog/2016/nov/26/london-cycling-and-the-by-chance-success-of-amsterdam (accessed 26 November 2016).

48 *New Cyclist*, Spring 1989, p. 43; August 1992, p. 8.
49 *Guardian*, 26 November 2016. https://www.theguardian.com/uk-news/davehillblog/2016/nov/26/london-cycling-and-the-by-chance-success-of-amsterdam (accessed 26 November 2016).
50 *New Cyclist*, April 1992, pp. 40–4.
51 *Guardian*, 11 July 1996, p. 7.
52 *New Cyclist*, Autumn 1990, p. 65.
53 *New Cyclist*, July/August 1991, p. 77.
54 Barker and Gerhold, *Rise and Rise*, p. 74.
55 *The Times*, 19 May 1989, p. 17; https://assets.publishing.service.gov.uk/government/uploads/system/uploads/attachment_data/file/8995/vehicles-summary.pdf (accessed 21 February 2019).
56 Barker and Gerhold, *Rise and Rise*, pp. 71–4.
57 *The Times*, 13 May 1989, p. 5.
58 *The Times*, 26 September 1989, p. 6.
59 *The Times*, 19 May 1989, p. 33.
60 *Guardian*, 19 May 1989, p. 22; *The Times*, 19 May 1989, p. 17.
61 MSS.328/N107/1, Don Mathew, 'Personal Biography'.
62 Robinson, 'Major Government, Minor Change', p. 47.
63 Ibid., chapter 4.
64 *New Cyclist*, Spring 1989, p. 23.
65 *New Cyclist*, May/June 1991, p. 85.
66 *New Cyclist*, September/October 1991, p. 23.
67 *New Cyclist*, Summer 1988, p. 52.
68 *New Cyclist*, Winter 1988, p. 35.
69 *New Cyclist*, April 1992, pp. 33–4.
70 *New Cyclist*, March 1992, p. 8.
71 https://fullfact.org/health/spending-english-nhs/ (accessed 21 February 2019).
72 *New Cyclist*, February 1993, p. 5.
73 Pete Alcock, 'Voluntary Action, New Labour and the "third sector"', in Matthew Hilton and James McKay (eds), *The Ages of Voluntarism: How we got to the Big Society* (Oxford: British Academy, 2011), pp. 158–79.
74 Ironically, the forum was chaired by Steve Norris who had worked previously selling cars and in 1997 was appointed head of the Road Haulage Federation on a £100,000 salary. Norris later stood for London mayor in 2000; one part of his manifesto was to ban lorries from the capital in the daytime. *Guardian*, 26 February 2000, section B, pp. 6–9.
75 In 2011 the Conservative–Liberal coalition abolished it.
76 http://webarchive.nationalarchives.gov.uk/20100409000639/http://www.dft.gov.uk/cyclingengland/who-we-are/our-board/ (accessed 22 August 2017).

77 http://webarchive.nationalarchives.gov.uk/20100408101934/http://www.dft.gov.uk/cyclingengland/who-we-are/ (accessed 22 August 2017).

78 At that time the standard amount of funding for cycling initiatives in English local authorities was around £1 per citizen, per year. In contrast, Dutch towns such as Amsterdam spent around £10–20 per year. Cycling City and Cycling Towns had a total budget of around £16 per citizen per year with match funding. http://webarchive.nationalarchives.gov.uk/20100408101526/http://www.dft.gov.uk/cyclingengland/cycling-cities-towns/ (accessed 23 August 2017).

79 Matt Seaton, *Two Wheels: Thoughts from the Bike Lane* (London: Guardian Books, 2007), pp. 207–14.

80 Seaton, *Two Wheels*, p. 213; John Urry, 'Social Engineering: Responding to Ken Livingstone', *Planning, Theory & Practice*, vol. 5, no. 4 (2004), pp. 506–9.

81 http://webarchive.nationalarchives.gov.uk/20100408101721/http://www.dft.gov.uk/cyclingengland/bikeability/ (accessed 23 August 2017).

82 Virginia Berridge, *Health and Society in Britain since 1939* (Cambridge: Cambridge University Press, 1999), p. 57.

83 Ibid.

84 *Guardian*, 11 April 2003, p. 25.

85 'Bicycles – UK – February 2013: Market Drivers', http://academic.mintel.com/display/655181/ (accessed 19 July 2017).

86 MSS.328/NL/FOTE, *Bicycles Bulletin*, September/ October 1982, p. 3.

87 Ibid., p. 2.

88 Ibid., p. 3, 15.

89 *New Cyclist*, January 1993, p. 51.

90 *New Cyclist*, Summer 1989, pp. 38–9.

91 *New Cyclist*, Spring 1989, p. 21.

92 Matthew Hilton and James McKay, 'The Ages of Voluntarism: An Introduction', in Matthew Hilton and James McKay (eds), *The Ages of Voluntarism: How We Got to the Big Society* (Oxford: British Academy, 2011), p. 16; Alcock, 'Voluntary Action', p. 160; Rachel Aldred, 'Governing Transport from Welfare State to Hollow State: The Case of Cycling in the UK', *Transport Policy*, vol. 23 (2012), pp. 95–102.

93 *Daily Mail*, 11 September 1995.

94 *Daily Mail*, 28 July 1997, p. 44.

95 *Daily Mail*, 5 July 1997, p. 60; 22 June 2000, p. 34.

96 'Bicycles – UK – February 2013: Market Drivers', http://academic.mintel.com/display/655181/ (accessed 19 July 2017).

97 http://apps.charitycommission.gov.uk/Accounts/Ends50/0000326550_AC_20130331_E_C.PDF (accessed 15 August 2017). See also, Anna Goodman, Shannon Sahlqvist and David Ogilvie, 'Who Uses New Walking and Cycling Infrastructure and How? Longitudinal Results from the UK iConnect Study', *Preventive Medicine*, vol. 57 (2013), pp. 518–24.

98 http://apps.charitycommission.gov.uk/Accounts/Ends50/0000326550_AC_20130331_E_C.PDF (accessed 15 August 2017).

99 'Bicycles – UK – February 2013: Market Drivers', http://academic.mintel.com/display/655181/ (accessed 19 July 2017).
100 See for example, https://onthelevelblog.wordpress.com/2009/01/26/the-problem-with-sustrans-how-a-grassroots-phenomenon-has-turned-into-a-private-unaccountable-corporation/ (accessed 26 September 2016).
101 Aldred, 'Governing Transport', pp. 95–102.
102 *Daily Mail*, 3 January 1987, p. 5.
103 MSS.328/C/1/11/1, Cyclists' Touring Club, Town and Countryside Committee, 1981-2, Minutes 5 September 1981.
104 *Guardian*, 10 June 2002, p. D4.
105 'Wheel Ambition: Cycling in London', *Economist*, 7 February 2016.
106 Rachel Herring, 'Governance, Sport and The City: Realising Mega Sporting Events in London' (Unpublished PhD: Middlesex University, 2006), p. 111, 274, 277.
107 *Guardian*, 26 February 2000, section B, p. 6.
108 Livingstone was readmitted to the Labour Party in 2005, after being expelled in 2000 for standing against the official Labour candidate, Frank Dobson.
109 Ken Livingstone, 'The Challenge of Driving through Change: Introducing Congestion Charging in Central London', *Planning Theory & Practice*, vol. 5, no. 4 (2004), pp. 490–8.
110 The Cyclists' Public Affairs Group (C-PAG) was the public policy group of the Cycle Campaign Network, CTC and London Cycling Campaign and represented cycle users nationwide. MSS.328/N107/3, Transport Select Committee, 24 April 1996, Risk Reduction for Vulnerable Road Users, Memorandum by the Cyclists' Public Affairs Group.
111 http://news.bbc.co.uk/1/hi/england/london/3915349.stm (accessed 18 August 2017).
112 https://www.standard.co.uk/news/london-bike-park-one-of-the-safest-in-world-6863966.html (accessed 18 August 2017).
113 https://tfl.gov.uk/info-for/media/press-releases/2004/september/cycling-safety-comes-first-in-childrens-competition (accessed 18 August 2017).
114 http://rachelaldred.org/wp-content/uploads/2012/10/cycling-review1.pdf (accessed 21 February 2019).
115 Ibid.
116 *Guardian*, 7 November 2015, http://www.theguardian.com/uk-news/davehillblog/2015/nov/07/waltham-forest-mini-holland-row-politics-protests-and-house-prices (accessed 7 November 2015).
117 'Bicycles – UK – February 2013: Market Drivers', http://academic.mintel.com/display/655181/ (accessed 19 July 2017).
118 *New Cyclist*, Spring 1990, p. 51.
119 Richard Ballantine, *Richard's Bicycle Book: A Manual of Bicycle Maintenance and Enjoyment* (London: Pan, 1972, 1933 edition), p. 18.
120 *Guardian*, 7 June 2013.

121 Ballantine, *Richard's Bicycle Book*, p. 19.
122 *New Cyclist*, July 1992, p. 27.
123 *New Cyclist*, June 1992, p. 27.
124 *New Cyclist*, Summer 1988, p. 8.
125 *New Cyclist*, Autumn 1989, p. 23.
126 Tom Bogdanowiz, 'Mountain Bikes – From Insider Cult to Centre Stage', in Tom Bogdanowiz (ed.), *The Off-Road Bicycle Book*, 3rd edn (Hawes: Leading Edge, 1992), pp. 3–4.
127 Rosen, *Framing Production*, p. 133.
128 *New Cyclist*, Spring 1990, p. 77. In 1989, more than 134,000 cycles were stolen in Britain; 15,219 (11.31 per cent) were found. Two years later over 210,000 were stolen. More than 20,000 (worth over £4 million) were from Greater London. *New Cyclist*, March/April 1991, p. 63; July 1992, p. 44.
129 *New Cyclist*, March 1992, pp. 56–65.
130 Guido Buenstorf, 'Designing Clunkers: Demand-Side Innovation and the Early History of the Mountain Bike', in J. S. Metcalfe and U. Cantner (eds), *Change, Transformation and Development* (Heidelberg: Physica, 2003), pp. 53–70.
131 Rosen, *Framing Production*, pp. 133–4.
132 *New Cyclist*, Spring 1989, p. 16.
133 *New Cyclist*, Autumn 1990, p. 69.
134 *New Cyclist*, Spring 1988, p. 14.
135 *New Cyclist*, Summer 1988, pp. 38–9. By 1988 there were over 40 companies employing cycle messengers.
136 *Daily Mail*, 10 March 1997, p. 45. Cyclists had to give right of way to pedestrians and horses.
137 *New Cyclist*, Spring 1989, p. 36.
138 Tony Hadland, 'Raleigh UK in the Last Quarter of the Twentieth Century', in *International Cycling History Conferences Proceedings*, No. 11, Osaka, 2000, p. 63-71.
139 *New Cyclist*, February 1993, p. 57.
140 Cox, 'Activism and Market Innovation'.
141 *New Cyclist*, Summer 1990, p. 16; May 1992, pp. 50–1.
142 *New Cyclist*, June 1992, p. 7.
143 *New Cyclist*, Winter 1990, p. 81. In 1992 the United States Cycling Federation initially allowed recumbents to race against conventional bicycles, but then changed its mind. *New Cyclist*, April 1992, p. 9; August 1992, p. 9.
144 Peter Cox with Frederick Van De Walle, 'Bicycles Don't Evolve: Velomobiles and the Modelling of Transport Technologies', in Dave Horton, Paul Rosen and Peter Cox (eds), *Cycling and Society* (Aldershot: Ashgate, 2007), p. 116.
145 *New Cyclist*, Winter 1989/90, p. 9; Spring 1990, p. 33.
146 *New Cyclist*, Autumn 1989, p. 9.

147 *New Cyclist*, May/June 1991, p. 25.
148 *New Cyclist*, March 1992, p. 115.
149 Cox, 'Activism and Market Innovation'. In 2017, while the permaculture side of their business survived, the cycling business did not. https://www.permaculture.org.uk/education/course/permaculture-design-course-2016-10-17 (accessed 19 May 2017).

Chapter 9

1 https://www.cyclingweekly.com/news/boris-bike-24-hours-challenge-18906 (accessed 28 February 2019).
2 https://www.youtube.com/watch?v=HUWCeAzkc2Q (accessed 28 February 2019).
3 For recent statistics on cycling use and patterns see https://www.cyclinguk.org/statistics
4 MSS.328/N/12, 'Cycle use in Britain', Symposium on Cycling as a mode of transport, Transport and Road Research Laboratory, 25 October 1978, File: TRRL – Transport and Road Research Laboratory; 'Two Wheels in Place of Four', Radio London, 19 October 1973.
5 *New Cyclist*, August 1992, p. 40.
6 http://www.cyclinguk.org/resources/cycling-uk-cycling-statistics (accessed 3 September 2017).
7 'BBC News – Cycling Industry Gives Economy £3bn Boost', 22 August 2011, http://www.bbc.co.uk/news/uk-14610857?print=true (accessed 26 August 2013).
8 'Bicycle Accessories – Executive Summary', *Mintel*, June 2015.
9 *New Cyclist*, August 1992, p. 40.
10 http://www.cyclinguk.org/article/campaigns-guide/cycling-levels-in-european-countries (accessed 3 September 2017).
11 http://www.cyclinguk.org/resources/cycling-uk-cycling-statistics (accessed 3 September 2017); Aldred, 'Governing Transport', p. 97, Table 1; MSS.328/N/12, 'Cycle use in Britain', Symposium on Cycling as a mode of transport, Transport and Road Research Laboratory, 25 October 1978, File: TRRL – Transport and Road Research Laboratory.
12 MSS.328/BCF/1/1/2, BCF Annual Meeting of the National Council, 11–12 December 1971, Finance and Management Committee Report.
13 MSS.328/BCF/1/1/2, BCF Annual Meeting of the National Council, 13–14 December 1980, Finance and Management Committee Report.
14 Leicester staged the track championships on both occasions at its now defunct Saffron Lane track. In 1970 the road races were at nearby Mallory Park, while in 1982 they took place at Goodwood in Sussex.
15 'Bicycles – UK – January 2008: Internal Market Environment', http://academic.mintel.com/display/317739/ (accessed 8 July 2017).

16 'Is British Success Inspiring a Generation of Cyclists?', http://academic.mint el.com/display/636751/ (accessed 1 July 2017).
17 'Bicycles – UK – February 2013: Market Drivers', http://academic.mintel.com/display/655181/ (accessed 19 July 2017).
18 https://www.britishcycling.org.uk/about/article/20160815-about-bc-news-British-Cycling-reaches-125-000-members-milestone-0 (accessed 3 September 2017).
19 'Bicycles – UK – February 2013: Market Drivers', http://academic.mintel.com/display/655181/ (accessed 19 July 2017).
20 Arthur McIvor, *Working Lives: Work in Britain Since 1945* (Basingstoke: Palgrave, 2013), p. 2.
21 Malcolm Smith and Fiona Browne, *General Household Survey 1990* (London: HMSO, 1992), Table 2.10, p. 23.
22 McIvor, *Working Lives*, pp. 1–2, 9–20.
23 *New Cyclist*, July/August 1991, Advertising Sheet. *New Cyclist* had various reincarnations. In 1994 it became *Cycling Today* and after further name changes ceased publication in 2000. For 1990, according to the Audit Bureau of Circulation it sold an average of 23,282 per issue. *New Cyclist*, May/June 1991, p. 7; June 1992, p. 7.
24 Richard Holt and Tony Mason, *Sport in Britain 1945-2000* (Oxford: Blackwells, 2000), p. 8.
25 A. J. Veal, *Sport and Recreation in England and Wales: An Analysis of Adult Participation Patterns in 1977* (Birmingham: University of Birmingham, 1979). Cycling was one of only five activities where the other non-manual group (37 per cent) was the most predominant.
26 Ibid., p. 47.
27 Anon., *Cycling to the Countryside: Annex to Report to the Countryside Commission, March 1978*, Dartington Amenity, Research Trust, June 1977, Table 9.
28 Each survey used different methodologies, so results can only be indicative rather than conclusive.
29 Smith and Browne, *General Household Survey 1990*, Table 8.10, p. 173.
30 *New Cyclist*, July/August 1991, Advertising Sheet.
31 *Guardian*, 1 July 2015.
32 'Bicycles – UK – November 2005: Consumer Attitudes and Typologies', http://academic.mintel.com/display/190261/ (accessed 7 July 2017).
33 'Bicycles – UK – January 2008: Attitudes Towards Cycling', http://academic.mintel.com/display/317750/ (accessed 8 July 2017).
34 Rebecca Steinbach, Judith Green, Jessica Datta and Phil Edwards, 'Cycling and the City: A Case Study of How Gendered, Ethnic and Class Identities can Shape Healthy Transport Choices', *Social Science & Medicine*, vol. 72, no. 7 (2011), pp. 1123–30.
35 It first published a brief report on cycling in 1995, before a second in 2001 and then producing four between 2003 and 2010. From 2012 there was a report every year up to 2017.

36 'Bicycles – UK – February 2013: Frequency of Riding a Bicycle', http://academic.mintel.com/display/655189/ (accessed 19 July 2017).
37 Anon., *City Cycling: London* (London: Thames and Hudson, 2013), pp. 6–7.
38 Seaton, *Two Wheels*, p. 142.
39 *New Cyclist*, Summer 1989, p. 43.
40 *New Cyclist*, Autumn 1988, p. 4.
41 Steinbach et al., 'Cycling and the City', pp. 1123–30.
42 *Daily Telegraph*, 21 September 2012.
43 https://theconversation.com/the-unbearable-whiteness-of-cycling-76256 (accessed 24 April 2017).
44 Information supplied by Deepa Carter.
45 MSS.328/N7/1/36, Cyclists' Touring Club, *passim*.
46 Holt and Mason, *Sport in Britain*, pp. 166–7.
47 McIvor, *Working Lives*, pp. 1–2.
48 For a discussion over the impact of the Wolfenden Report, see Kevin Jefferys, *Sport and Politics in Modern Britain: The Road to 2012* (London: Palgrave, 2012), pp. 53–76.
49 Matthew Hilton, 'The Fable of the Sheep, or, Private Virtues, Public Vices: The Consumer Revolution of the Twentieth Century', *Past and Present*, No. 174 (2002), p. 228.
50 Frank Mort, *Cultures of Consumption: Masculinities and Social Space in Late Twentieth-Century Britain* (London: Routledge, 1996).
51 In 1973 out of 850,000 cycles sold: 297,500 were adult machines; 552,500 children machines. MSS.328/N/12, Eric Claxton, 'Cycling in Wandsworth, 1974-75', Wandsworth Council, Box 6.
52 Tony Hadland, 'Raleigh UK', p. 64.
53 *The Times*, 14 March 1986, p. 10.
54 Herlihy, *Bicycle*, p. 400; Pryor Dodge, *The Bicycle* (New York: Flanmarion, 1996), pp. 200–1; *New Cyclist*, Autumn 1988, p. 34.
55 'BBC News – Cycling Industry Gives Economy £3bn Boost', 22 August 2011, http://www.bbc.co.uk/news/uk-14610857?print=true (accessed 26 August 2013). Since 2000, the UK bicycle market has been almost wholly supplied by overseas production, with UK production (which had been 1.2 million as recently as 2000) standing at 50,000 to 60,000 split by 2015, mainly between Brompton, Moulton and Pashley. 'Bicycles – UK – February 2013: Companies and Products', http://academic.mintel.com/display/655186/ (accessed 19 July 2017).
56 'Is British Success Inspiring a Generation of Cyclists?', http://academic.mintel.com/display/636751/ (accessed 1 July 2017).
57 'The Motor Industry: Statistics and Policy', Briefing Paper, Number 00611, House of Commons Library, 11 April 2017.
58 'Bicycles – UK – February 2013: Executive Summary', http://academic.mintel.com/display/655178 (accessed 19 July 2017); 'Bicycles – UK – March

2015: Type of Bicycle Ridden', http://academic.mintel.com/display/733992/?highlight#hit1 (accessed 1 July 2017).
59 'Bicycles – UK – February 2013: Executive Summary', http://academic.mintel.com/display/655178/ (accessed 19 July 2017).
60 'Bicycles – UK – February 2013: Retailer Consideration', http://academic.mintel.com/display/655191/ (accessed 19 July 2017).
61 'Bicycle Accessories – UK – June 2015: Executive Summary'.
62 *New Cyclist*, July 1992, p. 77.
63 Ibid., pp. 44–9.
64 *Observer*, 4 May 2014; *Guardian* 1 May 2017.
65 'Selling the Cycling Dream', 15 November 2007', http://academic.mintel.com/display/307158/ (accessed 07/07/2017).
66 'Bicycles – UK – June 2010: Internal Market Environment', http://academic.mintel.com/display/532965/ (accessed 01 July 2017); http://www.tweedrun.com/about/ (accessed 1 July 2017).
67 http://www.guardian.co.uk/environment/bike-blog/2013/jun/10/penny-farthings-making-comeback (accessed 10 June 2013).
68 'Bicycles – UK – June 2010: Internal Market Environment', http://academic.mintel.com/display/532965/ (accessed 01/07/2017).
69 Sportives are defined as amateur organized leisure rides of a specific distance, usually anything between 60 kilometres and 250 kilometres. The rides are often held in areas of outstanding natural beauty and enable people to explore a new area while at the same time tackling a challenging cycling route. 'Bicycles – UK – February 2013: Market Drivers', http://academic.mintel.com/display/655181/ (accessed 19 July 2017); 'Bicycles, Executive Summary – UK – March 2012', Mintel.
70 *New Cyclist*, September/October 1991, p. I, 'Guide to Charities' supplement'.
71 *New Cyclist*, June 1992, p. 77.
72 *New Cyclist*, July 1992, p. 11; August 1992, pp. 51–61. The largest annual bicycle ride in the world could be found in Montreal with 40,000 participants. The Tour de L'Ile – because the city is built on an island – had started in 1985 with 3,500 cyclists. The event allowed cyclists to use 60 kilometres of open, traffic-free road. *New Cyclist*, September/October 1991, pp. 81–2.
73 *New Cyclist*, January 1993, p. 22.
74 *New Cyclist*, May 1992, p. 29.
75 *Guardian*, 1 August 2016.
76 *New Cyclist*, July/August 1991, pp. 47–51.
77 'Bicycle Accessories – UK – 2015', http://academic.mintel.com/display/741921/?highlight (accessed 7 July 2017).
78 'Bicycles – UK – June 2010: Broader Market Environment', http://academic.mintel.com/display/532966/ (accessed 1 July 2017).

79 http://www.bbc.co.uk/sport/38884801 (accessed 20 March 2017); http://www.cyclingweekly.com/news/latest-news/14-per-cent-regular-cyclists-admit-taking-steroids-320653 (accessed 20 March 2017).
80 *New Cyclist*, October 1992, p. 7.
81 *New Cyclist*, Spring 1990, p. 21.
82 The couple were Chris and Rachael Mellor, who completed their 25,000 journey in 25 months. *New Cyclist*, October 1992, p. 72.
83 In 2012, for example, Bradley Wiggins' autobiography *My Time* (London: Yellow Jersey, 2012) placed 18th on Amazon's Best Sellers list. At number 71 was Tyler Hamilton's confessional, *The Secret Race: Inside the Hidden World of the Tour de France: Doping, Cover-Ups, and Winning at All Costs* (London: Bantam Press, 2012).
84 Cited in Jo Gill, 'Introduction', in Jo Gill (ed.), *Modern Confessional Writing: New Critical Essays* (London: Routledge, 2006), p. 6.
85 *New Cyclist*, January/February 1992, p. 28.
86 Ned Boulting, *How I Won the Yellow Jumper: Dispatches from the Tour de France* (London: Yellow Jersey Press, 2011), p. ix.
87 Robert Penn, *It's All about the Bike: The Pursuit of Happiness on Two Wheels* (London: Penguin, 2011), pp. 11–12.
88 Fotheringham, *Put Me Back On My Bike: In Search of Tom Simpson* (London: Yellow Jersey Press, 2002).
89 Carter, *Medicine, Sport and the Body*, p. 105.
90 For a broader discussion on doping in sport, see Paul Dimeo, *A History of Drug Use in Sport 1876–1976: Beyond Good and Evil* (London: Routledge, 2007).
91 'Bicycles – UK – February 2013: Market Drivers', http://academic.mintel.com/display/655181/ (accessed 19 July 2017).
92 For example, *Daily Mail*, 10 April 1999, p. 60; 8 April 2000, pp. 56–57; 22 June 2000, p. 34.
93 *Daily Mail*, 8 April 1997, p. 10.
94 *Daily Mail*, 13 January 1998, p. 6.
95 'Bicycles – UK – November 2005', http://academic.mintel.com/display/190253/ (accessed 1 July 2017).
96 Ibid.
97 https://www.bbc.co.uk/news/uk-wales-south-west-wales-36521289 (accessed 9 March 2019).
98 This section is largely based on https://www.ukbmxhistory.com (accessed 26 March 2019).
99 Mark Dyreson, 'World Harmony or an Athletic "Clash of Civilizations"? The Beijing Olympic Spectacle, BMX Bicycles and the American Contours of Globalisation', *The International Journal of the History of Sport*, vol. 29, no. 9 (2012), p. 1232.

100 https://www.ukbmxhistory.com/my-ukbmx-history-by-bill-baggs/ (accessed 26 March 2019).
101 Herlihy, *Bicycle*, p. 400; Dodge, *The Bicycle*, pp. 200–1; *New Cyclist*, Autumn 1988, p. 34.
102 Wade Nelson, 'Reading Cycles: The Culture of BMX Freestyle' (Unpublished PhD: McGill University, 2006), pp. 65–9.
103 Thomson, *Lost Freedom*, pp. 142–6.
104 Richard Moore, *Heroes, Villains and Velodromes: Chris Hoy and Britain's Track Cycling Revolution* (London: Harper Collins, 2008), chapter 1.
105 *Guardian*, 11 March 2016.
106 For a version of the amalgamation and an insight into the politics of BMX, see https://www.ukbmxhistory.com/my-ukbmx-history-by-bill-baggs/ (accessed 26 March 2019).
107 Nelson, 'Reading Cycles', p. 58; Wade Nelson, 'The Historical Mediatization of BMX-Freestyle Cycling', *Sport in Society*, vol. 13, nos. 7–8 (2010), pp. 1152–69.
108 For a historical example of this relationship see Stephen Hardy, 'Polo at the Rinks: Shaping Markets for Ice Hockey in America 1880-1900', *Journal of Sport History*, vol. 33, no. 2 (2006), pp. 157–74 and for an overview, see Porter, 'Entrepreneurship'.
109 Other teams included Edwardes, Youngs, Hotshot-Redline, Shenpar-JMC/Powerlite and then Cyclecraft, Alans-Robinson/Torker and Bunneys-GT. https://www.ukbmxhistory.com/rise1980/ (accessed 26 March 2019).
110 https://www.ukbmxhistory.com/the-early-years/ (accessed 26 March 2019).
111 Belinda Wheaton, 'Introducing the Consumption and Representation of Lifestyle Sports', *Sport in Society*, vol. 13, nos. 7–8 (2010), p. 1059.
112 Ibid., p. 1060.
113 BMX Freestyle was included in the Tokyo 2020 Olympics.
114 *New Cyclist*, September/October 1991, p. 71.
115 Rebecca Madgin, David Webb, Pollyanna Ruiz and Tim Snelson, 'Resisting Relocation and Reconceptualising Authenticity – The Experiential and Emotional Values of the Southbank Undercroft, London, UK', *International Journal of Heritage Studies*, vol. 24, no. 6 (2018), pp. 585–98.
116 Robert D. Putnam, 'Bowling Alone: America's Declining Social Capital', *Journal of Democracy* vol. 6 (January 1995), pp. 65–78.
117 https://www.youtube.com/watch?v=e0ZWhI7yrjs (accessed 10 March 2019).
118 https://www.youtube.com/watch?v=ycpRPIDwTr8 (accessed 29 March 2019)..
119 Interview with Shaun Carter, 15 March 2019.

Chapter 10

1 http://news.bbc.co.uk/sport1/hi/olympics2000/cycling/927385.stm (accessed 11 March 2019).

2   Quoted in Moore, *Heroes*, p. 132.
3   Collins, *Sport in Capitalist Society*, p. 120.
4   MSS.328/BCF/1/1/1-2, British Cycling Federation, *passim*.
5   Holt and Mason, *Sport in Britain*, p. 83; MSS.328/BCF/1/1/2, British Cycling Federation, Annual Meeting of the National Council, 13 December 1970. The 62 were those registered with the British Cycling Federation; the 1996 figure may have included cyclists from other disciplines. In 1970 there were a total of 5,121 riders who held a BCF racing licence, which included Men's amateur – 4,647; Professional – 62; Scottish Cycling Union – 354, plus 58 female riders.
6   In 2017 there were 17 British cyclists riding for World Tour teams.
7   Quoted in Tony Mason, *Only a Game? Sport in the Modern World* (Cambridge: Cambridge University Press), p. 42.
8   MSS.328/BCF/1/1-4, *passim*. It is perhaps worth noting that in 1957 the number of BLRC racing licences awarded was alone around 4,700. MSS.328/BLRC/1/1/3, BLRC NEC Minutes, 13 October 1957.
9   Minutes of Committee Meeting, 12 December 1970, http://www.anfieldbc.co.uk/minutes/m_1970.pdf (accessed 20 March 2019).
10 Nicholson, *The Professionals*, p. 104. It was only in 1964 that the rule not allowing any publicizing of time trials was abolished. Ibid., p. 102.
11 Ibid., p. 103.
12 Russell, 'Mum's the Word', p. 788.
13 Ibid., pp. 787–606.
14 Burton, *Personal Best*, p. 44.
15 In 1966 there was another failed attempt at amalgamation between the two. Instead, both the BCF and RTTC, along with the BCA and CTC, joined the newly formed Cycling Council of GB. MSS.328/BCF/1/1/2, BCF Annual Meeting of the National Council, 10 December 1966; BCF Annual Meeting of the National Council, 9 December 1967.
16 MSS.328/BCF/1/1/1, BCF, Annual Meeting of the National Council, 10 December 1960; MSS.328/BCF/1/1/1, BCF Annual Meeting of the National Council, 8 December 1962.
17 MSS.328/BCF/1/1/1, BCF Annual Meeting of the National Council, 8 December 1962; MSS.328/BCF/1/1/4, BCF Annual Meeting of the National Council, 13-14 December 1980. Four clubs received the bare minimum sponsorship of £250; half received up to £500.
18 *Observer*, 17 September 1967, p. 14.
19 MSS.204/1/1/37, British Cycle and Motor Cycle Industries Association, Joint Bicycle Publicity Committee Minutes, 15 March 1967.
20 Information via BBC Genome.
21 *World Sports*, July 1965, pp. 42–3.
22 BBC, *Death on the Mountain: The Story of Tom Simpson* (2005).
23 Fotheringham, *Put Me Back On My Bike*, p. 72.
24 The programme was first shown in July then repeated in August.

25 Fotheringham's *Put Me Back On My Bike*, p. 130.
26 See Benjamin D. Brewer, 'Commercialization in Professional Cycling 1950–2001: Institutional Transformations and the Rationalization of "Doping"', *Sociology of Sport Journal*, vol. 19 (2002), pp. 276–301.
27 For a fuller explanation see Eric Reed, *Selling the Yellow Jersey: The Tour de France in the Global Era* (Chicago: University of Chicago Press, 2015), pp. 121–4.
28 It later led to the rise of Brittany Ferries.
29 *Observer*, 30 June 1974, p. 23; *The Times*, 29 June 1974, p. 14; 1 July 1974, p. 8.
30 *The Times*, 1 July 1974, p. 8.
31 There was also considerable indirect funding for sport, especially from local authorities.
32 MSS.328/BCF/1/1/1, BCF, Annual Meeting of the National Council, 17 November 1961; Annual Meeting of the National Council, 7 December 1963. In 1964 the BCF received £800, increasing to £1,000 in 1965 to cover administration and coaching. In 1964 the BCF also received £500 from the Foreign Office towards the cost of sending a team to the world championships in Spain in 1965. MSS.328/BCF/1/1/1, BCF Annual Meeting of the National Council, 5 December 1964, https://www.bbc.co.uk/sport/cycling/20193300 (accessed 3 November 2012).
33 MSS.328/BCF/1/1/1, BCF Annual Meeting of the National Council, 5 December 1964.
34 It rained on the day and the track events had to be postponed.
35 Jefferys, *Sport and Politics*, pp. 121–2.
36 MSS.328/BCF/1/1/2, BCF Annual Meeting of the National Council, 11 December 1965. In total, the organization budget was £186,000. *Sports Argus*, 1 August 1970, p. 7.
37 *Birmingham Daily Post*, 27 June 1968, p. 29. While the track events were held at Saffron Lane in Leicester, the road races were hosted at Mallory Park, which was used for motor racing.
38 Department for Culture, Media and Sport (DCMS)/Strategy Unit, *Game Plan: A Strategy for Improving Government's Sport and Physical Activity Objectives* (London: Cabinet Office, 2000), pp. 16–17.
39 https://www.cyclingweekly.com/news/latest-news/from-paupers-to-kings-the-lottery-funded-revolution-93603 (accessed 14 March 2019).
40 The British Cycling Federation became British Cycling in 2001 after it merged with the British Cyclo-Cross Association, the British Mountain Bike Federation, the English BMX Association and the British Cycle Speedway Council.
41 https://www.theguardian.com/sport/blog/2012/dec/17/british-cycling-other-sports-learn (accessed 14 March 2019).
42 Moore, *Heroes*, p. 2.
43 Ibid., p. 111.

44 https://www.independent.co.uk/sport/general/others/cycle-of-success-how-britains-cyclists-won-the-lottery-800241.html (accessed 14 March 2019).
45 Carter, *Medicine, Sport and the Body*, chapter 4.
46 Ibid., chapter 5; Brewer, 'Commercialization in Professional Cycling 1950–2001', pp. 276–301.
47 Quoted on *Eurosport*, May 2019.
48 Foot, *Pedalare! Pedalare*, pp. 261–2. Moser later admitted that he underwent blood doping before his attempt.
49 Geoffrey Nicholson, *Tony Doyle: Six-Day Rider* (Huddersfield: Springfield, 1992), p. 164.
50 Chris Sidwells, *The Long Race to Glory: How the British Came to Rule the Cycling World* (London Andre Deutsch, 2013), pp. 183–7, chapter 7.
51 Moore, *Heroes*, p. 106.
52 Sidwells, *The Long Race to Glory*, p. 190.
53 https://www.theguardian.com/sport/blog/2012/dec/17/british-cycling-other-sports-learn (accessed 14 March 2019).
54 Moore, *Heroes*, pp.156–63, 191–2.
55 https://www.ft.com/content/7890fdf0-ac5f-11e6-9cb3-bb8207902122 (accessed 14 March 2019).
56 Boardman had not been the first to ride the Lotus Windcheetah. Another British rider, Bryan Steel, had finished 8th in a World Cup event on the bike. Moore, *Heroes*, p. 20.
57 Sidwells, *The Long Race to Glory*, pp. 165–6; *New Cyclist*, October 1992, pp. 38–40.
58 *New Cyclist*, Spring 1988, p. 27. Monocoques were 'legalised' in 1990.
59 Another of his designs was an 'around-town' bicycle, which fitted his low-maintenance philosophy. *New Cyclist*, June 1992, pp. 35–6.
60 *New Cyclist*, October 1992, p. 40.
61 Ibid., pp. 38–40.
62 Graeme Obree, *Flying Scotsman: The Graeme Obree Story* (Edinburgh: Birlinn, 2004 edition), p. 144.
63 Obree, *Flying Scotsman*, pp. 109–13; Sidwells, *The Long Race to Glory*, p. 168.
64 Their major honours on the track were Boardman won gold in the World 4,000 metres Individual Pursuit in 1994 and 1996 and the World Road Time-Trial in 1994, also breaking the World Hour Record (in its various guises) in 1993, 1996 and 2000; Obree won gold in the World 4,000 metres Individual Pursuit in 1993 and 1995 and broke the World Hour Record (in its various guises) in 1993 and 1994. Boardman also won three stages on the Tour de France and wore the yellow jersey.
65 https://www.cyclist.co.uk/chris-boardman/59/chris-boardman-interview (accessed 19 March 2019).
66 Moore, *Heroes*, p. 143.

67 In 2017 Lewis was awarded an OBE in recognition of his contribution to the performance of British athletes over the previous three Olympics. https://www.totalsimulation.co.uk/rob-lewis-awarded-obe/ (accessed 19 March 2019).
68 https://www.cyclist.co.uk/chris-boardman/59/chris-boardman-interview (accessed 19 March 2019).
69 https://www.bbc.co.uk/news/entertainment-arts-27923596 (accessed 6 August 2019).
70 https://www.cyclinguk.org/statistics (accessed 22 March 2019).
71 https://www.independent.co.uk/environment/green-living/the-rise-of-the-female-cyclist-from-the-medal-winning-track-speedsters-to-school-run-mums-9202631.html (accessed 22 March 2019).
72 *New Cyclist*, Winter 1990–91, p. 14.
73 She was born in Stotfold, Bedfordshire, and attended St. Mary's School, Stotfold, and Etonbury School, Arelsey.
74 Max Pendleton was a member of the Nomads (Hitchin) Cycling Club. In 1965 he won the Catford CC climb, the unofficial south of England championship. https://simdoyle.files.wordpress.com/2013/07/hncc_50_years.pdf
75 Raymond Boyle and Richard Haynes, *Power Play: Sport, the Media and Popular Culture Second Edition* (Edinburgh: Edinburgh University Press, 2009), p. 131.
76 Her teammate Rebecca Romero also posed naked riding a bike in *The Times* in 2008. Boyle and Haynes, *Power Play*, p. 131.
77 Ibid.
78 Martin Polley, *Moving the Goalposts: A History of Sport and Society since 1945* (London: Routledge, 1998), p. 109.
79 https://www.theguardian.com/sport/2008/mar/02/cycling.features1 (accessed 21 March 2019).
80 For an early account of the rise of Team Sky, see Richard Moore, *Sky's the Limit: Wiggins and Cavendish: The Quest to Conquer the Tour de France* (London: Harper Collins, 2012).
81 Reed, *Selling the Yellow Jersey*, pp. 139–40.
82 Richard Holt, Alan Tomlinson and Christopher Young, 'Introduction: Sport in Europe 1950-2010, Transformation and Trends', in Alan Tomlinson, Christopher Young and Richard Holt (eds), *Sport and the Transformation of Modern Europe: States, Media and Markets 1950-2010* (London: Routledge, 2011), p. 1.
83 Dauncey, *French Cycling*, pp. 233–5.
84 The book, *LA Confidential: Lance Armstrong's Secrets* (2004) by David Walsh and Pierre Ballester, was published in France, but Armstrong successfully sued against publication in Britain. https://www.theguardian.com/media/2014/apr/20/lance-armstrong-david-walsh-drug-addled-cycling (accessed 6 March 2019).
85 This is a perspective portrayed in the film on Armstrong, *The Program* (2015). It was based on Walsh and Ballester's book, *LA Confidential*.

86 Reed, *Selling the Yellow Jersey*, pp. 140–1.
87 In 2019 Team Sky was taken over by Team Ineos, which was bankrolled by British billionaire, Jim Radcliffe.
88 https://publications.parliament.uk/pa/cm201719/cmselect/cmcumeds/366/366.pdf (accessed 25 March 2019).

Conclusion

1 https://www.theguardian.com/music/2019/jun/29/stormzy-glastonbury-review-pyramid-stage (accessed 29 June 2019).
2 Figures differed throughout the UK. https://www.cyclinguk.org/statistics (accessed 29 June 2019).
3 Anon., *The Economic Value of the Bicycle Industry and Cycling in the United Kingdom: Report to the Bicycle Association of Great Britain* (March 2017), p. 12.
4 In 2017 it was found that young people aged 16–24 and those aged 35–44 cycled more than other people, and in every age group more people cycled for recreation than utility purposes. Anon., *The Economic Value of the Bicycle Industry and Cycling in the United Kingdom*, p. 13.

BIBLIOGRAPHY

Primary sources

Archives

Modern Records Centre, University of Warwick

MSS.204/1-3, British Cycle and Motor Cycle Manufacturers and Traders Union Ltd.
MSS.328/BCF, British Cycling Federation
MSS.328/BLRC, British League of Racing Cyclists
MSS.328/BU/1-6, National Cyclists' Union
MSS.328/C, Cyclists' Touring Club
MSS.328/C/10/2/2, Amateur Bicycle Club
MSS.328/C/6/3/1, Edinburgh Amateur Bicycle Club
MSS.328/M/1333, Cycling Clubs
MSS.328/M/249, Rosslyn Ladies CC
MSS.328/N/107, Don Mathew
MSS.328/N/12, Eric Claxton
MSS.328/N/17, British League of Racing Cyclists
MSS.328/N/45, Ernest Green Papers
MSS.328/N/55, Solihull Cycling Club
MSS.328/N/57/3/1/5, Cycling Memories of Arthur Cook
MSS.328/N/7/1/1-166, Derek Roberts Collection
MSS.328/N/90, Tom Flinn Diaries
MSS.328/N/99, South Lancashire Road Club
MSS.328/N10, Alexander Josey
MSS.328/N10/6/F, Women's Road Records Association
MSS.328/NL/BL, British League of Racing Cyclists
MSS.328/NL/CTC/DA, Cyclists' Touring Club, District Associations
MSS.328/NL/CYC, *Cycling Weekly* Periodical
MSS.328/NL/FOTE, Friends of the Earth
MSS.328/RTTC, Road Time Trials Council

The National Archives, Kew, London

TNA/BT 34/1025/42907, North London Cycling and Athletic Grounds Company Ltd, Liquidation 1900.

TNA/CAB 24/245/0/0033, Road Accidents, Memorandum by the Minister of Transport, November 1933

TNA/CAB 24/254/0/0014, Cabinet Papers, Mr. Lloyd George's Memorandum On Unemployment, Plans Submitted By The Right Hon. D. Lloyd George O.M., M.P., For Utilising The Depression To Reorganise and Develop our National Resources and to Improve National Conditions, 1935

TNA/ED 113/74, National Fitness Council-Minutes, Papers and Reports. Voluntary Organisations, The National Cyclists' Union

TNA/MT 34/131, Accidents, Order of the Road, Cyclists' Touring Club and National Cyclists' Union-Joint Committee Report.

TNA/MT 39/127, Cycle Tracks, Proposed construction, 1926-43

http://webarchive.nationalarchives.gov.uk/20100408101526/http://www.dft.gov.uk/cyclingengland/cycling-cities-towns/

http://webarchive.nationalarchives.gov.uk/20100408101721/http://www.dft.gov.uk/cyclingengland/bikeability/

http://webarchive.nationalarchives.gov.uk/20100408101934/http://www.dft.gov.uk/cyclingengland/who-we-are/

http://webarchive.nationalarchives.gov.uk/20100409000639/http://www.dft.gov.uk/cyclingengland/who-we-are/our-board/

Other archives

UK Data Archive

UKDA5404. Paul Thompson, *Family Life and Work Experience before 1918: Middle and Upper Class Families in the Early 20th Century, 1870-1977 2nd Edition* (Colchester, Essex: UK Data Archive, 2008) https://www.data-archive.ac.uk

Wolverhampton Archives

DB, Percy Stallard Papers

Newspapers and periodicals

Athletic News
Birmingham Daily Post
Birmingham Gazette
CTC Gazette
Cycling
Cycling Record
Daily Express
Daily Gazette (Middlesbrough)
Daily Mail
Daily Mirror

Daily Telegraph
Dundee Evening Telegraph
Guardian
Hendon and Finchley Times
Illustrated Sporting and Dramatic News
Leamington Spa Courier
Leeds Mercury
Lincolnshire Echo
Manchester Courier
New Cyclist
Northern Echo
Northern Whig
Observer
Pall Mall Gazette
Picture Post
Punch
Scottish Review
Sheffield Independent
Shields Daily News
Spectator
Sporting Life
Sports Argus (Birmingham)
Sunderland Daily Echo and Shipping News
The Bicycle
The Economist
The Leaguer: Official Journal of the British League of Racing Cyclists
The Review of Reviews
The Sketch
The Sportsman
The Times
The Tricyclist
Western Daily Press
Western Morning News
Windsor Magazine
World Sports
York Herald
Yorkshire Post

Government papers

'The motor industry: statistics and policy', Briefing Paper, Number 00611, House of Commons Library, 11 April 2017.

[Bill 214.] Committee. HC Deb 09 July 1878 Vol 241 Cc1078-83.

Department for Culture, Media and Sport (DCMS)/Strategy Unit, *Game Plan: A Strategy for Improving Government's Sport and Physical Activity Objectives* (London: Cabinet Office, 2000).

https://assets.publishing.service.gov.uk/government/uploads/system/uploads/attachment_data/file/8995/vehicles-summary.pdf
https://publications.parliament.uk/pa/cm201719/cmselect/cmcumeds/366/366.pdf

Secondary sources

Books

Addison, Paul, *No Turning Back: The Peacetime Revolutions of Post-War Britain* (Oxford: Oxford University Press, 2010).
Alderson, Frederick, *Bicycling: A History* (Newton Abbot: David & Charles, 1972).
Alexander, Anthony, *Britain's New Towns: Garden Cities to Sustainable Communities* (London: Routledge, 2009).
Andrew Ritchie, *King of the Road: An Illustrated History of Cycling* (London: Wildwood House, 1975).
Anon., *City Cycling: London* (London: Thames and Hudson, 2013).
Anon., *Cycling to the Countryside: Annex to Report to the Countryside Commission, March 1978*, Dartington Amenity, Research Trust, June 1977.
Anon., *The Economic Value of the Bicycle Industry and Cycling in the United Kingdom: Report to the Bicycle Association of Great Britain* (March 2017).
Anon., *Statistical Digest of the War* (London: HMSO, 1951).
Anthony, Scott, *Public Relations and the Making of Modern Britain: Stephen Tallents and the Birth of a Progressive Media Profession* (Manchester: Manchester University Press, 2010).
Ballantine, Richard, *Richard's Bicycle Book: A Manual of Bicycle Maintenance and Enjoyment* (London: Pan, 1972, 1983 edition).
Barker, Theo and Dorian Gerhold, *The Rise and Rise of Road Transport, 1700–1990* (Cambridge: Cambridge University Press, 1993).
Barr, John (ed.), *The Environmental Handbook: Action Guide for the UK* (London: Friends of the Earth, 1971).
Beaven, Brad, *Leisure, Citizenship and Working-Class Men in Britain, 1850–1945* (Manchester: Manchester University Press, 2005).
Berridge, Virginia, *Health and Society in Britain since 1939* (Cambridge: Cambridge University Press, 1999).
Bijker, Wiebe, *Of Bicycles, Bakelites and Bulbs: Towards a Theory of Sociotechnical Change* (London: MIT Press, 1995).
Blunden, Edmund, *Cricket Country* (London: The Imprint Society, 1945).
Bolsmann, Chris and Dilwyn Porter, *English Gentlemen and World Soccer: Corinthians, Amateurism and the Global Game* (London: Routledge, 2018).
Booth, James, *Philip Larkin: Life, Art and Love* (London: Bloomsbury, 2015).
Borsay, Peter, *A History of Leisure: The British Experience since 1500* (Basingstoke: Palgrave, 2006).
Boulting, Ned, *How I Won the Yellow Jumper: Dispatches from the Tour de France* (London: Yellow Jersey Press, 2011).
Bourke, Joanna, *Dismembering the Male: Men's Bodies, Britain and the Great War* (London: Reaktion, 1996).

Boyle, Raymond and Richard Haynes, *Power Play: Sport, the Media and Popular Culture Second Edition* (Edinburgh: Edinburgh University Press, 2009).
Burton, Beryl, *Personal Best* (Huddersfield: Springfield Books, 1986).
Bury, Viscount and G. Lacy Hillier, *Cycling, 2nd Edition* (London: Longmans, Green and Co., 1889).
Cannadine, David, *Class in Britain* (London: Penguin, 1998).
Carter, Neil, *Medicine, Sport and the Body: A Historical Perspective* (London: Bloomsbury Academic, 2012).
Collins, Tony, *A Social History of English Rugby Union* (London: Routledge, 2009).
Collins, Tony, *Sport in Capitalist Society: A Short History* (London: Routledge, 2013).
Colls, Robert, *George Orwell: English Rebel* (Oxford: Oxford University Press, 2013).
Colls, Robert, *Identity of England* (Oxford: Oxford University Press, 2002).
Conekin, Becky E., 'The Autobiography of a Nation': The 1951 Festival of Britain* (Manchester: Manchester University Press, 2003).
Cox, Peter, *Cycling: A Sociology of Vélomobility* (London: Routledge, 2019).
Cunningham, Hugh, *The Invention of Childhood* (London: BBC Books, 2006).
Dauncey, Hugh, *French Cycling: A Social and Cultural History* (Liverpool: Liverpool University Press, 2012).
Davidoff, Leonore and Catherine Hall, *Family Fortunes: Men and Women of the English Middle Class, 1780–1850* (London: Routledge, 1987).
Dee, David, *Sport and British Jewry: Integration, Ethnicity and Anti-Semitism 1890–1970* (Manchester: Manchester University Press, 2013).
Denning, Andrew, *Skiing into Modernity: A Cultural and Environmental History* (Oakland: University of California Press, 2014).
Dimeo, Paul, *A History of Drug Use in Sport 1876–1976: Beyond Good and Evil* (London: Routledge, 2007).
Dodge, Pryor, *The Bicycle* (New York: Flanmarion, 1996).
Edgerton, David, *The Rise and Fall of the British Nation: A Twentieth-Century History* (London: Penguin, 2019).
Edwards, Elizabeth, *The Camera as Historian: Amateur Photographers and Historical Imagination, 1885–1918* (London: Duke University Press, 2012).
Foot, John, *Pedalare! Pedalare! A History of Italian Cycling* (London: Bloomsbury, 2011).
Fotheringham, William *Put Me Back On My Bike: In Search of Tom Simpson* (London: Yellow Jersey Press, 2002).
Gardiner, Juliet, *The Thirties: An Intimate History* (London: Harper Press, 2010).
Griffin, Brian, *Cycling in Victorian Ireland* (Dublin: Nonsuch, 2006).
Gunn, Simon, *The Public Culture of the Victorian Middle Class: Ritual and Authority in the English Industrial City 1840–1914* (Manchester: Manchester University Press, 2000).
Hall, M. Ann, *Muscle on Wheels: Louise Armaindao and the High-Wheel Racers of Nineteenth-Century America* (Montreal: McGill-Queen's University Press, 2018).
Hamer, Mick, *Wheels Within Wheels: A Study of the Road Lobby* (London: Routledge & Kegan Paul, 1987).

Hamilton, Tyler, *The Secret Race: Inside the Hidden World of the Tour de France: Doping, Cover-ups, and Winning at All Costs* (London: Bantam Press, 2012).
Harris, Jose, *Private Lives, Public Spirit: Britain 1870–1914* (London: Penguin 1993).
Harrison, Brian, *Seeking a Role: The United Kingdom 1951–1970* (Oxford: Oxford University Press, 2009).
Herlihy, David, *Bicycle: The History* (New Haven: Yale University Press, 2004).
Hill, Jeffrey, *Sport, Leisure and Culture in Twentieth Century Britain* (Basingstoke: Palgrave, 2002).
Hilton, Matthew and James McKay (eds), *The Ages of Voluntarism: How We Got to the Big Society* (Oxford: British Academy, 2011).
Hilton, Tim, *One More Kilometre and We're in the Showers: Memoirs of a Cyclist* (London: HarperCollins, 2004).
Hoggart, Richard, *The Uses of Literacy: Aspects of Working-Class Life with Special Reference to Publications and Entertainments* (London: Penguin, 1957).
Holt, Richard, *Sport and the British: A Modern History* (Oxford: Clarendon Press, 1989).
Holt, Richard and Tony Mason, *Sport in Britain 1945–2000* (Oxford: Blackwells, 2000).
Horrall, Andrew, *Popular Culture in London c.1890–1918* (Manchester: Manchester University Press, 2001).
Horton, David, Paul Rosen and Peter Cox (eds), *Cycling and Society* (Aldershot: Ashgate, 2007).
Huggins, Mike, *The Victorians and Sport* (London: Hambledon, 2004).
Inglis, Simon, *Played in London: Charting the Heritage of a City at Play* (London: English Heritage, 2014).
James, Lawrence, *The Middle Class: A History* (London: Little, Brown, 2006).
Jefferys, Kevin, *Sport and Politics in Modern Britain: The Road to 2012* (London: Palgrave, 2012).
Jephcott, Pearl, *Some Young People* (London: George Allen, 1954).
Jones, Stephen, *Sport, Politics and the Working Class: Organised Labour and Sport in Inter-war Britain* (Manchester: Manchester University Press, 1988).
Jones, Stephen, *Workers at Play: A Social and Economic History of Leisure 1918–1939* (London: Routledge and Kegan Paul, 1986).
Keys, Barbara, *Globalizing Sport: National Rivalry and International Community in the 1930s* (Cambridge, MA: Harvard University Press, 2006).
Korr, Charles, *West Ham United: The Making of a Football Club* (London: Duckworth, 1986).
Kynaston, David, *Austerity Britain 1948–51: Smoke in the Valley* (London: Bloomsbury, 2007).
Langhamer, Claire, *Women's Leisure in England 1920–60* (Manchester: Manchester University Press, 2000).
Lightwood, James T., *The Cyclists' Touring Club Being The Romance of Fifty Years' Cycling* (London: The Cyclists' Touring Club, 1928).
Lineham, Thomas, *Communism in Britain, 1920–39: From the Cradle to the Grave* (Manchester: Manchester University Press, 2007).
Lloyd-Jones, Roger and M. J. Lewis with the assistance of Mark Eason, *Raleigh and the British Bicycle Industry: An Economic and Business History, 1870–1960* (Aldershot: Ashgate, 2000).

Lowerson, John, *Sport and the English Middle Classes 1870–1914* (Manchester: Manchester University Press, 1993).
Manners, William, *Revolution: How the Bicycle Reinvented Modern Britain* (London: Duckworth, 2018).
Martin, Simon, *Sport Italia: The Italian Love Affair with Sport* (London: IB Tauris, 2011)
Mason, Tony, *Association Football and English Society 1863–1915* (Brighton: Harvester Press, 1980)
Mason, Tony, *Only a Game? Sport in the Modern World* (Cambridge: Cambridge University Press)
Mason, William, *Marguerite Wilson: The Story of the First Star of Women's Cycling Told in Her Own Words and those of Her Admirers* (Self-published, 2014).
Matless, David, *Landscape and Englishness* (London: Reaktion Books, 1998).
McIvor, Arthur, *Working Lives: Work in Britain Since 1945* (Basingstoke: Palgrave, 2013).
McKibbin, Ross, *Classes and Cultures: England 1918–1951* (Oxford: Oxford University Press, 1998).
McWilliam, Rohan, *Popular Politics in Nineteenth Century England* (London: Routledge, 1998).
Meller, Helen, *Towns, Plans and Society in Modern Britain* (Cambridge: Cambridge University Press, 1997).
Messenger, Charles, *Ride and be Damned: Chas Messenger's Glory Years of the British League of Racing Cyclists* (London: Pedal Publishing, 1998).
Metcalfe, Alan, *Leisure and Recreation in a Victorian Mining Community: The Social Economy of Leisure in North-East England, 1820–1914* (London: Routledge, 2006).
Moore, Richard, *Heroes, Villains and Velodromes: Chris Hoy and Britain's Track Cycling Revolution* (London: Harper Collins, 2008).
Moore, Richard, *Sky's the Limit: Wiggins and Cavendish: The Quest to Conquer the Tour de France* (London: Harper Collins, 2012).
Mort, Frank, *Cultures of Consumption: Masculinities and Social Space in Late Twentieth-Century Britain* (London: Routledge, 1996).
Moxham, S. H., *Fifty Years of Road Riding (1885–1935): A History of the North Road Cycling Club, Ltd.* (Bedford: Diemer & Reynolds, 1935).
Nicholson, Geoffrey, *The Professionals* (London: Andre Deutsch, 1964).
Nicholson, Geoffrey, *Tony Doyle: Six-day Rider* (Huddersfield: Springfield, 1992).
O'Connell, Sean, *The Car and British Society: Class, Gender and Motoring 1896–1939* (Manchester: Manchester University Press, 1998).
Oakley, William, *Winged Wheel: The History of the First Hundred Years of the Cyclists' Touring Club* (Godalming: Cyclists' Touring Club, 1977).
Obelkevich, Jim and Peter Catterall, *Understanding Post-War British Society* (London: Routledge, 1994).
Obree, Graeme, *Flying Scotsman: The Graeme Obree Story* (Edinburgh: Birlinn, 2004 edition).
Oriard, Michael, *Reading Football: How the Popular Press Created an American Spectacle* (London: University of North Carolina Press, 1993).
Penn, Robert, *It's All about the Bike: The Pursuit of Happiness on Two Wheels* (London: Penguin, 2011).

Perkin, Harold, *The Rise of Professional Society: England Since 1880* (London: Routledge, 1989).
Perkin, Harold, *The Third Revolution: Professional Elites in the Modern World* (London: Routledge, 1996).
Plowden, William, *The Motor Car and Politics in Britain* (London: Penguin, 1971).
Polley, Martin, *Moving the Goalposts: A History of Sport and Society since 1945* (London: Routledge, 1998)
Pye, Denis, *Fellowship Is Life: The Story of the National Clarion Cycling Club* (National Clarion Publishing, 1995).
Radford, Peter, *1866 and All that ...: The Story of the World's First National Athletics Championships* (Birmingham: England Athletics, 2016).
Reed, Eric, *Selling the Yellow Jersey: The Tour de France in the Global Era* (Chicago: University of Chicago Press, 2015).
Ritchie, Andrew, *King of the Road: An Illustrated History of Cycling* (London: Wildwood, 1975)
Ritchie, Andrew, *Quest for Speed: A History of Early Bicycle Racing 1868–1903* (El Cerrito: Self-Published, 2011).
Robinson, Joe, *Tommy Turnbull: A Miner's Life* (Newcastle upon Tyne: TUPS Books, 1996).
Rosen, Paul, *Framing Production: Technology, Culture, and Change in the British Bicycle Industry* (Cambridge, MA: MIT Press, 2002).
Russell, Dave, *Football and the English: A Social History of Association Football in England, 1863–1995* (Preston: Carnegie, 1997).
Sampson, Anthony, *Anatomy of Britain* (London: Hodder and Stoughton, 1962).
Sandbrook, Dominic, *The Great British Dream Factory: The Strange History of Our National Imagination* (London: Penguin, 2015).
Seaton, Matt, *Two Wheels: Thoughts from the Bike Lane* (London: Guardian Books, 2007).
Sheridan, Eileen, *Wonder Wheels: The Autobiography of Eileen Sheridan* (London: Nicholas Kaye, 1956).
Sidwells, Chris, *The Long Race to Glory: How the British Came to Rule the Cycling World* (London: Andre Deutsch, 2013).
Simmonds, Alan G. V., *Britain and World War One* (London: Routledge, 2012).
Simpson, Tommy, *Cycling Is My Life* (London: Yellow Jersey Press, 2009).
Skillen, Fiona, *Women, Sport and Modernity in Inter-War Britain* (Oxford: Peter Lang, 2013).
Smith, Malcolm and Fiona Browne, *General Household Survey 1990* (London: HMSO, 1992).
Szreter, Simon and Kate Fisher, *Sex Before the Sexual Revolution: Intimate Life in England 1918–1963* (Cambridge: Cambridge University Press, 2010).
Taylor, Matthew, *The Leaguers: The Making of Professional Football in England, 1900–1939* (Liverpool: Liverpool University Press, 2005).
Thompson, Christopher, *The Tour de France: A Cultural History* (Berkeley and Los Angeles: University of California Press, 2006).
Thomson, Mathew, *Lost Freedom: The Landscape of the Child and the British Post-War Settlement* (Oxford: Oxford University Press, 2013).
Todd, Selina, *Young Women, Work, and Family in England 1918–1950* (Oxford: Oxford University Press, 2005).

Tosh, John, *A Man's Place: Masculinity and the Middle-Class Home in Victorian England* (London: Yale University Press, 1999).
Urry, John, *Mobilities* (Cambridge: Polity Press, 2007).
Veal, Anthony James, *Sport and Recreation in England and Wales: An Analysis of Adult Participation Patterns in 1977* (Birmingham: University of Birmingham, 1979).
Waters, Chris, *British Socialists and the Politics of Popular Culture 1884-1914* (Stanford: Stanford University Press, 1990).
Weeks, Jeffrey, *Sex Politics and Society: The Regulation of Sexuality since 1800, Second Edition* (London: Longman, 1989).
Weight, Richard, *Patriots: National Identity in Britain 1940–2000* (London: Macmillan, 2002).
Wells, H. G., *The Wheels of Chance; A Bicycling Idyll* (1896). www.gutenberg.org.
Whiteley, Nigel, *Reyner Banham: Historian of the Immediate Future* (Cambridge, MA and London: MIT Press, 2002).
Wiggins, Bradley, *My Time* (London: Yellow Jersey, 2012).
Willmott, Peter, *Adolescent boys of East London* (London: Routledge & Kegan Paul, 1966).
Wood, Jonathan, *The British Motor Industry* (Oxford: Shire, 2012).
Woollacott, Angela, *On Her Their Lives Depend: Munitions Workers in the Great War* (Berkley: University of California Press, 1994).
Zuelow, Eric, *A History of Modern Tourism* (London: Palgrave, 2016).
Zweiniger-Bargielowska, Ina, *Managing the Body: Beauty, Health, and Fitness in Britain, 1880–1939* (Oxford: Oxford University Press 2010).

Articles, book chapters and papers

Alcock, Pete, 'Voluntary Action, New Labour and the "third sector"', in Matthew Hilton and James McKay (eds), *The Ages of Voluntarism: How we got to the Big Society* (Oxford: British Academy, 2011), pp. 158–79.
Aldred, Rachel, 'Governing Transport from Welfare State to Hollow State: The Case of Cycling in the UK', *Transport Policy*, vol. 23 (2012), pp. 95–102.
Aldred, Rachel, 'Incompetent or Too Competent? Negotiating Everyday Cycling Identities in a Motor Dominated Society', *Mobilities*, vol. 8, no. 2 (2013), pp. 252–71.
Aldred, Rachel, '"On the outside": Constructing Cycling Citizenship', *Social & Cultural Geography*, vol. 11, no. 1 (2010), pp. 35–52.
Aldred, Rachel, 'The Role of Advocacy and Activism', in J. Parkin (ed.), *Cycling and Sustainability* (Bingley: Emerald Group Publishing Limited, 2012), pp. 83–107.
Anon., *Board of Trade Journal*, 12 January 1946, p. 24.
Anon., 'Cyclomania', *Chambers's Journal of Popular Literature, Science and Arts*, vol. 13, no. 655 (18 July 1896), pp. 458–61.
Bailey, Peter, 'Jazz at the Spirella: Coming of Age in Coventry in the 1950s', in Becky Conekin, Frank Mort and Chris Waters (eds), *Moments of Modernity: Reconstructing Britain 1945–1964* (New York: Rivers Oram, 1999), pp. 22–40.

Banham, Reyner, 'A Grid on Two Farthings', *New Statesman*, vol. 66, no. 1 (1 November 1963), p. 626.

Banham, Reyner, 'The Atavism of the Short-Distance Mini-Cyclist', in Penny Sparke (ed.), *Design by Choice: Reyner Banham* (London: Rizzoli, 1981), pp. 84–94.

Bateman, Anthony, '"Guilty, M'Lud, to Fiction": Neville Cardus and the Moment of Scrutiny', *Sport in History*, vol. 29, no. 2 (2009), pp. 259–76.

Beaven, Brad and John Griffiths, 'Creating the Exemplary Citizen: The Changing Notion of Citizenship in Britain 1870–1939', *Contemporary British History*, vol. 22, no. 2 (2008), pp. 203–25.

Bendixson, Terence, 'The Return of the Bicycle', *New Society*, 12 June 1975, pp. 651–2.

Biddle-Perry, Geraldine, 'Fashioning Suburban Aspiration: Awheel with the Catford Cycling Club, 1886–1900', *London Journal*, vol. 39, no. 3 (November 2014), pp. 187–204.

Biddle-Perry, Geraldine, 'The Rise of "The World's Largest Sport and Athletic Outfitter": A Study of Gamage's of Holborn, 1878–1913', *Sport in History*, vol. 34, no. 2 (2014), pp. 295–317.

Blair, Thomas L., 'Friends of the Earth', in John Barr (ed.), *The Environmental Handbook: Action Guide for the UK* (London: Friends of the Earth, 1971), pp. 325–6.

Blickstein, Susan and Susan Hanson, 'Critical Mass: Forging a Politics of Sustainable Mobility in the Information Age', *Transportation*, vol. 28 (2001), pp. 347–62.

Bogdanowiz, Tom, 'Mountain Bikes – From Insider Cult to Centre Stage', in Tom Bogdanowiz (ed.), *The Off-Road Bicycle Book*, 3rd edn (Hawes: Leading Edge, 1992), pp. 3–12.

Brewer, Benjamin D., 'Commercialization in Professional Cycling 1950–2001: Institutional Transformations and the Rationalization of "Doping"', *Sociology of Sport Journal*, vol. 19 (2002), pp. 276–301.

Buenstorf, Guido, 'Designing Clunkers: Demand-Side Innovation and the Early History of the Mountain Bike', in J. S. Metcalfe and U. Cantner (eds), *Change, Transformation and Development* (Heidelberg: Physica, 2003), pp. 53–70.

Claxton, Eric, 'The Future of the Bicycle in a Modern Society', *Journal of the Royal Society of Arts*, vol. 16 (1968), pp. 114–34.

Conekin, Becky E., Frank Mort and Chris Waters, 'Introduction', in Becky E. Conekin, Frank Mort and Chris Waters (eds), *Moments of Modernity: Reconstructing Britain 1945–1964* (London: Rivers Oram Press, 1999), pp. 1–21.

Cox, Peter with Frederick Van De Walle, 'Bicycles Don't Evolve: Velomobiles and the Modelling of Transport Technologies', in Dave Horton, Paul Rosen and Peter Cox (eds), *Cycling and Society* (Aldershot: Ashgate, 2007), pp. 113–31.

Cox, Peter, '"A Denial of Our Boasted Civilisation": Cyclists' Views on Conflicts over Road Use in Britain, 1926–1935', *Transfers*, vol. 2, 3 (Winter 2012), pp. 4–30.

Cox, Peter, 'Activism and Market Innovation: Changing Patterns in the Cycle Trade', Paper presented to 4th CSRG Symposium, at CTC Guildford, 7 September 2007.

Cox, Peter, 'Social Movement Activism, Social Change and Bicycling in the UK', paper presented at The Future of Mobilities: Flows, Transport and

Communication. T2M/ Cosmobilities joint conference, Caserta, Italy, September 2–15.

Cunningham, Michael, 'Ethos and Politics in the Youth Hostels Association (YHA) in the 1930s', *Contemporary British History*, vol. 30, no. 2 (2016), pp. 177–202.

Cunningham, Michael, '"Two Wheels Bad"? The Status of Cycling in the Youth Hostels Association of England and Wales in the 1930s', *Transfers*, vol. 8, no. 2 (2018), pp. 1–22.

Day, David, 'Kinship and Community in Victorian London: the "Beckwith Frogs"', *History Workshop Journal* (Advanced Access, 25 February 2011), pp. 1–25.

Dominici, Sara, '"Cyclo-Photographers", Visual Modernity, and the Development of Camera Technologies, 1880s–1890s', *History of Photography*, vol. 42, no. 1, (2018), pp. 46–60.

Dyreson, Mark, 'World Harmony or an Athletic "Clash of Civilizations"? The Beijing Olympic Spectacle, BMX Bicycles and the American Contours of Globalisation', *International Journal of the History of Sport*, vol. 29, no. 9 (2012), pp. 1231–42.

Ebert, Anne-Katrin, 'When Cycling Gets Political: Building Cycling Paths in Germany and the Netherlands, 1910–40', *Journal of Transport History*, vol. 33, no. 1 (June 2012), pp. 115–37.

Epperson, Bruce, 'A New Class of Cyclists: Banham's Bicycle and the Two-wheeled World it didn't Create', *Mobilities*, vol. 8, no. 2 (2013), pp. 238–51.

Finlayson, Geoffrey, 'A Moving Frontier: Voluntarism and the State in British Social Welfare 1911–1949', *Twentieth Century British History*, vol. 1, no. 2 (1990), pp. 183–206.

Garrard, John and Vivienne Parrott, 'Craft, Professional and Middle-Class Identity', in Alan Kidd and David Nicholls (eds), *The Making of the British Middle Class? Studies of Regional and Cultural Diversity since the Eighteenth Century* (Stroud: Sutton, 1998), pp. 148–68.

Geary, Dick, '"Beer and Skittles?" Workers and Culture in Early Twentieth-Century Germany', *Australian Journal of Politics and History*, vol. 46, no. 3 (2000), pp. 388–402.

Gill, Jo, 'Introduction', in Jo Gill (ed.), *Modern Confessional Writing: New Critical Essays* (London: Routledge, 2006), pp. 1–10.

Goodall, Robert, 'Cycling Clubs of North Yorkshire and South Durham, 1876–1914', *Bulletin of the Cleveland and Teesside Local History Society*, No. 57 (Autumn 1989), pp. 20–34.

Goodman, Anna, Shannon Sahlqvist and David Ogilvie, 'Who Uses New Walking and Cycling Infrastructure and How? Longitudinal Results from the UK iConnect Study', *Preventive Medicine*, vol. 57 (2013), pp. 518–24.

Gregson, Keith and Mike Huggins, 'Ashbrooke Whit Sports, Sunderland and Its Records: A Case Study of Amateurism in Late Victorian and Edwardian Athletic and Cycling Competition', *International Journal of the History of Sport*, vol. 31, no. 9 (2014), pp. 994–1011.

Gunn, Simon, 'The Buchanan Report, Environment and the Problem of Traffic in 1960s Britain', *Twentieth Century British History*, vol. 22, no. 4 (2011), pp. 521–42.

Gunn, Simon, 'People and the Car: The Expansion of Automobility in Urban Britain, c.1955–70', *Social History*, vol. 38, no. 2 (2013), pp. 220–37.

Hadland, Tony, 'Raleigh UK in the Last Quarter of the Twentieth Century', in *International Cycling History Conferences Proceedings*, No. 11 (Osaka, 2000), pp. 63–71.

Hall, Peter, 'Equal Rights for Bikes', *New Society*, 12 August 1971, pp. 280–2.

Hallenbeck, Sarah, 'Riding Out of Bounds: Women Bicyclists' Embodied Medical Authority', *Rhetoric Review*, vol. 29, no. 4 (2010), pp. 327–45.

Hardy, Stephen, 'Polo at the Rinks: Shaping Markets for Ice Hockey in America 1880–1900', *Journal of Sport History*, vol. 33, no. 2 (2006), pp. 156–74.

Harrison, A. E., 'Joint-stock Company Flotation in the Cycle, Motor-vehicle and Related Industries, 1882–1914', *Business History*, vol. 23, no. 2 (1981), 165–90.

Hill, Jeffrey, '"What shall we do with them when they're not working?": Leisure and Historians in Britain', in B. Bebber (ed.), *Leisure and Cultural Conflict in Twentieth-Century Britain* (Manchester: Manchester University Press, 2012), pp. 11–40.

Hilton, Matthew, 'Politics Is Ordinary: Non-governmental Organisations and Political Participation in Contemporary Britain', *Twentieth Century British History*, vol. 22, no. 2 (2011), pp. 230–68.

Hilton, Matthew, 'The Fable of the Sheep, or, Private Virtues, Public Vices: The Consumer Revolution of the Twentieth Century', *Past and Present*, No. 174 (2002), pp. 222–56.

Hilton, Matthew and James McKay, 'The Ages of Voluntarism: An Introduction', in Matthew Hilton and James McKay (eds), *The Ages of Voluntarism: How we got to the Big Society* (Oxford: British Academy, 2011), pp. 1–26.

Hilton, Matthew, James McKay, Nicholas Crowson and Jean-Francois Mouhot, '"The Big Society": Civic Participation and the State in Modern Britain', http://www.historyandpolicy.org/papers/policy-paper-103.html

Holt, Richard, 'The Amateur Body and the Middle-class Man: Work, Health and Style in Victorian Britain', *Sport in History*, vol. 26, no. 3 (2006).

Holt, Richard, 'The Bicycle, the Bourgeoisie and the Discovery of Rural France, 1880–1914', *British Journal of Sports History*, vol. 2, no. 2 (1985), pp. 352–69.

Holt, Richard, Alan Tomlinson and Christopher Young, 'Introduction: Sport in Europe 1950–2010, Transformation and Trends', in Alan Tomlinson, Christopher Young and Richard Holt (eds), *Sport and the Transformation of Modern Europe: States, Media and Markets 1950–2010* (London: Routledge, 2011), pp. 1–17.

Horton, Dave, 'Fear of Cycling', in Dave Horton, Paul Rosen and Peter Cox (eds), *Cycling and Society* (Aldershot: Ashgate, 2007), pp. 133–52.

Howkins, Alun, 'The Discovery of Rural England', in Robert Colls and Philip Dodd (eds), *Englishness: Politics and Culture 1880–1920* (Breckenham: Kent, 1986) pp. 62–88.

Huggins, Mike, 'More Sinful Pleasures? Leisure, Respectability and the Male Middle Classes in Victorian England', *Journal of Social History*, vol. 33, no. 3 (Spring 2000), pp. 585–600.

Huggins, Mike, 'Second-Class Citizens? English Middle-Class Culture and Sport: A Reconsideration', *International Journal of the History of Sport*, vol. 17, no. 1 (2000), pp. 1–35.

Kay, Joyce, 'A Window of Opportunity? Preliminary Thoughts in Women's Sport in Post-war Britain', *Sport in History*, vol. 30, no. 2 (June 2010), pp. 196–217.

King, Laura, 'Future Citizens: Cultural and Political Conceptions of Children in Britain, 1930s-1950s', *Twentieth Century British History* (Advance Access published 31 May 2016), pp. 1–23.

Kinsey, Fiona, 'Reading Photographic Portraits of Australian Women Cyclists in the 1890s: From Costume and Cycle Choices to Constructions of Feminine Identity', *International Journal of the History of Sport*, vol. 28, nos. 8–9 (2011), pp. 1121–37.

Kinsey, Fiona, 'Stamina, Speed and Adventure: Australian Women and Competitive Cycling in the 1890s', *International Journal of the History of Sport*, vol. 28, no. 10 (2011), pp. 1375–87.

Law, Michael, '"The car indispensable": The Hidden Influence of the Car in Inter-war Suburban London', *Journal of Historical Geography*, vol. 38 (2012), pp. 424–33.

Livingstone, Ken, 'The Challenge of Driving through Change: Introducing Congestion Charging in Central London', *Planning Theory & Practice*, vol. 5, no. 4 (2004), pp. 490–8.

Loudon, Irvine, 'Doctors and their Transport, 1750–1914', *Medical History*, vol. 45 (2001), pp. 185–206.

Madgin, Rebecca, David Webb, Pollyanna Ruiz and Tim Snelson, 'Resisting Relocation and Reconceptualising Authenticity- The Experiential and Emotional Values of the Southbank Undercroft, London, UK', *International Journal of Heritage Studies*, vol. 24, no. 6 (2018), pp. 585–98.

Marland, Hilary, '"Bicycle-Face" and "Lawn Tennis" Girls', *Media History*, vol. 25, no. 1 (2019), pp. 70–84.

McCarthy, Helen, 'Associational voluntarism in inter-war Britain', in M. Hilton and J. McKay (eds), *The Ages of Voluntarism: How we got to the Big Society* (London: British Academy, 2011), pp. 47–68.

McKibbin, Ross, 'Why was there no Marxism in Great Britain?' *English Historical Review*, vol. 99, no. 391 (April 1984), pp. 297–331.

Mills, William J., 'Cycling', in James Rivers (ed.), *The Sports Book 3* (London: MacDonald, 1949), pp. 51–66.

Naylor, Gillian, 'The Banham Factor: The Ninth Reyner Banham Memorial Lecture', *Journal of Design History*, vol. 10, no. 3 (1997), pp. 241–52.

Nelson, Wade, 'The Historical Mediatization of BMX-Freestyle Cycling', *Sport in Society*, vol. 13, nos. 7–8 (2010), pp. 1152–69.

Newlyn, Lucy, 'Dorothy Wordsworth', paper presented at De Montfort University History seminar, 28 January 2015.

Norcliffe, Glen, 'The Technical and Social Significance of the Tricycle', in *International Cycling History Conferences Proceedings*, No. 17 (Toronto/Canada – 2006), pp. 59–67.

Oddy, Nicholas, 'The Flaneur on Wheels?' in Dave Horton, Paul Rosen and Peter Cox (eds), *Cycling in Society* (Aldershot: Ashgate, 2007), pp. 97–112.

Oldfield, Samantha-Jayne, 'Running Pedestrianism in Victorian Manchester', *Sport in History*, vol. 34, no. 2 (2014), pp. 223–48.

Oosterhuis, Harry, 'Cycling, Modernity and National Culture', *Social History*, vol. 41, no. 3 (2016), pp. 233–48.

Park, Jihang, 'Sport, Dress Reform and the Emancipation of Women in Victorian England: A Reapraisal', *The International Journal of the History of Sport*, vol. 6, no. 1 (May 1989), pp. 10–30.

Parratt, Catriona, 'Little Means or Time: Working Class Women and Leisure in Late Victorian and Edwardian England', *International Journal of the History of Sport*, vol. 15, no. 2 (1998), pp. 22–53.
Pennell, Elizabeth Robins, 'Cycling', in Beatrice Violet Greville (ed.), *Ladies in the Field: Sketches of Sport* (New York: D. Appleton and Co., 1894), pp. 247–65.
Pennell, Joseph and Elizabeth Robin, 'Cycling: Past, Present, And Future', *The New Review*, vol. 4, no. 21 (February 1891), pp. 171–80.
Porter, Dilwyn, 'Entrepreneurship', in John Nauright and Steve Pope (eds), *Routledge Companion to Sports History* (London: Routledge, 2012), pp. 197–215.
Porter, Dilwyn, 'Revenge of the Crouch End Vampires', *Sport in History*, vol. 26, no. 3 (2006), pp. 406–28.
Priestley, John Boynton, 'When Work Is Over', *Picture Post*, 4 January 1941, pp. 39–40.
Putnam, Robert D., 'Bowling Alone: America's Declining Social Capital', *Journal of Democracy*, vol. 6, no. 1 (January 1995), pp. 65–78.
Ritchie, Andrew, 'The Origins of Bicycle Racing in England: Technology, Entertainment, Sponsorship and Advertising in the Early History of the Sport', *Journal of Sport History*, 26, no. 3 (Fall 1999), pp. 489–520.
Rix, Alicia, '"Henry's Bicycle": Cycling and Figurations of Exposure in "The Papers"', *The Henry James Review*, vol. 39, no. 1 (2018), pp. 23–36.
Robinson, Emily, Camilla Schofield, Florence Sutcliffe-Braithwaite and Natalie Thomlinson, 'Telling Stories about Post-war Britain: Popular Individualism and the "Crisis" of the 1970s', *Twentieth Century British History*, vol. 28, no. 2 (2017), pp. 268–304.
Rubinstein, David, 'Cycling Eighty Years Ago: A Change in Social Habits when the New Bicycle Replaced the Old Penny-Farthing', *History Today*, August 1978, pp. 544–7.
Rubinstein, David, 'Cycling in the 1890s', *Victorian Studies* (Autumn 1977), pp. 47–71.
Russell, Dave, 'Deeply Honoured: The Rise and Significance of the British Sporting Award, 1945-c.1970', *Sport in History*, vol. 29, no. 3 (September 2009), pp. 479–99.
Russell, Dave, 'Mum's the Word: The Cycling Career of Beryl Burton, 1956–1986', *Women's History Review*, vol. 17, no. 5 (2008), pp. 787–806.
Russell, Dave, '"Interesting and Instructive Reading"? The FA Book for Boys and the Culture of Boyhood, 1945–1973', *Journal of Sport History*, vol. 34, no. 2 (2007), pp. 231–52.
Simpson, Clare S., 'Capitalising on Curiosity: Women's Professional Cycle Racing in the Late-Nineteenth Century', in Dave Horton, Paul Rosen and Peter Cox (eds), *Cycling and Society* (Aldershot: Ashgate, 2007), pp. 47–66.
Snape, Robert, 'The New Leisure, Voluntarism and Social Reconstruction in Inter-War Britain', *Contemporary British History*, vol. 29, no. 1 (2015), pp. 51–83.
Steinbach, Rebecca, Judith Green, Jessica Datta and Phil Edwards, 'Cycling and the City: A Case Study of How Gendered, Ethnic and Class Identities can Shape Healthy Transport Choices', *Social Science & Medicine*, vol. 72, no. 7 (2011), pp. 1123–30.
Taylor, Matthew, 'Sport and Civilian Morale', *Journal of Contemporary History*, vol. 53, no. 2 (2016), pp. 315–38.

Trainor, Richard, 'Neither Metropolitan nor Provincial: The Inter-war Middle Class', in Alan Kidd and David Nicholls (eds), *The Making of the British Middle Class? Studies of Regional and Cultural Diversity since the Eighteenth Century* (Stroud: Sutton, 1998), pp. 203–14.

Urry, John, 'Social Engineering: Responding to Ken Livingstone', *Planning, Theory & Practice*, vol. 5, no. 4 (2004), pp. 506–9.

Weight, Richard and Abigail Beach, 'Introduction', in Richard Weight and Abigail Beach (eds), *The Right to Belong: Citizenship and National Identity in Britain, 1930–1960* (London: IB Tauris, 1998), pp. 1–18.

Wheaton, Belinda, 'Introducing the Consumption and Representation of Lifestyle Sports', *Sport in Society*, vol. 13, nos. 7–8 (2010), pp. 1057–812.

Wilton, Iain, '"A Galaxy of Sporting Events": Sport's Role and Significance in the Festival of Britain, 1951', *Sport in History*, vol. 36, no. 4 (2016), pp. 459–76.

Zweiniger-Bargielowska, Ina, 'The Making of a Modern Female Body: Beauty, Health and Fitness in Interwar Britain', *Women's History Review*, vol. 20, no. 2 (2011), pp. 299–317.

PhDs and Master's Dissertations

Bellégo, Marine, 'Bicycles and Bodies in Britain at the Fin-de-Siècle' (Unpublished MPhil: Cambridge University, 2013).

Bray, Tom, 'The Pleasure Factory and Delights of the Game: The Intersections of Health, Leisure and Environment in Interwar England' (Unpublished MA Dissertation: University of Warwick, 2013).

Budd, Catherine, 'The Growth of an Urban Sporting Culture – Middlesbrough, c.1870-1914' (Unpublished PhD: De Montfort University, 2012).

Crump, Jeremy, 'Amusements of the People: The Provision of Recreation in Leicester, 1850–1914' (Unpublished PhD: University of Warwick, 1985).

Ensor, Rob, '"The Champion Club of the Midland Counties": A Social Study of the Nottingham Chess Club, 1829 – c.1904' (Unpublished MA Dissertation: De Montfort University, 2016).

Goodall, Robert, 'Cycling in North Yorkshire and South Durham 1869–1914' (Unpublished MA Dissertation: University of Teesside, 1989).

Heller, Michael, 'London Clerical Workers 1880–1919: The Search For Stability' (Unpublished PhD: University College London, University of London, 2003).

Herring, Rachel, 'Governance, Sport and The City: Realising Mega Sporting Events in London' (Unpublished PhD: Middlesex University, 2006).

Knuts, Stijn, 'Converging and Competing Courses of Identity Construction: Shaping and Imagining Society through Cycling and Bicycle Racing in Belgium before World War Two' (Unpublished PhD: University of Leuven, 2014).

Millward, Andrew, 'Factors Contributing to the Success of the UK Cycle Industry, 1870–1939' (Unpublished PhD: University of Birmingham, 1999).

Nelson, Wade, 'Reading Cycles: The Culture of BMX Freestyle' (Unpublished PhD: McGill University, 2006).

Osborne, Carol, 'Gender and the Organisation of British Climbing c.1857-1955' (Unpublished PhD: University of Lancaster, 2004).

Robinson, Nicholas, 'Major Government, Minor Change: The Politics of Transport, 1990–1997' (Unpublished PhD: University of Warwick, 1998).

Sheets, Diana, 'British Conservatism and the Primrose League: The Changing Character of Popular Politics, 1833–1901' (Unpublished PhD: Colombia University, 1986).
Simpson, Clare S., 'A Social History of Women and Cycling in Late-Nineteenth Century New Zealand' (Unpublished PhD: Lincoln University, New Zealand, 1998).
Threlfall-Sykes, Judy, 'A History of English Women's Cricket, 1880–1939' (Unpublished PhD: De Montfort University, 2016).

Oxford Dictionary of National Biography https://www.oxforddnb.com

Bartrip, PWJ, 'Jeffreys, William Rees (1871–1954)'
Dawkins, Laura, 'Bidlake, Frederick Thomas (1867–1933)'
Donovan, Paul, 'Quigley, Janet Muriel Alexander (1902–1987)'
Mason, Tony, 'Veitch, Colin Campbell McKechnie (1881–1938)'
Nahum, Andrew, 'Moulton, Alexander Eric [Alex] (1920–2012)'
Pollard, AF, 'Keppel, William Coutts, seventh earl of Albemarle and Viscount Bury (1832-1894)', rev. H. C. G. Matthew
Rennick, Tony, 'Bailey, William James (1888–1971)'
Robbins, Keith, 'Belisha, (Isaac) Leslie Hore-, Baron Hore-Belisha (1893–1957)'
Sinker, Robert, 'Ion Grant Neville Keith-Falconer (1856–1887)', rev. John Gurney
Skillen, Fiona, 'Fleming [née Bartram; first married name Dovey], Lillian Irene [Billie] (1914–2014)'

Internet sources

Web articles:

'BBC News - Cycling industry gives economy £3bn boost', 22 August 2011, http://www.bbc.co.uk/news/uk-14610857?print=true
'Cycle speedway: The 'skid kids' who raced bicycles on WW2 bomb sites', http://www.bbc.co.uk/news/magazine-31013387
Harold Briercliffe, David Renney and Paul Stanbridge, *The Nomads (Hitchin) Cycling Club: The first 50 years* https://simdoyle.files.wordpress.com/2013/07/hncc_50_years.pdf
http://autobus.cyclingnews.com/features/?id=2006/woodland_greaves
http://news.bbc.co.uk/1/hi/england/london/3915349.stm
http://news.bbc.co.uk/sport1/hi/olympics2000/cycling/927385.stm
http://rachelaldred.org/wp-content/uploads/2012/10/cycling-review1.pdf
http://www.bbc.co.uk/news/uk-14610857?print=true
http://www.bbc.co.uk/sport/38884801
http://www.cyclingweekly.com/news/latest-news/14-per-cent-regular-cyclists-admit-taking-steroids-320653
http://www.guardian.co.uk/environment/bike-blog/2013/jun/10/penny-farthings-making-comeback

http://www.independent.co.uk/news/uk/this-britain/were-not-deviants-say-the-cycling-ladies-308628.html?printService=print
http://www.theguardian.com/uk-news/davehillblog/2015/nov/07/waltham-forest-mini-holland-row-politics-protests-and-house-prices
https://theconversation.com/the-unbearable-whiteness-of-cycling-76256
https://www.bbc.co.uk/news/entertainment-arts-27923596
https://www.bbc.co.uk/news/uk-wales-south-west-wales-36521289
https://www.bbc.co.uk/sport/cycling/20193300
https://www.cyclingweekly.com/news/boris-bike-24-hours-challenge-18906
https://www.cyclingweekly.com/news/latest-news/from-paupers-to-kings-the-lottery-funded-revolution-93603
https://www.cyclist.co.uk/chris-boardman/59/chris-boardman-interview
https://www.ft.com/content/7890fdf0-ac5f-11e6-9cb3-bb8207902122
https://www.independent.co.uk/environment/green-living/the-rise-of-the-female-cyclist-from-the-medal-winning-track-speedsters-to-school-run-mums-9202631.html
https://www.independent.co.uk/sport/general/others/cycle-of-success-how-britains-cyclists-won-the-lottery-800241.html
https://www.mirror.co.uk/news/uk-news/britains-longest-married-couple-celebrating-18850524
https://www.standard.co.uk/news/london-bike-park-one-of-the-safest-in-world-6863966.html
https://www.theguardian.com/environment/2017/mar/18/torrey-canyon-disaster-uk-worst-ever-oil-spill-50tha-anniversary
https://www.theguardian.com/media/2014/apr/20/lance-armstrong-david-walsh-drug-addled-cycling
https://www.theguardian.com/sport/2008/mar/02/cycling.features1
https://www.theguardian.com/sport/blog/2012/dec/17/british-cycling-other-sports-learn
https://www.theguardian.com/uk-news/davehillblog/2016/nov/26/london-cycling-and-the-by-chance-success-of-amsterdam
https://www.totalsimulation.co.uk/rob-lewis-awarded-obe/

Websites:

http://classiclightweights.co.uk/
http://thepedalclub.org/archives/
http://www.airedaleolympic.co.uk
http://www.anfieldbc.co.uk
http://www.bidlakememorial.org.uk/
http://www.centuryroadclub.org.uk/history.html
http://www.concordecc.org.uk/history1.htm
http://www.earthday.org/about/the-history-of-earth-day/
http://www.johnmajorarchive.org.uk
http://www.moidigital.ac.uk/reports/wartime-social-survey/wartime-social-survey-rg-23-62/idm140133747457344/

http://www.sheilahanlon.com
http://www.tweedrun.com/about/
http://www.visionofbritain.org.uk
https://fullfact.org/health/spending-english-nhs/
https://roadswerenotbuiltforcars.com
https://tfl.gov.uk/info-for/media/press-releases/2004/september/cycling-safety-comes-first-in-childrens-competition
https://www.britishcycling.org.uk
https://www.cyclinguk.org
https://www.permaculture.org.uk
https://www.rospa.com
https://www.ukbmxhistory.com

Mintel sources

'Bicycles - UK - November 2005: Consumer Attitudes and Typologies', http://academic.mintel.com/display/190261/
'Bicycles – UK – November 2005', http://academic.mintel.com/display/190253/
'Selling the cycling dream', 15 November 2007', http://academic.mintel.com/display/307158/
'Bicycles - UK - January 2008: Attitudes Towards Cycling', http://academic.mintel.com/display/317750/
'Bicycles - UK - January 2008: Internal Market Environment', http://academic.mintel.com/display/317739/
'Bicycles - UK - June 2010: Broader Market Environment', http://academic.mintel.com/display/532966/
'Bicycles - UK - June 2010: Internal Market Environment', http://academic.mintel.com/display/532965/
'Is British success inspiring a generation of cyclists?', March 2012, http://academic.mintel.com/display/636751/
'Bicycles - UK - February 2013: Companies and Products', http://academic.mintvel.com/display/655186/
'Bicycles - UK - February 2013: Executive Summary', http://academic.mintel.com/display/655178
'Bicycles - UK - February 2013: Frequency of Riding a Bicycle', http://academic.mintel.com/display/655189/
'Bicycles - UK - February 2013: Market Drivers', http://academic.mintel.com/display/655181/
'Bicycles - UK - February 2013: Retailer Consideration', http://academic.mintel.com/display/655191/
'Bicycle Accessories – Executive Summary', *Mintel*, June 2015
'Bicycle Accessories – UK – 2015', http://academic.mintel.com/display/741921/?highlight
'Bicycles - UK - March 2015: Type of Bicycle Ridden', http://academic.mintel.com/display/733992/?highlight#hit1

Film

BBC, *Death on the Mountain: The Story of Tom Simpson* (2005)
http://www.britishpathe.com/video/cycling-the-thames-miss-zetta-hills
http://bufvc.ac.uk
https://www.youtube.com/watch?v=-lEnGQxP8zs
https://www.youtube.com/watch?v=e0ZWhI7yrjs
https://www.youtube.com/watch?v=HUWCeAzkc2Q
https://www.youtube.com/watch?v=jDXgv3pqPcw
https://www.youtube.com/watch?v=JlEm4tEodhU
https://www.youtube.com/watch?v=QPkT0paGEnQ
https://www.youtube.com/watch?v=QXT83ne4fHM
https://www.youtube.com/watch?v=qyz5d3entBw
https://www.youtube.com/watch?v=XjNzpWph-io
https://www.youtube.com/watch?v=ycpRPIDwTr8

INDEX

Abercrombie, Patrick 70, 171
Aberdeen 24, 111, 129
Abrahams, Adolphe 160, 163, 300 n.128
Active Travel Consortium 200
Acts of Parliament
  Clean Air Act (1956) 188
  Countryside Act (1968)
  Cycle Racing and Highways Act (1963) 235
  English Highways and Locomotives Amendment Act (1878), 'Red Flag Act' 57, 58, 61
  Finance Act (1999) 198
  Local Government Act (1888) 37, 56–7, 58, 62, 76
  Municipal Franchise Act (1869) 32
  National Parks and Access to the Countryside Act (1949) 132
  New Towns Act (1946) 171
  Physical Training and Recreation Act (1937) 111, 242
  Road Traffic Act (1930) 84
  Road Traffic Act (1934) 83
  Trunk Roads Act (1936) 83
Ades, Rose 202
advertising 159, 162, 174–5
ALARM UK 195
Albemarle, Lord aka Viscount Bury, William Coutts Keppel 6, 31, 58
Albin 45
Aldred, Rachel 6, 9
Alexander, Dr W. P. 180
Algemeene Wielrijders Bond (ANWB) 87, 265 n.90

Alliance Internationale de Tourisme 73, *see also* International Union of Touring Clubs
Alness report, *Prevention of Road Accidents* (1939) 87, 179
Amateur Athletic Association (AAA) 50–1, 76, 125
Amateur Athletic Club (AAC) 20, 33, 48
amateur cycling championships 48
amateurism 4, 11, 24–5, 32, 48, 54, 67, 76, 253
  clubs 19, 21
  Cyclists' Touring Club 24–5
  middle-class identity 14, 33, 39–40, 51
  sport 3, 49–51, 53, 55, 64–5, 67, 119–21, 123, 131, 135, 140–1, 216, 233, 235
  time trial 116, 120
Ammaco Mongoose 228
Amsterdam 25, 170, 193, 310 n.78
Anglophilia 25
anti-modern critique 74, 90, 131, 133, 185, 204, *see also* modernity
anti-urban critique 38, 106, 225
Apps, Geoff 204, 206
Armaindo, Louise 56
Armitstead, Lizzie 245
Armstrong, Lance 251–2, 253, 322 nn.84, 85
  It's Not About the Bike (2000) 252
  LA Confidential: Lance Armstrong's Secrets (2004) 322 n.84
Ashton, Martyn 225

associational life, club culture 25–8, 32–3, 44, 76, 90, 101–6, 118, 122, 146–8, 173, 235
Austin, Herbert 66, 145
Automobile Association 80, 81, 278 n.65
Aylesbury 197

Bailey, Peter 93
Bailey, William (Bill) 67, 124
Balfour, Arthur 15, 18, 22, 25, 263 n.34
Ballantine, Richard 203–4, 207, 246
Ballard, J. G., *Crash* 186
Banham, Reynar 93, 177, 190, 204
Bare, Jack and Joan 154
Barrington, Richard 228
Bartleet, H. W. J. 76, 82, 276 n.39
Bates, J. E. L. 64
Bath-to-Britton railway line 199
BBC
    BBC website 220
    Beryl: A Love Story on Two Wheels (2012) 248–9
    The Bicycle (1991) 222
    Me and My Bike (1989) 221
    Pedal Power (1974) 190
    radio 79, 92, 136, 143, 148, 161, 250
    Sports Personality of the Year 161, 234, 239, 252
    television 190, 221, 224, 234, 237–8, 239, 249
Beeching Report (1963) 170, 199
Belgium 3, 25, 81, 85, 126, 129, 159, 192, 254
Bell, Graham 208
Bernal, Egan 253
Best All-Rounder (BAR) 121–3, 129, 173, 235, 289 nn.41, 43
    BAR concert 123, 289 nn.47, 50–1
    women's BAR 140, 161–2, 236, 301 n.140
Beveridge Report (1942) 169
bicycle, the, early history 7–8
bicycle companies, *see also* Dunlop
    BSA 91, 124, 204
    Claud Butler 159, 160

Coventry Bicycles Ltd. 95
Coventry Machinists Co. Ltd. 13
European Sewing Machine Company 13
Hercules 91, 123, 124, 160, 161–2, 300 n.133, 301 n.148
Humber 18, 25, 64, 66, 153
Raleigh 1, 91, 165, 173, 176, 177, 181, 207, 229, 236, 261 n.37
Rover 8, 41, 66, 247, 266 n.118
Rudge-Whitworth 96, 143
Singer 66
Sturmey-Archer Gears Ltd. 124
TI 173
bicycle designs
    ATB 204
    centre cycle 43
    Chopper, Raleigh 1–2, 177, 183
    electric 207, 256
    fixed-wheel (fixie) 218–19
    hybrid 205, 217
    Lotus Windcheetah 246–7, 321 nn.56, 58
    Michaux velocipede 13
    Moulton bicycle 176–7, 190, 227, 247, 315 n.55
    ordinary 8, 15, 18, 28, 30, 41, 45, 50, 55, 76, 139, 149, 206, 221, 268 n.2
    Pashley Princess 213, 218
    penny-farthing 218, 261 n.31 (*see also* bicycle designs, ordinary)
    recumbent 207–8, 312 n.143
    road bicycle (racer) 91, 96, 165, 176, 203, 217, 229
    roadster 46, 66, 91, 92, 144, 217
    Rover Safety bicycle, 8, 41, 247, 256, 266 n.118, 268 n.2
    velocipede 7–8, 13, 18, 35
    Zike design 207 (*see also* mountain bike (MTB); safety bicycle; tandem cycles; tricycle)
bicycle hire schemes 192, 203
    London 202, 209
bicycle industry 13, 65–6, 91–2, 217, 315 n.55
bicycle ownership and sales 14, 92, 177–8, 205, 210, 216–17, 256, 304 n.74, 315 n.51

INDEX

Bicycle Polo Association   135
bicycle theft   18–19, 205, 312 n.128
Bicycle Touring Club (BTC)   17, 24, 50
Bicycle Union (BU)   49, 50
Bicycle United Motocross Society (BUMS)   226
Bidlake, Frederick Thomas (F. T.)   69–73, 74, 82, 105, 116–17, 118, 119, 124, 157
Bidlake Memorial Garden   69–70, 73, 77
Bidlake Memorial Prize   72, 73, 74, 124, 141, 160, 162, 236, 296 n.176
Bikeability   197
Birmingham   21, 31, 65, 75, 78, 97, 101, 145, 149, 158, 181, 192
  Spaghetti Junction   170
Birmingham and Midland, NCU centre   138
Blackpool   61, 180
Blackwell, Henry   17
Blair, James   61
Blair, Thomas L.   188
Blake, Vernon   126, 290 n.72
Blatchford, Robert   21, 22
Blenheim Palace   128, 291 n.94
Bloch, Stella   157
Blunden, Edmund   130
BMX   6, 216, 225, 226–30, 318 n.109
  BMX Freestyle   229–30
  bodies, English BMX Association   320 n.40
  lifestyle   229
  NBMXA, UKBMX   228
  urban culture   230
Boardman, Chris   203, 224, 244–5, 246–8, 321 nn.56, 64
Boer War   46
Bogdanowiz, Tom   204–5
Booty, Ray   141
Bordeaux to Paris   64, 65, 235
Bottomley, Peter   195–6
Boulting, Ned   223
boxing   46, 178
Brachi, Philip   191
Bradford   21, 24, 95–6

Brailsford, Dave   234, 245–6, 248, 250–1, 252, 253
Bramall, John   152
Breithaupt, Scot   226
Brighton   197
Bristol   81, 192, 197, 198–9
British Cycle and Motor Cycle Industries Association   173, 174, see also Cycle and Motor Cycle Manufacturers and Traders' Union Ltd.
British Cycling   233, 243, 244, 245, 248, 250, 252, 320 n 40
  membership   211–12, 231, 249
British Cycling Federation (BCF)   115, 133, 137, 139, 172, 174–5, 210–11, 226, 235, 237, 241–3, 319 n.15, 320 n.32
  membership   172–3, 210–11, 249, 319 n.5, 320 n.40
British Cyclo-Cross Association   320 n.40
British League of Racing Cyclists (BLRC)   96, 125, 130, 132–9, 146, 293 nn.125, 129
  membership   134, 319 n.8
British Medical Association (BMA)   196
British Medical Journal   15
British Pathé   148, 162, 301 n.144
British Workers' Sport Federation (BWSF)   98–9
Brotton   53
Brown, Gordon   198
Brown, Mick   228
Buchanan, Colin   170
Buchanan Report, *Traffic in Towns* (1963)   170
Buenstorf, Guido   205
Bureau of Commercial Information Ltd.   175
Burl, Bill   129, 292 n.88
Burnett, Kendall   24
Burrows, Mike   246, 247, 321 n.58 n.59
Burton, Beryl   141, 235–7, 248–9, 287 n.7, 296 n.176
  Charlie, Denise   236
Burton, Maurice   214
Butler, H. P.   266 n.106

Cambridge 191
 Cambridge University 49, 55, 145
Camm, F. J. 133
Campaign for Lead Free Air (CLEAR) 189
Campaign for Nuclear Disarmament 189
Campbell, Malcolm 85
captain, role of 27, 102, 103, 127
Cardiff 111, 200
Cardus, Neville 74
Carmichael-Riddell, Bob 215
Carter, G. 54
Carter, Teddy 93
Cavendish, Mark 1, 211, 218, 234
Central Council for Physical Recreation 242
Channel 4 228, 238
Channon, Paul 194
Chester 44
Chichester College 244
children 2, 6, 93–4, 111, 176, 177–84, 189, 195, 197, 200, 216, 306 n.108, *see also* BMX
Choice, Jessie 31, 32, 35
Chudasama, Jaiprakash 214
citizenship and cycling 71, 85–6, 110–12, 123, 163, 178, 216, *see also* National Cycling Proficiency Scheme (NCPS)
Clancy, Ed 245
Clarion Cycling Club (CCC), National 21–2, 92, 99–100, 105, 112
 clubs 21–2, 86, 96, 97, 98
Claxton, Eric 171–2, 190
Clement, Ernie 134
coaching and sports science, 233, 241–2, 243–8, 250
 technological innovation 246–8
Cobb, G. F. 49
Cocker, Jarvis and Pulp, *Common People* 1
Cody, Samuel Franklin 53
Col du Galibier 127, 149
commercialism 25, 34–5, 43, 47–51, 65, 67, 120–1, 123–5, 131, 133, 233, 237–8, 251–3, *see also* BMX; Team Sky

Communist Party of Great Britain 99, 283 n.78
Conabeer, S. 151
Connelly, Billy 221
Conservation Society 189
Conservative-Liberal coalition 309 n.75
Conservative Party 22, 196, 200, 211, 242
consumerism 12, 23, 35, 80, 144, 165–8, 186, 198, 204, 209–10, 215–21, 226–30, 251, 255, 257
Cook, Arthur 75, 101–2, 105, 109–10, 119, 120, 127, 153–4, 158, 173
Cook, Nellie, *see* Kimmance, Nellie
Cook, William Pagan (W. P.) 'Billy' 72–3, 75, 119
Cooke, Nicole 234
Cookson, Brian 233
Cooper, Fred 49
Copenhagen 82, 170, 193
Coppi, Fausto 140, 223, 295 n.175
Coronation Street 1
Cortis, Herbert 49
Cosens, William 24
Cotterell, J. A. 29
Council for the Preservation of Rural England 71
Coventry 8, 43, 58, 76, 78, 93, 162, 170, 174, 203, 276 n.39
Cowal Highland Games 128
Cowan, Sally 248
Cox, Peter 6, 58, 80, 207, 208
Cozens, Syd 124, 125
Crane, Edmund 123
cricket 3, 14, 47, 48, 51, 74, 125, 132, 135, 140, 155, 234, 237
Critical Mass 185, 192
Cross, Len 137–8
Crowe, H. N. 125, 129, 291 n.86
Cuca Cocoa 24-hour race 51–2
Cycle and Motor Cycle Manufacturers and Traders' Union Ltd. 66
Cyclebag 192, 198–9
cycle paths 4, 79–83, 85–8, 99, 105, 169, 171–2, 191–3, 199, 203, *see also* Harlow; Stevenage

INDEX

cycle speedway 6, 92, 226
  British Cycle Speedway
    Council 320 n.40
Cycle Superhighways scheme 203
Cycle to Work Alliance 198
Cycling (journal), 33, 45, 52, 65,
    69, 71, 72, 73–4, 75–6, 77–8,
    79, 82, 86, 98, 104, 107, 109,
    110, 112–13, 118, 119, 121–2,
    127, 129, 130, 131, 135, 137,
    139–40, 147, 148, 150, 151,
    154, 155, 156–7, 160, 161, 162,
    168, 220
  Cycling and Mopeds 182
  Cycling and Motoring 65
  Cycling Weekly 214, 220, 224,
    225
  Diamond Jubilee 139–40
  poll, 1938 292 n.106
cycling accidents, fatalities 15,
    27, 55, 59, 60, 81, 132, 180,
    183, *see also* road accidents,
    fatalities
cycling activism 3, 6, 190–3, 207,
    210, 255, *see also* cycling lobby;
    politics and cycling; Sustrans
cycling and diversity 213–15
cycling and the law 37, 56–62,
    116–17, 120, 136–7, 235,
    see also cycle paths; Local
    Government Act (1888); massed-
    start racing (MSR); Ministry of
    Transport (MoT); police
  Cycle Racing and Highways Act
    (1963) 235
  Cycle Racing on Highways
    regulations (1960) 137
cycling attire, fashions, uniforms 134,
    218, 288 n.34
  male 33–5, 108–10
  female 35–7, 149–53
cycling booms 18–19, 22, 30, 36,
    38–40, 42–6, 51, 55, 65–7,
    209–11
cycling clubs 19–20, 53, 97, 102,
    117, 211, 293 n.129
  Airedale Olympic CC 96
  Amateur BC 20
  Amateur Velocipede Club 20

Anfield BC 72, 75, 100, 117,
    118, 119, 126, 235, 287 n.13,
    288 nn.20, 24
Ariel BC 20
Astley CC, Seaton Delaval 43
Barnesbury CC 137
Belfast Cruisers CC 41
Bishop Auckland Cyclists and
    Tourists Club 97
BLRC 137–8, 295 n.160
Bradford BC 20, 24
Bradford Racing CC 134,
    293 n.125
Brent Jewish Road Club 100
Cambridge University BC 48–9
Canonbury CC 17
Catford CC 21, 45, 78, 287 n.13,
    322 n.74
Century Road Club 72, 287 n.13,
    288 n.24, 292 n.111
Charlottevile CC 50, 122
Comet CC 97, 101–3, 104–5, 109,
    119–20, 173, 284 n.114
Concorde Racing CC 137, 138
Coventry CC 161
Dark Blue BC, Oxford
    University 48
Edinburgh Amateur BC
    (EABC) 20, 26–7, 34,
    265 n.95
Essex Roads CC 101
Forest CC 101
Forty Plus CC 106
Hartlepool Co-operative CC 97
Hartlepools Social CC 56
Knaresborough CC 236
Leeds Road Club 156
Liverpool Velocipede Club 19
London County Cycling and
    Athletic Club Ltd. 50
Manchester Road Racing
    Club 146
Middlesbrough BC 20
Middlesbrough Clarion CC 97
Middlesbrough Co-operative
    CC 97
Middlesex BC 16
Monckton CC 122
Morley CC 236

New Delaval Black Diamond Amateur BC 53
Nomads (Hitchin) CC 101, 250, 322 n.74
North London CC 52–3, 118
North London Tricycle Club 21, 32–3
North of Ireland Cricket Club, Belfast 41
North Ormesby and Middlesbrough CC 34
North Road Club 64, 72, 116, 119, 121, 124, 126, 157
Norwood Paragons CC 122
Peterborough CC 19
Pickwick Club 19
Polytechnic CC 122, 271 n.73
Red Wheelers CC 99
religious 100
Richmond CC 97
Sharrow CC 28
Solihull CC 97, 100, 138, 154
South Lancashire Racing Club 137
South Lancashire Road Club 97, 102, 104, 106, 107, 127
South London Tricycle Club 31
Spartacus CC 99, 100
Stanley Club 27, 44, 50, 270 n.57
Temple BC 20–1
Thornaby CC 56
Tyne Dock Belle Vue CC 9
Vegetarian CC 20, 95, 124
Walthamstow Town CC 101
Watford CC 146
West Bradford CC 96
Wolverhampton Racing Club 133
Yorkshire Century CC 104
Yorkshire Road Club 129, 133, 156 see also women's cycling clubs
Cycling Demonstrations Towns 197
Cycling England 197
cycling entertainment, music hall, variety acts 45, 46, 51, 105, 123, 139, 158
cycling levels, activity 16–17, 19, 92–4, 172, 200, 201, 210–11, 217, 249, 256, 257
   females 148
cycling lobby 170–2, 179, 190, 192, 195, 199
Cycling Safety League 181, 306 n.108
Cycling towards Health and Safety (1992) 196
cycling tracks, velodromes and venues 52, 271 n.77
   Agricultural Hall, Islington 45, 47
   Alexandra Palace 103
   Brooklands 128, 132, 291 n.94
   Catford Cycle and Athletic Ground 52, 53, 66, 271 n.77
   Crystal Palace 45, 47–8, 52, 67, 118, 128
   Donnington Park 128, 129, 132, 291 n.94
   Herne Hill 50, 52, 66, 72, 139, 159
   Lillie Bridge 48, 52
   Manchester velodrome, Reg Harris Stadium 233, 237, 243, 252
   Memorial Ground, Canning Town 52, 66, 133
   Molineux Grounds 47
   Olympia 56
   Paddington 41, 52, 66
   Phoenix Park 128
   Putney 52
   Stamford Bridge 52
   Wembley Empire Pool 112
   Westminster Aquarium 45, 56
   White City 52, 67
   Wood Green 52–3, 66–7
cyclists, honours 73, 168, 234, 322 n.67
Cyclists' Parliamentary and Municipal Association 59–60
Cyclists' Public Affairs Group (C-PAG) 202, 311 n.110
Cyclists' Touring Club (CTC) 10, 14, 15, 17–18, 22–6, 28–9, 34, 36–9, 44, 46, 54, 58–63, 72, 75–8, 83, 85–7, 90, 94, 98–9, 101–2, 103–4, 107, 111–12, 146–52, 156, 161, 173–5, 181, 190, 194, 201, 214–15, 219, 264 n.76, 265 n.87, 273 nn.115, 131, 286 n.156, 311 n.110, 319 n.15
CTC 'Cyclists Special' 90, 167

CTC Gazette 15, 23, 24, 25, 34, 46, 59, 60, 63, 72, 73, 76, 98, 102, 106, 127, 148, 168, 175, 179
CTC Manchester DA 103, 147, 149
CTC membership 17–18, 23–4, 26, 29, 92, 98, 101, 167, 172, 211, 262 n.24, 308 n.29
CTC membership, female 29
CTC North Metropolitan DA 102, 103, 108
CTC Rochdale DA section 103–4, 107
CTC uniform, male 34–5, female 35–6
CTC West Metropolitan DA 147–8
CTC York Rally 174
Cycletouring 175, 214–15
Loiterers, The 103, 105–6, 108
tours and touring 38–9
Cyclists' War Memorial 72, 78

Daily Mail 38, 45, 59, 85, 225, 270 n.63
Darlington 20, 97, 197
Darnton, Philip 197
Daventry 191
Davies, Victor 174
Denmark 3, 184, 192, 257
Denson, Vin 239
Department of Transport 193–4, 195, 197, 199, 310 n.78, *see also* Ministry of Transport (MoT)
Derby 197
Dew, Josie 221
disability and cycling 94–6, 214
Doncaster 24, 95
doping 12, 220, 224, 239–40, 242, 245, 250–3
Dovey, Billie 96, 143, 148, 300 n.124
Doyle, Tony 244
draisine 7
Dredge, Lillian 106, 159, 160, 161, 163, 300 n.124
Du Cros, Harvey, family 41
Duffield, David 227–8
Duke of Edinburgh 242
Dunham, Katherine 294 n.145

Dunlop, John Boyd 8, 41
company 8, 41–2, 52, 112
Durham 43, 44, 239
Durlacher, Lutz 100–1

Earnshaw, Harry 'Shake' 122, 124, 161, 300 n.133
Earth Day, 1970 188
Earth First 136
Edge, S. F. 64
Edwards, John 225
Egerton, Wilbraham 58
Elton, Ben, *Gridlock* 186
employment patterns, workforce 84, 167–8, 211–12, 215
women 144
England, Harry 82, 124, 131, 140, 159, 168, 182
Englishness 11, 37–9, 69–71, 74, 88, 187, 239, *see also* anti-urban critique; rural idyll
cycle paths 79–88
English Schools Cycling Association 175
The Environmental Handbook (1971) 189
environmentalism 185–93, 203, 207, 208, 232
Environmental Transport Association 189
European cycling, sport 251, *see also* Giro d'Italia; Tour de France
European Union 210
Common Market 139
European Economic Community 218, 240
Eurosport 227, 238, 251
Evans, Arthur 61
Evans Cycles 198, 220
Exeter 197

Fancourt, James 129
Fellowship of Old-Time Cyclists 72, 147
Fellowship of the Wheel 86
Femina, journalist 153
Ferris, Sid 124, 160
Festival of Britain 110, 112, 139
Fignon, Laurent 246

films, documentaries 182, *see also* BBC
  Chain of Events (1954) 182
  Cyclists Special (1955) 90
  No Short Cut (1964) 183–4
  On Any Sunday (1971)
  The Program (2015) 322 n.85
  Saturday Night and Sunday Morning (1960) 165
  A Sunday in Hell (1976) 246
  Wheels of Chance (1973) 183–4
Fiola, Eddie 230
First World War 37, 46, 74–5, 78, 87, 90, 98, 118, 126, 144, 145, 146, 150, 163, 179
Fisher, Gary 205
Fleming, Billie, *see* Dovey, Billie
Flinn, Tom 93
football 3, 14, 21, 26, 46, 47, 48, 50, 51, 52, 55, 65, 66, 71, 72, 76, 100, 122, 125, 135, 139, 155, 167, 175, 212, 223, 229, 234, 235, 237–8, 241, 242, 245, 249, 252
Ford, J. E. 104, 137
Fort William 225
Foster, Ken 153
Fotheringham, William 1, 239
  In Search of Tom Simpson 223–4
Fox, Charles 133, 293 n.126
France, French cycling 3, 7, 13, 16, 26, 38, 55, 57–8, 60, 64–5, 67, 70, 85, 121, 126–8, 129–30, 132, 149, 163, 165, 167, 174, 188, 210, 218, 223, 228, 242, 251, 252, 253, 264 n.73, 271 n.72, 290 n.72, 322 n.84, *see also* Tour de France
  Union des Sociétés Françaises de Sports Athlétiques 65
  Union Velocipedique de France 65, 265 n.90
Friends of the Earth 10, 188–90, 191, 194, 199, 201, 204, 219
Froome, Chris 253
Fry, Maxwell 169

Gachon, P. 291 n.88
Gainsborough 93

Gamage's 35, 52
Gambley, Jessie 56
Game Plan (2002) 242
Gardner, Scott 245
Garrett-Anderson, Elizabeth 31, 143
gender relations 14, 29–30, 39, 101, 146–7, 152, 153–4, 250
Germany 3, 21, 70, 86
  East Germany 242, 245
  West Germany 167
Gilligan, Andrew 203
Gjers, John 20
Gladstone, Herbert 59
globalisation, cycling 250–3
Godwin, Tommy 241
Goodwin, Harry 123, 139, 140
Gordon, Patrick 169
Grahame, Kenneth, *The Wind in the Willows* 71
Grant, H. 124
Grant, Richard 204
Great Northern Bike Ride 219
Great North Road, A1, 69, 74, 79
Greaves, Walter 95–6, 133, 282 nn.48, 54, 293 n.125
Green, C. E. 106
Green, Kate 156
Greenpeace 188, 189
Grimshaw, John 197, 201
Groom, Tom 21, 99
Guardian 73, 74, 91, 180, 193, 194, 213, 223, 224
Gurney, William 24

Hackney 158, 201
Halfords 198, 214, 217, 227–8
Hall, Peter 189–90
Hamilton, David 76–7
Hamilton, Tyler 317 n.83
Hampton Court parades 16, 34, 44
Harberton, Viscountess 36
Hardriders 104
Hardy, Jay 227, 229
Harlow 171, 191
Harman, C. A. 17
Harris, Reg 140
Harrod's 35
Harrogate meeting 24, 44

health, physical and mental 14–16, 23, 29, 30–1, 35, 59, 74–5, 79, 109, 110, 111–12, 113, 143, 151–2, 160, 196, 204, 208, 210
Heath, Edward 242
Heppleston, Cyril 123, 300 n.133
Hertfordshire 44, 104, 192
Higginson, Arnold 227
Highway Code 86, 111, 179
Hillier, George (G.) Lacy 6, 30, 31, 32, 33, 50, 63, 65, 76, 116, 270 n.63
Hillman, Mayer 196
Hills, Zetta 148–9, 297 n.53
Hilton, Tim 73–4, 101, 102, 130, 223, 292 n.103, 299 n.113
Hipster Spice Route 213
Hoban, Barry 239, 240
Hodgson, Mabel 147, 148, 150, 156
Hoggart, Richard 89, 107
 The Uses of Literacy (1957) 89
Holbein, Montague 64
Holden, Rob 209, 224
Holdsworth, J. E. 112, 286 n.165
Holland, *see* Netherlands, the
Holland, Charles 128, 129, 291 n.88, 292 n.120, 293 n.121
Holley, E. T. 65
Holmes, Jack 129
Holme Valley Wheelers 222
Holt, Richard 9, 14, 19
Home Office 136, 179
homophobia 214–15
Hooley, E. T. 65
Hore-Belisha, Leslie 83–4, 86
Hornby, Nick, *Fever Pitch* 223
Horsham 43
House of Commons 18, 194, 224, 253
House of Keys 128, 291 n.81
House of Lords 179
Houses of Parliament 57, 59, 85, 201, 273 n.117
Howard, Ebenezer 171
Howell, Denis 242
Howell, Richard 48
Hoy, Chris 226, 234, 235, 243, 248, 253
human powered vehicles (HPV)
Hume, William 41

Hylton, Kevin 214
Hyman, Dorothy 161, 236

Ingle, Ken 282 n.54
International Cycling Association (ICA) 64–5
international cycling touring clubs 264 n.73, 265 nn.89, 90
International Road Congress 81
International Touring Congress 25–6
International Union of Touring Clubs 25–6, 265 n.89, 90
Ireland 20, 41, 75, 128, 159, 238, 264 n.76
Isle of Man 127, 128, 291 nn.81, 94
Isle of Wight 103
Italy, Italian cycling 3, 126, 130, 140, 167, 238, 239, 244
 Giro d'Italia 3, 125, 140, 253, 289 n.40
ITV 1, 174, 200, 223, 233

James, Dr Eric 180
James, H. 124
James, Henry 18
James, Rebecca 249
Jarvis, Michael and Sue 228
Jeffreys, William Rees 62
Jerome, J. K. 17
Johnson, Boris 202–3
Johnson, Robert 66
Josey, Alex (KMD) 79, 131–2, 161, 277 n.52, 292 n.111
Joy, Ken 140, 141, 301 n.142

Kain, Jimmy 133
Katsanis, Dimitris 248
Keen, John 46, 47, 49
Keen, Peter 244–5, 247
Keith-Falconer, Ion 48–9
Kelly, Sean 238
Kemps, Richard 300 n.133
Kennedy, Ludovic 239
Kenny, Jason 249, 252
Kimmance, Nellie 158, 159
Kinder Scout trespass 132, 192
Kuklos, *see* Wray, William Fitzwater (Kuklos)
Kynaston, David 89

Labour party 196–8, 211, 241, 242, 249, 311 n.108
Ladies' Cyclists' Rally 147, 150, 156, see also rallies, women
Lake District 38, 74, 104
Lallement, Pierre 7
Lambert, Zeta 145
Lancaster 197
Lancet 8
Land's End to John O'Groats 17, 47, 49, 95, 124, 159, 160–3, 175, 222, 227, 262 n.22, 299 n.91, 301 n.143
Lane, Arbuthnot 109
Lane, Eddie 139
lantern lectures 74, 75, 103
Larkin, Philip 168
League of American Wheelmen 25, 65, 265 nn.88, 90
Leicester 20, 47–8, 118, 211, 214, 216, 242, 313 n.14, 320 n.37
Leisure for Living (1959) 215
Le Mond, Greg 246, 251
L'Etape du Tour de France 219
Levene, Edward 18–19
Lewis, Rob 248, 322 n.67
liberalism 60, 186, 258
lightweight bicycle 8, 91–2, 144, 153
Lightwood, James T. 37
Ligue Internationale De Cyclisime 133
Lincoln 95, 282 n.52
Linden, Enid 145
Lingdale 53–5, 272 n.94
literature and cycling 222–5, 317 n.83
Liverpool 61, 74, 85–6, 152, 191
 Liverpool Police athletic meeting 41
 Liverpool Time-Trial Cycling Association 149
Liverton Mines 55
Livingstone, Ken 202, 311 n.108
Lloyd, T. Lee 74
Lloyd George, David 84
London 10, 15, 18, 19, 20, 26, 36, 41, 45, 47, 52–3, 56, 57, 58, 66, 75, 80–1, 90, 92, 94, 97, 101–5, 110, 112, 125, 146, 147, 153–4, 156, 158, 172, 175, 177, 185, 190, 192, 193, 194, 201–3, 206, 209, 213, 214, 218, 219, 222, 223, 224–5, 255
 Greater London Assembly 201–2
 Greater London Council 190, 194, 201, 312 n.128
 London County Council 180
 London mayors 111, 201–2, 203, 309 n.74
 London Cycling Campaign 201, 230, 311 n.110
 London Ringway scheme 170
 London Safety First Council 179, 305 n.87
 London to Brighton 13, 146, 219
 London to Findon 156
Longcraine, Richard 207
Lonsbrough, Anita 161, 236
Loughborough University 244
Low, Percy 119
Lusty, Albert 157

McGurn, Jim 207, 208, 220
McKibbin, Ross 21, 71
MacLean, Craig 243
Maddox, R. D. 98
magazines, periodicals and journals 224–5, 228
Maitland, Bob 137
Major, John 69, 195, 242
Manchester 100, 145, 152, 203
 Greater Manchester Police 195
 Manchester Grammar School 180
Manpower Services 199–200
maps, Ordnance Survey, 37–8
March, Tim 229
March Racing Developments 229
Marsh, D. 288 n.22
Martin, Alfred 122
Mason, Tony 93
massed-start racing (MSR) 10, 11, 65, 125–41, 294 n.155, 295 nn.158, 170
 opposition to 130–2, 134–9
 Tripartite Agreement 295 n.171
Mathew, Don 190, 194
Mathews, Joyce 145
Matlock Bath Parochial Church Council 153

Mayall, J.   13
MCC   51
meanings of cycling   9–10, *see also* amateurism; Clarion Cycling Club (CCC), National; Englishness; Patterson, Frank; Robinson, Walter MacGregor (Wayfarer); rural idyll; Worpole, Ken; Wray, William Fitzwater (Kuklos)
  communism   99–100
  socialism   21–2
Mellor, Chris and Rachael   317 n.82
Menzies, Rene   96
Merckx, Eddy   240, 246
Mercredy, Robert   41
Meredith, Leon   121
Meriden   77–8
Michaux, Pierre   7
Middle-Aged Men In Lycra (MAMIL)   209
middle classes   14, 17–18, 49, 71, 97, 104, 107–8, 119, 126, 135, 153, 185, 201, 211–12, 217–20, 234, 255, 256, 257
  amateurism   18, 22–4, 51, 67, 80–2, 93, 120
  Cyclists' Touring Club   22–5, 63, 98
  identity and values   3, 4–5, 15–17, 19–26, 37–40, 60, 70, 74–5, 77–8, 80, 82, 90, 98–9, 110, 169, 180, 205, 209–10, 211–13, 217, 220–1, 231, 256–7
  literature   223–6
  motoring   5, 49, 65, 67, 71, 100
  Primrose League   22
  touring   37–9
  women   28–35, 39, 144–5, 148, 150–1, 155–6, 163
Middlesbrough   20, 43, 97, 191
Millar, Robert   238
Milliken, Ernie   124
Mills, Billy   123, 133
Mills, G. P.   64
mini-Holland scheme   203
Ministry of Education   182, 241
Ministry of Transport (MoT)   80, 82, 83–4, 136, 165, 168, 177, 179, 180–1, *see also* Department of Transport

Minneapolis   81
Mintel, market research   212–13, 314 n.35
Miroir des Sports   130
Miroir-Sprint   130, 292 nn.102, 103
Mitchell, Eric   137
modernity   5, 11, 38–9, 46, 55, 65, 67, 70–1, 80, 112, 165, 166, 169, 178, 184, *see also* anti-modern critique; planning
  cycling   13, 51, 67, 76, 113–15, 121, 125, 130–1, 133, 134, 139, 166, 174, 238, 241, 257
  motoring   65, 67, 70–1, 80
  women and cycling   155, 159, 160, 163
Modley, Albert   95
Moerenhout, Jeff   300 n.133
Moore, James   47, 64
Morris, William (Lord Nuffield)   66
Moser, Francesco   244, 321 n.48
motor car, *see* motoring
motoring   1, 2, 3, 4, 5, 11, 18, 60–2, 65, 66, 67, 70, 71, 73, 76, 80–3, 84–6, 87, 91, 92, 166–71, 177, 184, 185, 188, 190, 203, 204, 217, 222, 225, 230, 251, 256, 257
motoring lobby   4, 80, 84–6, 179, 184, 225, *see also* road lobby
Mottram, Simon   218
Moulton, Alex   176, *see also* bicycle designs
Mount Ventoux   209, 224, 239
mountain bike (MTB)   8, 186, 203–7, 208, 220, 225, 256
  British Mountain Bike Federation   320 n.40
Moxham, S. H.   119

Naseby   90
National Athletic Union   51
National Bicycle Publicity Scheme   173–4
National Bicycle Week   110–11
National Cycle Network   200–1, 225
National Cycle Show   66
National Cycling Forum   197
National Cycling Proficiency Scheme (NCPS)   178–84, 304 n.80

National Cycling Strategy 193–7, 202
National Cyclists' Union (NCU) 10, 14, 17, 24, 31, 41, 50–1, 53–4, 56, 58–64, 65, 67, 85–6, 97, 98, 111–12, 116–17, 119, 121, 125, 128–9, 132–3, 135–9, 149, 180, 181–2, 268 n.2, 270 n.56, 273 nn.115, 117, 285 n.124, 286 n.156, 288 n.20, 291 nn.80, 86, 293 n.124, 295 nn.158, 171, *see also* British Cycling Federation (BCF); British League of Racing Cyclists (BLRC); Road Time Trials Council (RTTC)
  NCU, founding clubs 270 n.57
  NCU membership 17, 18, 92, 101, 172–3, 262 n.24, 275 n.167, 280 n.16, 281 n.22, 291 n.96, 293 n.133
  women 156
National Fitness Council 110, 111–12
National Health Service (NHS) 169, 196, 198, 246
National Lottery 200, 233, 242–3, 249
National Maccabi Cycling Centre 100
National Safety Congress 179, 180
National Safety First Association 85, 180, 305 n.87, *see also* London Safety First Council; Royal Society for the Prevention of Accidents
National Trust 187, 188, 189, 195
National Union of Teachers 181
National Workers' Sport Association (NWSA) 99
Nelson, Gaylord 188
Nelson, Wade 228
neoliberalism 4, 187, 198, 211, 231, 234
Netherlands Cyclists' Union 25
Netherlands, the 3, 70, 85, 86–7, 172, 184, 192–3, 210, 228, 257, 310 n.78
Newcastle-upon-Tyne 9, 44, 77
New Cyclist 204, 208, 211, 212, 314 n.23
New Left 189
Newlyn, Lucy 76

newspapers, *see also* magazines, periodicals and journals
  cycling 45
New Woman 29, 55
Nicholson, Geoffrey 235
Nicholson, Ossie 96, 282 n.48
Norris, Steve 202, 309 n.74
Northcliffe, Lord (Viscount Rothermere) 45, 270 n.63
Northern Cyclist Battalion 77
Northern Ladies' Rally 147
Northumberland 43, 53, 56, 64
North Yorkshire 43, 145
North Yorkshire and South Durham, NCU centre 54, 97
Norton Bicycle Gymkhana 56
Norwich 93
Nottingham 165, 203

Obelkevich, Jim 169
Obree, Graham 247, 321 n.64
O'Connell, Sean 80, 256
Oddy, Nicholas 67
Office of the Third Sector 197
Oldenziel, Ruth 193
Oliver brothers, 7
Olympics, 161, 230, 241, 243, 245, 322 n.67
  1908 244
  1928 122
  1932 122
  1936 131
  1948 137, 291 n.80
  1952 162
  1984 249
  1992 244
  2000 233, 243, 247
  2004 248
  2008 226, 243, 250
  2012 1, 185, 192, 202, 211, 219, 234, 243, 250, 252
  2020 318 n.113
One Hour Record 47, 321 n.64
Opperman, Hubert 124, 126, 132, 162, 290 n.58, 301 n.143
opposition to road racing 63–4
Order of the Road 86, 279 n.106
Orwell, George 69, 79
outdoor movement 106–8

Palmer, Eileen   153
Parkes, H. W. (Petronella)   148, 155, 299 n.92
pastoralism   57, 74, 75, 78, 79, 107, 116, 130
　motoring pastoral ideal   71, 81
Patterson, Frank   73–4, 116
Pattison, Zelle   56
Paul, Andre   291 n.89
Peak District   74
Peake, Maxine, *Beryl: A Love Story on Two Wheels*   248–9
Pease, Alfred   54
Pease, Joseph   53
Pedal Club   79
Pedestrian and Cyclist's Protection Society   61
pedestrianism   47
Pendleton, Max   250, 322 n.74
Pendleton, Victoria   211, 234, 250
Penn, Robert   223
Pennell, Elizabeth Robins   56, 63
performance enhancing drugs (PED), *see* doping
Peterborough   183, 191
Peters, Steve   245
Petronella, *see* Parkes, H. W.
Pfanner, Mlle   297 n.53
photography   39, 107–8
Pinkerton, John   221
Planned Public Relations Ltd.   174
planning   71, 85–6, 88
pneumatic tyres   8, 41–2, 50, 116, 268 n.1
police   44, 54, 60–2, 116, 118, 135–7, 180, 195, 240, 291 n.86
　fines   61, 274 n.140
political culture, *see* liberalism; neoliberalism; socialism; Thatcherism; voluntarism; welfarism
politics and cycling   79–88, 170–2, 185–203, *see also* cycling activism; cycling and the law; National Cycling Proficiency Scheme (NCPS)
Poole and Co.'s Ibex Quad   52, 53
Poplars Corner   69
Poppe, Henk   240
Porter, Eric   103

Post Office   43–4, 269 n.16
Powers Brothers   45
Priestley, J. B.   88, 131, 168, 169
　English Journey (1934)   88
Primrose League Cycling Corps   22
The Principles and Practices of Town and Country Planning   191
professional cyclists, Britain   47–8, 64, 123–5, 134, 139–40, 235, 240, 300 n.133, 319 n.6
professionalism   47–51, 54, 64–5, 120–1, 123, 125, 140, 216, *see also* amateurism
public health   111, 196, 197–8, 216, *see also* National Health Service (NHS)
public relations   84, 85, 174
pugilism   47
Punch   61
Putnam, Robert   230
Pybus, John   83

Queally, Jason   233
Quigley, Janet   79

racism   214
Radbury   230
Radcliffe, Jim   323 n.87
railways   57, 90, 195, 199, 273 n.125
Raising the Game (1995)   242
rallies, women   147–8
Rapha   218
Rea, Lillian   146
Redditch   227–8
Rees, Neville   194
Reigate, Surrey   61
Renshaw, Joyce   146
Reynolds, Tessie   36
Richard's Bicycle Book (1972)   204, 207, 246
Richardson, Dr   14, 16
Riga, Celestine   300 n.133
Rigby, Harold   297 n.50
Ripley, Surrey   76
Ritchie, Andrew   6, 8, 42, 50, 51, 165
road accidents, fatalities   81–4, 85, 105, 179–80, 183, 191
road lobby   62, 170, 184, 187, 194–6, 257, *see also* motoring lobby

road races   287 n.13
  Bath Road CC   100, 121
  Brighton to Glasgow Victory Marathon   96, 134
  Liège–Bastogne–Liège   65, 125
  Llangollen to Wolverhampton race   115, 135
  Nations Road Race   121
  Otley CC 12-hour   287 n.7
  Paris-Roubaix   65, 125, 256
  Tour of Britain   3, 134, 136, 235, 238, 254
  Tour of Flanders   3, 239
  Tour of Lombardy   239
  Tour of the Peaks   134
  University CC 100   122, see also North Road CC
road racing, see British League of Racing Cyclists (BLRC); massed-start racing (MSR); road races; Road Racing Council (RRC); Road Time Trials Council (RTTC); time trial; Tour de France
Road Racing Council (RRC)   119–21
road records   299 n.91
  Cardiff to London   176
  Land's End to London   124
  London Portsmouth   124
  London to Brighton   124
  London to John O'Groats   17
  London York   124
  1,000 miles   124, 161, (see also Land's End to John O'Groats)
Road Records' Association (RRA)   62, 123–4
roads and traffic   57–8, 61–2, 92, 172, 194–5
Roads Improvement Association   62, 81, 83
Roads to Prosperity (1989)   194
Road Time Trials Council (RTTC)   92, 117, 96, 120–1, 131, 133–6, 138, 235–7, 293 n.124, 295 n.171, 236, 301 n.140, 319 n.15
  membership   92, 120, 235
Roberts, Derek   6, 215, 260 n.16
Robinson, Brian   130, 140, 239

Robinson, Walter MacGregor (Wayfarer)   75–6, 78, 79, 82, 86, 108, 153, 168, 204, 206
Roche, Stephen   238, 243–4
Rodgers, Nellie   156
role of the state, sport   241–3
Romero, Rebecca   322 n.76
Rough Stuff Fellowship   75
Royal Albert Hall   122, 139, 156, 235
Royal Automobile Club   62, 278 n.65
Royal Commission on Environmental Pollution   189
Royal Commission on Motor-Cars (1905)   61
Royal Society for the Prevention of Accidents (RoSPA)   180–2, 305 n.87, 306 n.114, see also National Safety First Association
Royal Society for the Protection of Birds   195
Ruffell, Andy   228–9
rugby   90–1
  rugby league   234
  rugby union   46, 47, 51, 77, 98, 132, 135, 213, 234
Rumney, A. W.   75
rural idyll   11, 38–9, 57, 70, 71, 73–9, 88, 90, 100, 106, 110, 112–13, 116, 206, 256, see also anti-urban critique; Englishness; pastoralism

Safe Cycling (1957)   181
safety bicycle   8, 30, 36, 39, 41, 50, 55, 176
safety discourse   80–5, 178–84, 195–6
sale   97
Salvarani team   239
Salzwedel, Heiko   245
Sampson, Anthony   168, 176
Samuel, Marcus   83
Sandy   69
Scherens, Jef   140
Schools Eco-Action Group   189
Scotland   15, 24, 92, 103, 128, 158, 183, 208, 264 n.76, 289 n.43, 291 n.84
  Scottish Amateur Cycling Association   129, 291 n.84

INDEX

Scottish Cycling Union   319 n.5
   massed-start racing   128–9
Seaton, Matt   213–14, 223
Seaton Delaval   43, 53, 56
Second World War   74, 79, 89, 90, 92, 132, 178
Selfridges   35
Shaw, George Bernard   18, 262 n.28
Shaw, Pat   138
Sheffield University Sports Engineering Research Group   248
Sheridan, Eileen   107, 140, 141, 161–3, 174, 236, 249
Shipton, E. R.   15, 63
Shortland, Frank   52
Sillitoe, Alan   165
Simpson, Clare   55
Simpson, Tom   138–9, 209, 223–4, 238–40, 295 n.171
Sinclair, Clive   207
singletrackworld.com   225
Sisley, Charles   45
Smith, Don   228
Smith, Paul   218
sociability *see* associational life, club culture
sociable, *see* tricycle
socialism   20–1
social media   225, 230
Society for Rational Dress   35, 36
Southall, Frank   117, 122–4, 161, 162, 289 n.55, 290 n.65, 292 n.118
South Shields   9
South Yorkshire   122
Spain   3, 139, 238, 320 n.32
   Vuelta a España   253
Spastics Society   214
speedway   92, 125, 131, 227
Spencer, Charles   13, 16, 17
sport, British cycling, 47–9, 51–6, 66–7, 124–5, 233–54, *see also* road races; road racing role of the state, sport
Sport England   210
sportives   219–20, 316 n.69, 72
Sports Council   216, 228, 241
Springall, Jessie   127, 149, 155, 160, 163
Staff, Jamie   226

Stallard, Percy   10, 115, 128, 132–3, 137
Stancer, George Herbert (G. H.)   72, 73, 82, 85–7, 98–9, 117, 127, 152, 156, 157, 159, 162, 168, 299 n.92
Stanley, Lottie   56
Stanley, Oliver   83
Stanley Show   44, 45, 274 n.161
Stansell, W.   159
Stanton, David   47
Stanway, A. W.   137
Starley, James   8, 30, 266 n.118
Starley, John Kemp   8, 266 n.118
Steel, Bryan   321 n.56
Stevenage, cycle paths   171–2, 190, 191
Stewart, Jackie   184
Stewart, Mary   158
Stockton Wheelers   97
Stonehenge   63
Stormzy, Vossi Bop   255
Stout, Ben   214–15
Strava   220
Sturmey, Henry   19, 64
Sunderland   96
Sustrans   197, 198–201, 225
   Connect2   200
Sutton, Shane   245
Sweden   192
swimming   55–6, 160, 161, 297 n.45
   Swimming Association of GB   50
Switzerland   192
Sydenham   31, 47
Sydney   81, 233
Symington, G. H.   56

Tallents, Stephen   174
tandem cycles   18, 28, 44, 45, 53, 103, 153, 158, 208, 221
Tatler   148, 297 n.45
Taylor, Major   52
Team Ace   223
Team Ineos   323 n.87
Team Sky   250–3
Thatcher, Margaret   187, 191, 195
   Thatcherism   186, 195, 208, 218
The Times   13, 86, 194, 224
The Tricyclist   30
   amalgamation   50

Thomas, Geraint   245, 253
Thomas, Gordon   140
Thorne, Will   22
Tilley, Vesta   158
time trial
    history   11, 62, 70, 72, 74, 115, 116–25
    races   287 n.13, *see also* road racing
Tomkins, J. C.   151
Torrey Canyon disaster   188
Torry, J. W.   124
Tour de France   1, 3, 65, 115, 125–7, 129–30, 131–2, 140, 149, 185, 209, 211, 217, 222–3, 224, 234, 238–40, 244, 246, 250–3, 254, 289 n.40, 290 n.69
    Britain   129–30, 240
Tour d'Elephant   230
touring   23, 25–6, 37–9, 43, 75, 87, 91, 94, 98, 103–4, 107–8, 122, 130, 147, 157, 206, 221, *see also* cycling clubs; Cyclists' Touring Club (CTC); Englishness
    decline   172–3, 175
track cycling   47–9, 51–6, 66–7, 124–5
Trades Union Congress   215
Trans Pennine Trail   199
Transport 2000   195, 201, 202
Transport Advisory Committee   72, 76
Transport for London (TfL)   202
tricycle   8, 16, 18, 29–33, 35, 39, 41, 43, 44, 47, 51, 55, 58, 60, 92, 94–5, 97, 204, 207, 228, 262 n.23, 270 n.56
    Lever Tricycle   30
    Salvoquadricycle   30
    Tricycle Association   72, 106
Trott, Laura   249
Tufty Club   181–2, 306 n.114
Turnbull, Tommy   9–10
Turner, Dr E. B.   76
Turner, Josiah   13
Turner, Rowley B.   13
Tweed Run   218
Tyneside   9–10

UK Sport   244, 245
Union Cycliste Internationale (UCI)   65, 119, 128, 131, 136, 195, 207, 247, 252, 288 n.20, 291 n.89
United Kingdom economy   42, 217
United Kingdom population   42, 70
United States Cycling Federation   312 n.143
United States of America (USA)   3, 7, 25, 41, 45, 53, 55–6, 57, 72, 140, 226, 227, 230, 242
    Chicago   41, 57, 65
    San Francisco   81, 186, 192, 220
urbanization   5, 38, 42, 57, 107, 187, 256
Urry, Frank   168
Urry, John (cyclist)   82
US Postal Team   253
USSR   242

van Eijden, Jan   245
Veitch, Colin   21
Vienna   192
voluntarism   19–22, 110–11, 116, 123, 235

Wales   74, 75, 92, 97, 149, 200, 206, 264 n.76
Walthamstow   103
Washington DC   81
water cycle   44, 148–9, 297 n.50
Wayfarer, *see* Robinson, Walter MacGregor
Webb, Beatrice and Sidney   18
The Weekly Dispatch Cup   67
Welch, Mrs   56
welfarism   4, 110, 113, 168, 169, 178, 190, 234, 241
Wellbye, Reginald   112
Wells, H. G.   17, 46
    The Wheels of Chance (1896)   17, 35, 36, 46, 183
Western Avenue cycle path   80, 83, 85
Whitby   180
Wiggins, Bradley   1, 185, 211, 217, 234, 250, 253, 317 n.83
Wilson, Des   189
Wilson, Harold   242

Wilson, Marguerite 124, 148, 150, 160–2, 236, 300 nn.124, 133, 301 nn.144, 143
Wolfenden Report (1960) 216, 241, 286 n.163
Wolverhampton 47–8, 115, 132–3
women and cycling 28–33, 55–6, 143–63, *see also* rallies, women; Women's Road Records' Association (WRRA)
  American 56
  French 35, 56
  journalists, female 148
  Ladies' Cyclists' Rally 147, 150, 156
  Lady Cyclists' Association 16
  sport 154–8, 248–50
women's cycling, medical theories 29–30
women's cycling clubs
  Heatherbell Ladies' CC 158
  Ladies' CC 16
  Rosslyn Ladies' Cycling Club 158–9, 299 n.113, 300 n.118
  Ross Wheelers Ladies' CC 158
  Southern Ladies' Road Club 143, 158
Women's League of Health and Beauty 143
Women's Road Records' Association (WRRA) 106, 127, 149, 154–5, 159, 161, 301 nn.140, 148
Women's Tour de France 249
Wood, Fred 48
Woodburn, John 176, 222
Woodhead, Nancy 208

Woods, Alan 227
Wordsworth, Dorothy 38
working classes 1, 5, 6, 13, 22, 28, 33, 43, 47, 49, 50, 63, 66, 75, 77, 78, 80, 82, 89–113, 118, 119–22, 135, 144, 165, 169, 177, 183, 210, 212, 215, 258, 277 n.62
  women 144, 148, 150, 152, 155, 158
world championships, 48
  1893 163
  1904 67
  1922 118–19, 128
  1937 293 n.121
  1965 320 n.32
  1970 210–11, 216, 238, 242, 320 nn.34, 36, 37
  1993 247, 252, 321 n 64
  1994 321 n.64
  1995 321 n.64
  women 1953 163, 249
Worpole, Ken 222
Wrath-Sharman, David 206
Wray, William Fitzwater (Kuklos) 75, 86, 204

X Games 229–30

Yates, Simon 245, 253
York 80, 95, 174, 191, 199
Yorkshire 43, 104, 105, 236
Young, H. Collings 78, 151
Younger, George 193
Youth Hostels Association (YHA) 106–7, 130, 285nn.124, 126

www.ingramcontent.com/pod-product-compliance
Lightning Source LLC
Chambersburg PA
CBHW061705300426
44115CB00014B/2567